MIPAM ON BUDDHA-NATURE

Mipam on Buddha-Nature

The Ground of the Nyingma Tradition

Douglas S. Duckworth

STATE UNIVERSITY OF NEW YORK PRESS

Published by
State University of New York Press, Albany

Printed in the United States of America

For information, contact State University of New York Press, Albany, NY
www.sunypress.edu

Production by Ryan Morris
Marketing by Michael Campochiaro

Library of Congress Cataloging in Publication Data

Duckworth, Douglas S., 1971–
Mipam on Buddha-nature : the ground of the Nyingma tradition / Douglas S. Duckworth.
p. cm.
Includes bibliographical references and index.
ISBN 978-0-7914-7521-8 (hardcover : alk. paper)
ISBN 978-0-7914-7522-5 (pbk. : alk.paper) 1. Mi-pham-rgya-mtsho, 'Jam-mgon 'Ju, 1846-1912. 2. Rñin-ma-pa (Sect)—Doctrines. 3. Madhyamika (Buddhism) 4. Buddhahood. I. Title.

BQ972.I457D83 2008
294.3'420423—dc22

2007037662

10 9 8 7 6 5 4 3 2 1

Contents

PREFACE

I have gathered here Mipam's writings on Buddha-nature from a variety of sources to show the central role of Buddha-nature in his works. In doing so, I do not stray far from his texts and include many excerpted translations. In the notes and text, I use the Wylie system to transliterate Tibetan into English. Also, I have adopted the THDL system of phonetic transcription developed by David Germano and Nicolas Tournadre to render Tibetan into English (hence, "Mipam" not "Mipham"). When relevant, I include Sanskrit technical terms parenthetically with the Tibetan.

As with all things, this book is the result of many causes and conditions. I would like to first express my deepest gratitude to Chökyi Nyima Rinpoché, and his late father, Tulku Urgyen, without whom I would not have had the inspiration to take on such a study as this. This book evolved out of my Ph.D. dissertation, entitled "Buddha-Nature and a Dialectic of Presence and Absence in the Works of Mi-pham" (University of Virginia, 2005); it would not have been possible without my peerless advisor, Professor Jeffrey Hopkins. I also owe a debt of gratitude to Professor David Germano, who has helped me over the years in many significant ways. Professors Hopkins and Germano have both consistently challenged me to deepen my understanding of texts and traditions in critical and creative ways. Professors Karen Lang and Robert Hueckstedt also gave me invaluable feedback in the early stages of this project.

My studies were made possible due to many learned Tibetan scholars, who I list in the order that I met them: the late Nyoshül Khenpo, Khenpo Orgyen Trinlé, the late Khenpo Jadrel, the late Khenpo Petsé, Khenpo Chöying Lhündrup, Khenpo Tupten Yeshé, Khenpo Yeshé

Trinlé, Khenpo Sherap Özer, Khenpo Nyima Töndrup, Khenpo Namdröl, Khenpo Tsültrim Dargyé, Aku Rapgyé, the late Khenpo Yönten Zangpo, Khenpo Jampa Lodrö, Khenpo Sherap Zangpo, Khenpo Sherap Dorjé, Khenpo Pema Sherap, Khenpo Kātyāyana, Khenpo Wangchuk Sönam, Khenpo Apé, Trülku Nyima Gyeltsen, Khenpo Tsülnam, and last but not least, Khenpo Tsültrim Lodrö. All these teachers, and others not mentioned, shared their wisdom with great kindness.

My interest in the academic study of Buddha-nature was sparked by my undergraduate professor, Sallie King, whom I would like to thank as a teacher, friend, and mentor. I am also grateful to Fulbright-Hays for providing me with a fellowship to do research in Nepal and India. Also, a summer stipend from the National Endowment for the Humanities helped me to bring this project to completion. I owe a special thanks to Professor John Dunne, who tutored me in Tibetan when I was first traveling in India after college. I would also like to thank Nawang Thokmey, a South Asian librarian at the University of Virginia, for helping me locate Tibetan texts, and Gene Smith, who introduced me to Jonang teachers and texts.

I wish to express my gratitude to all my other teachers, colleagues, friends, and family who have given me guidance over the years. In particular, communications with Thomas Doctor, Adam Pearcy, and Karma Phuntsho have helped my understanding of Mipam. Also, Cortland Dahl, David Duckworth, James Gentry, Charlie Orzech, Jimmy Pittard, Amanda Porterfield, and Jann Ronis have given me valuable feedback on this work. This book is dedicated to my family, and to anyone whose hair stands on end upon hearing about emptiness.

INTRODUCTION

This book addresses the relationship between presence and absence (emptiness) in Buddhist thought. It focuses on the Nyingma (*rnying ma*) tradition of Tibet as articulated in the works of Mipam (*'ju mi pham rgya mtsho*, 1846–1912), a great synthesizer of Buddhist doctrine and Nyingma philosophy. Mipam incorporates an extraordinarily wide range of discourses into his grand, systematic interpretation of Buddhist doctrine. I draw widely from his writings on the Middle Way (*dbu ma, madhyamaka*), epistemology (*tshad ma, pramāṇa*), and tantra to discuss the significance of an ontological "ground" (*gzhi*), or Buddha-nature, as the central theme in his overall interpretative scheme. I present Mipam's view across a range of topics to underscore Buddha-nature and a dialectic of presence and absence as a central thread that runs through his interpretative system.

The presence of Buddha-nature as intrinsic within the ground of existence is a predominant feature of the discourses of tantra in the Nyingma tradition of Tibet, and in particular, the Great Perfection (*rdzogs chen*). The Great Perfection is a textual and meditative tradition that affirms the nature of mind as the Buddha, and offers a radically direct approach to actualizing this reality. The view of the Great Perfection consistently evades systematic analysis and in a fundamental way is antithetical to abstract conceptual determination. While Mipam did not write extensively on the Great Perfection as an isolated topic, he elucidates the view of the Great Perfection in his exoteric writings by creatively formulating the esoteric discourses that have defined the Nyingma tradition—namely, the Great Perfection—in terms of central exoteric discourses of monastic Buddhism: Buddha-nature, the Middle Way, and Buddhist epistemological systems.

He skillfully incorporates esoteric discourses of Mantra (*sngags*) characteristic of his Nyingma predecessors into his commentaries on Indian śāstras.

Buddhist epistemology, a system that delineates the authentic means of knowing reality, plays an important role in Mipam's exegesis across both domains of esoteric and exoteric doctrines. Mipam integrates aspects of the Buddhist epistemological tradition with a view of Mantra, and associates the view of the Great Perfection with Prāsaṅgika-Madhyamaka. The Great Perfection is the Nyingma tradition's highest esoteric teaching and Prāsaṅgika-Madhyamaka is the philosophy commonly accepted in Tibet as the highest exoteric view. By integrating the esoteric teachings of Nyingma tantra with Buddhist epistemology and Prāsaṅgika-Madhyamaka, Mipam affirms the Nyingma as not only a tradition of tantric exegesis and ritual practice, but also as grounded within the rigorous intellectual traditions of Buddhist exoteric philosophy.

While discussing Mipam's treatment of Buddha-nature, or the ground, across a number of issues in his works, we will address in detail his representation of affirmation and negation. The English terms "affirmation" and "negation" refer to the realm of linguistic representation. To depict the issues at stake in a more meaningful way, I use the words "presence" and "absence," which have more of an ontological connotation—*what is* rather than simply its linguistic representation. Presence as such can be understood in two ways:

1. as a reified presence—the realm of conceptual or linguistic knowledge.
2. as an indeterminate presence—the realm of the mystical or divine ground of being.

We will see how the former presence is rejected, and discuss implications of the latter presence in Mipam's interpretation of Buddhist doctrine. In particular, we will look into the tension, or resonance, between the problem intrinsic to formulating such presence conceptually (or linguistically) as well as its fundamental place within the Buddhist tradition. A central concern here is the nature of philosophical reasoning and intellectual inquiry into Buddhist scriptural traditions.

Presence and Absence

In the course of this book, we will see how a dialectic of presence and absence is a central theme in Mipam's works. The relationship between emptiness and divine presence involves a fundamental tension in Buddhist exegetical discourse. For Mipam, a key to the resolution of this tension is the unity of emptiness and divine presence. The ground, or Buddha-nature, is a focal point around which he articulates this unity.

The topic of Buddha-nature spans the domains of metaphysics, theology, and philosophical anthropology. An etymology of the term "Buddha-nature" (*tathāgatagarbha*)[1] reflects the variable status and complexity of the subject matter. The Sanskrit compound *tathā + gata,* meaning "the thus gone one" (i.e., Buddha), is the same spelling as the compound *tathā + āgata,* meaning "the thus *come* one"; the term reveals the dual quality of a transcendent Buddha thus gone and an immanent Buddha thus come. Also, *garbha* can mean "embryo," "womb," and "essence." On the one hand, as an embryonic seed it denotes a latent potentiality to be *developed* and the subsequent consummation in the attainment of Buddhahood. As a womb, it connotes a comprehensive matrix or an all-embracing divine presence in the world to be *discovered.*

Academic scholars have described Buddha-nature in a number of ways. David Ruegg addresses a dual function of Buddha-nature in a dialectic between a *soteriological* point of view, in which the absolute is immanent in all beings, and a *gnoseological* point of view, in which it is altogether transcendent.[2] We can see that Buddha-nature is at once transcendent, a future potential, and at the same time immanently present. As such, Buddha-nature functions as a mediating principle spanning both the absolute and phenomenal worlds.

Another term for the Buddha-nature is "heritage" (*gotra*). Ruegg cites three main meanings of the term *gotra* in Buddhist usage: (1) germ, seed; (2) family, clan, lineage; (3) mine, matrix. He also mentions that the term *gotra* is designated *extensionally* as a soteriological or gnoseological category, and *intensionally* as the spiritual factor or capacity that determines the classification into that category.[3] The topic of Buddha-nature also is a basis for promoting "one vehicle" (*ekayāna*) of the Buddha, an inclusivist system of the Mahāyāna that incorporates all Buddhist traditions. The role of Buddha-nature as the single heritage of all beings distinguishes the Buddha-nature from Vijñānavāda (Mind-Only) traditions that accept five distinct heritages within three final vehicles (*śrāvaka, pratyekabuddha, bodhisattva*).

Another scholar, Florin Sutton, delineates three other roles of Buddha-nature: from a *theoretical* point of view, Buddha-nature is an extension of the Self/no-self debate, "providing the Yogācāras with a new, positive platform of defense against both the Hindu Eternalists and the Buddhist Nihilists"; from a *didactic* (or *practical*) point of view, it functions as an intermediate step between a narrowly defined notion of Self (*ātman*) and a more thorough understanding of no-self (*anātman*); and from an *ethical* point of view, it provides a philosophical basis for altruism in the Mahāyāna. Sutton also explains Buddha-nature to function in three ways: (1) as an essence, an "underlying ontological Reality, or essential nature behind phenomena"; (2) as an "embryo" or "seed"—a dynamic, evolving potential; and (3) as a "matrix" or "womb," an "intermediate" meaning (between the first two meanings), equated with the universal ground consciousness (*ālayavijñāna*).[4]

The discourse of Buddha-nature, as a pure essence abiding in temporarily obscured living beings, is a considerable diversion from the negative language found in many other Buddhist texts. The unchanging, permanent status attributed to Buddha-nature is a radical departure from the language emphasizing impermanence within the discourses of early Buddhism. Indeed, the language of Buddha-nature is strikingly similar to the very positions that Buddhists often argue against, demonstrating a decisive break from the early Buddhist triad of impermanence (*anitya*), suffering (*duḥkha*), and selflessness (*anātman*). The *Uttaratantra* (*ca.* fourth century), the first known commentarial treatise to deal explicitly with this topic, states: "The qualities of purity (*śubha*), self (*ātman*), bliss (*sukha*), and permanence (*nitya*) are the transcendent results."[5] Such affirmations are conspicuously absent in many other Buddhist texts. However, these terms are found in sūtras such as the *Laṅkāvatāra*, *Gaṇḍavyūha*, *Aṅgulimālīya*, *Śrīmālā*, and the *Mahāparinirvāṇa*, where they are used to describe the Buddha (*tathāgata*), the Truth Body (*dharmakāya*), and the Buddha-nature.[6] Furthermore, the *Laṅkāvatāra* uses the term "supreme Brahman" to describe the ultimate state of existence (*niṣṭhābhāvaḥ paraṃ brahma*).[7]

While the Perfection of Wisdom (*prajñāpāramitā*) Sūtras can be seen to function as an overturning of early Buddhist literature by depicting all phenomena as empty, Buddha-Nature Sūtras mark another radical inversion with the use of *ātman* in a positive light. This language has been said to have soteriological "shock value," to uproot reified conceptions of emptiness.[8] Nathan Katz has fittingly termed this phenomenon of contradictory claims as "hermeneutical shock."[9] The tension between the discourses of presence, as in the Buddha-Nature Sūtras, and emptiness, in the Perfection of Wisdom Sūtras, is a rich source from which divergent interpretations grew, and one that has a long history in the developments of Buddhist discourse. In an important way, opposed opinions and sectarian debates on this issue create and maintain the dynamic vitality of Buddhist traditions.

A lively dialectical tension between Buddha-nature and emptiness has continued in Tibet in terms of the competing doctrines of "other-emptiness" (*gzhan stong*) and "self-emptiness" (*rang stong*). The language of other-emptiness—which portrays the ultimate truth in affirming language—explicitly conflicts with the orthodox Geluk (*dge lugs*) formulation of the ultimate as a mere absence of inherent existence. A central issue concerning the status of other-emptiness is a recurring tension between presence and absence, which in Buddhist terms gets expressed in various ways such as appearance and emptiness, conventional and ultimate truth, Buddha-nature and emptiness, and other-emptiness and self-emptiness. This issue can be seen to have a history extending back to India in the competing depictions of the absolute as qualified (*saguṇa*) or unqualified (*nirguṇa*). A major tension in Tibetan thought is found between the positions that the ultimate truth must be a simple emptiness—a negation—in contrast to the positively framed depictions of ultimate reality as a divine presence existing at the ground of all. Across this spectrum we find a wide array of positions.

The most famous proponents of other-emptiness are found within the Jonang (*jo nang*) tradition, and Dölpopa (*dol po pa shes rab rgyal mtshan,* 1292–1361) in particular.[10] A view of other-emptiness in general involves affirming an ultimate ground of reality as a metaphysical presence that is empty of all phenomena that are extrinsic to it. We will discuss Dölpopa's view of other-emptiness in chapter 3, as well as look into the views of a Jonang scholar of the last century, Khenpo Lodrö Drakpa (*mkhan po blo gros grags pa,* 1920–1975).[11]

Tsongkhapa (*tsong kha pa blo bzang grags pa,* 1357–1419) and his Geluk followers were major critics of the Jonang, the emblematic tradition of other-emptiness. In contrast to the Jonang depiction of other-emptiness as a metaphysical presence, Tsongkhapa consistently argued that the ultimate truth is necessarily a mere absence.[12] He offered a clear delineation of what ultimate truth is: the lack of inherent existence. We will see how other traditions portray the ultimate truth in more affirming language, and offer a less delimited portrayal of ultimate reality than the one championed by the Geluk tradition following Tsongkhapa.

In order to fully appreciate the dialectical tension between presence and absence in Tibetan thought, we need to recognize the central role that the works of Dharmakīrti (600–660) and Candrakīrti (600–650) have played in Tibet. Representations of exoteric Buddhist discourse in Tibet have been dominated by the commentaries of Dharmakīrti and Candrakīrti. It is important to not only recognize this fact, but also to acknowledge its implications for how Buddhism is interpreted.

In Tibet, the negative dialectics of the Middle Way are typically identified with Candrakīrti's interpretation of Nāgārjuna, and systematic epistemology is associated with Dharmakīrti. These two figures are also held to be authoritative commentators on a univocal doctrine of Buddhism. Even though Candrakīrti explicitly criticized Buddhist epistemological systems in his *Prasannapadā*,[13] Buddhists in Tibet have integrated the theories of Candrakīrti with Dharmakīrti's epistemology in unique ways.[14] Within this integration, there is a tension between the epistemological system-building on the one hand, and "deconstructive" negative dialectics on the other. The integration of an epistemological system within the Middle Way is an important part of Mipam's philosophical edifice. He calls the integration of these two systems "the intertwined necks of the lions of the Middle Way and valid cognition."[15]

Along with Candrakīrti and Dharmakīrti, an important Indian figure for Mipam in particular is Śāntarakṣita (*ca.* eighth century), who synthesized components of epistemology with the Middle Way in a system of Yogācāra-Madhyamaka. Mipam explains that Śāntarakṣita's *Madhyamakālaṃkāra* is a treatise that demonstrates the essential point of all Mahāyāna, Sūtra and Mantra.[16] He states:

> Such a scripture as this is the universal path of the Mahāyāna, integrating the viewpoints of the scriptures of the two chariot traditions like water mixed with water. In particular, both (1) ultimate valid cognition in the way that Nāgārjuna asserts and (2) conventional valid cognition in the way that Dharmakīrti asserts are combined as one taste in the great ocean of reason.[17]

Śāntarakṣita's system of Yogācāra-Madhyamaka is important for Mipam in significant ways: not only does Yogācāra play a fundamental role in his systematic presentation of exoteric Buddhism, but it plays an important role in the narrative structure of the entire Buddhist path by putting forward wisdom as the ground and fruition of the Buddhist path. Moreover, the synthetic approach of Yogācāra is instrumental to the way that Mipam incorporates various systems of Buddhist thought in Tibet.

However, it is the reconciliation of Buddha-nature—particularly the affirmations of presence in tantra and the *Uttaratantra*—with depictions of emptiness in Candrakīrti's *Madhyamakāvatāra* that is a central part of

Mipam's exegesis. Mipam weaves together aspects of Dharmakīrti, Candrakīrti, and the *Uttaratantra* into his unique exegesis of Buddhist doctrine.

A number of scholarly works on Mipam have surfaced in the past decade. One example is Karma Phuntsho's recently published *Mipham's Dialectics and the Debates on Emptiness*. He discusses Mipam's works in light of polemical exchanges with Geluk scholars, and his work is an excellent source for Mipam's treatment of emptiness. Also, John Pettit's *Mipham's Beacon of Certainty*, which is focused around a translation of one of Mipam's texts with an annotated commentary, offers biographical information and provides a general background to central issues in Mipam's writings.

Another book-length study of Mipam was done by Paul Williams, whose work deals with the notion of "reflexive awareness" (*rang rig*) in Mipam's commentary on the ninth chapter of the *Bodhicaryāvatāra*.[18] In his book, Williams makes a case that Mipam can be understood as a proponent of "other-emptiness."[19] Matthew Kapstein, however, questions the usefulness of the indigenous labels of "self-emptiness" and "other-emptiness" in interpreting Buddhist thought, and cites a danger in overly generalizing these categories. As an alternative, he suggests that it is important to document the precise usages of such terms as they are employed by indigenous traditions.[20] In chapter 3, I have tried to document some ways in which "other-emptiness" and "self-emptiness" have been used by the specific Jonang and Nyingma authors I address, in order to further the understanding of how emptiness is represented in these traditions in general, and Mipam's position in particular.

There has been little written directly concerning the topic of Buddha-nature in the Nyingma tradition, particularly in Mipam's works. I intend to clarify the central role of Buddha-nature in his works through a broad-based representation of Mipam's view of Buddha-nature that takes into account his treatment of epistemology, negative dialectics, and tantra. By drawing upon a wide range of discourses that he treats, my aim is to provide a holistically-oriented account of Mipam's view of Buddha-nature.

Historical Survey

In the nineteenth century, what came to be known as a "nonsectarian" (*ris med*) movement developed in the eastern Tibetan province of Kham (*khams*). Alliances of a ritual, intellectual, literary, and institutional character formed among the traditions of the Kagyü (*bka' brgyud*), Sakya (*sa skya*), and

Nyingma following the political ascendancy of the Geluk tradition in central Tibet. This era of Tibetan history witnessed an intellectual and literary renaissance driven by a wave of creative doctrinal syntheses and new institutional movements toward formalized monastic education. The Nyingma tradition came to play a particularly influential role at this time, and a central figure and primary architect of the era was Mipam.

Mipam's Nyingma tradition identifies its origins within the dynastic period of the eighth century, although a self-conscious Nyingma tradition, known as the "old school," actually developed in response to attacks on the legitimacy of its translations by the Sarma tradition, the "new schools," which began to develop in Tibet from the activities of the famous translator Rinchen Zangpo (*rin chen bzang po,* 958–1055) in the eleventh century. Efforts to affirm the legitimacy, and superiority, of the Nyingma tradition are evident from early on in the works of Rongzom (*rong zom chos kyi bzang po, ca.* eleventh century) and Nyangrel (*myang ral nyi ma'i 'od gzer,* 1124–1192).

The Nyingma, with a textual tradition of translations dating back to the early dissemination of Buddhism in Tibet, claim a distinctive connection with the imperial age of Tibet—a theocratic polity populated by the enlightened figures of the Dharma King Trisong Detsen (*khri srong lde'u btsan*) and Padmasambhava—as well as translators who had privileged access to the living tradition of Buddhism in India before its destruction at the hands of Muslim invaders in the eleventh century. The Nyingma have been able to periodically reinvigorate their tradition to serve the contingencies of history through their "close lineage" (*nye brgyud*) of revealed teachings. In this close lineage, Buddhist canonical teachings are not limited to a specific set of texts, nor a specific individual in history, but remain within a tradition of an ongoing revelation, that in principle is open to anyone, at anytime.

Before Mipam, the Nyingma tradition was largely defined by their esoteric transmissions, particularly those of the *Guhyagarbhatantra.*[21] While many scholars of the Nyingma tradition certainly studied the exoteric texts of Buddhist sūtras and śāstras, they did not commonly write commentaries that focused on such exoteric texts. An important part of Mipam's contribution to his Nyingma tradition was to provide commentaries on exoteric texts that incorporated a Nyingma esoteric view.

Rongzom and Longchenpa (*klong chen rab 'byams,* 1308–1364) are Mipam's main Tibetan sources. Rongzom, an eleventh-century Nyingma apologist, composed a commentary on the main tantra of the Nyingma tradition, the *Guhyagarbhatantra.*[22] In his *Establishing Appearances as Divine,*[23] Rongzom notably draws upon Buddhist epistemology, exemplifying a unique relationship between tantra and Buddhist epistemology in Nyingma exegesis. Longchenpa, the fourteenth-century systematizer of Nyingma thought, also wrote a commentary on the *Guhyagarbhatantra*,[24] and is renowned for his writings on the Great Perfection, such as the "Seven Treasuries."[25] Mipam wrote catalogues for the publications of the Collected Works of Rongzom[26] and the "Seven Treasuries" of Longchenpa.[27] The influences of Rongzom and Longchenpa are prominently reflected in Mipam's works, particularly Longchenpa and the tradition of the Great Perfection. In many ways, his works can be seen as an extended commentary upon the writings of Longchenpa.[28]

Another important figure in the Nyingma tradition was Lochen Dharmaśrī (*lo chen dharmaśrī,* 1654–1717). Lochen and his brother, Terdak Lingpa (*gter bdag gling pa 'gyur med rdo rje,* 1646–1714), both of whom took ordination from the Fifth Dalai Lama (1617–1682), were important figures in the transmission of the Nyingma canon (*bka' ma*).[29] Terdak Lingpa founded the Nyingma monastery of Mindröling in 1670.[30] Lochen wrote commentaries of the *Guhyagarbhatantra*,[31] as well as a commentary on the three vows by Ngari Paṇchen (*nga ri paṇ chen padma dbang rgyal,* 1487–1542),[32] which we will address in the context of discussing the view of "other-emptiness" in contrast to Mipam's representation of emptiness.

We will also look briefly into the works of Getsé Paṇchen (*dge rtse paṇ chen, 'gyur med tshe dbang mchog grub,* 1761–1829), a Nyingma scholar from Kaḥtok (*kaḥ thog*) monastery, who set forth a view of other-emptiness that he says accords with the Great Perfection.[33] An explicit adoption of other-emptiness can be found in the Nyingma tradition affiliated with Kaḥtok monastery, which apparently stemmed from the works of Tsewang Norbu (*tshe dbang nor bu,* 1689–1755) in the eighteenth century. The popularity of other-emptiness in the nineteenth century seems to have been largely due to Tsewang Norbu.[34] He told Situ Paṇchen (*si tu paṇ chen chos kyi 'byung gnas,* 1699–1774) that if he upheld the view and practice of other-emptiness, then his activity would be certain to flourish, and he would bring benefit to the teachings and beings.[35] Situ Paṇchen was the founder of Pelpung (*dpal spungs*) monastery and the editor of the Degé (*sde dge*) edition of the Tibetan translations of the Buddha's Word (*bka' 'gyur*). Gene Smith conveys that Situ Paṇchen blended Mahāmudrā with a view of other-emptiness that he propagated throughout the Karma Kagyü traditions in Kham.[36]

Kongtrül (*kong sprul blo gros mtha' yas,* 1813–1899), one of Mipam's teachers, was a prominent figure at Pelpung in the following century. Kongtrül took up a view of other-emptiness as a means to unify the various sectarian views in Tibet.[37] His *Encyclopedia of Knowledge*[38] is a tremendous resource on different views and systems of thought throughout Tibet. Gene Smith credits Kongtrül's *Encyclopedia of Knowledge*, finished in 1864, as likely "the earliest statement of nonsectarian thought."[39]

Along with Kongtrül, another of Mipam's teachers, Jamyang Khyentsé Wangpo (*'jam dbyangs mkhyen brtse'i dbang po,* 1820–1892), was a prolific figure in nineteenth-century Kham. Among the many texts Khyentsé composed in his massive, twenty-four volume Collected Works, he wrote a summary of the other-emptiness view of the Jonang.[40] It is significant that the text immediately following this one in the volume is an exposition of the view and philosophy of Tsongkhapa, who is known as the founding father of the Geluk tradition and a prominent critic of the Jonang view.[41] Such an eclectic character is a predominant feature of the nonsectarian movement.

Monastic Education and the Nonsectarian Movement

Before the nineteenth century, the Nyingma tradition was mainly defined by its practice and exegesis of tantra, in particular, the *Guhyagarbhatantra.* This central tantra of the Nyingma tradition embraces what may be called a pantheistic vision of the world as an expression of divinity.[42] The institutional transformation of the Nyingma tradition in the late nineteenth and early twentieth centuries was a complex process of a systematization, or domestication, of the tantric vision of divine unity. Before the developments in monastic education during this time, the Nyingma tradition was more of a meditative, contemplative, and ritual tradition centered on the mystical vision of tantra. Mipam's work is a product of the synergy between the wild, divine world of tantra and the structured, analytic rigor of monastic education.

Mipam's work can be seen as a synthesis of two polarities that form the contours of Buddhism in Tibet: the esoteric discourses of tantra and the exoteric discourses of monastic education. His treatment of Buddha-nature plays a particularly important role in this synthesis. Through his exegesis of Buddha-nature, Mipam shows the compatibility of esoteric discourses such as the Great Perfection with the exoteric discourses of valid cognition (*tshad ma, pramāṇa*) and the Middle Way, which in his day played a prominent role in monastic education.

Earlier in the nineteenth century, Gyelsé Zhenpen Tayé (*rgyal sras gzhan phan mtha' yas,* 1800–1855?) had played an important role in the revitalization of Nyingma monasticism. He published the Nyingma canon (*bka' ma*) for the first time in ten volumes, founded Śrī Singha college at Dzokchen monastery, and instituted the rituals for the three foundations of the Vinaya at the monastery: the biweekly ritual of the vows for individual liberation, summer retreat, and the ritual for summer retreat recess. He rebuilt Dzokchen monastery with the support of the rulers of Degé, among others, after it was destroyed by an earthquake in 1842.[43] Many large monastic colleges soon followed the model at Dzokchen.[44]

Along with Dzokchen, another source of Nyingma monasticism comes from Kaḥtok, the oldest Nyingma monastic tradition, which stems back to the twelfth century. At Kaḥtok monastery, the Norbu Lhünpo (*nor bu lhun po*) monastic college, or "the tantric college of one hundred scriptures," was founded in 1906. This college was founded by Mipam, along with Kaḥtok Situ (*kaḥ thog si tu chos kyi rgya mtsho,* 1880–1923/25), and extending from this college, twenty-five monastic colleges were founded through Kaḥtok Situ's work.[45]

The hermeneutical principle of other-emptiness, adopted from the Jonang tradition by Kaḥtok Tsewang Norbu and Situ Paṇchen Chökyi Jungné, came to be employed by Nyingma scholars at Kaḥtok and Kagyü scholars at Pelpung. Nyingma scholars at Kaḥtok monastery appear to have drawn upon the exegetical language of other-emptiness more so than those at Dzokchen.

Mipam offers a uniquely Nyingma interpretative style that differs not only from other-emptiness, but also from Khenpo Zhenga (*mkhan po gzhan dga',* 1871–1927), a prominent professor at Dzokchen and an important figure in the revitalization of monastic education.[46] Nyoshül Khenpo (*smyo shul mkhan po 'jam dbyangs rdo rje,* 1931–1999) delineates two traditions of explanation in the Nyingma tradition: (1) the transmission of Khenpo Zhenga, which is the manner that Indian scriptures such as the thirteen great scriptures are explained, and (2) the transmission of Mipam, which is the manner of explanation mainly based on Tibetan commentaries such as Longchenpa, Rongzom, and Ngari Paṇchen. He states that many from Kaḥtok mainly follow the latter tradition.[47]

Khenpo Zhenga is famous for compiling textbooks for monastic colleges comprising his interlinear commentaries on "the thirteen great scriptures," Indian treatises that were considered to be the important texts representing the spectrum of major Buddhist discourses—namely, the Abhidharma, the Vinaya, the profound view (of the Middle Way), and the "five treatises of Maitreya."[48] Khenpo Zhenga concerns himself with an exposition upon Indian sources, not the Tibetan layers of commentary, in an attempt to interpret the Indian texts on their own terms.[49] His commentaries can be seen as a means to circumvent sectarian disputes by appealing to Indian originals rather than some specific strand of nearly one thousand years of Tibetan commentary.[50] His work contrasts not only with Kongtrül, who embraced an explicit other-emptiness interpretation, but also with Mipam. Mipam's works have a stronger Nyingma sectarian identity.

Nyoshül Khenpo quotes Mipam as stating that his own works were composed to ensure the legacy of the Nyingma tradition in future generations, whereas Khenpo Zhenga's transmission "maintains the viewpoint of Candrakīrti and both Rongzom and Longchenpa as the life-force, and spreads the continuum of explanation and practice in all directions."[51] In this light, Mipam's works can be seen to maintain a stronger sectarian identity than Khenpo Zhenga's; Mipam's own works explicitly draw from the Nyingma works of Rongzom and Longchenpa.

In contrast to the uniquely Nyingma identity concerning the commentarial tradition of Buddhist exoteric texts that Mipam had forged for Nyingma monasteries in Kham, several Nyingma monasteries in Amdo (*a mdo*), including the Dodrup (*rdo grub*) tradition, adopted Geluk exegesis for their exoteric curriculum while maintaining Nyingma tantric studies as their esoteric base.[52] The reliance on Geluk exegesis, however, became a target of Mipam's polemical works. Although he promoted an inclusivist agenda characteristic of the nonsectarian movement, he affirmed a strong Nyingma identity.

Before we turn to Mipam's life and works, I should mention that what it means to be nonsectarian is complex. It clearly does not mean that all traditions are seen as equal on all levels. Rather, attention to a broad range of interpretations can be seen as a general quality of what it means to be nonsectarian in Tibet. Such attention to a plurality of interpretations does not (necessarily) mean a coercive amalgamation of others' views with one's own, but involves a move in the direction of inclusiveness that contrasts with a more insular model of scholarship that frames the boundaries of discourse within a more narrowly delineated tradition of interpretation.

A unique quality of Mipam's form of (non)sectarianism is the level of his engagement in dialogue with his main "opponent," the Geluk: he appropriates certain aspects of Geluk thought, yet argues against what he finds to be problematic with their system of interpretation. His approach contrasts with four other ways of responding to the dominance of Geluk tradition, such as: (1) a more hostile attitude toward Geluk positions, such as found in the works of Gorampa;[53] (2) a more submissive attitude to Geluk authority on exoteric exegesis, such as found in the Dodrup tradition; (3) a more dismissive attitude that excludes Geluk from the conversation and remains focused solely within one's own tradition, such as what may be seen in the case of Padmavajra,[54] one of Mipam's teachers; and (4) a fourth alternative—wholesale conversion to Geluk (willed or forced). Mipam forged an alternative response to Geluk dominance by selectively appropriating certain features of the Geluk tradition while contesting others. It is this response that has become the formula for the enduring legacy of non-Geluk monastic colleges.

The nonsectarian tradition of Tibet is not univocal, and what it means to be nonsectarian is not so clearly delineated. A broader range of particular texts and traditions needs to be documented before we can understand the nature of a nonsectarian stance of Tibet. Also, further research into the sociohistorical matrix of nineteenth- and early twentieth-century Kham will be necessary before we can better assess the (non)sectarian climate of this time period.

Because newly formed alliances and shifting territories were characteristics of nineteenth- and early twentieth-century Tibet, it may be that it was an ideology of alliance that characterizes the so-called nonsectarian movement. In Kham, the proliferation of incarnation lineages exemplifies this. There, we witness the emergence of a system developing from one recognized incarnation to three (body, speech, mind) and five (quality and activity), as multiple incarnations of deceased teachers were recognized within other sectarian traditions.[55] Actively forming alliances between disparate sectarian traditions helped strengthen feeble traditions. After the devastation of the Nyakrong wars in the middle of the nineteenth-century,[56] Kham, which is sandwiched between the two dominant forces of China and central Tibet, proved to be a contested territory. It was in this turbulent and creative time that Mipam lived.

Life and Works of Mipam

Mipam was born to an aristocratic family in Degé in eastern Tibet.[57] He memorized Ngari Paṇchen's *Ascertaining the Three Vows* (*sdom gsum rnam nges*) when he was about six years old. He also studied Indian and Chinese systems of astrology at a young age. When he was ten, it is said that he was "unobstructed in reading and writing," and composed a few short texts.[58] He became a novice monk when he was twelve, entering the monastery of Jumohor (*'ju mo hor gsang sngags chos gling*), a branch of Zhechen (*zhe chen*) monastery connected with the lineage of Mindröling. There, he was a child prodigy, and came to be known as "the little scholar-monk."[59]

After doing a retreat for eighteen months at Junyung (*'ju nyung*) on Mañjuśrī, the Lion of Speech, it is said that he achieved signs of accomplishment. From then on, he knew the scriptures without studying, and did not need to study other than simply receiving reading transmissions (*lung*). He went to Golok (*mgo log*) in 1859, due to the onset of the Nyakrong wars. In 1861, he went to Lhasa on pilgrimage, and studied at the Geluk monastery of Ganden (*dga' ldan*) for about a month.[60]

He studied with a number of prominent teachers of his day, including Khyentsé, Peltrül (*dpal sprul o rgyan chos kyi dbang po,* 1808–1887), and Kongtrül.[61] With Peltrül, he studied the *Bodhicaryāvatāra*; and later composed a commentary on the ninth chapter of the *Bodhicaryāvatāra*, the Wisdom Chapter. His commentary became a source of contention with some scholars in the Geluk tradition.[62] Mipam studied the common arts, such as grammar, with Kongtrül, as well as various extraordinary practices of ripening and liberation. With Dzokchen Khenpo Padmavajra (*padma badzra,* 1867–1934), he studied a wide range of scriptures: Sūtra, Mantra, and the arts.[63]

When Mipam studied the *Madhyamakāvatāra* with Geshé Ngawang Jungné, he asked for only the reading transmission, saying that he need not bother with a detailed commentary. After hearing the teacher read the text just once, Mipam then explained it all from the beginning. The teacher responded, "Although I have the title of 'Geshé' (doctor, professor), I don't have even a fraction of the intellect of this one!"[64]

Mipam is a unique figure of his time because he was not endorsed as an incarnate lama (*sprul sku*), at least not while alive. Also, unlike many other prominent figures of his day, such as Kongtrül, Khyentsé, and Chokgyur Lingpa (*mchog gyur bde chen gling pa,* 1829–1870), Mipam did not actively promote the new traditions of treasure text (*gter ma*) revelations; he neither discovered earth treasure texts (*sa gter*) publicly nor wrote extensive commentaries on them.[65] Rather, he wrote numerous commentaries on a variety of diverse topics, ranging from logic, poetics, the Middle Way (both Prāsaṅgika and Yogācāra), medicine, astrology, including a sex manual; in short, he was a polymath.[66] He also wrote on Tibetan translations of Indian texts, including tantras from the "new schools" (*gsar ma*),[67] the *Guhyagarbhatantra* of his own Nyingma tradition, and Buddha-nature, which is the primary focus of this book.

Mipam wrote on a variety of subjects. His literary output, which has been reproduced in twenty-seven volumes, is among the largest of any Tibetan author. A catalogue of his works divides his texts into four cycles: (1)

the cycle of narratives and eulogies, (2) the cycle of ordinary arts, (3) the cycle of the inner art (i.e., Buddhism), and (4) the cycle of dedications, auspicious verses, and prayers. The first cycle, which is said to foster faith, has four sections concerning:

1. eulogy
2. narrative
3. worship
4. miscellaneous supplications[68]

The second cycle of ordinary arts, which is said to foster comprehensive knowledge, has two parts: (1) the four major arts and (2) the subsidiary arts. The four major arts are:

1. linguistics
2. epistemology
3. material arts
4. healing, together with additional topics[69]

The subsidiary arts are:

1. poetics
2. astrological divination
3. counsel
4. miscellany[70]

The third cycle is divided into four sections (the first of which is the primary topic of this book). The four sections are:

1. Commentaries on the viewpoint of the Vehicle of Characteristics:[71]
    - Commentaries on the general meaning of scriptures
    - Commentaries on the specific scriptures
2. The Vajrayāna of the common inner-tantras and outer-tantras[72]
3. The extraordinary Vajrayāna of the quintessential instructions of the *Kālacakratantra*[73]
4. Oral instructions on practice within the unexcelled Nyingma:
    - Explanatory commentarial notes[74]
    - Ritual accomplishment texts[75]

- Quintessential instructions on the activities[76]
    - Specific four activities:
        - pacifying
        - enriching
        - magnetizing
        - subjugating
    - Common variety
- Oral instructions on practice.[77]

The last of the four main sections of Mipam's corpus is the cycle of dedications, auspicious verses, and prayers.[78]

While we are left with a voluminous corpus of his literary output, Mipam's life story describes him as not studying very much, and spending a lot of time in retreat. He was encouraged to write commentaries on the major Indian and Tibetan treatises by his teacher, Jamyang Khyentsé Wangpo.[79] He states that he wrote the texts to fulfill his teacher's wishes. Also, he says that he wrote them due to the fact that the teachings of the Nyingma tradition had dwindled to near extinction, and that most people were simply following after what others say.[80] Unlike the other prominent sectarian traditions in Tibet, the Nyingma did not have an authoritative commentarial corpus on the central exoteric Buddhist treatises from India before Mipam.

His texts have been very influential and many of his works came to be adopted within the curriculum of Nyingma monastic colleges. Mipam's works have continued to play an important part in the monastic colleges in India, Nepal, and Tibet up to the present day. His texts constitute about 25 percent of the entire course of study at Larung Gar (*bla rung gar*), which lies in the eastern Tibetan region of Serta (*gser rta*) and is currently the largest monastic college in the world.[81] Also, the curriculum of the Ngagyur Nyingma Institute in Mysore, India, which is currently the largest Nyingma monastic college in exile, includes Mipam's commentaries on Indian treatises such as the *Abhidharmakośa*, *Madhyamakālaṃkāra*, *Pramāṇavārttika*, *Mahāyānasūtrālaṃkāra*, the ninth chapter of the *Bodhicaryāvatāra*, and *Kāvyādarśa*. Their curriculum also includes his commentaries on Longchenpa's *Wish-Fulfilling Treasury* and *Guhyagarbha* commentary, as well as Mipam's compositions such as *Gateway to Scholarship*, *Sword of Supreme Knowledge*, *Beacon of Certainty*, and *Lion's Roar: Exposition of Buddha-Nature*, among others.[82] His works have come to play a prominent role in Nyingma monastic education.

Two events in Mipam's life in particular directly relate to the topic of this book. The first is his dream of Sakya Paṇḍita, a thirteenth-century Sakya scholar, upon his reading of Dharmakīrti's influential text on Buddhist epistemology, the *Pramāṇavārttika*. In his dream, Sakya Paṇḍita tells Mipam, "What is to be known about epistemology in the *Pramāṇavārttika*? It is negation and affirmation."[83] He then divided the text in two and told Mipam to put the two parts of the text together. When he did, they became a sword and all objects of knowledge appeared before him. He swung the sword once and cut through them all unobstructedly. Henceforth, there was not a word in the *Pramāṇavārttika* that he did not know.[84]

Within Mipam's visionary experience, we get a hint of the import of the all-inclusiveness of negation and affirmation in the system of epistemology set up by Dharmakīrti. Dharmakīrti put forth a binary system of knowledge: (1) the real and (2) the unreal. The real and the unreal correspond to the radical dichotomy of (1) particulars and (2) universals, respectively. These two are validly known by either (1) direct perception or (2) inference; exclusively by means of either (1) nonconceptual, "affirming engagement" or (2) conceptual, "eliminative engagement" (negating contradistinctions). All these dichotomies boil down to negation and affirmation.

The dichotomy of negation and affirmation is a central part of the structure of Dharmakīrti's epistemology. Negation and affirmation constitute the two means of conventional valid knowledge, and understanding this dichotomy is fundamental to understanding Buddhist epistemology, at least as it functions on the ordinary level.[85]

Another significant moment in Mipam's life story is when he debated with Japa Dongak (*'ja' pa mdo sngags*), with Peltrül acting as moderator. The debate appeared to be even, so Peltrül suggested that they turn to the topic of "the universal form of the Great Perfection" (*rdzogs pa chen po'i spyi gzugs*) because Japa Dongak had written a commentary on this. It is during the debate on this topic, "the universal form of the Great Perfection," that Mipam won the debate.[86]

Here we see that the Great Perfection is not simply an anti-intellectual meditative practice that rejects reasoned inquiry; it can involve analysis and polemical exchange. Indeed, the dialectical inquiry into the Great Perfection has a prominent place in Mipam's works. Herein we find his significant contribution to Nyingma philosophy, and it is this topic that distinguishes the unique character of his view. The meaning of the Great Perfection, as conveyed through the ground (*gzhi*) and Buddha-nature, is central to the Nyingma view.

Summary of Contents

The dialectical unity[87] of presence and absence is a theme that runs through Mipam's works. This central theme can be seen in his treatment of a variety of topics: appearance versus emptiness, authentic versus inauthentic experience, sūtra (the last vs. middle "wheels of doctrine"), śāstra (Yogācāra vs. Prāsaṅgika), an ontology of emptiness (other-emptiness vs. self-emptiness), an epistemology of Buddha-nature (extraordinary logic vs. ordinary logic), Mahāyoga Tantra (purity vs. equality), and the Great Perfection (spontaneous presence vs. primordial purity). The structure of the chapters follows somewhat of a historical progression of the development of these topics; it can also be seen as a dialectical ascent into a deepening ground of subjectivity, which in Buddhist terms is expressed as wisdom.

We will also look at how Mipam's works are interpreted through the writings of Bötrül (*bod sprul mdo sngags bstan pa'i nyi ma,* 1898–1959), a scholar from the eastern region of central Tibet called Dakpo (*dwags po*), who was a prominent commentator on Mipam's works. Bötrül was recognized to be an incarnation of Peltrül by his teacher, Khenpo Künpel (*kun bzang dpal ldan,* 1870/2–1943), who was Mipam's direct disciple.[88] In his main work, *Distinguishing the Views and Philosophies* (*lta grub shan 'byed*), Bötrül elucidates Mipam's view on a number of topics discussed below.

Chapter 1 discusses Mipam's interpretation of Buddhist sūtras in terms of the "wheels of doctrine" (*chos 'khor, dharmacākra*) and the two truths. The chapter begins by looking at how Longchenpa represents the three wheels of doctrine, and then turns to how Mipam integrates the middle wheel and the last wheel of doctrines through his interpretation of Buddha-nature. This chapter introduces Mipam's important delineation of two models for the two truths. One two-truth model is based on a distinction between appearance and emptiness (*snang stong bden gnyis*), and the other is in terms of authentic and inauthentic experience (*gnas snang bden gnyis*). The first model can be seen as dealing with ontology, or what is, and the latter model can be seen as dealing with epistemology, or the way we know. We will see how Mipam shows the compatibility of emptiness and Buddha-nature through these two models of the two truths.

The chapter also discusses theories of interpretation based on the categories of "definitive meaning" (*nges don, nītārtha*) and "provisional meaning" (*drang don, neyārtha*). We will see how Bötrül describes the two-truth model according to Candrakīrti's *Madhyamakāvatāra* as concerning appearance and emptiness. He aligns this model with the middle wheel of doctrine, for which the explicit teaching is emptiness. As such, any appearance is necessarily a relative truth. In contrast, he depicts the two truths according to the *Uttaratantra* as the model of authentic/inauthentic experience, in accord with the two truths in Buddha-Nature Sūtras of the last wheel of doctrine. In this case, the ultimate truth is not only emptiness because appearances that accord with reality are the ultimate truth, as is the subject that experiences reality authentically. Conversely, inauthentic experience and distorted modes of being are relative. Through integrating both models of two truths from the *Madhyamakāvatāra* and the *Uttaratantra*, appearance/emptiness and authentic/inauthentic experience, respectively, Bötrül shows how (1) Buddha-nature is the ultimate truth as authentic experience and (2) Buddha-nature is the unity of the two truths of appearance/emptiness.

Chapter 2 discusses the Middle Way in contrasting depictions of Prāsaṅgika-Madhyamaka and Yogācāra-Madhyamaka. It begins by introducing how Mipam distinguishes Prāsaṅgika from Svātantrika. The relationship between Prāsaṅgika and Svātantrika, as distinctive approaches to the Middle Way, is a disputed topic in Tibet.[89] A key point of Mipam's delineation of Prāsaṅgika and Svātantrika is his distinction between two types of ultimate truth: the "categorized ultimate" (*rnam grangs pa'i don dam*) and the "uncategorized ultimate" (*rnam grangs ma yin pa'i don dam*). The categorized ultimate is emptiness that is known conceptually and the uncategorized ultimate is emptiness that is beyond language and thought.

In the contexts of language and thought, the two truths are distinct; however, the two truths are not distinguished in the context of nonconceptual meditative equipoise. Mipam delineates the Prāsaṅgika as a discourse emphasizing the uncategorized ultimate, in accord with the perspective of wisdom in meditative equipoise. In contrast, he depicts the Svātantrika as a discourse emphasizing the categorized ultimate, which accords with the contexts of postmeditation when the two truths are divided and the ultimate truth can only be conceptually known. We come to see how he makes a distinction between wisdom (*ye shes*), as the context emphasized by Prāsaṅgika, and ordinary consciousness (*rnam shes*), as the context emphasized by Svātantrika. We will also see how in Yogācāra, wisdom is held to be the ultimate truth in contrast to consciousness.

Mipam also depicts Prāsaṅgika as an instantaneous means to eliminate conceptual constructs, in contrast to the progressive path emphasized in Svātantrika. Other than different means of approaching the ultimate truth, however, he does not delineate a distinct view for Prāsaṅgika that is different from Svātantrika. He emphasizes the compatibility of Prāsaṅgika and

Svātantrika by stating that the unique object of negation for the Prāsaṅgika is only the conception of the two truths as distinct. In this way, Mipam emphasizes the unity of the two truths as a characteristic of Prāsaṅgika discourse.

Yogācāra also has an important place in Mipam's characterization of ultimate truth as the authentic experience of wisdom. Moreover, Yogācāra plays a central role in his formulation of conventional reality as Mind-Only. We will see how Mipam situates the discourse of Prāsaṅgika to represent the nonconceptual unity of the two truths; it functions to deconstruct the distinction between the two truths. Yogācāra, in contrast, plays a *constructive* role in his systematic representation of two truths. As opposed to Prāsaṅgika, Yogācāra provides a comprehensive structure to his systematic interpretation, within which the conceptual is distinguished from the nonconceptual, and consciousness is distinguished from wisdom. He draws from both Prāsaṅgika and Yogācāra in his characterization of the Middle Way.

Chapter 3 explores Mipam's depiction of emptiness in more detail. In particular, it addresses the categories of "self-emptiness" and "other-emptiness." The chapter begins by introducing depictions of self-emptiness and other-emptiness in the works of two Jonang scholars: Dölpopa and Khenpo Lodrö Drakpa. Then it looks into the representations of self-emptiness and other-emptiness in the works of a Nyingma scholar, Lochen Dharmaśrī. By discussing these different depictions of emptiness, we are able to provide some contrast with Mipam's descriptions of emptiness and ultimate reality. We will see that Mipam is a proponent of self-emptiness in terms of the way he characterizes "self-emptiness."

This chapter looks in detail at the way Mipam articulates the view of emptiness. We will see that Mipam emphasizes the *unity* of emptiness and appearance; he argues against the notions of a non-empty appearance and a non-appearing emptiness. He also consistently emphasizes that emptiness is beyond any conceptual or linguistic referent. He argues that any conception of emptiness is not the genuine emptiness, and represents genuine emptiness as beyond dichotomies such as existence and nonexistence or substance and quality. He also makes an important distinction between conventional assertions—where things appear to be distinct and are said to exist as such—and assertions concerning the ultimate in which no such divisions are made.

Chapter 4 addresses the explicit topic of Buddha-nature. Mipam depicts Buddha-nature as the suchness (*chos nyid, dharmatā*) of mind and reality. Buddha-nature, like emptiness, is the unity of appearance and emptiness. He affirms that the qualities of Buddha are primordially present, but are simply not manifest for sentient beings. He distinguishes his view of Buddha-nature from other views and adopts a view of Buddha-nature that reflects Longchenpa's depiction of the ground of the Great Perfection. Buddha-nature thus represents the ground of indivisible truth—empty, or "primordially pure" (*ka dag*), and "spontaneously present" (*lhun grub*) from the beginning.

Chapter 5 begins with a discussion of Mipam's use of reasoning to establish the existence of Buddha-nature. The reasoning that he uses draws upon the epistemological tradition of valid cognition. Mipam integrates an epistemological system of valid cognition with what he claims is beyond conceptual frameworks. We will see how he incorporates valid cognition into his exegesis of Buddha-nature and Mantra. In this integration, he portrays consciousness' ordinary reason as only a provisional means of knowledge; true knowledge is the inner wisdom that is Buddha-nature, which is present from the beginning. His use of reasoning to establish the presence of Buddha-nature is similar to the reasoning he uses to establish the divine nature of appearances in Mantra. This use of valid cognition to establish appearances as divine is a unique quality of the Nyingma tradition, as Mipam states, which he attributes to the works of Rongzom.

In this chapter, we will consider Mipam's treatment of Buddha-nature in light of exoteric Buddhism (Mantra). We will discuss Mipam's distinction between Sūtra and Mantra as well as see how he integrates them.[90] In particular, we will see how he delineates two types of conventional valid cognition, based on "confined perception" (*tshur mthong*) and "pure vision" (*dag gzigs*), respectively. His two conventional valid cognitions are similar to his two ultimate valid cognitions, those that concern the categorized and uncategorized ultimate, in that the division is grounded in two distinct modes of understanding: (1) a delimited, conceptual mode of mind and (2) an inconceivable mode of wisdom. In this we see again how he juxtaposes conceptual mind and nonconceptual wisdom.

Each of the chapters deals with a distinct dialectical tension in Buddhist doctrine and discusses Mipam's resolution of each of these tensions: chapter 1 treats the two truths in the middle and last wheels of sūtra—the relationship between emptiness and Buddha-nature; chapter 2 explores the relationship between Prāsaṅgika's radically negative dialectic and Yogācāra's substantialist epistemology; chapter 3 deals with the nature of emptiness—as "other-emptiness" or "self-emptiness"; chapter 4 addresses the relationship between appearance and reality in a discussion of the explicit topic of

Buddha-nature, and chapter 5 discusses the relationship between tantra and epistemology, and addresses the fundamental role of subjectivity—reality as grounded within the divine versus a world of ordinary perception.

In the course of the chapters, we will see that the monistic[91] resolution of duality is central to Mipam's exegetical system. A common theme in his exegesis is a twofold schema, with an ultimately false dichotomy of two opposed factors and a unified ground that emerges from their dissolution. Two provisionally opposed factors, such as the two truths, saṃsāra and nirvāṇa, self and other, appearance and emptiness, and so on, are resolved in a synthesis in which each of the two distinctions is ultimately untrue, because they are actually indivisible from the beginning. His manner of representing the indivisible ground, however, goes through a virtual "detour" of dichotomization. Thus, such a system is not a simple monism but is better understood as a *dialectical monism*.[92] The detour through ultimately unreal dichotomies is a process that involves everything that falls under the rubric of conventional reality—all that can be physically acted upon, verbally spoken of, and mentally thought about. In Mipam's depictions of the indivisible ground, these provisional divisions are part of a process toward the complete realization of the single ultimate truth of a unified ground—Buddha-nature.

The End of the Beginning

When we inquire into Buddhist thought, it is not hard to see that Buddhist discourse does not sustain such dichotomies as religion versus philosophy, *mythos* versus *logos*, the premodern versus the modern, and so on. The topic of Buddha-nature in particular has a meaning that is both objective and subjective or, in other words, it does not fall only within the domain of either "philosophy" or "religion." We should acknowledge that such categories are bound up with modern (northwest European) cultural traditions; they are not natural categories and thus are not always helpful for reaching an understanding of another cultural tradition.

I suggest that Mipam's work can be more fully appreciated when not seen as a response to an issue in the distant past—of a medieval, "premodern" situation. The presence of a mature epistemological system in Buddhism, its radical suspicion of language, along with its deep-rooted tradition of reasoned critique that incorporates a strong presence of logical and empirical skepticism, are all factors that problematize the categorization of Buddhism as premodern. However, Buddhism is not rightfully labeled "modern" either because there is no such appeal to a distinct realm of objective truth within a strict subject-object duality; Buddhist truth is immanently grounded in subjectivity. Furthermore, without the reductionist conception of the world as a mechanistic system, Buddhists like Mipam never detached themselves from the notion of a "sacred cosmos."[93]

What alternative is available for this tradition of Buddhism apart from a traditional dichotomy of the premodern *mythos* grounding being in a sacred cosmos and the *logos* of a modern critical consciousness? It may be the category of the "postmodern" that is more relevant to Mipam's late nineteenth- and early twentieth-century interpretation of Buddhism than the other two alternatives. I use the category postmodern to refer specifically to a constructive, postcritical consciousness in religious hermeneutics. Here, I follow David Klemm's characterization of postmodern hermeneutics as a process of negotiating the space between participation in meaning and objectifying critical reflection.[94]

An important point to this postmodern gesture is acknowledging the role of *participation in understanding*. Such an approach to meaning contrasts with a precritical approach to meaning as the literal or figurative content of symbols (premodern), or the view that meaning is a distant and distinct object of critical observation (modern). By recognizing that understanding is necessarily *participatory*, we can appreciate how an inquiry into Buddha-nature presumes the act of participation. That is, we can see how an understanding of Buddha-nature happens *within* Buddha-nature, and how knowing Buddha-nature is a reflexive act. In this light, our understanding of Buddha-nature in some way entails *Buddha-nature knowing itself* (*oneself*).[95]

For Mipam, knowledge of Buddha-nature is not only via a subjective mystical wisdom, but an intersubjective critical consciousness also plays an important role. We can see this interplay of critical consciousness and wisdom in Paul Ricoeur's characterization of a postcritical hermeneutics:

> Thus, hermeneutics, an acquisition of "modernity," is one of the modes by which that "modernity" transcends itself, insofar as it is forgetfulness of the sacred. I believe that being can still speak to me—no longer, of course, under the precritical form of immediate belief, but as the second immediacy aimed at by hermeneutics. This second naïveté aims to be the postcritical equivalent to the precritical hierophany.[96]

It is useful to see Mipam's portrayal of Buddha-nature as a postcritical approach to being. The approach is not naïve and uncritical but is something like Ricoeur's "second naïveté" that *incorporates and transcends* a critical component. In this light, we can see how Mipam's representation of Buddha-nature can be situated within a central problematic of postmodern religious hermeneutics, in terms of how he configures the relationship between (1) critical consciousness and (2) participation in a meaningful existence within a sacred cosmos. As such, we can recognize how he positions critical consciousness as an integral, albeit provisional, part of meaningful understanding. Also, we can come to appreciate how critical consciousness and religious meaning need not be polarized into a dichotomous relationship of mutual incompatibility.

In the following chapters, I will try to present Buddha-nature in a scholarly way that allows for a meaningful encounter with what is arguably the most central topic of Buddhism. My agenda is to present an interpretation of Buddha-nature that can be considered in a way that avoids the pitfalls of a naïve nostalgia for a premodern vision of sacred unity, as well as a cool objectivity of disembodied reason in a modern world of dispassionate truths.

CHAPTER ONE

Buddha-Nature and the Unity of the Two Truths

The whole of philosophy is nothing else but a study of the definition of unity.

—G. W. F. Hegel, *Lectures on the Philosophy of Religion, Volume 1*

Introduction

Conflicting depictions of truth, and how ultimate reality should be best expressed—through negation or affirmation—is a contested issue in Mahāyāna Buddhism. In particular, this issue concerns the relationship between the affirmations of a true presence of divine wisdom on the one hand, and the negating discourse of emptiness, as evinced in scriptures such as the Perfection of Wisdom Sūtras, on the other. The competing interpretations of the relationship between contrasting descriptions of ultimate reality—as a presence and an absence—are fueled by the polysemy of Buddhist scriptures and the agenda to systematize them into a comprehensive whole.[1] This is clearly evident in how traditions in Tibet interpret Buddhist sūtras in terms of three wheels of doctrine, and in particular, how they distinguish between the "middle wheel" and the "last wheel."

An influential scripture for interpreting scriptures for Buddhists in Tibet is the *Saṃdhinirmocanasūtra*,[2] "the scripture explaining the intent," within which the Buddha gives guidelines for interpreting scriptures. A section of this text outlines three distinct "wheels of doctrine," offering a resolution to the conflicting literal statements of Buddhist teachings. The following citation from this text is a common source for the delineation of Buddha's teaching into three sections:

> Thereupon, the bodhisattva Paramārthasamudgata said to the Blessed One, "Initially, the Blessed One at Deer Park, in the region of Vārāṇasī, taught the four noble truths to the ones who fully engage in the vehicle of the Auditors. He fully turned the miraculous and amazing wheel of doctrine in a way unlike anything that had been turned in this world before by anyone, human or deity. Furthermore, this wheel of doctrine that the Blessed One turned is surpassed, affords an occasion [of refutation], is the provisional meaning, and is the subject of dispute.
>
> "Based on the essencelessness of phenomena, and based on non-arising, unceasing, primordial peace, and naturally complete nirvāṇa, the Blessed One turned the greatly miraculous and amazing second wheel of doctrine, with the feature of the discourse of emptiness, for those who fully engage in the Mahāyāna. Furthermore, this wheel of doctrine that the Blessed One turned is surpassed, affords an occasion [of refutation], is the provisional meaning, and is the subject of dispute.
>
> "However, based on the essencelessness of phenomena, and based on non-arising, unceasing, primordial peace, and naturally complete nirvāṇa, for those who fully engage in all of the vehicles, the Blessed One taught the completely amazing and miraculous third wheel endowed with the excellent differentiation. This wheel of doctrine turned by the Blessed One is unsurpassed, affords no occasion [of refutation], is the definitive meaning, and is not the subject of dispute."[3]

Longchenpa, an important figure in shaping the Nyingma tradition, characterizes the first two wheels of the Buddha's Word as involving what is to be abandoned, and the last wheel as affirming what is:

> The first Word, the category of the doctrine of the four truths, is mainly intended for the engagement of novices and for those with slightly inferior intellects; it clearly teaches the methods of practicing the stages of abandonment and remedy. The middle Word, the category of the doctrine of signlessness, is mainly intended for the

stages of engagement of those who have trained slightly and those with mediocre faculties; it teaches the antidote of the category of naturelessness and the apprehensions of self as non-arising. The last Word, the category of the doctrine of the definitive meaning, is mainly [intended] for the stages of engagement of those who fully [train in all] vehicles and for those of sharp faculties; it extensively teaches the category of the basic nature as it is. The first [Word] shows the path that counteracts what is to be abandoned—the character of saṃsāra. The middle [Word] shows, from what is to be abandoned, the abandonment of cognitive obscurations through the nature of apprehension lacking essence. The last [Word] shows the essential nature as it is.[4]

In this way, he shows a progression of the three wheels of doctrine in which the first two wheels show what is to be abandoned—the character of saṃsāra and cognitive obscurations—and the last wheel shows what is, the essential nature. Similarly, in his autocommentary of his *Resting in the Nature of Mind*, Longchenpa also states that the three wheels of doctrine are intended for those of differing capacities: the first wheel is intended for those of inferior faculties, the middle wheel is intended for those of mediocre faculties, and the last wheel is intended for those of sharp faculties.[5] Longchenpa again shows the preeminence of the last wheel in his autocommentary of his *Treasury of Words and Meanings:*

> From the three wheels of doctrine taught by the Victorious One, this topic was taught in the last wheel that ascertains the ultimate, yet you have failed to understand this. If solely emptiness were the ultimate, then what sense does it make that the Buddha taught three wheels separately? He taught emptiness as a provisional meaning, with the intention of merely negating fear of the abiding reality, and apprehension of self by novices.[6]

Longchenpa argues that solely emptiness, a mere absence, is not the ultimate. He states here that the topic of the last wheel of doctrine is the ultimate and that emptiness is a provisional meaning. Distinguishing the category of "the definitive meaning," as opposed to "provisional meanings," is a common way Buddhists differentiate what is really true from what is only *provisionally*, or *heuristically*, true. In his autocommentary of his *Resting in the Nature of Mind*, Longchenpa says that emptiness is not the definitive meaning: "Although you fixate upon no-self and emptiness, these are merely antidotes to the self and the non-empty; they are not the definitive meaning."[7] Also, in the *Treasury of Philosophies*, he states:

> Seeing the nature of that which is the expanse of the ultimate truth is called "seeing the ultimate truth," the ultimate truth is not an emptiness that is nothing whatsoever. That [emptiness] is taught to immature beings and to novices as an antidote to ego-clinging, etc. In actuality, it should be known that the luminous and clear expanse exists as unconditioned and spontaneously present.[8]

In these texts, Longchenpa explicitly states that *emptiness alone* is not the ultimate truth. We will return to the works of Longchenpa later, as he is perhaps the most significant influence on Mipam's writings. We will also look in some detail in this chapter at Bötrül's commentary on Mipam's work. First we will turn to Mipam.

Mipam's Synthesis

Mipam takes Longchenpa's explanations as a foundation for his interpretation that integrates the middle and last wheels of doctrine. Mipam does not relegate the status of *either* emptiness in the middle wheel *or* wisdom in the last wheel of doctrine as a provisional meaning. Rather, he argues that *both* are definitive:

> The emptiness taught in the middle wheel and the exalted body and wisdom[9] taught in the last wheel should be integrated as a unity of emptiness and appearance. Without dividing or excluding the definitive meaning subject matters of the middle and last wheels, both should be held to be the definitive meaning in the way of just this assertion by the omniscient Longchen Rapjam.[10]

Mipam cites Longchenpa as a source to support his interpretation of the unity of emptiness and wisdom as the definitive meaning of the middle and last wheels.[11] Mipam explains that the last wheel's status as the definitive meaning does not refer to everything taught in the last wheel, but specifically concerns the teaching of Buddha-nature:

> Even though the reasoning that analyzes the ultimate establishes the emptiness of all phenomena, it does not negate the qualities of [Buddha-]nature, because although the sublime qualities exist, they are also claimed to be essentially empty. Therefore, the meaning demonstrated by the middle wheel that all the phenomena of thorough affliction and complete purification are taught to be empty is established as such because Buddha-nature is also the nature of emptiness. However, since this teaching of [Buddha-]nature—characterized as neither conjoined with nor separable from the appearances of the empty-natured exalted body and wisdom—is the viewpoint of the definitive meaning sūtras of the last wheel, then by merely this fact it is superior to the middle wheel. Although the meaning of the last wheel is praised in the sūtras and commentaries, [this does] not [refer to] everything in the last wheel, but is spoken in this way concerning the definitive meaning position of demonstrating the [Buddha-]nature.[12]

Mipam says that the last wheel is superior to the middle because of the distinctive teaching of Buddha-nature as inseparable from the empty appearances of the exalted body and wisdom.[13] He also states that through integrating the middle and last wheels of doctrine as noncontradictory in this way, such an understanding of Buddha-nature becomes the crucial point within the quintessential instructions of the Vajrayāna:

> By maintaining both of these [wheels] to be the definitive meaning, there is not only no contradiction that one [wheel] must be held as the provisional meaning, but having integrated them, there is the essential point of the quintessential instructions of the Vajrayāna through the Buddha-nature as such taken as the meaning of the causal continuum.[14] Therefore, you should know how the teachings of the Buddha converge on this single essential point and that this consummate meaning is the single viewpoint of the Sublime Ones such as Nāgārjuna and Asaṅga, for it can be clearly understood through [Nāgārjuna's] *Dharmadhātustotra, Bodhicittavivaraṇa,* etc., and [Asaṅga's] commentary on the *Uttaratantra* and so forth.[15]

Through his interpretation of Buddha-nature, he shows the compatibility of the middle wheel and last wheel, as well as the convergence of Nāgārjuna and Asaṅga upon a single viewpoint.[16] The inseparable unity of Buddha-nature and emptiness is a central issue for Mipam:

> The single essential point of all the doctrines of Sūtra and Mantra is only this all-pervasive Buddha-nature . . . when speaking, the Sugata teacher sometimes elucidated the essence (*ngo bo*) of the Buddha-nature by means of teaching emptiness, and at other times elucidated the nature (*rang bzhin*) of the Buddha-nature through the aspect of teaching the [Buddha's] qualities of the powers and so forth as a primordial endowment. These two need to be integrated without contradiction. However, due to the influence of not having found conviction in the extremely profound of profound essential points—the indivisibility of the two truths—some people view the Buddha-nature as a permanent phenomenon that is not essentially empty, while others, holding onto a mere void, remain in the denigrating position of a view of annihilation that cannot posit the primordial endowment of the inseparable qualities of wisdom.[17]

Mipam states that it is important to integrate as noncontradictory the Buddha's teachings of emptiness, which elucidate the essence of Buddha-nature, with the teachings of the primordial endowment of qualities, which elucidate the nature of Buddha-nature.[18] He reveals that the essential point to the resolution of the issue of Buddha-nature and emptiness is the indivisibility of the two truths.

Two Truths

A central theme in Buddhism is the doctrine of two truths: (1) the ultimate and (2) the relative, or conventional, truth. An important part of Mipam's interpretation is his unique model that renders the two truths in two distinct ways:

> There are two ways in which the two truths are stated within the [Buddha's] Word and śāstras: (1) from the perspective of valid cognition analyzing the ultimate abiding reality, emptiness is called "ultimate" and appearance is called "relative," and (2) from the perspective of conventional valid cognition analyzing the mode of appearance, the subjects and objects of the incontrovertible accor-

dance between the modes of appearance and reality [i.e., authentic experience] are called "ultimate" and the opposite [i.e., inauthentic experience] are called "relative."[19]

Mipam describes one two-truth scheme as a dichotomy of appearance and emptiness. In the division of the two truths within this scheme, emptiness is the *only* ultimate and *all* appearances are relative. He defines the "relative" and "ultimate" as follows:

> The relative is the mode of appearance which is like an illusion, a dream, or a floating hair—while lacking intrinsic nature, appearing that way—like production, etc. The ultimate is the mode of reality lacking production, etc., when the nature of those appearances are analyzed.[20]

This two-truth scheme equates emptiness with the ultimate and appearances with the relative. In this scheme, the ultimate is only emptiness—the lack of intrinsic nature of phenomena when their nature is analyzed.

Bötrül, an influential commentator on Mipam's works, explains the two truths as appearance/emptiness by means of the evaluated object (*gzhal don*) of ultimate valid cognition[21] being authentic or not:

> The two truths are divided by means of appearance and emptiness through the evaluated object of ultimate valid cognition analyzing the mode of reality being authentic or not: emptiness, which is the authentic evaluated object, is "ultimate truth"; appearances, which are not authentic, are "relative."[22]

The two truths here are delineated by means of ultimate valid cognition, where emptiness alone is the authentic object of evaluation. The nature of appearances is not found when analyzed; upon ultimate analysis of phenomena, nothing is found—only emptiness. Mipam states: "The phenomena that are the realm of thought and speech, when analyzed are lacking; therefore, they are empty like an illusion and are never able to withstand analysis."[23]

Ultimate analysis negates whatever the mind takes as a perceived object. There is nothing that withstands such analysis: "An object which the mind takes as support that cannot be refuted by Middle Way reasoning is impossible."[24] Even so, emptiness, as the lack of inherent nature in the face of ultimate analysis, does not disrupt appearances, but is the necessary condition for appearance. Mipam states:

> All phenomena are just dependent arisings: existent entities are dependent productions (*brten nas skyes ba*) and nonentities are dependent imputations (*brten nas btags pa*). In this way, all phenomena that are comprised by dependent arisings lack inherent nature because if they had inherent nature, dependent arisings would not be reasonable.[25]

Existent entities arise in dependence upon something else; they are dependent arisings. "Nonentities" like space are also dependent because they are imputed in dependence upon entities.[26] This interdependence does not make phenomena go away, but is the necessary condition for their arising. Also, this is why phenomena lack any truly established, individual essences.

Appearances are not found when they are analyzed; therefore, they are empty. However, emptiness is not some separate reality *behind* appearances. Rather, in the appearance/emptiness dichotomy of two truths, the two truths are in actuality an inseparable unity. Mipam states: "If there is no appearance, then there is also no emptiness of that [appearance]. Mutually, both appearance and emptiness are such that one is impossible without the other; if there is one, there is the other."[27] In this way, emptiness and appearance are also interdependent.

Mipam describes the relationship between the relative and the ultimate as being "essentially the same with different contradistinctions" in the appearance/emptiness model of the two truths:

> From the perspective of supreme knowledge's analysis of what is authentic,
> Both appearance and emptiness—
> Together present, together absent—are asserted as essentially the same, and
> Divisible into different contradistinctions.[28]

He further states:

> All appearances are mere imputations;
> Emptiness[29] is also merely imputed by the mind.[30]

Thus, the two truths are not actually distinct but are only conceptually distinct; in other words, they are "two sides of the same coin." He also states:

> "Appearing" and "relative" are the same in meaning because appearance should be understood as appearing yet not truly established as it appears. One should understand that the phrase "not truly existent" also does not have to indicate erroneous appearances, because "not truly existent" designates what is empty. If it [appearance] were established the way it appeared and were true as it appeared, then the designation "relative"[31] would not be appropriate. In that way it would not be empty and the manner of the impossibility of a nonempty entity being an object of knowledge is authentically established by reason; therefore, it is impossible within this sphere of what can be known for a phenomenon to be exclusively one part which is detached from both appearance and emptiness.[32]

In this way, emptiness and interdependently arising phenomena are coextensive. For Mipam, there is nothing that appears and is not empty, nor is there any emptiness that does not appear; they are mutually present or mutually absent:

> If there is appearance, the emptiness of that [appearance] is designated as "emptiness," but the meaning of emptiness is not a lack of appearance, such as a horn of a rabbit, because that is nonexistent conventionally. Hence, the words "emptiness of horn" is applied to the rabbit horn, but it is [just] the meaning of utter absence. Emptiness is the suchness of all conventionally existent phenomena. . . . Therefore, this emptiness is what is to be established as the intrinsic nature, or abiding reality, of all conventionally existent phenomena; it is not at all to be established as the suchness of that which does not exist conventionally.[33]

Here he describes emptiness as not something else that is separate from conventionally existent phenomena. Furthermore, Mipam cites Longchenpa stating that when ascertaining the emptiness of a phenomenon, it does not help if the phenomenon's emptiness is (erroneously) thought to be something different from the phenomenon—just as it does not affect the presence of anger toward an enemy to know that space is empty:

> In the *Precious Wish-Fulfilling Treasury*, when refuting the traditions of those who accept appearance and emptiness as different, such as the master Śrīgupta in the class of lower Svātantrikas,[34] the powerful victor, Longchen Rapjam states reasons that (1) an emptiness that is not an appearance is impossible as either of the two truths, (2) nor is it suitable to be realized, and (3) if [emptiness and appearance are] different, [emptiness] is not reasonable to be an antidote for what is abandoned because knowing the emptiness of something else, while holding onto the ground of false appearance, does not help at all—as it does not help to know the emptiness of space when anger arises towards an enemy, there is no purpose in realizing such an emptiness.[35]

In Mipam's appearance/emptiness model, only what appears (or is perceived) is empty; there is no substrate of emptiness that is beyond perceptible reality:

> There is no ultimate apart from the relative,
> There is no relative at all other than the ultimate.
> Whatever appears is necessarily empty,
> Whatever is empty necessarily appears
> Because appearance that is not empty is impossible
> And emptiness as well is not established without appearance.[36]

He depicts the quality of emptiness as an essential property of all objects of knowledge. In this way, he preserves the integrity of the Buddhist claims to the universality of emptiness in the middle wheel of doctrine.

The ultimate truth is not privileged in the two truths as appearance/emptiness because the two truths here are not actually distinct. Thus, in this characterization of the two truths as emptiness/appearance, neither of the two truths is superior to the other:

> The unreal appearances are called "relative" and the emptiness that is the lack of intrinsic nature is called "ultimate." Without being regarded with a qualitative difference, both of these are equally applied [to all phenomena] from form to omniscience. If you know this, there is certainly nothing more important to know within the sphere of what can be known.[37]

The unity of appearance and emptiness is an important part of Mipam's interpretation that we will return to again.

In his other scheme, Mipam represents the two truths not as appearance/emptiness, but as a dichotomy of appearances in accord or not with reality (i.e., authentic/inauthentic experience). Appearances that accord with reality, that is, pure appearances that are not bifurcated into a separate subject and object, are the ultimate truth. Dualistic appearances are the relative truth. In this way, emptiness is not the only ultimate because appearances can be both ultimate (e.g., pure, nondual appearances) and relative (e.g., impure, dualistic appearances). The two truths as authentic/inauthentic experience are not delineated from the perspective of ultimate analysis, but from a conventional perspective:

> Positing (1) both the objects and subjects for which the mode of appearance is in accord with the mode of reality as ultimate and (2) both the objects and subjects for which appearance and reality are not in accord as relative, should be posited as such due to being conventionally nondeceptive or deceptive.[38]

Expanding upon this distinction, Bötrül states:

> Also, concerning analyses of the manner of appearance, by means of its evaluated object being authentic or not at the time of evaluation from the perspective of a conventional valid cognition, the two truths are divided: (1) as the authentic mode of the abiding reality, both appearance and emptiness are ultimate, such as the emptiness-object and the wisdom-subject for which appearance is in accord with reality, and (2) as inauthentic modes of appearance, the aspects of distortion are relative, such as the subjects and objects for which appearance is not in accord with reality.[39]

In this scheme, the ultimate is defined as "authentic experience" (*gnas snang mthun*)[40]—literally, "the mode of appearance in accord with the way it is" (and the subject that experiences it as such). The relative is the opposite of this, "inauthentic experience" (*gnas snang mi mthun*)—"the mode of appearance not in accord with the way it is" (and the subject that experiences it as such). This distinction is an appearance-reality distinction such that experience in meditation is true in contrast to the distorted perceptions of nonmeditative states.

In the two-truth model of authentic/inauthentic experience, we can see how the two truths are not qualitatively the same, but are a hierarchy—the ultimate truth is undistorted truth while the relative truth is distorted and false. This treatment of relative truth reflects the meaning of "relative" (*kun rdzob, saṃvṛti*) as concealing. In this two-truth model, we find a context in which the ultimate truth is privileged above the relative truth and is not just the empty quality of appearance. Mipam relates this dichotomy of two truths to the dichotomy of saṃsāra and nirvāṇa:

> It is suitable to posit that all phenomena of nirvāṇa, which are attained through the power of appearance in accord with reality, are ultimate; and that all phenomena of saṃsāra, which arise through the power of appearance that does not accord with reality, are relative.[41]

He clearly states two ways in which the two truths are to be understood: (1) as emptiness and appearance and (2) as what is distorted and what is undistorted:

> The appearances which are included in the relative also need to be distinguished as distorted or undistorted, deceptive or nondeceptive—not everything that is relative must necessarily be a distorted appearance. Nor must everything with the name ultimate be solely empty because the two ways to arrive at the distinctive names in [two] manners of assessing the relative and ultimate are widely proclaimed in the great sūtras and śāstras.[42]

In this way, he depicts two models of the two truths.

Mipam accommodates the presence of wisdom in his second two-truth scheme of authentic/inauthentic experience. Thereby, he does not reduce the ultimate truth to a mere absence, nor does he categorically reject as ultimate the presence of the authentic experience of wisdom. By this, descriptions of ultimate truth are not limited to only negations, but the presence of wisdom can be affirmed as ultimate truth because wisdom is ultimate—as an authentic and undistorted experience of reality—in the two-truth model of authentic/inauthentic experience. In this way, this model provides a context for asserting the ultimate truth as an undistorted reality (and *not just a negation* of distortion).

Mipam validates nonconceptual wisdom as ultimate truth due to its presence in ultimate reality. While doing so, he also preserves the appearance/emptiness two-truth scheme and a context for the critique of the ontological status of all reality, including the presence of wisdom. Mipam does not curtail the universality of emptiness. Rather, he states: "The latter ultimate [authentic experience] also is empty of essence."[43] In this way, he synthesizes two models of two truths. We can see that instead of an "either/or" interpretation of the presence of wisdom and emptiness, he adopts a "both/and" position by means of these two models of two truths:

> In the great scriptures there are two ways in which the two truths are posited: (1) the term "ultimate" designates reality as non-arising and the term "relative" designates the conventional mode of appearance, and (2) in terms of conventional apprehension, the term "ultimate" designates both the subject and object of authentic experience and the term "relative" designates both the subject and object of inauthentic experience. In this manner, whether in Sūtra or Mantra, the term "ultimate" also applies to the subject . . . although the terms "ultimate" and "relative" are the same in these two systems, the way of presenting the meaning is different. Therefore, if one does not know how to explain having made the distinction between the viewpoints of each respective system, the hope of fathoming the great scriptures will be dashed—like a mind as narrow as the eye of a needle measuring space.[44]

These two systems of two truths support Mipam's interpretation of the compatibility of the emptiness taught in the middle wheel and the wisdom taught in the last wheel as both the definitive meaning. Emptiness as the ultimate truth in Mipam's appearance/emptiness model supports his exegesis of emptiness in the middle wheel of doctrine and the unity of the two truths. The inclusion of wisdom as ultimate truth in Mipam's authentic/inauthentic experience model supports his exegesis of wisdom in the last wheel of doctrine and Buddha-nature, as will be further shown below.

Buddha-Nature as the Unity of Appearance and Emptiness

Buddha-nature is a topic discussed in both the *Madhyamakāvatāra* and the *Uttaratantra*, two important exoteric Buddhist texts of Indian śāstra. The former represents a systematic commentary on the sūtras of the middle wheel of doctrine, and the latter is a commentary on the sūtras of the last wheel of doctrine. We will see how Bötrül, following Mipam, brings these two treatises together around the topic of Buddha-nature.

Bötrül explains Candrakīrti's description of the ultimate in the *Madhyamakāvatāra*, the object of authentic seeing, as the ultimate truth of the two truths as appearance/emptiness:

> The viewpoint of the root text and [auto]commentary of Candrakīrti, which is the meaning-commentary on the great śāstra, the *Prajñāmūlamadhyamaka*[-*kārikā*],[45] is also the two truths as appearance and emptiness; it is not seen otherwise. From the *Madhyamakāvatāra*:
>
> > [Buddha] said that all entities found by authentic and false seeing are apprehended as two essences:
> > That which is the object of authentic seeing is ultimate; false seeings are relative truths.[46]
>
> Authentic seeing, which is only the emptiness that is an object of the wisdom of meditative equipoise, is posited as ultimate; false seeings are all aspects of appearance, like an illusion or a dream, posited as relative. Such an emptiness, which is the ultimate truth, is ascertained through the ultimate valid cognition that analyzes the mode of reality [through] the negation of production by means of the four extremes, etc. However, there is not a single word in the "Collection of Reasonings"[47] of the Middle Way, or the root text and [auto]commentary of the *Madhyamakāvatāra*, that is a presentation that posits the two truths in which the ultimate [is] nirvāṇa and the relative [is] saṃsāra by means of pure conventional valid cognition analyzing the mode of appearance. Therefore, it is established that this manner of dividing the two truths as appearance/emptiness is the unsurpassed viewpoint of these scriptures.[48]

In this way, Bötrül states that Candrakīrti delineates the two truths as appearance/emptiness. He also characterizes the appearance/emptiness model of the two truths as the viewpoint of the middle wheel of doctrine:

> The manner of positing the two truths by means of appearance/emptiness is the viewpoint of the profound, definitive meaning sūtras of the middle Word of signlessness such as the extensive, middling, and condensed Mother [Perfection of Wisdom Sūtras]

> because of mainly teaching the topic—the positing of all appearances from form to omniscience as relative phenomena, and emptiness, which is the nonestablished essence of those, as the ultimate truth.[49]

In contrast, Bötrül characterizes the authentic/inauthentic model of the two truths—appearance in accord with reality or not—as the manner of positing the two truths in the definitive meaning sūtras of the last wheel:

> The manner of positing the two truths by means of whether or not appearance accords with reality is [the viewpoint] of the definitive meaning sūtras of the last Word, such as the ten [Buddha-]Nature Sūtras, for which:
>
> - the distinction of the definitive meaning Buddha-nature is asserted as the ultimate which is appearance in accord with the reality—from the empty aspect it is the nature endowed with the three gates of liberation, the essentially empty, objective expanse of phenomena (*yul chos kyi dbyings*); and from the aspect of appearance, it is inseparable from the qualities of knowledge, love, and powers, the natural luminous clarity of the subjective wisdom (*yul can ye shes*), and
> - the aspect of adventitious defilements, the distorted appearances which are the nature of saṃsāra—the subjects and objects that are the separable aspects that do not abide in the foundational nature of reality—are asserted as the relative which are appearances that do not accord with reality.[50]

Bötrül says here that, from the aspect of emptiness, Buddha-nature is the objective expanse of phenomena that is essentially empty. From the aspect of appearance, Buddha-nature is the subjective wisdom that is not empty of the inseparable qualities of naturally luminous and clear wisdom, yet is empty of the adventitious defilements that are the distorted appearances of the nature of saṃsāra.

Bötrül further expands upon Mipam's delineation of the two models of truth in his interpretation of Buddha-nature. Bötrül states that in terms of appearance in accord with reality (the two truths as authentic/inauthentic experience), Buddha-nature is ultimate; in terms of the two truths as appearance/emptiness, Buddha-nature has aspects of both of the two truths:

> Both the appearing and empty aspects of heritage, the basic element, [Buddha-]nature, etc. are posited as ultimate from the aspect of appearance in accord with reality; however, through the manner of delineating the relative from the aspect of appearance and the ultimate from the empty aspect, it has [aspects of] both the truths of appearance and emptiness.[51]

In the former model of authentic/inauthentic experience, Buddha-nature is only the ultimate truth as authentic experience; in the latter model of appearance/emptiness, Buddha-nature has aspects of both relative and ultimate truth because Buddha-nature is empty and it appears.

Bötrül states that traditions that only accept the two truths as appearance/emptiness, without accepting the two truths as authentic/inauthentic experience, have cast away the profound meaning of Buddha-nature and tantra:

> These days, the two truths of appearance and emptiness is only widely known, but it is rare to perceive one who knows the profound two truths of whether or not appearance accords with reality (i.e., authentic/inauthentic experience). It appears that the positions that accept the indivisibility of appearance and emptiness are cast far away: such as the presentation of the profound meaning intended by the definitive meaning sūtras and tantras, Buddha-nature—the unity of appearance and emptiness—as ultimate, and the Mahāyoga tradition's presentation of the indivisibility of purity and equality as the ultimate truth.[52]

His polemical claim apparently addresses the widespread dominance of Geluk commentaries that emphasize a model of the two truths as appearance/emptiness. Misrepresenting his distinction as a confession, John Pettit cites that Bötrül "admits [that the authentic/inauthentic experience distinction], is unusual,"[53] implying that this distinction is somehow heterodox. On the contrary, it is clear that this model of the two truths and the appearance/emptiness model are both important in Bötrül's and Mipam's works. In fact, the authentic/inauthentic experience model is a principal way the two truths are represented in the exegeses of the last wheel and tantras.[54] Moreover, far from heterodox, this distinction is also found in the predominant Geluk tradition.[55]

Furthermore, Bötrül says that the tradition of Prāsaṅgika accepts both two-truth models:

> In the scriptures of the Prāsaṅgika tradition, as was just explained, since the commentaries on the middle Word, such as the "Collection of Reasonings" and the root text and [auto]commentary of the *Madhyamakāvatāra*, posit the two truths by means of appearance and emptiness, and the commentaries on the last Word, such as the root text and commentary of the *Uttaratantra*, posit the two truths by means of whether or not appearance is in accord with reality, both manners of positing the two truths are accepted as one essential point without contradiction; only accepting either one and rejecting the other is not done. For this very reason, both: (1) scriptures of Candrakīrti, such as the root and [auto]commentary of the *Madhyamakāvatāra*, and (2) the *Uttaratantra* scripture of the supreme, great regent Maitreyanātha, also are within one essential point, without contradiction, scriptures of the Mahāyāna Prāsaṅgika.[56]

Bötrül states that Candrakīrti delineates the two truths as emptiness/appearance, while the *Uttaratantra* delineates the two truths as whether or not appearance is in accord with reality (i.e., authentic/inauthentic experience). He argues that both texts have the same viewpoint. Furthermore, in his *Notes on the Essential Points of [Mipam's] Exposition* [*of Buddha-Nature*], Bötrül states:

> If it is asked, "Well, which is the manner of positing the two truths in the Prāsaṅgika tradition?" Both are posited without contradiction. Moreover, Candrakīrti, emphasizing the former [appearance/emptiness model], elucidated the empty essence of all phenomena. The *Uttaratantra*, although emphasizing the latter [authentic/inauthentic experience model], is in accord with the former because the nature of emptiness is established as luminous clarity (*'od gsal ba*). Therefore, this is the reason why both the *Madhyamakāvatāra* and the *Uttaratantra* fall to one essential point, without contradiction, as Prāsaṅgika scriptures.[57]

He explains that the nature of emptiness is luminous clarity; this is the reason why there is no contradiction between Candrakīrti's *Madhyamakāvatāra* and the *Uttaratantra* as both Prāsaṅgika texts.[58] Thus, Buddha-nature, as the unity of emptiness and luminous clarity, is an important topic around which Bötrül synthesizes the *Madhyamakāvatāra* and the *Uttaratantra*, and establishes them both as Prāsaṅgika texts. We will look further at Prāsaṅgika in the next chapter and continue here with Mipam's interpretation of Buddha-nature.

A stanza that is frequently cited to support that Buddha-nature is not empty is found in the *Uttaratantra:*

> The basic element (*khams*) is empty of those adventitious
> [phenomena] that have the character of separability,
> But not empty of the unexcelled properties that have the character
> of inseparability.[59]

Mipam glosses this stanza as follows:

> All of the faults of saṃsāra arise from the deluded mind which apprehends a personal self or a self of phenomena. Since this deluded mind also is adventitious like clouds in the sky, from the beginning neither mixing nor polluting the luminous clarity of the primordial basic nature, these faults are individually distinguished from the basic element and are suitable to be removed. Therefore, the essence of the basic element is empty of these faults; it is untainted. Without depending on the polluting delusion, it is luminous and clear by its own nature; self-existing wisdom permeates the thusness of all phenomena. It is not empty of that which it is inseparable from, the basic element of consummate qualities, because in its essence this is the basic nature from which it is inseparable—like the sun and light rays.[60]

Mipam states that the basic element (Buddha-nature) is empty of adventitious defilements, yet not empty of consummate qualities. These consummate qualities are inseparable from the suchness of phenomena that is luminous clarity and self-existing wisdom.

Bötrül explains that the first half of the stanza from the *Uttaratantra* previously quoted shows distorted phenomena of duality as relative, and the second half shows Buddha-nature as ultimate:

> Also in the context of the *Mahāyāna-Uttaratantra*, ". . . But not empty of the unexcelled properties that have the character of insepa-

> rability," shows as ultimate: the luminous clarity that is the self-vibrancy (*rang gdangs*) of the empty essence, the Buddha-nature—the heritage which is the basic element—inseparable from the qualities of the Truth Body that is a freed effect (*bral 'bras*); and, "The basic element is empty of those adventitious [phenomena] that have the character of separability," shows as relative: the defilements which do not abide in the foundation—the distorted phenomena of perceived-perceiver [duality]—which are separable through the power of training in the path of the antidote.[61]

Bötrül shows that the *Uttaratantra* demonstrates Buddha-nature, the unity of luminous clarity and emptiness, as ultimate. Since both the empty and appearing aspects are ultimate in this context, Buddha-nature also reflects the ultimate truth as authentic experience.

In addition to the stanza from the *Uttaratantra,* another source to support the interpretation of the empty quality of Buddha-nature is found within Candrakīrti's autocommentary on the *Madhyamakāvatāra* (VI.95). Mipam cites this passage in the context of refuting the view that Buddha-nature is truly established and not empty.[62] In this citation, originally found in the *Laṅkāvatārasūtra,* Mahāmati asks the Buddha how Buddha-nature is different from the Self proclaimed by non-Buddhists. The Buddha answers as follows:

> Mahāmati, my Buddha-nature teaching is not similar to the non-Buddhists' declaration of Self. Mahāmati, the Tathāgatas, Arhats, and completely perfect Buddhas teach Buddha-nature as the meaning of the words: emptiness, the authentic limit, nirvāṇa, non-arising, wishlessness, etc. For the sake of immature beings who are frightened by selflessness, they teach by means of Buddha-nature.[63]

Bötrül states that, from the empty aspect, Buddha-nature is not like the Self of the non-Buddhists because it is inseparable from the great emptiness distinguished by the "three gates of liberation" (i.e., empty essence, signless cause, wishless effect). He says that from the aspect of appearance, Buddha-nature is not without qualities, as in the tradition of the Nirgrantha,[64] because it has a nature with the qualities of luminous clarity distinguished by knowledge, love, and powers:

> From the aspect of appearance, unlike the Nirgrantha, [Buddha-nature] is distinguished by the qualities of the luminous and clear

> nature—knowledge, love, and powers; and from the empty aspect, unlike the Self of the non-Buddhists, [Buddha-nature] is distinguished by the essence of great emptiness—the three gates of liberation.[65]

Bötrül shows that Buddha-nature is not like the Self of the non-Buddhists due to the empty aspect. The emphasis on the empty aspect of Buddha-nature reflects the ultimate in the two truths of appearance/emptiness that Bötrül delineates as the manner that Candrakīrti posits the two truths. The unity of the empty and appearing aspects of luminous clarity reflects the ultimate in the two truths of authentic/inauthentic experience that Bötrül delineates as the manner that the two truths are posited in the *Uttaratantra*. Thus, through Mipam's twofold depiction of the two truths, Bötrül synthesizes Candrakīrti's treatment of Buddha-nature in the *Madhyamakāvatāra* with the description from the *Uttaratantra*.

Furthermore, Bötrül's teacher and Mipam's student, Khenpo Künpel, states as follows in his commentary on Mipam's *Beacon of Certainty:*

> In general, if the essence of Buddha-nature were not empty, it would not be different from the permanent Self of the non-Buddhists; therefore, the nature of the three gates of liberation was taught. Also, if the wisdom of luminous clarity did not exist, being an utterly void emptiness like space, there would be no difference from the Nirgrantha; therefore, the unconditioned wisdom of luminous clarity was taught. Thus, the definitive scriptures of the middle and last Word of the teacher show the empty essence and the natural clarity.[66]

Thus, the meaning of Buddha-nature, like the meaning of emptiness, is explained as not only an absence, but as the unity of appearance, or clarity, and emptiness.

Buddha-Nature as the Definitive Meaning

Bötrül describes such a Buddha-nature as the definitive meaning. He shows the criteria for distinguishing the definitive meaning from a provisional meaning by stating that it is a provisional meaning if the literal teaching has three features: (1) a basis within an [other] intention (*dgongs gzhi*), (2) a purpose (*dgos pa*), and (3) explicit invalidation (*dngos la gnod byed*):

> Concerning the manner of positing the provisional and the definitive in general, sūtras are provisional meanings when the meaning of the literal teaching has all three complete: a basis within an [other] intention, a purpose, and explicit invalidation. The opposite of this is posited as the definitive meaning.[67]

Bötrül states that in accordance with the viewpoint of middle wheel sūtras such as the *Samādhirājasūtra*,[68] Candrakīrti explained the distinction between provisional and definitive meanings by means of what is and is not invalidated by ultimate valid cognition. As such, sūtras that mainly express emptiness as the explicit topic are said to be the definitive meaning, and sūtras that mainly express relative truths (i.e., appearances) are provisional meanings:

> In accord with the viewpoint of the *Samādhirājasūtra* and so forth, by means of what is or is not invalidated by the valid cognition of ultimate analysis, Candrakīrti accepts sūtras that mainly express the topic of emptiness as the definitive meaning, and sūtras that mainly express the topic of the conventional, [or] relative, truths as provisional meanings:
>
> > Whatever sūtras have the meaning that does not explain thusness
> > Know those to also explain the relative, what is provisional.
> > Know those that have the meaning of emptiness as the definitive meaning.[69]
>
> Therefore, the manner of positing is by means of the topic: the first Word is provisional, the middle is definitive, and the last is a mix of provisional and definitive meanings. Hence, it does not follow that a meaning taught in a sūtra that Candrakīrti has said to be a provisional meaning is necessarily nonexistent conventionally because all presentations of relative truth are the expressed meanings of a provisional meaning.[70]

Thus, it does not follow that whatever is a provisional meaning in this context—including pillars, pots, the presence of wisdom, and so on—is necessarily nonexistent conventionally because all appearances are relative truths in this context. Furthermore, Bötrül states:

> The manner of positing the topic as the definitive meaning by means of appearance and emptiness in the middle Word is as follows: by means of emptiness, the object found by valid cognition of ultimate analysis being supremely authentic or not, there is the way of dividing the two truths in which relative phenomena are [posited] from the aspect of appearance and ultimate phenomena are [posited] from the empty aspect. From this, sūtras with emptiness, the ultimate truth, as the main topic of explicit teaching—the Perfection of Wisdom Sūtras of the middle wheel—are the definitive meaning.[71]

Bötrül states that in terms of ultimate valid cognition, the ultimate is posited from the aspect of emptiness and relative phenomena are posited from the aspect of appearance. The ultimate truth is the empty quality, and thus the definitive meaning in this context is delineated as the sūtras that have the explicit teaching of emptiness as their main topic. He explains that this is the way that the definitive meaning is delineated in the middle wheel, and by Candrakīrti, but not in the last wheel.

Bötrül explains that the commentaries on the last wheel, such as the *Uttaratantra* and the *Dharmadhātustotra*,[72] explain the distinction between the provisional and definitive meaning by means of what is and is not invalidated by the conventional valid cognition of pure vision. In this way, Buddha-nature, as appearance in accord with reality, is the definitive meaning:

> In accordance with sūtras that show the heritage, the basic element, through the metaphor of cleansing a jewel, the *Uttaratantra* and the *Dharmadhātustotra* and so forth assert sūtras that teach the consummate definitive meaning, Buddha-nature, as the definitive meaning by means of whether there is or is not invalidation through the [conventional] valid cognition of pure vision in accord with what is found by the valid cognition of pure vision. Hence, the last Word teachings in which the definitive meaning Buddha-nature is the topic—the nature of inseparable appearance and emptiness and the ultimate that is appearance in accord with reality—are the definitive meaning because [Buddha-nature] is the object found by the valid cognition of pure vision.[73]

Here Bötrül states that commentaries on the last wheel explain the distinction between the provisional and definitive meanings by means of what is and is not invalidated by the conventional valid cognition of pure vision (authentic vs. inauthentic experience). Thus, in terms of appearance in accord with reality (authentic experience), Buddha-nature, as the topic of indivisible appearance and emptiness, is the definitive meaning. Furthermore, he states:

> The manner of positing the topic as the definitive meaning by means of appearance in accord with reality in the last Word is as follows: by means of the object found by the conventional valid cognition of pure [vision] being supremely authentic or not, there is the way of dividing the two truths in which relative phenomena are [posited] from the aspect of being appearances that do not accord with reality, and ultimate phenomena are [posited] from the aspect of being appearances that accord with reality. From this, the sūtras with luminous clarity, the ultimate truth, as the main topic of explicit teaching—the sūtras teaching Buddha-nature of the last wheel—are the definitive meaning.[74]

In this way, the Buddha-Nature Sūtras of the last wheel are also definitive. Thus, it is not *only* emptiness that is definitive, but the definitive meaning is stated in terms of the indivisibility of appearance and emptiness as known when reality is experienced authentically, when appearance accords with reality.

Bötrül argues that there is no contradiction in the delineations of what is definitive in the two wheels of doctrine because they are not based on the same criterion: the middle wheel describes the definitive meaning in terms of the ultimate that is understood as the empty aspect of empty appearance, what is validated by ultimate valid cognition. The last wheel, however, explains what is definitive in terms of the ultimate that is understood as authentic experience, what is validated by the conventional valid cognition of pure vision. He states that the two manners are completely compatible:

> In short, as for the topic of the middle and last Word, based on the distinctive manner of stating the main topic of the explicit teaching—Buddha-nature from the aspect of appearance or the expanse of phenomena from the empty aspect—there are two ways of positing the middle wheel as the definitive meaning and the last wheel as the definitive meaning. Based on the level of emphasis upon the topic, other than just the distinctive way in which they are respectively distinguished temporarily (*gnas skabs*), as for the consummate

> meaning, the two are also accepted within a single essential point, without contradiction, as definitive meaning sūtras.[75]

In this way, Bötrül states that sūtras of both the middle and last wheels are the definitive meaning. The main topic that is explicitly taught in the last wheel is Buddha-nature from the appearing aspect, while in the middle wheel it is the expanse of phenomena from the empty aspect. Both express the same consummate meaning, yet are distinguished by emphasizing one or another aspect—the empty or appearing aspect. Furthermore, Bötrül depicts the middle wheel as eliminating the extreme of permanence and the last wheel as eliminating the extreme of annihilation:

> The supreme definitive meaning of the middle wheel
> Is the expanse of phenomena endowed with the three gates of liberation.
> "The mind is devoid of mind . . ."[76]
> The essence of mind itself abides as empty.
>
> From the two truths as appearance/emptiness
> The ultimate emptiness is the supreme freedom from constructs.
> Since it is the object found by the valid cognition that analyzes the ultimate,
> It is free from the extreme of the truth of permanent entities.
>
> The supreme definitive meaning of the last wheel
> Is the heritage of the Buddha endowed with knowledge, love, and powers.
> ". . . The nature of mind is luminous clarity"
> Is the nature that abides as the great luminous clarity.
>
> From the two truths of authentic/inauthentic experience,
> It is the supreme ultimate of the concordant modes of appearance and reality.
> Since it is the object found by pure conventional valid cognition,
> It is free from the extreme of annihilation as nothing at all.
>
> The supreme noncontradiction of the middle and last wheels
> Is the unity of appearance and emptiness—the basic element of the essential nature.

From the purity and impurity of mind itself,
It abides as the great interdependent arising of compassionate resonance (*thugs rjes*).

It is the supreme meaning of the noncontradiction of the two truths
Of appearance/emptiness and authentic/inauthentic experience.
Since it is not the domain of confined valid cognition,
It is free from all adventitiously constructed phenomena.[77]

He asserts that the two modes of two truths do not conflict. The integration of the middle and last wheels of doctrine is an important way that Bötrül distinguishes the Nyingma tradition:

> In the tradition of the Great Middle Way, in accord with the meaning of the viewpoint of sūtras such as the *Akṣayamatisūtra*,[78] and great śāstras such as the *Madhyamakāvatāra*, the middle Word is accepted as the definitive meaning; and in accord with the meaning of the viewpoint of sūtras such as the *Dhāraṇīśvararāja*,[79] and great śāstras such as the *Uttaratantra*, sūtras of the last wheel that teach Buddha-nature are accepted as the definitive meaning—the meaning of the viewpoint within a single essential point, without contradiction, is the general [way of] Nyingma scriptures.[80]

Bötrül states that such an integration of the middle and last wheels of doctrine as both the definitive meaning is a feature of "general Nyingma scriptures."

In contrast to Bötrül's two criteria for the definitive meaning, Mipam uses a general criterion to delineate the definitive meaning: "Definitive meaning sūtras are those that indicate a non-referential emptiness, and the sūtras that indicate a relative referent object are provisional."[81] As we will see in the following chapters, the qualification of emptiness as non-referential delineates emptiness as not simply an empty quality, but as the inconceivable unity of emptiness and appearance that is known in authentic experience.

Bötrül highlights the inclusive quality of Mipam's interpretive system through integrating the statements of emptiness in the middle wheel with Buddha-nature in the last wheel. He states that although all of the great scholars of the early and later traditions have the same viewpoint in the end, at times for the purpose of destroying the aspect of thorough affliction (*kun nyon phyogs 'joms pa*) and at other times to increase the aspect of complete purification (*rnam byang phyogs 'phel ba*), they emphasize the empty aspect or the appearing aspect in their distinctive commentaries.[82]

Conclusion

Mipam formulates an interpretation of Buddhist doctrine that clearly articulates two models of the two truths: (1) the two truths as appearance/emptiness and (2) the two truths as authentic/inauthentic experience. The former scheme is in terms of the mode of reality—the way things are—as known by ultimate valid cognition. The latter scheme is in terms of the mode of appearance—the way things appear—as known by conventional valid cognition.

Commenting on Mipam's work, Bötrül states that the first two-truth model is the model found in the middle wheel of sūtra and in Candrakīrti's *Madhyamakāvatāra*—the doctrines that present the explicit teaching of emptiness. The second two-truth model is the model found in the last wheel of sūtra and in the *Uttaratantra*—the doctrines that present the explicit teaching of Buddha-nature. The integration of the *Madhyamakāvatāra* and the *Uttaratantra* represents the harmony between the Perfection of Wisdom Sūtras of the middle wheel and Buddha-Nature Sūtras of the last wheel as both the definitive meaning. In this way, these two wheels do not cancel each other out, but are mutually illuminating.

Mipam's two models of two truths support his interpretation of the compatibility of emptiness and Buddha-nature. The indivisibility of the two truths, empty appearance, is Buddha-nature; and the unity of appearance and emptiness is what is known in authentic experience. His two models of truth are a key part of his integration of the ultimate truth as a presence (ultimate qua authentic experience) and the ultimate truth as an absence (ultimate qua empty quality of appearances). Within his interpretation of the two wheels of doctrine, and the two models of truth, we find a dialectic of emptiness and presence at the heart of his Nyingma exegesis.

CHAPTER TWO

MIDDLE WAY OF PRĀSAṄGIKA AND YOGĀCĀRA

It is equally deadly for a mind to have a system or to have none. Therefore, it will have to decide to combine both.

—Friedrich Schlegel, in Kevin Hart, *The Trespass of the Sign*

INTRODUCTION

This chapter addresses in more detail the relationship between affirmations and denials of ultimate reality in Mipam's writings. Before we look further into the explicit topic of Buddha-nature, which is the topic of chapter 4, we will first look in more depth into the discourse of negation in the Middle Way, and the Prāsaṅgika-Madhyamaka in particular. The predominant role of the negative side of the dialectic—emptiness—is a distinctive feature of Buddhist philosophy and is an important part of Mipam's presentation of Buddha-nature.

To further understand the way he presents Buddha-nature in relationship to emptiness and the Middle Way, we will begin by looking at some significant features of his characterization of Prāsaṅgika. Prāsaṅgika is a discourse of radical negation par excellence. Central themes of Mipam's interpretation can be seen through his depiction of emptiness within the relationship between Prāsaṅgika and its counterpart, Svātantrika. In his depiction of Prāsaṅgika, Mipam emphasizes the inconceivable unity of the two truths as appearance/emptiness in authentic experience. With the Svātantrika, he emphasizes a progressive approach to truth, a truth represented in thought and language. He depicts the Svātantrika approach to truth as one based on the two truths of appearance and emptiness *conceived separately*. The domain of Svātantrika discourse plays a principal role in Mipam's formulation of conventional reality, where appearance is known and discussed as separate from emptiness. In particular, the Yogācāra subdivision of Svātantrika, in which the conventional mode of reality is asserted as Mind-Only, plays an important role in his systematic formulation of conventional reality.

We will see that Mipam represents Prāsaṅgika-Madhyamaka as a discourse that emphasizes what transcends conceptuality. Svātantrika-Madhyamaka, on the other hand, emphasizes the component of dialectical inquiry, a discourse at play within the conceptual structures of thought. As such, Svātantrika, and Yogācāra in particular, play an important role in Mipam's systematic interpretation of each of the two truths. Yogācāra not only plays an important part in his portrayal of conventional truth as Mind-Only, but also in his portrayal of ultimate truth as the authentic experience of wisdom. Moreover, following Longchenpa, he associates Prāsaṅgika with the manner of ascertaining primordial purity in the Great Perfection.[1] To fully appreciate Mipam's interpretation of the Middle Way, we need to keep in mind that his work is deeply rooted within the tradition of the Great Perfection inherited from Longchenpa.

In his depiction of the Svātantrika-Prāsaṅgika distinction, we will see that Mipam juxtaposes consciousness and wisdom, and the conceptual and the nonconceptual. This all-important distinction between mind (*sems*) and wisdom (*ye shes*), which is a central theme in the Great Perfection, comes into play in his portrayal of Yogācāra-Madhyamaka, too. In this we can see how the Great Perfection informs his representations of the exoteric discourses of the Middle Way.

Svātantrika-Prāsaṅgika

We will begin by looking into Mipam's representation of ultimate truth in order to introduce his discussion of Prāsaṅgika. The distinction between a conceptual negation and a negation that is free from all conceptual constructs (*spros bral*) is a central part of Mipam's depiction of ultimate truth. The former refers to a mere absence as a negative representation of the ultimate, the "categorized ultimate." In contrast to this *concept* of nonexistence, the "uncategorized ultimate" is nonconceptual:

> The ultimate truth that is categorized, merely a negation as an absence of true establishment, is an object of mind and an object of language. The uncategorized is the unity of appearance and emptiness that does not fall to the side of either appearance or emptiness. It is signified by the words such as "unity of the two truths," "freedom from constructs," "the Middle Way," but these are merely indicators, like the finger pointing to the moon; the meaning is far beyond the domain of language and thought.[2]

The "uncategorized" is indicated by words such as the unity of two truths, but it has no linguistic or conceptual referent. Its meaning defies affirmation and negation, and any other conceptual formulation.

Mipam's division of ultimate truth into the *categorized* and *uncategorized* ultimate reflects two distinct modes of understanding. The first, the categorized ultimate, is the ultimate that is known in the perspective of a "postmeditation phase" (*rjes thob*) of determinate experience, in which emptiness and appearance are known separately. The second, the unique "category" of the uncategorized ultimate, is the ultimate known from a nonconceptual state of meditative equipoise (*mnyam bzhag*), wisdom's perspective on reality, in which the two truths are indivisible:

> In short, in accord with the meaning found in meditative equipoise beyond thoughts and words, in the context of the indivisible truth that is the consummate reality, the two truths do not need to be distinguished. Therefore, as when replying in the manner of not saying anything at all, non-assertion is established in the authentic [condition] free from all conventions—inexpressible, free from constructs, equality—because all phenomena appear as such from the beginning free from any assertions whatsoever, such as negations and affirmations that are existential (*med*) or predicative (*min*). However, in the context of the way things appear, the objects of thoughts and words in postmeditation, if one needs to reflect upon the presentations of the ground, path, and fruition, etc., and also speak to others, the two valid cognitions are divided, and it is impossible to deviate from operating by way of affirmation and negation.[3]

There are no assertions, positive or negative, in the context of the way things are—the indivisible truth—in meditative equipoise free from conceptual engagement. However, when reflecting on conventional reality and the way things appear in postmeditation, the two truths are divided and one operates by means of thoughts and words. Mipam states that as long as the aspects of appearance and emptiness are distinct, there is conceptual apprehension and assertions are made:

> Hence, due to the fact that (1) the aspect of a non-implicative negation (*med dgag*), which is the emptiness of true existence that merely eliminates the object of negation, and (2) the aspect of interdependent arising separately exist as if separate and distinct, this manner also has apprehensions and assertions.[4]

He distinguishes the mere aspect of a negation, in which emptiness is separate from appearance, from the indivisible truth of empty appearance, in which emptiness is indivisible with interdependent arising. He makes this delineation in a distinction between a mere absence (*med tsam*) and the lack of intrinsic nature (*rang bzhin med pa*):

> Although it is possible for a mere absence that is the elimination of the object of negation to appear in a novice's mind, a person who has gone to the essential point through Middle Way analysis will distinguish well between the lack of intrinsic nature and a mere absence. Through doing so, a mode of apprehension (*'dzin stangs*), distinguished by the certainty that an absence of intrinsic nature and an interdependent arising are indivisible in meaning, will be an antidote that clears away the precipice-like extremes of permanence and annihilation. However, as long as it is together with an affirming or negating mode of apprehension, it will not be the nature that is free from the conceptual constructs of the four extremes.[5]

A mere absence is a negation, which is held within a conceptual mode of apprehension. However, the meaning of the indivisibility of interdependent arising and the lack of intrinsic nature is beyond negation and any such conceptual mode of apprehension.

By distinguishing the nonconceptual from (conceptual) negation in this way, Mipam creates a space for the absolute transcendence of an ultimate truth that is free from conceptual modes of apprehension and from constructs (*spros bral*): "This elimination of the object of negation, the entity, is merely a reflected image in the mind, an other-exclusion[6] that excludes existence, and therefore does not go beyond conceptual constructs."[7] Negations are relegated to the categorized ultimate because what is nonconceptual is beyond negation and affirmation. Since emptiness as the categorized ultimate is an object of thought and linguistic utterance, it is merely a relative truth: "The emptiness that is a non-implicative negation is posited as relative in relation to the genuine ultimate which is free from all conventions."[8] Emptiness that is the uncategorized ultimate, however, is not conceptual and is hence not a negation.

In his article assessing Mipam's position in relation to Prāsaṅgika-Madhyamaka, Dreyfus insightfully portrays the categorized ultimate as an issue of the limits of linguistically bound expressions:

> Moreover, a negation exists only in opposition to an affirmation. Hence, if emptiness were a negation, it would have to exist on the same level as other conventional phenomena and would be just another elaboration, a phenomenon captured by the dichotomies such as "is" and "is not." . . . Such descriptions cannot be taken literally, for they are still prisoners of the essentialist temptation to pin down reality through determinate description. To conceive of ultimate truth as being merely the fact that phenomena do not exist intrinsically is to assume a negative essence and to remain captive of binary oppositions.[9]

Mipam depicts a qualitative difference between the two ultimates by describing the categorized ultimate within the context of novices:

> The context such as the analysis whether the ultimate is within the domain of mind or not refers to the uncategorized ultimate; the categorized ultimate is not the expressed meaning because the categorized ultimate is in the context of a novice progressively engaging in emptiness from merely a conceptual perspective. As such, it cannot roam in the territory of a mind like the nonconceptual meditative wisdom of a Sublime One, for which duality has subsided, like a beggar that has no power to sit on the universal emperor's throne.[10]

The categorized ultimate concerns a perspective within a conceptual framework. In the context of discursive (i.e., conceptual) analysis, the categorized ultimate is known within that framework, whereas there is no such framework demarcating the uncategorized ultimate. In this way, Mipam portrays a provisional nature to conceptual categories:

> For a conventional phenomenon, other than asserting that it is either existent or nonexistent, permanent or impermanent, etc., it is not suitable to say that it is both or neither [existent and nonexistent]. At the time of expressing the non-assertion of the four extremes as the reality that transcends conventions and has completely pacified constructs, is it not extremely absurd if one must refute the Buddha's Word [which describes a reality that transcends conventions] by means of introductory logic primers?[11]

He suggests that laws of ordinary logic, including the law of the excluded middle, are trumped by the authority of scriptures (and the experiences of meditative equipoise) that are witness to a reality beyond conceptual categories.

He delineates the categorized and uncategorized ultimate in terms of the subject (*yul can*) as well as the object (*yul*):

> We also assert that in terms of the subject, whether or not dualistic experience has subsided or not, the names "categorized" and "uncategorized" are appropriate. In terms of the object, the difference between the two ultimates is the freedom from a partial domain of constructs and the freedom from the entire domain of constructs. In terms of the subject, having seen the meaning of the freedom from constructs as it is, the subject for whom dualistic experience has subsided is called the uncategorized ultimate, and oppositely, [the subject] with dualistic experience is called the categorized ultimate.[12]

He describes the two contexts of the ultimate as categorized or uncategorized in terms of the *object:* (1) whether it is free from constructs partially, or (2) free from all constructs; and in terms of the *subject:* whether dualistic apprehension is present or not. Both subjects and objects within the realm of conceptual experience are called "categorized." The subjects and objects beyond conceptual experience are "uncategorized."

Mipam associates discourse on the uncategorized ultimate with meditative equipoise:

> At the time that Prāsaṅgikas explain with an emphasis on the uncategorized ultimate, the great Middle Way free from assertions, it is in the context based upon ultimate analysis . . . ascertaining whatever appears in accord with the sacred domain of meditative equipoise free from constructs and without reference (*dmigs pa med pa*).[13]

He describes the distinction between the discourses emphasizing a context of meditative equipoise or postmeditation as the difference between Svātantrika and Prāsaṅgika:

> Therefore, one should know Prāsaṅgika and Svātantrika as they are the manners of explanation emphasizing: (1) wisdom of meditative equipoise for which the two truths are one taste, and (2) supreme knowledge of postmeditation for which the two truths are distinctively discerned.[14]

He associates the wisdom of meditative equipoise with the manner of explanation emphasized in Prāsaṅgika. In contrast, he associates a postmeditative perspective, where the two truths are separately discerned, with the manner of explanation emphasized in Svātantrika. He depicts the main distinction of Prāsaṅgika and Svātantrika as follows:

> The defining character (*mtshan nyid*) of Svātantrika is explanation that emphasizes the categorized ultimate together with assertions. The defining character of Prāsaṅgika is explanation that emphasizes the uncategorized ultimate free from all assertions. In the context of positing the defining characters for these two, positing a distinction such as whether or not [phenomena] are established by their own character conventionally, and the manners of forming evidence, and so forth, are merely ancillary divisions subsumed within the defining characters above. Also, due to this [emphasis on the categorized or uncategorized] itself, which was just explained, is also the key point of:
>
> - whether or not there are assertions
> - whether or not there is acceptance of establishment by own character conventionally
> - the manner of forming evidence establishing the lack of intrinsic nature as a consequence or an autonomous argument
> - whether or not the qualifier "ultimately" is applied to the object of negation.[15]

He characterizes Svātantrika as discourse that emphasizes the categorized ultimate truth. In contrast, he characterizes Prāsaṅgika as discourse that emphasizes the uncategorized ultimate truth. Thus, he describes the transcendent quality of the ultimate as *uncategorized* in the discourse emphasized in

Prāsaṅgika, in accord with a perspective in which no position is held, while maintaining an ultimate truth that can be conceptually discerned in the discourse emphasized in Svātantrika. In this way, discourse in accord with the discursive contexts of postmeditation, in which the ultimate is expressible in terms of an autonomous argument (*rang rgyud kyi sbyor ba, svatantraprayoga*) and determinate in analytical inquiry, is the emphasis of Svātantrika.

For Mipam, the Prāsaṅgika view is not necessarily different from that of the Svātantrika: "If Prāsaṅgika texts only indicated the categorized ultimate [and not the uncategorized], then among the two, Prāsaṅgika and Svātantrika, Svātantrika would have to be accepted as a higher viewpoint."[16] Thus, the Svātantrika texts also can indicate the uncategorized ultimate, but the *emphasis* is placed on the categorized ultimate.

The Prāsaṅgika and Svātantrika respectively emphasize discourses within the contexts of: (1) the way things are seen by wisdom—the unified truth, and (2) the way things appear to consciousness—distinguished as two truths:

> Thus, the meaning of the consummate ultimate
> Is without assertion, but in the way of appearance
> Each of the two truths are also conventionally asserted.
> However, compared with the reality of the indivisible two truths
> [The two truths] are merely separate in the manner of appearance.
> Compared with the wisdom that sees the indivisible meaning,
> Both of the valid cognitions are also
> A partial domain because
> It is impossible for one to apprehend the two truths.[17]

Mipam distinguishes two contexts of the Middle Way as (1) wisdom, in meditative equipoise free from constructs, and (2) consciousness, within the domain of thoughts and language in postmeditation:

> The uncategorized ultimate free from all assertions appears as the object of meditative equipoise of a Sublime One, and the categorized ultimate appears in postmeditation certainty; the former is the domain of wisdom and the latter is the domain of consciousness. . . . In this way, there is a great essential point here that applies to the [difference between] the nominal and genuine ultimates, and postmeditation and meditative equipoise. If this is understood, one can also understand the essential point of whether or not apprehension has deconstructed (*zhig*).[18]

Based on the distinction between consciousness and wisdom there are the two ultimates—the nominal (categorized) ultimate and the genuine (uncategorized)—and the two contexts of postmeditation and meditative equipoise. He also distinguishes the contexts of consciousness and wisdom as: the "gross" and "subtle," and the "lesser" and "great" Middle Way:

> The distinction I make
> Differentiate between two: the Middle Way of the path and
> The Middle Way of meditative equipoise, the main part (*dngos gzhi*)—
> The gross and subtle, or the causal and resultant—
> The distinction is made between the lesser and great Middle Ways
> Which are the contexts of consciousness or wisdom.[19]

He states that the lesser Middle Way, together with assertions and the two truths distinct, is designated as the "Middle Way" due to it being the cause of the Middle Way:

> Therefore, the Middle Way together with assertions
> Of the respective two truths
> Is the lesser Middle Way of alternation,
> Which is the designation of a cause with the name of the result.[20]

He states that the Middle Way with assertions is the lesser Middle Way, in which the two truths are separate and known in alternation. The domain of thought and language is the causal Middle Way, which is given the name "Middle Way" due to being a cause of the Middle Way. The resultant Middle Way is the meditative equipoise of wisdom.

The key distinction between Mipam's two contexts of (nonconceptual) meditative wisdom and (conceptual) postmeditative consciousness is precisely how he distinguishes key themes related to the Svātantrika-Prāsaṅgika distinction such as: (1) whether or not there are assertions,[21] (2) whether or not the qualifier "ultimately" is needed to modify what is negated, (3) whether or not commonly appearing objects are accepted,[22] (4) whether or not autonomous arguments are appropriate in the ascertainment of the ultimate,[23] and (5) whether or not apprehension (*'dzin stangs*) is present in the ascertainment of the ultimate.[24] Within the realm of thought and language: there are assertions, the qualifier "ultimately" is applied when negating (conventionally existent) phenomena, there are commonly appearing objects, autonomous arguments can be used to ascertain the (categorized) ultimate, and apprehension is present.

Mipam describes the style of explanation in Svātantrika as gradual and Prāsaṅgika as sudden; otherwise, he says that they have the same consummate viewpoint: "Other than the manner of explaining the meaning of the freedom from constructs gradually or instantaneously, in the end, [both Svātantrika and Prāsaṅgika] have the same viewpoint—that very freedom from constructs."[25] He claims that the unique object of negation for the Prāsaṅgika is the perception of the two truths as distinct, and that there is nothing more to be developed in Prāsaṅgika beyond that:

> In this way, one should know that the Prāsaṅgika's unique object of negation is the aspect of apprehending the two truths as distinct because if the Svātantrikas were free from this object of negation, which is conceiving the two truths as distinct, then other than that view, there would not be the slightest thing to develop for even the Prāsaṅgikas, etc.[26]

Mipam depicts the Svātantrikas as emphasizing an approach to emptiness when the two truths remain distinct, a context of the conceptual mind and language. Discourse on the categorized ultimate, in which the ultimate is distinct from the relative, is the emphasis of the Svātantrika.

Prāsaṅgikas emphasize the discourse of the uncategorized ultimate, yet ironically, without making a distinction between the categorized and uncategorized ultimate. Mipam states: "One should know that in this context of Prāsaṅgika, since the emphasis is on the great Middle Way, which is a unity and free from constructs, there is no twofold distinction of the categorized and uncategorized ultimates in this tradition."[27] Thus, oddly enough, we are confronted with a paradox that the defining character of Prāsaṅgika, explanation with an emphasis on the uncategorized ultimate, is based on the distinction of an uncategorized ultimate that the Prāsaṅgikas themselves do not accept in such discourse! However, such distinctions are necessary when *theorizing about* Prāsaṅgika in this way (which is not Prāsaṅgika discourse); such distinctions fall within the discursive contexts of nonmeditative states, whereas there are no distinctions in the wisdom of meditative equipoise or the discourse that accords with it. In any case, we are left with the paradox of how a discourse that uses language can accord with what is nonconceptual.

We should recognize a certain degree of fluidity within the categories of Prāsaṅgika and Svātantrika in Mipam's interpretation, as the difference between them is a contextual one. An important point of Mipam's presentation of Prāsaṅgika is that it is not so much a *view*, but a *discourse in accord with a view*. Consequently, one is allowed the flexibility to proclaim a Prāsaṅgika discourse in the morning and a Svātantrika one in the afternoon, without being committed to one view at the exclusion of the other.

We can see that Mipam primarily delineates the Prāsaṅgika in terms of discourse on the ultimate. However, he also states that the valid establishment of conventionally existent phenomena is an implication of the conception of the two truths as distinct for Svātantrikas:

> When Svātantrikas explain with an emphasis on the categorized ultimate, due to the essential point that they accept the ultimate as a mere emptiness of true existence and the conventional as validly established (*tha snyad tshad grub*), they ascertain the Middle Way in accordance with postmeditation certainty together with assertions.[28]

As long as the conventional and ultimate perspectives remain distinct, conventional phenomena are established by valid cognition. However, he rejects the view that an assertion that conventional phenomena are established from their own side (*rang ngos nas grub pa*) entails that conventional phenomena are truly established (*bden grub*) for Svātantrikas.[29] He says that true establishment is determined only from the perspective of ultimate analysis:

> At the time of ultimate analysis, if even the slightest phenomenon is found to be established from its own side (*rang ngos nas grub*), it would be truly established. The Svātantrikas also do not accept anything to be established from its own side from the perspective of ultimate analysis; if they did, they would not be suitable to be proponents of the Middle Way, nor would they possess the path of liberation. Although an object may appear to be established by its own essence (*rang gi ngo bos grub*) from the perspective of conventional analysis, by this how would it be truly established? Conventions need to be validly established; if they were not established even from the perspective of conventional analysis, they would never be established.[30]

He argues that although an object may appear to be established by its own essence from the perspective of conventional analysis, this does not entail that it is truly established. True establishment is the concern of *ultimate* inquiry and nothing is truly established for Svātantrikas.

He asserts that Svātantrikas accept conventional production that is established by valid cognition and that such production is not invalidated by ultimate valid cognition:

> This conventional production is accepted to be validly established by Svātantrikas, and this is not invalidated [for them] even by ultimate analysis because through holding onto "the negation of ultimate production," they think that if there were no production conventionally, then conventional truth would be nonexistent. When Prāsaṅgikas examine by means of ultimate analysis, there is nothing at all that withstands analysis.[31]

Conventional production is not negated by ultimate analysis from a Svātantrika perspective where the two truths are distinct. However, nothing withstands Prāsaṅgika analysis. Thus, conventional production does not even conventionally exist when ascertaining the uncategorized ultimate, where there is no dichotomy of conventional and ultimate perspectives apprehending the two truths as distinct. Mipam states:

> In this way, upon analysis through the manner of the four extremes, the reasoning that ascertains that production not only does not exist ultimately, but does not exist even conventionally, ascertains the primordially non-arising and unceasing nature of these interdependently-arisen appearances that incontrovertibly exist in this way. Therefore, the uncategorized ultimate, beyond the mere absence of true existence that is the categorized [ultimate], is indicated as the indivisibility of the two truths—the freedom from constructs—which is the expanse of phenomena itself.[32]

The reason for not accepting the existence of production conventionally is due to the nature of the uncategorized ultimate, which is not demarcated as an ultimate reality separate from the conventional. The negation of production is unqualified as either ultimate or conventional because there is no such distinction between the two truths in the uncategorized ultimate, which is the expanse of phenomena.

Commenting upon Mipam, Bötrül explains that negating appearances while dividing the two truths is an overextension of the object of negation. However, this is not the case when the two truths are not divided:

> If having divided the two truths one also negates appearance, there ensues the fault of the over-pervasion (*khyab ches ba'i skyon*) of the object of negation. However, due to the essential point of not dividing the two truths, there is not only no ensuing fault of the over-pervasion of the object of negation, but it is this which hits the essential point that evokes the genuine indivisibility of the two truths.[33]

In this way, when the two truths are not divided, there is no fault of over-pervasion when negating appearance; however, negating conventional appearances when dividing the two truths falls to the extreme of annihilationism.

Mipam does not assert the necessity of a difference between Svātantrika and Prāsaṅgika with regards to conventional truth.[34] Rather, he emphasizes the compatibility of the Svātantrika and Prāsaṅgika discourses. His main emphasis is on the compatibility of Prāsaṅgika and Svātantrika, but the distinction he makes between them is an important one.

It is significant that Mipam depicts Prāsaṅgika as an approach similar to the manner of ascertaining primordial purity in the Great Perfection:

> The viewpoint of Candrakīrti—the profound view in which the fictional marks of convention dissolve into the expanse since all these appearances are pure just as they are—is similar to the manner of ascertaining primordial purity in the scriptures of the Great Perfection.[35]

He also shows a parallel between the emptiness of Prāsaṅgika and primordial purity in the Great Perfection:

> To conclusively settle upon primordial purity
> One needs to perfect the view of Prāsaṅgika;
> From only the aspect of being free from constructs
> The two[36] are said to not be distinct.[37]

We will now turn to Mipam's description of a progressive approach to understanding the Middle Way.

Dialectical Ascent

Mipam explains that it is "difficult" for ordinary beings to see the ultimate truth instantaneously, and describes a study and contemplation approach as a manner to progressively negate the four extremes:

> Through a direct manner of instantaneously negating
> The constructs of the four extremes,
> It is difficult for ordinary beings
> To see the innate expanse that transcends the mind.
> Therefore, negating the constructs of the four extremes
> In alternation is the way of the view of study and contemplation.[38]

In contrast to the instantaneous approach that characterizes the manner of Prāsaṅgika and the Great Perfection, Mipam presents a gradual approach in the way of study and contemplation.

He outlines a process of those who progressively engage in the meaning of nonconceptuality in a fourfold scheme that he calls "the four stages of the dawning of the Middle Way": "empty" (*stong*), "unity" (*zung 'jug*), "freedom from constructs" (*spros bral*), and "equality" (*mnyam pa nyid*).[39] He states that individuals cannot reach an understanding of the higher stages until they have ascertained the former stages: "These four are such that in dependence upon the former, the manners of the latter are engaged; without gaining certainty in the former, one will not ascertain the latter."[40]

He says that the first stage, "empty," is arrived at by a novice who analyzes objects, such as pots, in terms of whether they are singular or plural, and so forth. When the nature of a phenomenon is not found when analyzed, it is discovered that the phenomenon is not established—empty. As phenomena are analyzed, they are not found, so they are empty; however, phenomena incontrovertibly appear from the perspective of non-analysis:

> When novices properly investigate by means of the reasons which establish emptiness—such as [the reason of] being neither singular nor plural—through contemplating the meaning of the nonestablishment of a pot and so forth, they think that the abiding reality is nonestablishment itself because although existing in the perspective of non-analysis, nothing is found when analyzed. Therefore, in a manner alternating appearance and emptiness, the empty quality dawns.[41]

At the stage of "empty," Mipam states that the nonestablishment of apparent phenomena is thought to be the mode of reality, and one alternates between the two modalities of appearance (when not analyzing) and emptiness (when analyzing).

The next phase, "unity," is understood when the nonexistence of phenomena is itself recognized as a mere imputation, not truly established in reality. One gains certainty that while appearing, phenomena are empty, and while empty, they appear:

> At that time, by contemplating that the nonexistence of phenomena also is just a mere imputation not actually established, or the manner that things appear while empty from the beginning, one generates the distinctive certainty that while empty, they appear and while appearing, are empty—like [a reflection of] the moon in water. At that time, the absence of intrinsic nature and interdependent arising dawn as noncontradictory—"the understanding of unity" (*zung 'jug tu go ba*).[42]

At the stage of "unity," the noncontradiction of the empty nature of phenomena and their interdependent arising is the "understanding of unity." One comes to understand that, from the beginning, appearances of phenomena are inseparable from their emptiness(es).

He states that in the next phase, "freedom from constructs," one gains certainty in the manner that the two—the lack of intrinsic nature and the interdependent arising—are not essentially different. A freedom from constructs dawns as the natural deconstruction (*rang sar zhig*) of conceptual cognitions that distinctively apprehend emptiness as a negation, and phenomena as the basis of negation:

> At that time, certainty is generated in the manner that the two—the lack of inherent nature and interdependent arising—although different in the manner of expression by two phrases, are indivisible without the slightest essential difference. Thereby, the thought that apprehends appearance as the basis of negation, which is affixed with an object of negation that is eliminated, naturally deconstructs; and there dawns the qualities of a freedom from constructs, such as the ability to remain naturally free from negation and affirmation, adding and removing.[43]

At the stage of "freedom from constructs," the lack of intrinsic nature and interdependent arising are known as not essentially different; other than different ways of expression,[44] they are indivisible.

The last stage is "equality." Through becoming accustomed to a freedom from constructs, all notions of duality become no longer present as impinging upon the mind:

> Through becoming familiar with such a freedom of constructs again and again, all aspects of dualistic phenomena, in which one observes a domain of partiality concerning particular objects (*chos can*) and their distinctive suchnesses (*chos nyid*), are purified. Through bringing forth a distinctive certainty in the nature of all phenomena as equality, one reaches completion.[45]

The fourth stage, "equality," is thus an all-encompassing eradication of dualistic notions.

In contrast to the analytical approach of "the way of the view of study and contemplation," another method, a "quintessential instructions approach,"[46] does not require much analysis. Certain people of sharp faculties are able to instantly gain certainty in the meaning of the equality of emptiness and appearance by engaging in simple analysis, such as observing that the mind does not arrive from anywhere, abide in someplace, or go anywhere:

> Some people of sharp faculties, through analyzing the mind [in terms of] only arising, abiding, and going, instantly generate certainty in the meaning of the equality of appearance and emptiness through the sole power of experiencing the nature of the three gates of liberation, which is the emptiness of the three—cause, essence, and effect.[47]

This is an analysis often found in meditation instructional manuals in the tradition of the Great Perfection. Such contemplations also may involve searching for the mind in terms of shape, form, and so forth. However, Mipam is critical of what he sees as misappropriations of such an uncritical approach. He states:

> Since the mind has no form
> It is impossible for anybody to see the mind as having color, etc.
> It is a mistake to think that one has recognized emptiness
> By merely not seeing the mind to have color.[48]

In this, we can see how a distinction can be made between uncritical views: (1) an uncritical view that has not sufficiently engaged analysis (precritical), and (2) an uncritical view that *transcends* analysis (postcritical).[49] In a similar distinction that he makes regarding the meaning of "not apprehending anything" (*cir yang mi 'dzin*), he criticizes the former type of uncritical view that has not engaged analysis:

> At the time of sustaining the actual view
> Some people say, "Do not apprehend anything."
> The meaning of "Do not apprehend anything"
> Is twofold: (1) good understanding and (2) misconception.
> The first is a freedom from the constructs of the four extremes,
> In the presence of a Sublime One's wisdom
> Since nothing at all remains
> Apprehension naturally subsides—
> Like seeing the open, clear sky.
> The second is oblivion, the tradition of Hvashang.
> By resting blankly without analysis
> With no clarity-aspect of special insight,
> One remains like an ordinary stone at the bottom of the ocean.
> For example, like the statement "nothing at all"
> For a proponent of the Middle Way seeing absence
> And one aspiring to an absence that is an absence of form,
> Although in mere words these are the same,
> The meanings are as different as the earth and space.[50]

Mipam delineates two meanings for "not apprehending anything" in a similar way that he makes a distinction between the apparent sameness of two uncritical views. While they resemble each other due to the fact that they sound the same, he depicts an important and radical difference.[51] Furthermore, he states that the "bad view of not apprehending anything" does not eliminate obscurations:

> How can the bad view of not apprehending anything
> Generate certainty in the nonestablishment of any entity?
> That [bad view of not apprehending anything] cannot abandon obscurations.
> Therefore, the difference between these two also
> Is known through the manner of the development of abandonment and realization,
> As fire [is known] through the evidence of smoke.

> Since ordinary idiot meditation
> Is not a cause for abandonment and realization,
> It is an obstacle to the cultivation of virtue.[52]

He states that a distinction between the correct view and "ordinary idiot meditation" can be seen in the fruits of practice—the development of abandonment and realization. He consistently emphasizes such a distinction and affirms a central place of certainty induced by reasoned analysis. He states:

> One may think, "It is not suitable to grasp at any extreme!" And throw away the certainty induced by reasoned investigation that is the source of the nectar of profound emptiness, the antidote for all diseases within existence. Thinking, "It is not suitable to engage the mind at all!" is entering into a thick darkness of oblivion, where it is difficult to view, see, conceive, or experience this profound truth.[53]

Mipam also stresses the importance of reason in distinguishing the meanings of such terms as "freedom from constructs" in Buddhism, from the same terms used by non-Buddhists. He states:

> Although [we share] the mere words such as "illusory," "nonentity," "freedom from constructs," it does not help if you do not know the manner that the Buddhist emptiness is superior to the limited emptiness of non-Buddhists, through a firm conclusion (*phu thag chod*) with certainty induced by reason . . . Although the words may be similar, Buddhists and non-Buddhists cannot be separated by words; the difference—which is like the earth and space—is in the profound essential point.[54]

Moreover, he says that statements that Buddhists do not need reasoned analysis are the words of a demon:

> The Buddha . . . taught the mode of reality of entities without error and according to fact. His followers also need to ascertain the way it is by reason (*rigs pas*); this is the unerring tradition of Śākya[muni]. However, saying that in the inner art [of Buddhism] one does not need reasoned analysis in general, and valid cognition, etc. in particular, is a frightful spell of a demon that obstructs the practice of the excellence to be experienced, which is the valid cognition of the Buddha's Word purified by the three analyses.[55]

We saw earlier how he represents the (uncategorized) ultimate truth as transcending linguistic and conceptual structures of thought. Nevertheless, valid cognition, reasoned analysis, and a conceptual understanding of the ultimate also play an important role for Mipam. He states as follows in his commentary on the *Madhyamakālaṃkāra:*

> The genuine ultimate is not merely an absence, but is free from the constructs of the four extremes. However, there is no method to realize the great ultimate without the categorized ultimate, which is the mere absence of a true existence of entities that abides as an other-exclusion—the object of a conceptual mind. The term "ultimate" is used because it is the method, or cause, of realizing that [genuine ultimate].[56]

He advocates a conceptual approach to the ultimate as a means to transcend conceptuality. Furthermore, he states that as long as experience remains as a dualistic participation of an internal subject with external objects, the incontrovertible law of causality will be at work accordingly:

> Someone may think, "If all phenomena are unreal and like an illusion, then it is not reasonable to train in even the path, generosity, etc. It would be like toiling to buy an illusory horse, what is the use?!" . . . [In response] The appearing factor of saṃsāra and nirvāṇa is incontrovertible due to the power of dependent arising. Therefore, until the [dualistic] engagement of subject and object has dissolved into the expanse, for that long, these appearances are uninterrupted and are harmful or helpful to sentient beings.[57]

Thus, the unreality of phenomena does not entail a lack of causality. We will now turn to Mipam's presentation of Yogācāra-Madhyamaka to show how he integrates both Prāsaṅgika and Yogācāra into his description of the Middle Way.

Foundations of Yogācāra

Mipam presents Yogācāra-Madhyamaka as a system that makes a distinction between the conventional mode of appearance (*tha snyad snang tshul*) and the conventional mode of reality,[58] through which one can take account for the fact that although things *appear* to be external, they are not because their conventional mode of reality is Mind-Only. Mipam wrote commentaries on many texts that are often characterized as Yogācāra[59] in addition to the works that he wrote on texts characterized as Prāsaṅgika that emphasize the negative dialectics of the Middle Way.[60] This shows the importance he placed on the Yogācāra traditions. It is also noteworthy that he says "asserting the conventional as Mind-Only is established as the general way for all Mahāyāna."[61]

Mipam characterizes proponents of Mind-Only as asserting a nondual reflexive awareness as truly existent:

> There are also two [bodhisattva vehicles]: (1) proponents of the Middle Way, who have perfected the view of selflessness, and (2) proponents of Mind-Only, who have not perfected the subtle selflessness of phenomena due to asserting a nondual reflexive awareness as truly existent.[62]

He distinguishes Mind-Only from the Middle Way in terms of the belief in the true establishment of consciousness. He states: "The debate between the Middle Way and Mind-Only is not about external objects existing or not, but the debate is about consciousness being truly established or not."[63] Furthermore, he says: "The manner of Mind-Only is very much the true nature of conventional reality; however, the aspect of clinging to the nature of a self-illuminating (*rang gsal*) consciousness as truly established is what is to be negated."[64] Thus, the reification of a cognitive presence—clinging to the nature of consciousness as truly established—differentiates the Middle Way and Mind-Only.

In his commentary on the *Dharmadharmatāvibhāga*, Mipam affirms the similarity of the traditions of Mind-Only and the Middle Way:

> Thus, when the appearance of apprehended [objects] is established to not have an essence that is separate from the apprehending [subject], the appearance of the apprehending subject is also established as nonexistent. If [one wonders] why, it is because the apprehending [subject] is established in dependence upon the apprehended [object]; it is never established on its own. In this way, if proponents of Mind-Only have to realize the lack of all duality, the awareness free from subject and object, naturally luminous and clear, inexpressible and nondistinct from the nature of the thoroughly established nature free from

> the twofold self, then it is needless to mention that the proponents of the Middle Way realize this! . . . Merely the slight philosophical assertion that posits the essence of ineffable cognition as truly established remains to be negated; authentic proponents of the Middle Way assert the unity of the primordially pure luminous clarity of one's mind and the emptiness of that nondual cognition. Therefore, other than the distinction of whether this slight fixation is eliminated or not, the Middle Way and Mind-Only are mostly the same in terms of the practices of meditative equipoise and postmeditation.[65]

Thus, we can see that the distinction between Mind-Only and the Middle Way does not concern the presence of a nondual cognition, but rather the position that such a cognition is truly established. We will return in the next chapter to see how Mipam portrays the relationship between wisdom and mind, and the status of such cognitions as "reflexive awareness" (*rang rig*) and "innate mind" (*gnyug sems*). Here we will look into his treatment of Yogācāra-Madhyamaka, which relies on Mind-Only to describe the *conventional* mode of reality (not the ultimate mode of reality).

In his commentary on the *Madhyamakālaṃkāra,* Mipam cites a verse from the *Laṅkāvatārasūtra* that states that all of the Mahāyāna is contained within four topics: the five principles (*chos lnga*), the three natures (*mtshan nyid gsum*),[66] the eight consciousnesses,[67] and the twofold selflessness:

> All of the Mahāyāna is contained within
> The five principles and the three natures
> The eight consciousnesses and
> The two meanings of selflessness [person and phenomena].[68]

In his *Rapsel Rejoinder*, a text Mipam wrote in response to criticisms of his commentary on the ninth chapter of the *Bodhicaryāvatāra*, Mipam states that: "The two selflessnesses and the eight consciousnesses also are comprised within the five principles; and these five [principles] are also comprised within the three natures."[69] It is significant that he claims that all Mahāyāna can be contained within the three natures, a frequent Yogācāra depiction.

He uses Yogācāra discourse to offer a systematic representation of reality—both conventional and ultimate truth. The comprehensive and systematic quality of Yogācāra contrasts with Prāsaṅgika, which, as we saw above, is defined in reference to the (uncategorized) ultimate truth. Unlike the function of Yogācāra in his works, we can see that Prāsaṅgika functions to *deconstruct* systematic representation; it is a discourse that accords with meditative equipoise in that it *enacts* the nonconceptual, where all distinctions, including the distinction between the conventional and ultimate truth, have collapsed. Yogācāra, on the other hand, situates the nonconceptual state of meditative equipoise within an overarching structure of a system that distinguishes the conceptual and the nonconceptual. By doing so, Yogācāra is more suited to represent a comprehensive account of reality that accounts for distorted (conceptual) and undistorted (nonconceptual) experience. Before we further address the role of Yogācāra in relation to Prāsaṅgika, we will first look into Mipam's portrayal of Yogācāra and his explanation of the five principles and three natures.

The five principles are: (1) name (*ming*), (2) property (*rgyu mtshan*), (3) conceptuality (*rnam rtog*), (4) authentic wisdom (*yang dag pa'i ye shes*), and (5) thusness (*de bzhin nyid*).[70] "Name" refers to the nominal designation and "property" (etymologically "the reason [for the designation]") refers to the basis of designation. Mipam states: "Name is the mere imputation through terms such as 'pillar' and 'pot.' Property is a term's basis of imputation, such as that which functions to support beams or the appearance of a bulbous object."[71] He describes these first two of the five principles as the "imagined nature" (*kun btags, parikalpita*), among the three natures, because they are the dualistic appearances within the realm of words and thought: "These two [name and property] are the imagined nature because they are dualistic perceived-perceiver appearances of the domain of language and thought; when analyzed they are not truly existent."[72]

Mipam characterizes the third principle, "conceptuality," as the eight consciousnesses: "Conceptuality is the collection of eight consciousnesses."[73] Among the three natures, he says that conceptuality is exclusively the "dependent nature" (*gzhan dbang, paratantra*): "This [conceptuality] is exclusively the dependent nature because it is the basis of the appearances of the manifold appearances which are strictly conventional."[74] Furthermore, he characterizes the dependent nature as conceptual mind:

> In the perspective of thoroughgoing conceptuality, while there is dualistic appearance, the awareness that exclusively appears as such, but is not established in duality, is called "the dependent nature." It is the basis for the arising of distortion, the imagined nature.[75]

He states that the last two of the five principles, "thusness" and "authentic wisdom," refer respectively to the objective (*yul*) and subjective (*yul can*) components of the "thoroughly established nature" (*yongs grub, pariniṣpanna*), the last of the three natures.[76]

Mipam describes "thusness" as the expanse of phenomena that is the lack of intrinsic nature in all phenomena: "Thusness is the expanse of phenomena that is the lack of any intrinsic nature of the twofold self in these phenomena comprised by the internal and external."[77] He explains "authentic wisdom" as the reflexive awareness that is the subject (*yul can*) free from the imagination of the unreal (*yang dag min rtog*): "The individual reflexive awareness, the subject free from the imagination of the unreal which permeates that [thusness], is 'authentic wisdom'."[78] Authentic wisdom, "free from the imagination of the unreal," is thereby distinguished from mind (*sems*) because he explains "imagination of the unreal" to mean the dualistic experience of mind. He states this in his commentary on the *Madhyāntavibhāga*: "What is the imagination of the unreal? It is all minds (*sems*) and mental states (*sems byung*) of the three realms that have the dualistic experience of a perceived [object] and a perceiver."[79]

Among the three natures, Mipam states that the domain of pure wisdom is only the thoroughly established nature (*yongs grub*), not the other two natures (i.e., the imagined nature and the dependent nature):

> The exclusive object of pure wisdom is not the imagined or dependent natures, but is said to be only the thoroughly established nature because when that [thoroughly established nature] is the realm of experience, appearance accords with reality.[80]

As appearance in accord with reality (i.e., authentic experience), the thoroughly established nature is ultimate. Thus, only the thoroughly established nature is ultimate among the three natures:

> The ultimate, or the ultimate meaning, is only the thoroughly established nature among the three natures; the other two are not: (1) because [the thoroughly established nature] has the nature of nondual experience beyond ordinary consciousness and expression, or (2) because only this is appearance in accord with reality.[81]

Here, he depicts the thoroughly established nature as ultimate due to it being authentic experience, which he also describes as the nature of nondual experience. In this way, we can see that the distinction between consciousness (*rnam shes*) and wisdom (*ye shes*) is one way he delineates the two truths: "The subject of appearance in accord with reality is called 'wisdom,' being free from duality; 'consciousness' is the apprehending [subject] of appearance that does not accord with reality, being dualistic."[82] The ultimate as appearance in accord with reality—the ultimate of the authentic/inauthentic experience two-truth model—characterizes the two truths in this Yogācāra context.

In addition to the ultimate as the authentic experience of wisdom, Mipam also maintains the empty quality of such an ultimate when he says that the thoroughly established nature is not truly established:

> These latter two, subject [authentic wisdom] and object [thusness], are said to be "thoroughly established" (*yongs su grub*) not because of an essence that is truly established (*bden grub*), but are designated with that name because of being the unerring reality.[83]

In contrast to Mipam, Getsé Paṇchen (*dge rtse paṇ chen, 'gyur med tshe dbang mchog grub,* 1761–1829), a Nyingma scholar from Kaḥtok monastery, states that suchness is truly established (*bden grub*) due to being what is experienced by the undistorted wisdom of the Sublime Ones:

> Thus, the suchness that is the empty-ground of all phenomena
> Is truly established because it is just what is experienced
> By the undistorted wisdom of the Sublime Ones, and
> Permanent, steadfast, and eternal because it is unchanging.[84]

Many Nyingma scholars, particularly those affiliated with the Nyingma monastic tradition of Kaḥtok, draw upon such language that is typical of the view of "other-emptiness" championed by the Jonang tradition. Getsé Paṇchen, for instance, says that other-emptiness accords with the Great Perfection: "The abiding mode of the Great Perfection singlely accords with the Great Middle Way of other-emptiness."[85] Moreover, he describes the Great Perfection in terms of the three natures of Yogācāra, with the empty-ground as the thoroughly established nature:

> Of the three stages of the wheel of the Victorious One's doctrine
> The first teaches the relative and causality as incontrovertible
> The second teaches the self-empty relative and
> The third teaches the profound suchness, the other-empty ultimate.

> The awareness-wisdom of liberation—the great thoroughly established nature—is freed from
> The objects of delusion that appear yet do not exist—the imagined nature—and
> The subjects of deluded mind which are the eight collections [of consciousness]—the dependent nature—
> This is the definitive meaning, the distinctive doctrine of the Great Perfection.[86]

Mipam also treats the dependent nature as consciousness and the thoroughly established nature as wisdom. However, he emphasizes that Prāsaṅgika is (also) compatible with the Great Perfection.[87] In the following chapter, we will look into competing representations of emptiness in terms of "other-emptiness" and "self-emptiness." Before concluding this chapter, we will first consider Mipam's presentation of Yogācāra in relation to Prāsaṅgika.

Prāsaṅgika versus Yogācāra

As we saw in Mipam's Svātantrika-Prāsaṅgika distinction, Svātantrika is mainly characterized by discourse on the ultimate. Yogācāra, however, has distinctive characteristics in both domains of discourse on the ultimate (thoroughly established nature) and conventional (Mind-Only). It is significant to recall that the etymology of Yogācāra is "someone who practices yoga," in contrast to the etymology of Svātantrika, which comes from a logical form, "someone who uses autonomous arguments [to invoke ascertainment of the ultimate]." The distinctive domains of discourse for these two categories are reflected in their etymologies.

While Mipam defines the Svātantrika-Prāsaṅgika distinction with reference to the ultimate truth, his distinction not only reflects divergent approaches to ultimate truth, but also implicates a different way that conventional truth is represented. Bötrül elaborates on Mipam's Prāsaṅgika distinction not only in terms of ultimate emptiness, but also in terms of relative appearance. He makes a distinction between the way the relative truth is respectively asserted in the three traditions of (1) Mind-Only, (2) Yogācāra (Śāntarakṣita), and (3) Prāsaṅgika. He says that appearances are held to be mind in the Mind-Only tradition, and that the mind is conceived as truly established. In the Yogācāra, while the conventional mode of reality is mind, that mind is not held to be ultimately real. Finally, in the Prāsaṅgika, the appearances of relative truth are "merely self-appearance" (*rang snang tsam*).[88]

In contrast to the accounts of conventional reality in the Mind-Only and Yogācāra systems, "merely self-appearance" seems to be the concise and comprehensive delineation of conventional truth in the context of what is a *uniquely* Prāsaṅgika account of conventional reality. We are not given an elaborate discussion of conventional truth beyond "self-appearance"—perhaps necessarily so—because when we engage in discourses that theorize about conventional reality, we are no longer in the domain of Prāsaṅgika as it is defined: namely, a domain of discourse that emphasizes the uncategorized ultimate—the "content" of nonconceptual meditative equipoise.

We can see that unlike Yogācāra, a uniquely Prāsaṅgika discourse does not make an appearance-reality distinction between a conventional mode of appearance and a conventional mode of reality. Also unlike the systems of Mind-Only and Yogācāra, a uniquely Prāsaṅgika discourse does not offer the mind as the ontological ground for appearances *even conventionally*. Thus, there is no reality *behind* conventional appearances to ground reality in the Prāsaṅgika tradition; Prāsaṅgika is antirealist through and through.

So how do we understand Mipam, as a proponent of Prāsaṅgika or Yogācāra? We might think that the fact that he does not systematically develop a uniquely Prāsaṅgika position on conventional reality reflects his commitment to Yogācāra. However, rather than this fact being necessarily due to a categorical preference for Yogācāra over Prāsaṅgika, his representation of Prāsaṅgika apparently necessitates this.[89] As such, Mipam's representation of Prāsaṅgika can be seen as an antirealist move to allay the problems of both "realist" and "idealist" positions—or any other such rational account of conventional reality—by simply rejecting the substantialist premises of discursive practices as such. Seen in this light, he does not develop a systematic theory of conventional reality that is unique to Prāsaṅgika precisely because such theories necessarily involve substantialist presuppositions. Instead, he positions Prāsaṅgika as antithetical to the substantialist and discursive presumptions that system-building discourses such as Yogācāra involve.

We are left with a question of whether Mipam is a proponent of Prāsaṅgika-Madhyamaka or Yogācāra-Madhyamaka. When we confront this question carefully, we come up with a similar answer as we did to the issue of the two wheels of doctrine in the last chapter, that is, which wheel of doctrine does he accept as definitive, the middle or the last? Both. In this chapter, too, we see again how he undoes another dichotomy: the answer to the question of where he stands, as a proponent of Yogācāra or Prāsaṅgika, is another "both/and." As we saw with his Svātantrika-Prāsaṅgika distinction, his presentations of Yogācāra and Prāsaṅgika reflect a distinction based on different perspectival contexts rather than different ontological commitments. The question of whether he is a proponent of *either* Prāsaṅgika *or* Yogācāra is poorly formulated because neither necessarily precludes the other, and both discourses can be employed to demonstrate the authentic view of the Middle Way.

Conclusion

Mipam's discussion of Prāsaṅgika and Svātantrika draws upon a distinction between (nonconceptual) wisdom and (conceptual) mind. He characterizes Svātantrika as a discourse that emphasizes the categorized, or conceptual, ultimate truth. In contrast, Prāsaṅgika discourse emphasizes the uncategorized ultimate. As such, Prāsaṅgika is a discourse that accords with the experience of wisdom's meditative equipoise, where the two truths are not conceived as separate.

Mipam portrays Prāsaṅgika as a radical discourse of denial. Since the mind cannot conceive the "content" of nonconceptual meditative equipoise, Prāsaṅgika, as the representative discourse of meditative equipoise, negates any formulation of that state. In contrast, he positions Yogācāra as a discourse that situates the nonconceptual state of meditative equipoise within a systematic conceptual structure. Rather than a discourse that *enacts* the nonconceptual (like Prāsaṅgika), the discourse of Yogācāra situates the nonconceptual within an overarching system, a system that distinguishes between the conceptual and the nonconceptual.

Mipam affirms that the manner of Prāsaṅgika is in accord with ascertaining primordial purity in the Great Perfection, the pinnacle of his own Nyingma tradition. Nevertheless, Yogācāra-Madhyamaka also plays an important role in his delineation of ultimate truth as wisdom's authentic experience (appearance in accord with reality), as well as in his formulation of conventional reality.

Looking broadly at Mipam's works, we can see a dialectical tension between two perspectives: (1) a conceptual, or gradual, perspective of reason and (2) a nonconceptual perspective of wisdom. These two perspectives reflect a distinction between: (1) consciousness, a realm of discursive inquiry within a conceptual framework, and (2) wisdom, a realm beyond concepts. Mipam brings the discourses of these seemingly incompatible perspectives into conversation, which is a theme that runs throughout his interpretation. Such a dialectic is a prominent feature of his Nyingma tradition.

CHAPTER THREE

The Present Absence

> It is not existent because even the Victorious Ones do not see it,
> It is not nonexistent because it is the ground of all of saṃsāra and nirvāṇa.
> This is not a contradiction; it is the path of the Middle Way of unity—
> May we realize the suchness of mind free from extremes!
>
> —Rangjung Dorjé, The Third Karmapa

Introduction

Emptiness is a central topic in Mahāyāna Buddhism and also an extremely complex one. This chapter further addresses Mipam's interpretation of emptiness, which is a fundamental part of his representation of Buddha-nature. We will see how he describes two aspects of emptiness: (1) as a substrate and (2) as a quality of reality. We will also address a third meaning of emptiness: as the inconceivable unity of appearance and emptiness.

In the previous chapter, we discussed the categorized ultimate, emptiness as a conceived absence of true existence. In the case of emptiness that is the categorized ultimate, the empty aspect is *conceived as a quality* of phenomena. For instance, a cup's lack of intrinsic existence—its emptiness—is a quality of the cup. As such, a phenomenon (*chos*) is an empty-ground (*stong gzhi*); it is a ground *of* the empty-quality. Another way that emptiness can be conceived is as a lack of something in something else—emptiness as an absence *in some location*. For instance, like the absence of an elephant in this room. As such, the location of absence (e.g., the room) is empty of something that does not exist there (e.g., an elephant). In this case, the existing substrate that is empty of something is the empty-ground (*stong gzhi*); it is the ground *that is* empty of some quality. I will call this representation of emptiness a *locative absence*.

We can see how both conceptions of emptiness imply a relationship between a quality and a substrate, and how the referents of quality and substrate are interchangeable: both phenomena (*chos*) and suchness (*chos nyid*) can mutually be conceived as either an empty-quality or an empty-substrate. For example, in the case of the emptiness of a phenomenon such as a cup, emptiness can be thought of as the empty-quality of the cup, in which the cup is the empty-ground and the lack of a truly established nature of the cup, its emptiness, is the cup's quality. Alternatively, emptiness can be thought of as the empty-ground of all phenomena, in which emptiness itself is the underlying substrate of all phenomenal qualities, such as cups. A third alternative is emptiness that is inconceivable: emptiness that is beyond the substrate/quality dichotomy. Such an emptiness is beyond any linguistic and conceptual reference. The inconceivability of emptiness is what Mipam emphasizes in his representation of emptiness.

It might be helpful here to resort to a familiar analogy to illustrate the distinction between these three types of emptiness: "Is the cup half-empty or half-full?" This of course is used to show the centrality of perspective—how the role of the observer determines the content of perception: a pessimist says it is half-empty and an optimist half-full. Although the dependence of an objective world on subjective perceptions is also relevant to a discussion of emptiness, I want to use this example in a different and more straightforward way. With the example of the cup of water, the cup is a substrate, and its presence, or lack, of water is a quality of that substrate. By identifying this substrate/quality relationship, we can see more clearly into how emptiness can be represented in different ways.

In the example of the half-empty cup, the cup (here metaphorically understood as the reality of ultimate truth) is the substrate and water (here understood as the unreality of relative truth) is the quality. Other-emptiness can be simply stated as the ultimate truth's lack of the relative truth. The extent to which the cup of water analogy is applicable is limited, however, as all analogies are, because both the water and the cup are within the domain of relative truth. In the other-emptiness of Dölpopa's Jonang tradition, which we will consider in this chapter, the ultimate truth is utterly lacking of any and every phenomena of relative truth—including both the cup and the water. Thus, it is other-emptiness—radically "other"; ultimate truth is empty of what is other (i.e., relative truth). In this interpretation, the ultimate truth is a *substrate*, that which is empty of the quality of relative truth.

When we look into the Geluk tradition, we can see another way that emptiness is represented: as a *quality*. Continuing with the analogy of the half-empty cup of water, the cup and the water are different; they are other. The emptiness of one thing in another—the cup's emptiness of water—is not the meaning of emptiness according to a Geluk view. Tsongkhapa's Geluk tradition emphasizes that both the cup and water are empty: the cup is empty of an inherently existing cup and water is empty of inherently existing water. It is so because when sought after, no true ontological basis for anything is findable—no truly existent water is to be found or a true nature of cup. Even emptiness is not found when analyzed. Emptiness itself is not a real substrate; hence, it is not to be reified as a metaphysical entity; rather, emptiness itself is empty—as is stated by "the emptiness of emptiness." In this interpretation, emptiness is a quality of all phenomena; emptiness is even a quality of emptiness itself!

We can see a third representation of emptiness in Mipam's presentation: emptiness as an inconceivable unity. He contrasts his interpretation of emptiness with the former two emptinesses, which he represents as substrate and quality, and emphasizes that mind and language cannot access the consummate meaning of emptiness, which is beyond the dichotomies of quality/substrate and negation/affirmation. In this chapter, we will see how Mipam incorporates elements from both the Jonang and Geluk interpretations of emptiness and uses their representations to clarify the meaning of emptiness.

We will see how he addresses two aspects of emptiness: as a quality of appearance and as an empty-ground. We will also see how he depicts emptiness as beyond the dichotomy of (1) emptiness as an absent quality distinct from appearance and (2) emptiness as an empty-ground distinct from appearance. We will then be able to better appreciate his portrayal of the meaning of emptiness as the unity of emptiness and appearance. In order to appreciate Mipam's unique depiction of emptiness, we will first discuss a Jonang portrayal of "other-emptiness" to provide a context for contrast with Mipam's exegesis.

Other-Emptiness in the Jonang

Dölpopa clearly delineates two types of emptinesses in his *Ocean of Definitive Meaning:* "That which exists within the abiding reality (*gnas lugs la yod pa*) is other-empty, and that which does not exist within the abiding reality is self-empty."[1] Dölpopa depicts emptiness as a locative absence, an emptiness of something in another:

> The fifteenth [emptiness],[2] the emptiness of nonentities, is the meaning of the frequent statement, "that which does not exist in something, that something is empty of that." That which is the emptiness of own entity is the relative self-emptiness. The sixteenth, the emptiness that is the nature of nonentities, is the meaning of the frequent statement, "that which remains always exists here."[3] That which is the emptiness of another entity is the ultimate other-emptiness.[4]

Here we can clearly see Dölpopa's delineation of two types of emptiness. He characterizes: (1) "relative self-emptiness" as the absent phenomena in a location and (2) "ultimate other-emptiness" as the remaining location of the absence. Dölpopa delineates earlier statements of Buddhist doctrine (i.e., first and middle wheels) of emptiness as the nonexistence of one thing in another; he portrays later statements (e.g., last wheel) of non-emptiness as what remains as always existing. In this way, he shows how Buddhist scriptures are not contradictory:

> The earlier statements due to the perspective of trainees that all—liberation and so forth—do not exist, are empty, selfless, and so forth are in consideration of the nonexistence of something in something else, whereas the later statements of non-emptiness, the existence of self, and so forth are in consideration of that which is the remainder of that nonexistence (*med pa'i lhag ma*). Therefore, although earlier and later scriptures seem to be contradictory, when analyzed well, they are not contradictory.[5]

He says that later statements of non-emptiness refer to what is *the remainder* of nonexistence. Thus, an empty-ground is the remainder of absence. Such a negation that implies something else is, technically speaking, an "implicative negation" (*ma yin dgag*).[6] Dölpopa depicts an implicative negation within the ground of a non-implicative negation (*med dgag*):

> An implicative negation exists within the ground of a non-implicative negation, and wisdom complete with all innate qualities, thor-

> oughly established and pervading space, abides within the ground which from the beginning is naturally pure and relinquished of all faults.[7]

Here, Dölpopa states that the ground of a non-implicative negation is an implicative negation. He seems to be saying that the presence of language, even negation, necessarily presupposes an underlying reality. For Dölpopa, this reality is cognitive; it is wisdom. He claims that wisdom abides within the ground of negation from the beginning. We might say that the cognitive ground of wisdom is the substrate—or rather the *super*strate—of reality and its linguistic formulation.

Dölpopa asserts a presence of ultimate qualities abiding within the ground of emptiness: "All qualities of the ultimate, the empty-ground . . . always abide within the abiding reality."[8] He also presents the ground of emptiness as the Buddha: "The omnipresent expanse of phenomena—the ground, free from all extremes such as existence and nonexistence, and so forth—is the Buddha that is the abiding reality (*gnas lugs kyi sangs rgyas*)."[9] Thus, Dölpopa states that the ground of reality is not only cognitive, but is the ultimate mind—the Buddha. He says that an ultimate mind exists within reality:

> The ultimate mind is the mind that exists within the abiding reality; relative mind is a mind that does not exist within the abiding reality. Therefore, "the mind which is existent mind" is the ultimate mind of awakening, natural luminous clarity.[10]

Dölpopa depicts a cognitive presence, an ultimate mind, within reality. Furthermore, he describes this ground as Buddha-nature: "Moreover, this which is thusness, the Buddha-nature—having many synonyms such as suchness, and so forth—is the ground of all phenomena."[11] Dölpopa emphasizes the existence of Buddha-nature as the ground of phenomena. He also affirms the existence, or rather, negates the nonexistence, of a pure self (*bdag dag pa*), the self which he says is the great identity of the Buddha (*sangs rgyas kyi bdag nyid chen po*):

> Within the abiding reality, the ultimate Truth Body is not nonexistent because [within the abiding reality] thusness which is pure self, the self which is the great identity of Buddha, is not severed. Within

> the abiding reality, relative form bodies (*kun rdzob gzugs sku*) do not exist because [within the abiding reality] not any relative phenomena are established.[12]

Dölpopa depicts relative phenomena as utterly nonexistent in the abiding reality. This ultimate reality is "other-empty," it is empty of all relative phenomena. In this way, he portrays the relative as appearances that do not accord with reality. He states that relative phenomena are consciousness' distortions of reality:

> These karmic appearances mistaken by sentient beings are private phenomena for only sentient beings, yet they are utterly impossible within the abiding reality—like the horns of a rabbit, the child of barren woman, a space-flower, and so forth.[13]

Dölpopa claims that the view that relative phenomena exist within the abiding reality is the extreme of existence, a superimposition, and the view that the ultimate qualities of wisdom do not exist is the extreme of nonexistence, a denigration:

> Whereas relative phenomena do not at all exist within the abiding reality, the extreme of existence is the superimposition that they do. Whereas the irreducible, omnipresent wisdom of the expanse of phenomena always abides pervading everywhere, the extreme of nonexistence is the denigration that it does not exist, is not established, and is empty of its own essence. That which is the middle free from those extremes is the ground free from all extremes such as existence and nonexistence, superimposition and denigration, permanence and annihilation, and so forth, due to which it is the consummate Great Middle Way.[14]

He portrays the Great Middle Way as free from the extremes of existence and nonexistence, superimposition and denigration. He also depicts a third category (*phung po gsum pa*) of knowledge that is beyond dichotomies:

> Those who state that all objects of knowledge are strictly limited to two, entities and nonentities, simply do not realize suchness, the ultimate abiding reality, because although it is an object of knowl-

> edge, it is neither an entity nor a nonentity. Consequently, it is also established as just a third category, an in-between or middle.[15]

Through affirming a third category, an in-between, Dölpopa portrays an object of knowledge that is neither an entity nor a nonentity. In representing suchness in this way, we can see that he does not subscribe to the law of the excluded middle.

In Dölpopa's depiction of emptiness, there is no emptiness of suchness; suchness is sui generis. Suchness is unique because it is the ultimate ground of reality; there is no ground that is empty of suchness:

> An emptiness of everything does not occur because an emptiness of suchness does not occur. A ground that is empty of all phenomena occurs; it is suchness. A ground that is empty of suchness does not occur because that is invalidated by an immeasurable [number] of extremely absurd consequences. Therefore, empty of all and empty of all phenomena are extremely different because within the abiding reality there is an emptiness of phenomena but not an emptiness of suchness. This repudiates the assertion that phenomena and suchness are the same with different contradistinctions and also the assertion that they are utterly nondistinct because the two are different [in the sense of] negating that they are one entity (*ngo bo gcig pa bkag pa'i tha dad*).[16]

Dölpopa makes a distinction between emptiness of all and emptiness of all *phenomena;* the abiding reality is empty of phenomena, but is not empty of suchness. He states that the empty-ground of phenomena is suchness, but that there is no empty-ground of suchness. In this way, suchness is not a quality because it has no substrate; consequently, suchness is *only a substrate.* Moreover, Dölpopa claims that suchness is not related to phenomena in a way that the two are essentially the same with different contradistinctions (i.e., as conceptually distinct). Nor are phenomena and suchness utterly nondistinct. Rather, phenomena and suchness are "different in the sense of negating that they are one entity."[17] We will see how Mipam portrays the relationship between phenomena and suchness, but first we will look further into the Jonang tradition.

A twentieth-century Jonang scholar, Khenpo Lodrö Drakpa, defines "self-empty" as follows: "'Self-empty' refers to the claim that a non-implicative negation, which is the absence of true establishment, is the consummate ultimate."[18] He characterizes a "proponent of other-emptiness" as follows:

> "A proponent of other-emptiness" refers to: (1) one who claims that the ultimate nondual wisdom, the empty-ground, is not empty from its own side, and from the beginning is empty of all that is other—the conceptual constructs such as a perceived-perceiver [duality], and (2) in addition to claiming that adventitious phenomena comprising the relative are empty of the essence of the extrinsic ultimate, relative [phenomena] are also said to be empty of their own essences.[19]

Khenpo Lodrö Drakpa describes a proponent of other-emptiness as one who claims that the ultimate is not empty of its own essence but is empty of all conceptual constructs. Additionally, he says that proponents of other-emptiness not only claim that relative phenomena are empty of the extrinsic ultimate, but they also assert that relative phenomena are empty of their own essences. His characterization of other-emptiness explicitly affirms the claim that relative phenomena are empty of their own essences; hence, other-emptiness is not only the ultimate truth's emptiness of relative phenomena. The statement that other-emptiness incorporates relative phenomena as empty of their own essences is a crucial point. Without explicitly affirming such emptiness, the traditions of other-emptiness risk becoming characterized as accepting a naïve metaphysical realism that conflicts with a Buddhist view, particularly the view of emptiness as expressed in the middle wheel of doctrine.

Like Dölpopa, Khenpo Lodrö Drakpa states that ultimate reality is not reduced to simply a mere emptiness; he says that an implicative negation abides within the ground of a non-implicative negation:

> The consummate reality is not reduced to the nonestablishment of everything or simply a mere emptiness that is a nonexistence. Within the ground of a non-implicative negation, an emptiness of all relative constructs, the ultimate suchness of luminous clarity, which is an implicative negation, abides from the beginning.[20]

He affirms that the ultimate suchness of luminous clarity abides from the beginning within an absence of relative constructs. Thus, he portrays a non-implicative negation as contained within an implicative negation. As with

Dölpopa, we can see how he portrays language as implying, or *presupposing*, an underlying reality. In the case of the Jonang tradition, that reality is ultimate suchness, which is the cognitive ground of wisdom.

Khenpo Lodrö Drakpa makes a distinction between "Middle Way followers of the middle wheel" (*'khor lo bar ba'i rjes 'brang gi dbu ma pa*), a category under which he classifies the position of self-emptiness, and "Middle Way followers of the last wheel" (*'khor lo tha ma'i rjes 'brang gi dbu ma pa*), which he identifies with the position of other-emptiness.[21] In his *Roar of the Fearless Lion*, he characterizes the middle wheel of doctrine as mainly expressing the categorized ultimate, which he calls the "temporary definitive meaning" (*gnas skabs kyi nges don*). He says that the last wheel mainly expresses the uncategorized ultimate, "the consummate definitive meaning" (*nges don mthar thug pa*):

> The mode of the relative is what is principally the topic of the first [wheel], the mode of the categorized ultimate is what is principally the topic of the middle [wheel], and the consummate uncategorized definitive meaning is what is clearly, principally the topic of the last [wheel]. Hence, the sūtras of provisional and definitive meaning are posited in that way in consideration of what is the topic in the sequence of the three wheels in general, from the aspect of taking the provisional meaning, the temporary definitive meaning, and the consummate definitive meaning [respectively,] as what is principally the topic.[22]

Furthermore, he states that the Buddha merely taught "half of the definitive meaning" (*nges don phyed tsam*) in the middle wheel of doctrine, but he revealed "the ultimate definitive meaning" (*nges don don dam*) in the last wheel:

> In the first [wheel], the relative was taught in the manner of the ordinary four truths; in the middle [wheel], the expanse free from the constructs of all signs was taught, merely half of the definitive meaning; in the last [wheel], the ultimate definitive meaning was taught, the ground-expanse free from constructs, the great wisdom.[23]

Khenpo Lodrö Drakpa depicts the expanse free from constructs of all signs as "merely half of the definitive meaning," and states that the ultimate definitive meaning—the ground-expanse free from constructs, the great wisdom—

was taught in the last wheel. Furthermore, he states that the ultimate truth is shown to be truly existent in the last wheel of doctrine, "the wheel of doctrine of the thorough differentiation of the ultimate":

> In the last [wheel], the wheel of doctrine of the thorough differentiation of the ultimate, for disciples of sharp and extremely mature faculties who had trained their mental continua through all the vehicles, he mainly taught, through elegantly differentiating: (1) the ultimate truth itself as truly existing, meaning that it is permanent, steadfast, and eternal in the perspective of the wisdom of the Sublime Ones because it is the primordially unchanging essence of the indivisible expanse and awareness; and (2) relative phenomena comprising the perceiving [subjects] and perceived [objects] as not truly existing, meaning that they are primordially non-arising like reflections in a mirror—merely expressions (*rnam 'gyur*) of the ultimate.[24]

In this way, the last wheel distinguishes the ultimate truth that truly exists from relative phenomena that do not truly exist. Moreover, Khenpo Lodrö Drakpa does not differentiate between the scriptures of the last wheel of doctrine as "Mind-Only Sūtras" and those of the "Great Middle Way":

> There is no difference between the sūtra collections of those two [Mind-Only and Great Middle Way] because aside from the mere distinction between better and worse ways of explaining the viewpoint of one sūtra, actually there are no sūtras to be distinctly posited. For example, although the Vaibhāṣikas and the Sautrāntikas do not have different sūtra collections, [the difference] is merely how they adopt a viewpoint.[25]

He does not make a distinction between Mind-Only Sūtras and Buddha-Nature Sūtras in the last wheel; he makes a distinction based on a viewpoint, not based on sūtras. He distinguishes the Great Middle Way from what he describes as "Mind-Only realists" (*dngos smra'i sems tsam*) as follows:

> It does not follow that the subject, the supreme sūtras of the last Word, the [Buddha-]Nature Sūtras and so forth, become the tradition of the Mind-Only realists through the mere teaching that generally the nondual wisdom is truly established (*bden grub*) because there is a great difference in the utterly dissimilar ways of establish-

> ing as true (1) the truly established wisdom that is the subject of the teaching of the last wheel and (2) the truly established dependent and thoroughly established natures in the tradition of the Mind-Only realists. This is so because (1) the wisdom that is the subject of the last teaching is truly established due to being true in the abiding reality of the basic nature as the object of ultimate reflexive awareness free from constructs; and (2) since the truly established dependent and thoroughly established natures in the Mind-Only tradition are posited from a philosophy that is not beyond the appearance factor of consciousness, from the aspect of [their] observing signs as true entities, which is an object of negation [in our tradition]—there is a manner of great difference.[26]

Khenpo Lodrö Drakpa says that the manner that wisdom is truly established in the Great Middle Way is different from the manner of true establishment for Mind-Only realists. Mind-Only realists assert the truly established dependent and thoroughly established natures from a philosophy that observes signs (*mtshan ma*) as true entities. Wisdom in the Great Middle Way, on the other hand, is truly established due to being true in the abiding reality as the object of ultimate reflexive awareness free from constructs.

Thus, we can see a difference between the ways that the dependent and thoroughly established natures are depicted by Mind-Only realists and in the Great Middle Way. Here we can also see a difference between two ways of identifying the empty-ground: (1) as the thoroughly established nature or (2) as the dependent nature. Dölpopa claims that the dependent nature is the empty-ground of the imagined nature *temporarily* (*re zhig*). He identifies the thoroughly established nature with suchness, the final (*mthar*) empty-ground:

> Temporarily, it is said that the aggregates, constituents, and sense-fields, which are contained within the dependent nature, is the ground that is empty of the imagined nature, the self, and self-possessions. In the end, the ground that is empty of even the dependent nature is suchness, the thoroughly established nature. . . . In this way, the ground that is empty of the imagined nature is the dependent nature. The ground that is empty of the dependent nature is the thoroughly established nature. A ground that is empty of suchness, the thoroughly established nature, is utterly impossible because it is the thusness that abides as spontaneously present, all the time and everywhere.[27]

Although the dependent nature is *temporarily* the ground of the imagined nature, the *final* empty-ground is the thoroughly established nature, which is the ground of the dependent nature. Dölpopa states that a ground that is empty of the thoroughly established nature is impossible because it is the reality that abides everywhere, all the time. In this way, it is the ground of all, the existent and the nonexistent.

Other-Emptiness and the Nyingma: Lochen Dharmaśrī

We will now consider a discussion of other-emptiness in the works of the Nyingma scholar, Lochen Dharmaśrī (*lo chen dharmaśrī,* 1654–1717). Through this we can begin to explore the view of emptiness in the Nyingma tradition in general, and see the relationship between Lochen's Nyingma view and the view of other-emptiness as presented by the Jonang tradition. This will allow us to better understand Mipam's interpretation of emptiness, as well as help us assess his treatment of other-emptiness.

Lochen delineates self-emptiness and other-emptiness as two manners of eliminating constructs (*spros pa gcod lugs*). He states:

> Concerning the manner of eliminating constructs there are two: self-emptiness and other-emptiness. [Proponents of] self-emptiness assert that the emptiness that is a non-implicative negation is ultimate because however phenomena may appear, they are empty of their own essences right from their mere appearance.[28]

He states that proponents of self-emptiness assert a non-implicative negation as ultimate. As for other-emptiness, Lochen delineates two traditions of identifying the empty-ground (*stong gzhi*) due to a difference in asserting all objects of knowledge: (1) in terms of the three natures or (2) condensing objects of knowledge into two, the imagined and the thoroughly established natures:

> In the traditions of the Middle Way that ascertain other-emptiness, due to the difference of asserting all objects of knowledge within the three natures or condensing objects of knowledge into the imagined and thoroughly established natures, there are two ways of identifying the subject (*chos can*): (1) in Yogācāra texts, the empty-ground is the dependent nature, the imagined nature is the object of negation, and the emptiness of the imagined nature in the dependent nature is

> the thoroughly established nature; (2) in texts such as the *Uttaratantra*, suchness, the thoroughly established nature, is empty of the imagined nature. Therefore, in the essence of the thoroughly established nature—which is the ultimate expanse and the suchness of mind—there are no defilements to remove, nor previously absent qualities to newly establish, because it is primordially pure by nature and has qualities that are spontaneously present.[29]

Lochen describes two traditions of other-emptiness for which he delineates (1) the empty-ground as the dependent nature that is empty of the imagined nature in Yogācāra texts and (2) the suchness that is empty of the imagined nature in texts such as the *Uttaratantra*. The latter resembles what we see in the Jonang presentations, and is also adopted by some Nyingma scholars, such as Getsé Paṇchen, as their own tradition of the "Great Middle Way."[30]

Moreover, similar to Khenpo Lodrö Drakpa's statement that the middle wheel is "merely half the definitive meaning,"[31] Lochen states that in his own tradition, the middle wheel is "half-definitive and half-provisional" (*drang nges phye ma*) or "definitive for the time being" (*gnas skabs pa'i nges don*):

> Although there are a lot of discordant assertions regarding what are the definitive or provisional [meanings] of the middle and last [wheels], since there is no scripture of sūtra that clearly states that the middle [wheel] is the definitive meaning and the last [wheel] is a provisional meaning, and [this] also would contradict the intended meaning of the metaphors of the patient's medicine and learning to read, my tradition asserts that the middle [wheel] is half-definitive and half-provisional, or definitive for the time being, and the last [wheel] itself is the definitive meaning because it is clearly explained in sūtras such as the *Saṃdhinirmocanasūtra*, the *Mahāparinirvāṇasūtra*, and the *Aṅgulimālīyasūtra*.[32]

Lochen says that there is no scripture that clearly states that the middle wheel is definitive and the last is a provisional meaning;[33] as such it would conflict with the meaning of the metaphors of learning to read [progressively][34] and medicine.[35] He affirms that his tradition asserts the last wheel as the definitive meaning.[36]

Lochen also shows a difference between the middle and last wheels of doctrine in terms of the view of what is to be experienced in meditation. He states:

> Regarding the view of what is to be experienced in meditation, according to the explicit teaching of the middle wheel explained in the way of [Nāgārjuna's] "Collection of Reasonings" (*rigs tshogs*), since the definitive meaning is accepted as a non-implicative negation, meditating on nothing whatsoever is said to be meditation on emptiness, and seeing nothing at all is said to be the realization of thusness. According to the viewpoint of the last wheel explained in the way of the texts of Maitreya, Asaṅga and [half-]brother [Vasubandhu], as well in Nāgārjuna's "Collection of Praises" (*bstod tshogs*), meditating on just the wisdom which is free from duality is what is to be experienced, and this also accords with the viewpoint of the profound tantras of Secret Mantra.[37]

He depicts two views of what is to be experienced in meditation: (1) according to the explicit teaching of the middle wheel, in which the definitive meaning is accepted as a non-implicative negation, meditation on emptiness is said to be meditating on nothing whatsoever and seeing nothing at all is said to be the realization of suchness, and (2) according to the viewpoint of the last wheel and the profound tantras, meditating on wisdom that is free from duality is what is to be experienced. Thus, he points out a difference between the middle and last wheel in terms of what is experienced in meditation.

Furthermore, Lochen cites Longchenpa, saying in the *Wish-Fulfilling Treasury* and the *Treasury of Philosophies* that it is not contradictory that the Prāsaṅgika method is more effective when ascertaining what is to be identified in study while also accepting the reflexive wisdom free from duality when ascertaining what is to be experienced in meditation:

> If one thinks, "In the scriptures such as the *Treasury of Philosophies* and the root and [auto]commentary of the *Wish-Fulfilling Treasury*, is it not a contradiction that: (1) in the context of identifying what is to be ascertained by means of study, Prāsaṅgika-Madhyamaka is established as the pinnacle of the Causal Vehicle of Mahāyāna, and (2) in the contexts of ascertainment by means of meditative experience, individual reflexive wisdom free from perceived-perceiver [duality] is asserted?" There is no contradiction because it is difficult for an ordinary being to deconstruct the reifications of the mind at the time of ascertaining the view by means of study and contemplation. Therefore, in negating these [reifications of the mind] through the supreme knowledge that arises through study and contempla-

> tion, Prāsaṅgika is a sharper awareness that cuts through superimpositions. Also, at the time of ascertaining by experience [the supreme knowledge] that arises in meditation, the view of the Middle Way taught in the last wheel itself is profound and much better because: (1) the naturally pure expanse, the ultimate truth that is the self-existing wisdom, is itself the primordial mode of reality of all phenomena, and (2) it is also in accord with the practice of the view that is accepted in the profound tantras of Secret Mantra.[38]

Here he makes a distinction based on two contexts: (1) study and contemplation and (2) meditation. In the contexts of study and contemplation, he portrays Prāsaṅgika-Madhyamaka as a more incisive means of cutting through superimpositions. However, in the contexts of meditation, he says that the view of the Middle Way taught in the last wheel is better because (1) self-existing wisdom is itself the primordial mode of reality and (2) that view accords with the practice of the view that is accepted in the profound tantras.[39]

Dölpopa also makes a distinction in the applied practice of the meaning of the last two wheels:

> Although the meaning of the last two wheels of doctrine are the same as the Vajrayāna, when they are practiced, one sets in equipoise in the conclusive profound suchness free from constructs in accord with the middle wheel, and then when making distinctions in postmeditation, one discerns phenomena in an authentic way, at which time one makes identifications upon differentiating well in accord with what is said in the last wheel and in the Vajrayāna.[40]

Dölpopa affirms that the meaning of both wheels is the same as the Vajrayāna, yet he makes a distinction between the ways the last two wheels of doctrine are practiced. He depicts a practice in accord with the middle wheel as setting in equipoise in the suchness free from constructs. In postmeditation, he states that one makes distinctions in accord with what is said in the last wheel and in the Vajrayāna. In this way, both the middle and last wheels are compatible with the Vajrayāna in different contexts.

Before we turn to Mipam, there is one more point Lochen raises that is important to address. Lochen states how certain practices of his tradition accord for the most part with Nāgārjuna; however, he raises a question as to whether the view in the Nyingma tradition is in accord with Nāgārjuna:

> In general, due to the essential point that the manner of taking the bodhisattva vow stated in the tantras of Secret Mantra, and also the enumerated trainings, are in accord for the most part with the tradition of Nāgārjuna, our tradition of early translations following the master Padmasambhava appears to be in accord with Nāgārjuna also in the ritual practice for generating the mind of awakening. However, it is not certain that the [Nyingma] view is [in accord with] his because even though it does not contradict Nāgārjuna's "Collection of Praises," [the Nyingma] for the most part are in accord with the way that Asaṅga and his [half-]brother [Vasubandhu] explain because of (1) taking the uncategorized ultimate as not a non-implicative negation, but taking it as an emptiness that is an implicative negation, and (2) accepting the last wheel as the definitive meaning.[41]

Lochen suggests that the fact that the Nyingma (1) accept the last wheel as the definitive meaning and (2) take an implicative negation as the uncategorized ultimate problematizes a simple identification with the view of Nāgārjuna.

In accord with Lochen's delineation of the Nyingma view, Mipam accepts Buddha-Nature Sūtras of the last wheel (along with the middle wheel sūtras) as the definitive meaning; however, whether or not he takes an implicative negation as the uncategorized ultimate is a moot point. As we saw earlier, Mipam states that the uncategorized ultimate is beyond affirmations and negations. Therefore, he explicitly states that the uncategorized ultimate is not a negation, implicative or non-implicative. However, for Mipam the ultimate is not a mere absence; he does claim that there is a reality of ultimate wisdom that is beyond thought and language. It may be argued that his claim of the existence of this ultimate wisdom does in fact entail that the ultimate is an implicative negation, because the reality of non-conceptual wisdom is implied, or presumed, in the negation of conceptual constructs. Indeed, this issue of whether the ultimate is indicated by an implicative negation or a non-implicative negation is at the heart of the debates between proponents of "other-emptiness" and "self-emptiness."

The difference between self-emptiness (via non-implicative negation) and other-emptiness (via implicative negation), however, is not necessarily one of mutual incompatibility. Like the difference between the Svātantrika and Prāsaṅgika we saw in the previous chapter, the difference can be seen as one of different perspectival contexts rather than a radical difference necessitating irreconcilable ontological views. Even in the case of emptiness interpreted as a substance (through an implicative negation) or a quality (through a non-implicative negation), the two need not be incompatible: a non-implicative negation can be taken to indicate the *absence* of conceptual constructs in the nonconceptual (what is negated) while an implicative negation indicates the nonconceptual *presence* (the wisdom that remains). This is in fact suggested in the words of another Nyingma scholar, Getsé Paṇchen, who claimed that: "The two modes of emptiness [self-emptiness and other-emptiness] are the same in that they both assert that the essence of the view is inexpressible, unspeakable, and inconceivable."[42] While Getsé Paṇchen explicitly endorses other-emptiness, he says that self-emptiness and other-emptiness need not involve conflicting views.[43]

We will now turn to assess Mipam's position on other-emptiness. We will begin by looking at how Mipam distinguishes his view of emptiness and the way he aligns his view with the Nyingma tradition.

Another Emptiness? Emptiness of Self/Other

Mipam places himself within the tradition of Nāgārjuna, Rongzom, and Longchenpa. He states: "I don't have any burden of establishing the view of other-emptiness; [I am] in accord with the texts of Nāgārjuna, Longchenpa, and Rongzom."[44] Nevertheless, he also wrote a text that explicitly defends a view of other-emptiness, called *Lion's Roar: Affirming Other-Emptiness,*[45] in which he states:

> First it is necessary to ascertain the lack of intrinsic nature of all phenomena in accordance with the scriptures of the protector Nāgārjuna; because if this is not known, one will not be able to ascertain the manner that relative [phenomena] are empty from their own side and the manner that the ultimate is empty of what is other. Therefore, one should first ascertain the freedom from constructs which is what is known reflexively.[46]

Here Mipam delineates two manners of emptiness: (1) the manner that relative phenomena are empty of their own essences and (2) the manner that the ultimate is empty of what is other. He states that first one should ascertain the freedom of constructs, the lack of intrinsic nature of phenomena in accordance with the scriptures of Nāgārjuna. Furthermore, he states: "Certainty in the equality of appearance and emptiness—the Great Perfection—is seen only through the excellent scriptural tradition of Nāgārjuna."[47] In this way, he firmly aligns his Nyingma tradition with Nāgārjuna.

We will first assess Mipam's view of emptiness by looking at the positions of other-emptiness he critiques. Mipam characterizes the position of other-emptiness as leaving an empty-ground:

> Saying, "A pillar is not empty of pillar" or
> "Suchness is empty of pillar"
> Is leaving an empty-ground, which is other-emptiness.
> These are (1) other-emptiness in words and (2) other-emptiness in meaning.[48]

Saying that a pillar is empty of true establishment, but not empty of itself is a statement of other-emptiness in that it conveys that something is empty of something else. In the same way, stating that the ultimate nature, suchness, is not empty of itself, but is empty of phenomena like pillars also shares the meaning of other-emptiness. Both of these claims represent an other-emptiness view: emptiness held as negating some extrinsic quality while leaving a (non-empty) ground. The latter claim characterizes other-emptiness in the Jonang tradition, where the ultimate suchness of reality is stated to be empty of all relative phenomena. Mipam also calls this "ultimate other-emptiness" (*don dam gzhan stong*).[49] The former claim characterizes a Geluk view, in which relative phenomena like pillars are the empty ground(s) of the ultimate quality of emptiness (that is, the lack if true establishment). Mipam also enlists this view as having the meaning of other-emptiness by associating other-emptiness with the claim that a pot is not empty from its own side, but is empty of another—true establishment.[50] When a (non-empty) ground of emptiness is taken as an implication of such claims as "a pillar is not empty of pillar," in effect it becomes an other-emptiness view.[51] He also calls such a view "relative other-emptiness" (*kun rdzob gzhan stong*), and states that while the Jonang tradition accepts ultimate other-emptiness and relative self-emptiness, this view accepts relative other-emptiness and ultimate self-emptiness.[52]

Mipam distinguishes the meaning of emptiness from the locative absence of other-emptiness by stating that an absence of one thing in another is not the meaning of emptiness:

> If a pot is not empty from its own side, but is empty of another phenomenon, this is not sufficient (*go mi chod*) as the emptiness of a

> pot itself. Just as a cow is absent in a horse, but this is not sufficient as the emptiness of a horse itself; or while the horn of an ox is empty of a rabbit horn, this is not sufficient as the emptiness of an ox horn. Among the seven types of emptinesses stated in the *Laṅkāvatārasūtra*,[53] it is inferior—such as a temple's emptiness of a spiritual community; it is to be abandoned.[54]

The lack of one thing in another is inferior and is not sufficient as the meaning of emptiness; an emptiness of another does not necessarily contain an emptiness of itself. Longchenpa also cites in his *Wish-Fulfilling Treasury* the statement from the *Samādhirājasūtra* that: "An emptiness of one thing in another is a lesser emptiness."[55] However, in his autocommentary of *Resting in the Nature of Mind*, Longchenpa cites Asaṅga's commentary on the *Uttaratantra*[56] in an approving portrayal of Buddha-nature as the absence of something in another:

> While Buddha-nature is empty of all that is divisible, separable, and disturbed, it is said to be not empty of the inconceivable, indivisible, and inseparable qualities of Buddha which are more numerous than the sands of the river Ganges. In this, one sees authentically that which does not exist in something, that something is empty of that; and one authentically knows as it is that which remains always exists there[57] (*de la*).[58]

We can see a similarity between the depictions of a locative absence (1) as an inferior view of emptiness and (2) as Buddha-nature. Perhaps a distinction can be made between the two as to whether or not the emptiness of another also contains within it an emptiness of itself. We will see how Mipam distinguishes his view of Buddha-nature from mistaken conceptions of it in the next chapter. Here we will look into his delineation in terms of emptiness. First, we will discuss his treatment of the ultimate in the view of other-emptiness.

Phenomena and Suchness

Mipam characterizes the tradition of other-emptiness as accepting something that ultimately exists. In contrast, he says that nothing ultimately exists in the tradition of self-emptiness. With this distinction, he identifies himself with the tradition propounding self-emptiness:

> In the tradition of self-emptiness, since there is only the ultimately nonexistent, an ultimately existing phenomenon is impossible. In the tradition of other-emptiness, what is ultimately nonexistent is the relative, and what is ultimately existent is the ultimate itself. My tradition is clear in the *Rapsel Rejoinder*,[59] the tradition propounding self-emptiness.[60]

In this way, he identifies his tradition as asserting self-emptiness; and thus he denies that anything ultimately exists.

When we consider Mipam's depiction of emptiness in light of the categories of "self-emptiness" and "other-emptiness," we can see that according to Khenpo Lodrö Drakpa's definitions of a proponent of self-emptiness (claiming a non-implicative negation as the consummate ultimate) and other-emptiness (claiming wisdom as not empty of its own essence),[61] Mipam is a proponent of *neither* self-emptiness nor other-emptiness. However, according to Lochen's definitions of self-emptiness and other-emptiness,[62] we see how Mipam can be said to be a proponent of *both* self-emptiness and other-emptiness!

In order to make sense of Mipam's interpretation of emptiness in relationship to the categories of self-emptiness and other-emptiness, we need to identify what these terms mean in the works of the respective authors who use them. It is clear that Mipam defines himself as a proponent of self-emptiness—as one who propounds that there is nothing ultimately existent—in accord with his definition of the term.[63] We will see below a distinction he makes between language and view (in the context of non-implicative vs. implicative negations), which problematizes the identification of Mipam's *view* with a view of self-emptiness. As we saw in the previous chapter in his discussion of Prāsaṅgika, there is an important distinction to be made between (1) view and (2) language in accord with a view, and Mipam is careful to distinguish the two.

Although Mipam states that emptiness is the ultimate truth, he does not affirm that anything, even emptiness, ultimately exists. Furthermore, he says: "The manner of establishing the ultimate of other-emptiness is by means of whether or not appearance accords with reality."[64] In his delineation of the two models of the two truths (i.e., appearance/emptiness and authentic/inauthentic experience), he states that appearance in accord with reality (authentic experience) is called "ultimate" from the perspective of conventional valid cognition:

> From the perspective of conventional valid cognition analyzing the mode of appearance, the subjects and objects of the incontrovertible accordance between the modes of appearance and reality are called "ultimate" and the opposite are called "relative."[65]

Thus, according to this delineation, the ultimate in other-emptiness is ultimate from the perspective of *conventional* valid cognition. Moreover, he argues that conventional valid cognition cannot establish something to be not empty of its own essence. Conventional valid cognition does not assess whether something is truly established or not; rather, that status is assessed by *ultimate* valid cognition. He states that what is truly established—not empty of its own essence—cannot be established by any valid cognition:

> Not empty of its own essence, being truly established it is completely impossible to be the suchness of an extrinsic phenomenon, etc. It also cannot be the outcome of ascertainment by the valid cognition of ultimate analysis because the affirmation of something truly established is not accurate as a handprint [result] of the analysis of all phenomena lacking true existence—like darkness [arising] from light. True establishment is not established by conventional valid cognition either because even though [it may appear to be] truly established from that [conventional] perspective, by merely that there is never an ability to establish phenomena to be non-empty. Without being able to be established by the two valid cognitions, the means of establishment has gone the way of a [nonexistent] space-flower; therefore, establishing this becomes meaninglessly tiresome.[66]

He states that something truly established and not empty of its own essence cannot result from ultimate valid cognition, which establishes the lack of true existence.[67] Nor can conventional valid cognition establish something to be not empty of its own essence, despite appearing that way from a perspective of conventional valid cognition.

However, in his *Lion's Roar: Affirming Other-Emptiness*, he shows how the claim of a non-empty ultimate can be supported. He argues that just as someone may assert that true establishment is to be negated, but not its *absence*, in a similar way, one can assert that the distorted relative is to be negated, but not the undistorted ultimate:

> The assertion that although true establishment is negated, the absence of true existence is not negated, not to be negated, nor is appropriate to be negated, is similar to [the assertion that] although the relative distortions are negated, the undistorted ultimate is not negated, not to be negated, nor is suitable to be negated.[68]

He argues that an assertion that one should not negate the absence of true existence is similar to the assertion that one should not negate the ultimate itself. In this way, he shows a correlation between the two claims that: (1) the absence of true existence (the ultimate in the appearance/emptiness two-truth model) is not to be negated and (2) the undistorted ultimate (the ultimate in the authentic/inauthentic experience two-truth model) is not to be negated. Furthermore, he uses a similar parallel consequence in his response to a hypothetical qualm:

> If a [conventional phenomenon like a] pot, were empty of pot, then would it not be that a pot would not be a pot, and thus a pot would not exist conventionally? [Response:] So be it. Hence, in the same way, if the ultimate truth were empty of ultimate truth, then the ultimate truth would not be ultimate truth, and thus the ultimate would not exist even conventionally.[69]

He again shows how a consequence that is used to defend the conventional existence of phenomena also can support a defense of the (conventionally existent) ultimate truth: he shows the conventional nonexistence of the ultimate as an absurd consequence that would follow if the ultimate truth were empty of ultimate truth. In this way, he shows how an assertion that the ultimate truth is (conventionally) not empty of itself is supported by the same logic that is used to defend a pot's conventional non-emptiness of itself. In doing so, he depicts how affirmations of the ultimate can be conventionally true, a move on par with an assertion that emptiness conventionally exists.

In this way, we can see how a distinction can be made between ultimate truth and ultimate existence. A similar distinction can also be made between conventional truth and conventional existence. For instance, Mipam states that a pot is not empty of pot in terms of the conventional: "In terms of the conventional, I assert that a pot is not empty of pot, because if it were empty conventionally, the pot would become nonexistent."[70] Moreover, he says that from a conventional perspective, a pot is truly established as a pot: "A pot is necessarily truly established (*bden grub*) as pot through conventional valid cognition, just like the truth of causality and the truth of the three jewels."[71]

According to Mipam, what is "conventional" is the realm of thought, words, and physical actions: "The conventional is posited as what is known, expressed, and acted upon by means of the mind, speech, and body."[72] Thus, a pot can be said to be a conventionally existent phenomenon (since it can be thought, expressed, and acted upon) and a conventional truth (from the aspect of its appearance). Also, the emptiness of the pot, as an empty quality that is a referent of thought and expression, can be said to be the (categorized) ultimate truth and conventionally existent. Although he does not make this distinction explicit in this way, we can see how such a distinction is made in his treatment of existence (*yod pa*) and truth (*bden pa*). This distinction between existence and truth in Mipam's works reveals an affinity with Tsongkhapa.[73] This affinity is often overlooked due to the fact that most of Mipam's polemics target views held within the Geluk tradition.

Mipam delineates the criterion for existence through an epistemological definition: via valid cognition, conventional or ultimate:

> In short, the conventional [existence] of that which is established to exist in the perspective of conventional valid cognition cannot be refuted by anyone at all. The conventional existence of that which is invalidated by conventional valid cognition cannot be established by anyone at all. Nobody at all can affirm that something is ultimately existent which has been established to not exist by ultimate valid cognition.[74]

We can see a distinction between ultimate existence and ultimate truth through his framework of valid cognition. For Mipam *nothing is ultimately existent*—not wisdom, or even emptiness. Nevertheless, in his authentic/inauthentic two-truth model, *wisdom is the ultimate truth*.

Moreover, a distinction between ultimate existence and conventional existence also plays a part in Mipam's depiction of reflexive awareness (*rang rig*) and the universal ground (*kun gzhi*). He states that reflexive awareness and the universal ground are conventionally existent, not ultimately existent:

> In the ascertainment of the ultimate, reflexive awareness and the universal ground are not necessary. However, they are indispensable

> in the analysis of a conventional presentation; and moreover, if it is established by valid cognition analyzing the conventional, there is no reason to negate it, saying "it does not conventionally exist."[75]

He argues that the universal ground and reflexive awareness, while not necessary in the ascertainment of the ultimate, are indispensable in an analysis of conventional reality.[76] Mipam's position here directly contrasts with Tsongkhapa, who included the rejection of both reflexive awareness and the universal ground among his eight unique assertions of Prāsaṅgika.[77]

For Mipam, conventional existence plays an important role in the way that he shows how conventions in tantra such as "innate mind" (*gnyug sems*) and "great bliss" (*bde ba chen po*) can be compatible with Prāsaṅgika:

> In general in the Prāsaṅgika tradition, the collection of six consciousnesses is accepted, and there is no presentation of reflexive awareness and so forth, as is clear from their texts. Yet how is it that just because there is no assertion conventionally in that [tradition] that one must necessarily understand that [these] definitely do not exist conventionally? For example, like the fact that although there is no point in using conventions such as innate mind and great bliss in the Prāsaṅgika tradition, it is not that these are conventionally unreasonable.[78]

Through the status of existing conventionally, he shows how such conventions as reflexive awareness, innate mind, and great bliss are not necessarily incompatible with the Prāsaṅgika tradition. In this way, he uses a *perspectival* system to integrate Prāsaṅgika and tantra. Such a perspectival system can be seen as an extension of Śāntarakṣita's integration of Dharmakīrti and Nāgārjuna. In Mipam's case, however, it extends to become an integration of Candrakīrti and Padmasambhava.

Furthermore, in a compilation of Mipam's oral instructions entitled *Trilogy of Innate Mind*, Mipam states that suchness is called "the great permanence" (*rtag pa chen po*) conventionally, but that this does not designate a permanent entity or an impermanent entity:

> Although suchness, together with the appearances that arise from the self-expression of suchness, are all ultimately beyond the extremes of entities and nonentities, conventionally, there is the designation "the great permanence"; it is neither a momentary imper-

> manent entity, nor a permanent, eternal entity. Although it is unchanging, it is not a mere absence that is a nonentity either. Therefore, since the basis of imputation of great permanence exists, it is not like the assertion of nonentities as "permanent" because when the imputation of the permanence of [nonentities] such as space is analyzed, it exists as the mere inverse of what is impermanent, but there is no basis of imputation at all for permanence.[79]

Mipam affirms that *conventionally* there is a basis of designation for "great permanence," which is unlike a permanent entity and unlike what is merely the inverse of what is impermanent imputed as "permanent." This is similar to Dölpopa's characterization of suchness as a third category that is neither an entity nor a nonentity. However, Mipam does not affirm that it exists *ultimately*.

Mipam also delineates the ultimate and conventional in a description of the relationship between mind and wisdom, reflecting his tradition of the Great Perfection. In this, we see how Mipam depicts the relationship between phenomena (*chos can*) and suchness (*chos nyid*): "The suchness of consciousness is wisdom."[80] He states that mind and wisdom are conventionally not the same, but ultimately are not different:

> Therefore, the two: (1) phenomena, which are the eight collections of consciousness, and (2) the wisdom that is suchness, which is the nature of those [consciousnesses], are not asserted as either the same or different. As Longchen Rapjam stated in accordance with the words in the *Saṃdhinirmocana*:
>
>> The character of the conditioned realm and the ultimate,
>> Is the character free from being the same or different;
>> Thus, those who conceive [them] as the same or different
>> Have entered into an improper view.[81]
>
> Therefore, conventionally, the two are not the same because (1) wisdom, the suchness of mind, is not realized by merely realizing the mind and (2) [mind and wisdom] are phenomena and suchness. Ultimately, they are not different because, due to the nature of mind being wisdom, (1) when wisdom is realized, the mind is also not observed as different from that [wisdom] and (2) when wisdom is realized, the mind arises as self-liberated.[82]

He states that consciousness and wisdom are not the same conventionally because they are related as phenomena and suchness; however, ultimately they are not different because the nature of mind itself is wisdom. Furthermore, he says:

> One should understand that wisdom does not arise from mind, but is the abiding reality of mind, which is naturally luminous and clear; in the way that emptiness—the suchness of all entities—does not arise from entities, but is the abiding reality of entities.[83]

In this way, Mipam depicts the relationship between mind and wisdom in the same way he describes the relationship between phenomena and suchness—neither the same nor different; that is, neither (conventionally) the same nor (ultimately) different. As with mind and wisdom, neither saṃsāra and nirvāṇa, nor the two truths as authentic/inauthentic experience, are a unity in ordinary conventional terms; the presence of one entails the absence of the other. He states: "It is not at all possible to conventionally be both the mistaken saṃsāra and the unmistaken nirvāṇa."[84] Thus, the two truths are a unity in terms of the two truths as appearance/emptiness, but the two truths as authentic/inauthentic experience are a different case.[85]

Mipam's emphasis on the unity of the two truths distinguishes his works from Dölpopa's representation of the view. Dölpopa emphasizes more of a radical separation between two distinct realities—the relative and the ultimate. Reflecting the separation between the relative and ultimate, Dölpopa makes a distinction between the universal ground consciousness (*kun gzhi'i rnam shes*) and the universal ground wisdom (*kun gzhi'i ye shes*).[86] This "universal ground wisdom" is a distinctive term used in the Jonang that I have not seen used in the Nyingma works of Longchenpa or Mipam. This terminology reflects how the Jonang preserve a form of dualism in their explanations—a radical dichotomy of (1) the nonexistent relative and (2) the existent ultimate. Such a dichotomy is unlike the strong monism we find in the Great Perfection, where the ultimate and relative are nondistinct.

Moreover, Mipam does not assign the ultimate truth of suchness a privileged status apart from the relative truth of appearance; suchness is ultimately not different from appearances. We find a precursor to this undivided ground of truth in Longchenpa's characterization of a "general ground" (*spyi gzhi*) as the ground of both saṃsāra and nirvāṇa.[87] Longchenpa states that from the aspect of its being the basis for both saṃsāra and nirvāṇa, it is the "general ground"; from the aspect of its being the basis of liberation, it is the "ground of liberation"; and from the aspect of its being the basis of sentient being's confusion, it is "the ground of confusion."[88] He also describes the support for both saṃsāra and nirvāṇa as the "ultimate universal ground" (*don gyi kun gzhi*), which is a synonym for Buddha-nature.[89] Mipam refers to such a ground as the "ground of the primeval beginning" (*ye thog gi gzhi*).[90]

Rather than a *dichotomous* relationship between a separate ground of the ultimate and relative, we can say that Mipam maintains a *dialectical* relationship between the two truths, a dialectical unity. As such, the ultimate and the relative have a common ground; they are only virtually distinct, but not actually so. The difference between the Great Perfection-inspired work of Mipam and the other-emptiness of the Jonang also corresponds with how Dölpopa derides a view that concepts are the Truth Body,[91] whereas an integral relationship between concepts and the Truth Body is more characteristic of the discourses of the Great Perfection.[92]

De/limiting Emptiness

Another difference between Mipam and Dölpopa is Mipam's consistent critiques of linguistic and conceptual formulations of the ultimate. Mipam frequently criticizes mistaken conceptions of suchness as an empty-ground. For instance, in his commentary on the *Madhyamakālaṃkāra,* he states:

> Without gaining certainty in primordial purity, merely an impassioned thought of a ground that is neither existent nor nonexistent will bring you nowhere. If you hold onto such a ground, which is empty of both existence and nonexistence, as separate and established by its own essence, whether it is called the inconceivable Self, Brahma, Viṣṇu, Īśvara, wisdom, etc., it is merely a different name for a similar [mistaken] meaning. The abiding reality that is free from the four extremes—the luminous clarity of the Great Perfection which is realized reflexively—is not at all like that.[93]

He claims that without gaining certainty in primordial purity, holding onto an empty-ground as the abiding reality is not the correct view. Furthermore, he states: "Although traditions may claim to be free from extremes, in the end since they constantly depend upon a conceptual reference for a Self, or Brahma, etc., how could this manner be the Middle Way?"[94] Mipam distinguishes the manner of the Middle Way as beyond conceptual reference. He says that "the middle" is not a referent object: "'The middle' expresses the lack of reference to any extreme."[95] Furthermore, he states: "It is said that 'the middle' should not be identified as a referent object that abides like the space between two aligned pillars; the middle is not what is observed."[96] In contrast to Dölpopa's emphasis on the ultimate as an other-empty presence, Mipam emphasizes that emptiness is beyond reference and conceptuality. A freedom from conceptual constructs is a central part of Mipam's characterization of emptiness.

Mipam also claims that "Middle Way reasoning will inevitably refute whatever object the mind takes as support."[97] He depicts the meaning of emptiness as distinct from determinate conceptions of a metaphysical referent. Thus, emptiness is not what is held as either (1) a substrate or (2) a quality of absence. In his *Lion's Roar: Affirming Other-Emptiness*, he states:

> Just as the assertion of the absence of true existence can become an incorrigible view of emptiness as a reified sign of a nonentity, similarly, the assertion of a freedom from constructs can become an incorrigible view in which emptiness is a referent object of an ineffable entity.[98]

He argues that emptiness can be reified as a sign of a nonentity; similarly, it can become a referent object of an "ineffable" entity. In this way, he emphasizes that suchness is beyond conceptual reference: "As long as the mind remains with reference or with a perceived-perceiver [duality], appearance does not accord with reality; suchness is not the object of a mind with a perceived-perceiver [duality]."[99] Appearance does not accord with reality when the mind remains with reference or is dualistic. Thus, the ultimate, or suchness, is not an object of a dualistic mind. Furthermore, he states:

> Those who emphatically claim that an inferential cognition analyzing the ultimate, or a wisdom that realizes the ultimate through direct perception, sees the essence of an object or even finds it, no matter how much they refute other-emptiness, the heart of their own view has fallen under the power of other-emptiness and they just don't know it.[100]

In this way, he portrays other-emptiness as affirming a determinate ultimate. In contrast, he emphasizes the transcendence of the ultimate by characterizing the ultimate as that which transcends thought and language: "The ultimate mode of reality of entities—free from all extremes of existence, non-existence, both, and neither—is therefore not the domain of mind; mind and language are relative, not ultimate."[101] Mipam describes the ultimate mode of reality as beyond the domain of mind. He states that conventionally the ultimate can be said to be an object of knowledge, but not ultimately:

> Conventionally, based on taking the meditative equipoise of the Sublime Ones as the subject and the expanse of phenomena as the object, it is suitable to say "[the ultimate] is an object of knowledge (*shes bya*)"; however, if this [ultimate] is said to be ultimately what is perceived or known by a meditative equipoise without perceived-perceiver [duality]—are these words not explicitly and implicitly in contradiction? Moreover, the claim that the ultimate is an object of knowledge, because the basis of division of the two truths is objects of knowledge,[102] is also by exclusion (*rnam gcod*). Here it is [said to] not [be] an object of knowledge determined by inclusion (*yongs gcod*); therefore, there is no contradiction. If one accepts that [the ultimate] is also an object of knowledge determined by inclusion, then emptiness is asserted as an entity.[103]

He states that the ultimate asserted as an object of knowledge is an object of knowledge *by exclusion;* it is known through explicitly negating what it is not. The ultimate cannot be an object of knowledge as determined *by inclusion*—through affirming what it is—because that would turn emptiness into an entity. Here we can see a tension between the status of the ultimate as a presence and an absence. Mipam incorporates assertions that the ultimate both is and is not an object of knowledge by stating that they are not necessarily a contradiction when the former is the ultimate that can be known through exclusion and the latter is the ultimate that cannot be known through inclusion.

The delineation of the ultimate as not the domain of mind is found in a description of the two truths from Śāntideva's *Bodhicaryāvatāra:*

> The relative and the ultimate, these are asserted as the two truths.
> The ultimate is not the domain of mind; the [domain of] mind is relative.[104]

Incorporating the *Madhyamakāvatāra* with the way the two truths are represented in the *Bodhicaryāvatāra,* Bötrül brings to light two ways in which the ultimate is expressed:

> In the root text and [auto]commentary of the *Madhyamakāvatāra*, the defining character of the ultimate is posited by means of inclusion; in the context of the Wisdom Chapter of the *Bodhicaryāvatāra*, the defining character of the ultimate is indicated by means of exclusion. Both scriptures indicate the defining character of the relative by means of inclusion.[105]

Bötrül says that the ultimate delineated in the *Madhyamakāvatāra*—the object of authentic seeing—is indicated by means of inclusion. The ultimate delineated in the *Bodhicaryāvatāra*—not the domain of mind—is indicated by means of exclusion. Both texts indicate the relative by means of inclusion, namely, false seeings in the *Madhyamakāvatāra* and the [domain of] mind in the *Bodhicaryāvatāra.*[106]

Bötrül describes the relationship between the two truths in the Svātantrika tradition, based on the categorized ultimate, as "essentially the same with different contradistinctions" (*ngo bo gcig la ldog pa tha dad*), only conceptually distinct. In the Prāsaṅgika tradition, based on the uncategorized ultimate, he states that the two truths are "essentially neither one nor many" (*ngo bo gcig du bral*), meaning that they are neither the same nor different. Also, he says that there is another way the relationship is described, as "the negation of being one" (*gcig pa bkag pa*). This latter delineation is by means of whether or not it is established in the abiding reality (*gnas lugs la grub ma grub*), which is the two truths of authentic/inauthentic experience. Such a delineation accords with the ultimate in other-emptiness—the object of the conventional valid cognition of pure vision:

> In general, based upon the Svātantrika tradition's ultimate that depends upon two truths—which is the object of valid cognition analyzing the categorized [ultimate]—it is not appropriate for the two truths to be divided other than as essentially the same with different contradistinctions. However, the two truths are asserted as essentially neither one nor many in relation to the consummate Prāsaṅgika tradition's view of the ultimate, which is the object of valid cognition analyzing the uncategorized. Moreover, in certain contexts concerning the two truths of phenomena that appear in accordance with reality—which are the objects of conventional valid cognition of pure vision—by means of whether or not they are established in the mode of reality, the two: (1) the phenomena of nirvāṇa, which is the natural purity of appearances in accord

> with reality, and (2) the phenomena of saṃsāra, which is the natural impurity of appearances that do not accord with reality, are asserted, like an entity and a nonentity, as the negation of being one. However, it appears that in [Mipam's] *Exposition [of Buddha-Nature]* and so forth, the two—saṃsāra and nirvāṇa—are also asserted to be neither one nor many in the manner of phenomena and suchness.[107]

Bötrül states that in texts such as the *Lion's Roar: Exposition of Buddha-Nature,* Mipam asserts the relationship between the two truths as neither one nor many, which accords with the Prāsaṅgika. He associates the Svātantrika with the relationship between the two truths as essentially the same with different contradistinctions, which was the way Tsongkhapa delineated them.[108] We saw earlier how Dölpopa articulated the relationship between suchness and phenomena as "different in the sense of negating that they are one entity,"[109] which is Bötrül's third delineation. We also saw that Dölpopa stated that an implicative negation exists within the ground of a non-implicative negation,[110] and we will now discuss how Mipam depicts implicative and non-implicative negations.

Emptiness as the Unity of Appearance and Emptiness

Mipam does not delimit emptiness as a substrate that is detached from phenomena or as merely the quality of absence separate from appearance. Emptiness is not separate from appearance. He states that an emptiness that is understood as separate from appearance is an implicative negation. He claims that an implicative negation does not have the meaning of unity because it establishes the essence of another phenomenon:

> An indication that entities lack intrinsic nature is a non-implicative negation because an implicative negation establishes the essence of another phenomenon; as such it does not have the meaning of unity. Although appearances are designated as lacking intrinsic nature, if this is understood to mean something empty separate from appearance, even though it may be called a "non-implicative negation" it has become an implicative negation. Appearance itself appears while nonexistent, it is a unity—marvelous—thus, through abiding as the ineffable indivisibility of appearance and emptiness, it

> is beyond the mind because it is free from negation and affirmation in the consummate meaning.[111]

He asserts that an indication that entities lack intrinsic nature is a non-implicative negation, not an implicative negation. He thus depicts non-implicative negations as better indicators of emptiness (qua absence) than implicative negations. In this way, he emphasizes that emptiness is beyond mind.

He states that in terms of *only* the manner of emptiness, the Nyingma view is a non-implicative negation, and adds that Candrakīrti and Rongzom both affirm the great emptiness of primordial purity:

> It is said that the Geluk (*dge ldan*) view is a non-implicative negation,
> Other traditions speak of an implicative negation—
> If one asks, "Which is the tradition of the early translations [of Nyingma]?"
> Considering only the manner of emptiness
> When questioned [what is the Nyingma view], it is only a non-implicative negation.
> The glorious Candrakīrti in the Noble Land [of India]
> And Rongzom Chözang in Tibet
> Established with one viewpoint and one voice
> The great emptiness of primordial purity.[112]

He affirms that, concerning only the manner of emptiness, the Nyingma view is a non-implicative negation. However, he also states that since wisdom transcends the mind and is not the domain of thoughts and words, there is no partiality for non-implicative or implicative negations, emptiness or appearance:

> Since wisdom transcends the mind,
> It is inconceivable by an extrinsic thought.
> Since it is not an object of language or thought
> There is no partiality for
> Non-implicative negations or implicative negations,
> Difference, appearance or emptiness, etc.[113]

Furthermore, he states:

> From the perspective of the great wisdom of unity,
> The elimination of the object of negation by "nonexistent"
> Implies neither a mere existential absence nor a predicative
> negation—
> What other phenomenon is there to imply by negation?
> Both of these are merely mental imputations;
> I assert neither as the [consummate] meaning.[114]

Mipam describes the view from the perspective of wisdom as neither a non-implicative negation nor an implicative negation. In this way, he represents emptiness within the *view* of wisdom as not a negation (since it is not the referent of thought or words). However, he describes the negative *language* used to express emptiness as only a non-implicative negation:

> In the context of indicating emptiness, the negation of form, etc. is only a non-implicative negation. Since an implicative negation is also in the end a fixation upon an entity, it is not suitable to be the meaning of emptiness. Therefore, while it is a non-implicative negation, due to appearing as an unfailing interdependent arising, it is the unity of emptiness and appearance so any apprehension of negation or affirmation should deconstruct.[115]

He states that the negating language expressed to indicate emptiness is only a non-implicative negation because an implicative negation is in the end a fixation on an entity. Thus, Mipam suggests that emptiness represented by an implicative negation leads to a reification of emptiness, not the authentic emptiness. Therefore, he does not accept implicative negations as adequate indicators of emptiness's quality of absence.

We can see that neither implicative nor non-implicative negations denote what Mipam characterizes as the *view* of consummate emptiness, which is the unity of appearance and emptiness beyond negation and affirmation. Overlooking this distinction between *view* and *language in accord with a view* leads to confusion as to how to place Mipam's view. He can certainly be understood as a proponent of self-emptiness in the way that he explicitly aligns himself with the tradition propounding "self-emptiness" (using the *language* of the tradition for which nothing ultimately exists). However, he does not depict the view of the ultimate as a simple negative; he characterizes the view of the ultimate as nonconceptual. Thus, we can see why he has no preference for a particular negation or affirmation in terms of the view that is beyond language and mind. Moreover, given that the view is nonconceptual, there is no reason why it could not be evoked by an implicative negation or even by an affirmation.[116]

In any case, Mipam argues that, in order to recognize the ultimate, it is necessary to firmly decide on the absence of true existence: "In order to recognize the own face of the ultimate, one must reach a firm conclusion (*phu thag chod*) on the absence of true existence."[117] We find that Tsongkhapa makes a similar statement in his *Great Exposition of the Stages of the Path:* "Realization of special insight (*lhag mthong*) will not occur without the certainty of the view that has reached a firm conclusion (*phu thag chod*) on the meaning of the absence of self."[118] We can see again how Mipam's approach here shares a close affinity with Tsongkhapa.

Also reflecting the importance he ascribes to reason, Mipam explains that it does not help to merely aspire to an absence, without knowing the manner of its absence. He uses as an analogy the way that just thinking, "there is no snake" does not remedy the confusion of seeing a multicolored rope as a snake, but through seeing the manner of its absence, the confusion is relinquished:

> Based on this clinging to self and other as real entities
> One continuously enters the stream of [cyclic] existence.
> The antidote that averts these
> Is the apprehension of the absence of self.
> Moreover, without knowing the manner of its absence
> Wishing for its absence does not help,
> Like when a multicolored rope is mistaken for a snake
> It does not help to think "there is no snake," but
> When the manner of its absence is seen, it is abandoned.[119]

The antidote that eradicates clinging to the entities of self and other is the apprehension of the absence of self. However, he argues that an emptiness that is apprehended solely as an absence is not the abiding reality:

> Only in the beginning, if a lack of true existence is not taught, there will be no method to extract the beginningless habit of the mistaken apprehension of entities; and if merely that [lack of true existence] is taught as the ultimate, some narrow-minded people will think, "The mere absence that is the elimination of the object of negation

> is the abiding reality!" Grasping at emptiness, this will become an incorrigible view. There are two ways to grasp also: grasping at emptiness as an entity and grasping at emptiness as a nonentity.[120]

Apprehending the absence of true existence eliminates the mistaken apprehension of entities; however, it is not the abiding reality. Although it is important, the empty-quality alone is not reality. He shows that the empty-quality conceived as distinct from an empty-substrate is not the meaning of emptiness. In this way, we can see how Mipam distinguishes his view from a view of emptiness as a substrate or a quality.

Mipam clearly delineates two contexts for the interpretation of words such as "abiding reality" (*gnas lugs*), "emptiness" (*stong nyid*), "suchness" (*chos nyid*), "freedom from constructs" (*spros bral*), "the expanse of phenomena" (*chos dbyings*), and "ultimate" (*don dam*). He states:

> "Abiding reality" that is the emptiness of entities and
> "Abiding reality" that is the indivisible two truths
> Although both are the same word,
> The meanings are as distinct as the earth and space.
> Likewise, "suchness," "expanse of phenomena,"
> "Emptiness," "freedom from constructs," "limit of cessation,"
> "Ultimate," etc., are similar expressions, yet
> Since the distinction is vast
> Between the consummate and the partial,
> Having delineated the distinctive context,
> They should be explained without error.[121]

He states that it is important to recognize two distinctive meanings of emptiness in their appropriate contexts because the two meanings of such terms are as different as "the earth and space." One is partial, referring to the emptiness of entities that is a quality of phenomena. The consummate meaning refers to the unity of appearance and emptiness. Likewise, he distinguishes: (1) emptiness as a distinctive quality of appearance from (2) emptiness as the indivisible truth of the unity of emptiness and appearance:

> Both the emptiness of true existence and the appearance of interdependent arising, which are the components of a division into two truths, are separate from the aspect of merely a contradistinction. However, just as impermanent phenomenon and product are not

> objectively separate, the pair of appearance and emptiness, being essentially of an indivisible nature within the uncontrived fundamental abiding reality that does not abide in any extreme, is called "the indivisible truth" or "the unity of the two truths."[122]

He states that a phenomenon's emptiness of true existence is essentially the same as its appearance—the two are only distinguished conceptually, as different contradistinctions. In reality, they are indivisible as "the unity of the two truths." However, unity is not to be understood (only) as a combination of the two aspects of appearance and emptiness:

> The appearance that is the object of conventional valid cognition,
> The emptiness that is the object of ultimate analysis, and
> The unity that is the aspect of the combination of those two,
> Since they are objects of words and concepts
> They are transcended in meditative equipoise.[123]

The unity that is understood as the aspect of a combination of (1) appearance, the object of conventional valid cognition, and (2) emptiness, the object of ultimate analysis, is still within the domain of language and concepts. The two truths known by distinct valid cognitions only apply in the context of knowledge in postmeditation. Such conceptions are transcended in meditative equipoise. Although appearance and emptiness are contradictory in the context of conventional valid cognition, Mipam affirms that in the perspective of wisdom, emptiness and appearance are not contradictory:

> Since this is the context of presenting
> The objects seen by conventional valid cognition,
> Existence and nonexistence are contradictory in that perspective, [but]
> The two truths existing upon one entity is not contradictory
> Due to being the object of wisdom.[124]

Emptiness and appearance are mutually exclusive in the context of conventional valid cognition, but not for wisdom. Wisdom is beyond dichotomies and perceives the unity of appearance and emptiness.

Thus, the empty quality alone is not what is meant by terms such as "suchness," "ultimate," and "emptiness"; these terms also refer to the indivisible unity of appearance and emptiness. In his *Trilogy of Innate Mind,* he affirms that the consummate meaning of suchness is only unity:

> Awareness (*rig pa*) and luminous clarity (*'od gsal*) are posited from the aspect of appearance, but are not separate from emptiness. Also, "emptiness" is not separate from appearance. In reality, unity alone is suchness; it is thoroughly important that neither emptiness nor appearance on its own is the great suchness, the consummate ultimate. From here the essential points of all of Sūtra and Mantra are unraveled.[125]

He affirms that suchness, as the unity of emptiness and appearance, is an important point through which the meaning of all the sūtras and tantras can be known. Thus, he says that suchness refers to unity: "The abiding reality is the unity of appearance and emptiness from the beginning."[126]

Conclusion

Mipam emphasizes nonconceptual unity as the meaning of emptiness. In his presentation, he critiques determinate conceptual and linguistic formulations of emptiness. We have seen how he critiques two delimited conceptions of emptiness: (1) as solely an absence separate from appearance and (2) as a location that is separate from appearance. These two conceptions of emptiness—emptiness as solely a quality or a substrate—are within the domain of mind. In contrast, the consummate meaning of emptiness cannot be known by the mind because it is the domain of wisdom. In this way, emptiness as such is beyond the substance/quality dichotomy; the consummate emptiness is the unity of emptiness and appearance.

While conventionally there can be said to be a referent of emptiness, and a difference between quality and substrate, ultimately, emptiness is not a referent object and there is no difference between quality and substrate. Thus, emptiness does not refer to an empty-ground separate from appearance nor is it only a quality of an appearance distinct from that appearance. Rather, emptiness refers to the indivisible unity of emptiness and appearance. The nature and content of the appearing aspect of emptiness bring us squarely into the subject matter of Buddha-nature. We are now ready to turn to the explicit topic of Buddha-nature in Mipam's works.

CHAPTER FOUR

Buddha-Nature and the Ground of the Great Perfection

> To know God and not oneself to be God, to know blessedness and not oneself to enjoy it, is a state of disunity, of unhappiness. Higher beings know nothing of this unhappiness; they have no conception of what they are not.
>
> —Ludwig Feuerbach, *The Essence of Christianity*

Introduction

Buddha-nature is a unifying theme woven throughout Mipam's interpretations of Buddhist doctrines; it is forged as the common ground of saṃsāra and nirvāṇa, and the unifying principle of transcendence and immanence. Mipam depicts Buddha-nature as the unified suchness of reality in the same way that he depicts emptiness. While emptiness (as unity of emptiness and appearance) is also the meaning of Buddha-nature, this chapter will discuss the *explicit* topic of Buddha-nature.

We will begin our discussion by looking at how Mipam distinguishes his view of Buddha-nature from other views of Buddha-nature. We will then assess his depiction of Buddha-nature in light of Longchenpa's representation of the ground of the Great Perfection, followed by a discussion of Mipam's treatment of Buddha-nature within his distinction of appearance and reality. We will see that Mipam conveys the ground of the Great Perfection—the unity of primordial purity and spontaneous presence—through his representation of Buddha-nature.

Distinguishing the Views on Buddha-Nature

We will begin by discussing Mipam's text entitled *Lion's Roar: Exposition of Buddha-Nature*. This text, which is translated in its entirety in the back of the book (see Appendix 1), is a focal point around which most of the discussions in this chapter revolve. In a section of this text, Mipam positions his view of Buddha-nature in contrast to others' views. We will look into this now to see how he contrasts his view with depictions of Buddha-nature (1) as truly established and not empty, (2) as a mere void emptiness, and (3) as impermanent and conditioned.

He first criticizes the interpretation of a non-empty Buddha-nature that is truly established, as we saw in the previous chapter:

> Also by reasoned analysis, due to the essential point that Buddha-nature is essentially empty, it impartially appears in all aspects of quality: it is suitable to be the suchness of mind, all-pervasive everywhere, permanent as long as time, inconceivable. However, while not empty of its own essence, being truly established it is completely impossible to be the suchness of an extrinsic phenomenon, etc. It also cannot be the outcome of ascertainment by the valid cognition of ultimate analysis because the affirmation of something truly established is not accurate as a handprint [result] of the analysis of all phenomena lacking true existence—like darkness [arising] from light. True establishment is not established by conventional valid cognition either because even though [it may appear to be] truly established from that [conventional] perspective, by merely that there is never an ability to establish phenomena to be non-empty. Without being able to be established by the two valid cognitions, the means of establishment has gone the way of a [nonexistent] space-flower; therefore, establishing this becomes meaninglessly tiresome.[1]

In this way, he argues that a non-empty Buddha-nature cannot be established by either of the two valid cognitions. The prominent role of valid cognition is a distinctive feature of Mipam's portrayal of Buddha-nature. The view that Buddha-nature is truly established and not empty of its own essence is a view held in the Jonang tradition.[2] Since we addressed his arguments against a truly established substance in the previous chapter, we will not discuss this further here.

Mipam also argues against the interpretation of Buddha-nature as a mere absence, the aspect of the mind's lack of true establishment.[3] Such a view was taken up by the Geluk tradition stemming from a disciple of Tsongkhapa, Khedrupjé (*mkhas grub rje,* 1385–1438).[4] Mipam agrees that if the mind were truly established, there would be no potential to be a Buddha. However, since all things, even physical objects like rocks, are empty of true existence, the mere absence of true existence is not sufficient to establish that such things are potential Buddhas:

> [The assertion that] the essential point of the lack of true existence establishes the potential to be a Buddha is also nonsense. Although it is true that if the mind were truly established, there would simply be no potential to be a Buddha, even so, in lacking true establishment, [the potential of] being Buddha is undetermined because even though all phenomena—earth, rocks, etc.—also lack true existence, who is able to establish that everything that lacks true existence is a potential Buddha?[5]

In his *Trilogy of Innate Mind*, Mipam also affirms that a mere non-implicative negation is not suitable to be identified as the meaning of Buddha-nature: "In general, the mere aspect of a non-implicative negation that is the emptiness of true existence is not suitable as the Buddha-nature because there is no cognitive quality in that; therefore, it is not the meaning of Buddha-nature."[6] He argues that the meaning of Buddha-nature is not merely an absence because a non-implicative negation in itself has no cognitive quality. For Mipam, Buddha-nature contains an intrinsic cognitive presence, similar to what we saw in the previous chapter in Dölpopa's depiction. Mipam states as follows in his *Lion's Roar: Exposition of Buddha-Nature:*

> Calling such a non-implicative negation "Buddha-nature" is a senseless assertion because it becomes a heritage shared with Auditors and Self-Realized Ones. Through this, the potential to be a Buddha is not established because: (1) there is no ability in merely this to establish any legitimacy for the occurrence of omniscient wisdom after abandoning cognitive obscurations (*shes sgrib*), and (2) since there is no cognitive quality within the essence of a non-implicative negation, it is impossible for that to know anything whatsoever even at the time of being a Buddha.[7]

Also, if the heritage[8] were merely an absence of existence, there would be no means to legitimate the presence of a Buddha's wisdom; such wisdom does not occur from a void absence. A mere absence cannot establish the potential to be a Buddha because an absence in itself has no cognitive quality. He also argues that a heritage that is a mere negation would be a heritage shared with Auditors and Self-Realized Ones, not the Mahāyāna heritage that is the potential in all beings to be a complete and perfect Buddha.

Furthermore, Mipam states that it is not reasonable to think of heritage as a mere absence that is the potential for the transformation of a sentient being into a Buddha. It is due to the aspect of being a conditioned, functional entity that transformations take place conventionally. However, the aspect of absence is not what is said to affect change conventionally, just as a seed's lack of true existence—which is unconditioned and lacking functional capacity—can never be somehow transported to a sprout:

> The mere categorized emptiness does not at all have the meaning of heritage. This follows because from the perspective of this thinking, one asserts that this heritage is the potential to newly produce [a Buddha] when conjoined with the conditions of the path despite now having no qualities of Buddha whatsoever—like a seed that is transported to a sprout. Yet such a quality [of potential transformation] is not at all feasible in the contradistinctive aspect of a non-implicative negation, which is an emptiness of true existence—an unconditioned phenomenon that lacks the ability to perform a function. It is like the way that the aspect of a conditioned seed may conventionally transform into a sprout, but the aspect of a seed's lack of true existence can never transform into a sprout.[9]

He states again that a mere absence is not the meaning of heritage. Without having any qualities whatsoever, it is not reasonable for a mere lack of true existence, which is unable to perform any function, to be the heritage that is the potential to be a Buddha. Mipam's statements here challenge the Geluk interpretation of Buddha-nature as an absence and a cause.[10]

Moreover, he states that rather than conceiving the heritage as a mere absence, it would be better to conceive it as a conditioned potential in all beings. A conditioned potential—such as knowledge of benefit and harm, and love for one's own children—can be seen to progressively develop into the love, wisdom, and powers of a Buddha. In a conception of heritage as this kind of impermanent entity, heritage is efficacious, unlike a heritage conceived as an impotent negation:

> In considering this manner of the transforming conditioned heritage (*gnas 'gyur 'dus byas kyi rigs*), rather than asserting a non-implicative negation as the heritage, it is better to assert a seed of wisdom, love, and powers in the mental-continua of all beings from beginningless time—even wild beasts, ogres, etc. possess such [qualities] of love for their children and recognition of benefit and harm—such that when further developed, through conjoined with the path and freed from obstacles, it is merely that which is the potential to become a Buddha endowed with limitless knowledge, love, and powers. This follows because once the causality of production is necessitated, to disregard the momentary entity which is a productive cause and assert an unproductive, unconditioned non-entity as the cause is indeed astonishing![11]

In terms of transformation that necessitates a causal relationship of producer and produced, he states that it is better to assert a momentary entity as the heritage rather than a mere negation. However, he does not accept that the qualities of a Buddha are in essence a new production, so in reality there is no such causal relationship.

The primordial endowment of the qualities of Buddha in sentient beings is a central part of Mipam's presentation of Buddha-nature. This is an important aspect of his interpretation that he shares in common with the Jonang tradition.[12] In contrast, exegetes in the Geluk tradition argue that scriptural statements that depict a Buddha-nature that is a permanent exalted body, with the qualities of the Buddha existing in sentient beings, are the provisional meaning. In the Geluk Prāsaṅgika tradition, the definitive meaning of Buddha-nature is emptiness, that is, the mind's lack of true existence, and this emptiness is understood to be the basis of intention (*dgongs gzhi*) of Buddha-nature.[13] While emptiness is also the meaning of Buddha-nature according to Mipam, his interpretation of emptiness (as a unity) is different from the Geluk interpretation of emptiness as a mere absence. As with Mipam's representation of emptiness, his depiction of Buddha-nature also notably differs from this Geluk view. Before we turn to Mipam's own view of Buddha-nature, we will first continue with his refutations of others' views.

Mipam argues against a Sakya position that heritage is the abiding reality that is the indivisibility of emptiness and the clarity of mind (*sems*).[14] He acknowledges that he would agree with this depiction if mind were understood to refer to *wisdom* (*ye shes*) as distinguished from *consciousness* (*rnam shes*). However, he does not agree if one of the elements of the unity is the aspect of impermanent consciousness, which is thought of as something that "progressively transports" to a Buddha:

> If one thinks, "[Heritage] is not posited having distinguished the two truths because heritage is asserted as the abiding reality that is the indivisibility of (1) the quality-bearer (*chos can*), which is the clarity of mind, and (2) suchness (*chos nyid*), which is emptiness." If this also is asserted as the unconditioned, immutable wisdom, which is wisdom as distinguished from consciousness, then since this is established as such by scripture and reasoning, then it certainly is [heritage]. However, making the claim that the quality-bearer that is a unity with emptiness is the aspect of momentary consciousness, then thinking, "this progressively transports to a Buddha" is senseless because it would [absurdly] follow that the heritage would have both a conditioned and an unconditioned aspect. That being the case, the unconditioned, which has no use or ability, would become the nominal heritage, and the conditioned would become the genuine heritage capable of producing effects. Consequently, the viewpoint of all of the Mahāyāna Sūtras—which assert that the unconditioned naturally abiding heritage (*rang bzhin gnas rigs*) is the expanse of phenomena—would be relinquished.[15]

He argues that asserting an impermanent consciousness as a fundamental component of heritage, and thinking that this is what is progressively transported to a Buddha, is a mistaken conception. We can see here that Mipam emphasizes the naturally abiding heritage as the genuine heritage, as opposed to the developing heritage (*rgyas 'gyur rigs*), which is the appearance of development. This emphasis is important in his argument for the primordial endowment of the qualities of Buddha.

Also, an important aspect of his depiction of Buddha-nature is the distinction between consciousness and wisdom. In contrast to the characterization of heritage as the unity of *consciousness* and emptiness, in his *Gateway to Scholarship*, Mipam depicts the naturally abiding heritage as the unity of self-existing *wisdom* and the expanse of phenomena: "The naturally abiding heritage is Buddha-nature: its essence is the unconditioned, self-existing wisdom unified with the empty and aware expanse of phenomena that is inseparable from the exalted body and wisdom from the beginning."[16] Self-existing wisdom is a central element in his interpretation. He characterizes self-existing wisdom as follows: "Wisdom is designated as 'self-existing' [literally, 'self-arising'] due to the aspect of it being wisdom that does not arise from another nor from a cause; it does not arise from itself nor is it a new occurrence because it is non-arising."[17] The presence of wisdom that is not produced anew is a central part of his depiction of Buddha-nature. We will now take a closer look at Mipam's view of Buddha-nature and discuss his own depiction of heritage.

Buddha-Nature as Heritage, Buddha-Nature as the Ground

We will begin this discussion by first addressing how Mipam describes the manner that heritage exists in beings. This will help us to better understand how he represents the essence of heritage as such. In *Lion's Roar: Exposition of Buddha-Nature,* he identifies heritage with "the essential nature" (*snying po*) and says that heritage is the suchness of mind that abides in the manner of an extract, or essential core, enclosed by adventitious defilements:

> In terms of the essence of the abiding reality itself, all phenomena are encompassed within the expanse of suchness and the essence of suchness itself abides, without arising or ceasing, as equality; without temporal distinctions such as the past or future, or aspects such as the good or bad, here or there, self or other, greater and lesser, in saṃsāra and nirvāṇa, etc.—the expanse of phenomena is the unchanging, single sphere (*thig le nyag gcig*). Although the abiding reality is as such, in accord with the perspective of the appearances of adventitious delusion, even when bodies, minds, and domains of the three realms of saṃsāra appear in this way and the nature of suchness is not seen, it is not that suchness does not exist; it exists without deviating in the slightest from its own nature. Therefore, although the suchness of mind is as such, it is not actualized due to being enclosed by adventitious defilements. Even so, it abides in the manner of an extract or an essential core in the center and is called the "heritage" or the "essential nature"; for example, it is said to be

> known by illustration through the nine metaphors such as the underground treasure, etc.[18]

He states that heritage is illustrated through the nine metaphors, cited in the *Uttaratantra.*[19] He characterizes the heritage as the suchness of mind that is not actualized, or not manifest; it abides as an extract or essential core. In his *Trilogy of Innate Mind,* Mipam also calls this suchness of mind "Buddha-nature": "Existing in the minds of all sentient beings in the manner of suchness on the occasion when obscurations dwell as suitable to be removed, it is called 'Buddha-nature' because when this suchness of mind is realized, one becomes a Buddha."[20] The suchness, or nature, of mind is Buddha-naure. Self-existing wisdom is simply made manifest; it is not produced by a cause. In his *Lion's Roar: Exposition of Buddha-Nature*, Mipam says that even though the Truth Body appears to be a new production, when the obscuring conditions are removed, it is a freed effect:

> Self-existing wisdom is not produced by a cause because actually, the Truth Body freed from adventitious defilements is a freed effect. Although it appears to be newly produced by a cause, it merely appears as such in the way of appearance for those who are untransformed. However, in terms of the actual meaning, in the essence of the Truth Body, which is the nature of suchness without arising or disintegration, from the beginning all phenomena are—as equality—the actual Buddha, primordially nirvāṇa, naturally luminous and clear, etc. This consummate viewpoint of the profound sūtras is a topic that is difficult to fathom for pure beings, needless to mention ordinary people![21]

He states that the new development of the Truth Body is only in the way of appearance for those who are untransformed; in actual reality, all phenomena are primordially Buddha in the essence of the Truth Body, which is the suchness of all phenomena.

In his *Trilogy of Innate Mind*, he states that the qualities of Buddha-nature at the time of the ground (i.e., at the time of a sentient being) only potentially exist as manifest:

> The manifest appearance of the qualities of omniscient wisdom has the endowment of twofold purity, not only natural purity.[22] However, the qualities of that [omniscient wisdom] have to be asserted as

> present from the beginning, like the metaphor of a knife [in a sheath], etc. Therefore, one should know that at the time of the ground (*gzhi'i dus na*), the qualities of Buddha-nature only potentially exist as manifest.[23]

Thus, we can see a distinction between two types of potential: (1) the potential to *transform* into a newly produced Buddha and (2) the potential (of what is already present) to *manifest*. In his presentation of the way Buddha-nature exists for a sentient being, he rejects the former and accepts the latter. He states that the primordial qualities of wisdom are already present; they are an intrinsic endowment—like a knife has the ability to cut, a mirror to reflect, and a gemstone to shine:

> The primordial endowment of qualities such as the powers are spontaneously present by nature from the beginning [like] the quality of a functional knife to cut, the quality of a clear mirror to shine reflected forms, and the quality of a gem to be luminous and bestow desires; however, they are like the knife in a sheath, the mirror put in the box, and the gem covered with mud. When the obscurations are cleared, the qualities do not newly arise, but appear manifest as if newly arisen.[24]

He describes the qualities of the Buddha, such as powers, and so forth, as spontaneously present from the beginning. Yet like the qualities of a knife in a sheath, when the qualities are obscured they are not evident. Thus, while the qualities may appear to newly arise when their obscurations are removed, in reality they do not newly arise; they are simply made manifest. Furthermore, he states in his *Difficult Points of Scriptures in General:*

> If it is asked, "Well, do the continua of sentient beings such as dogs and pigs have the wisdom with the ten powers?" The Buddha-nature of their continua from the beginning has the qualities of wisdom with the ten powers because these are the qualities of its suchness. Therefore, if there is the basic element, there are qualities; however, [the qualities] are not manifest—like a knife has the ability to cut, even so, the ability to cut is not manifest when put in a sheath; and a mirror has the quality to potentially shine reflected forms, even so, it does not manifestly shine when put in a box.[25]

In this way, he describes heritage as the suchness of mind, endowed from the beginning with the qualities of Buddha's wisdom, together with the ten powers.[26]

Mipam's treatment of Buddha-nature should be considered in light of Longchenpa's works, so we will turn now briefly to Longchenpa. Longchenpa states that the Buddha is not an effect that is newly produced. In his *Treasury of Philosophies,* Longchenpa delineates two types of effects: (1) a produced effect and (2) a freed effect: "The Buddha also is a freed effect from a freeing cause (*bral ba'i rgyu 'bras*), and is not established as a produced effect by a producing cause (*bskyed bya skyed kyi rgyu 'bras*) because the Buddha is spontaneously present from the beginning."[27]

Longchenpa describes the Buddha as a freed effect because the Buddha is present from the beginning. A freed effect is not newly produced, but is simply made manifest when the conditions that obscure it are removed—like the sun freed from clouds. In contrast, a produced effect, or ripened effect, is a transformation—like a seed transforming into a sprout. Moreover, Longchenpa states as follows in his autocommentary of his *Treasury of the Expanse of Phenomena:*

> One may think, "Do [the exalted body and wisdom] not arise from the accumulations of merit and wisdom?" It is said as follows: the two accumulations, from the beginning already complete with the qualities of emptiness and appearance, are called "spontaneously present" because the adventitious accumulations, which are the mere aspect of the conditions that remove the defilements, are merely designated as "the two causal accumulations"—just as the washcloth and cleanser that clean a dirty gemstone are called "the causes of seeing the gem."[28]

In this way, the exalted body and wisdom of the Buddha are spontaneously present within sentient beings from the beginning; they are said to be "caused" only in the sense that they become manifest when the defilements that obscure them are removed. Longchenpa says that the suchness of mind of a sentient being is endowed with the qualities of Form Bodies from the aspect of appearance, and endowed with the qualities of the Truth Body from the aspect of emptiness. He states this in his autocommentary of his *Resting in the Nature of Mind:*

> At the time of a sentient being, the suchness of mind is completely endowed with the qualities of the Form Bodies from the aspect of

> appearance, and the qualities of the Truth Body from the aspect of emptiness. However, due to being obscured by defilements, it is not clearly manifest so it is called "the basic element" or "heritage," and due to being free from all defilements at the time of being a Buddha it is called "awakening." Even so, since it is unchanging, other than the essence, the nature of mind's potential, completely appearing or not, it is not asserted that qualities that were first nonexistent at the time of a sentient being are newly produced later.[29]

Longchenpa affirms that the suchness of mind is not manifest due to the obscurations of defilements. At that time, it is called "basic element" or "heritage" and when free from defilements at the time of a Buddha, it is called "awakening." He claims that there are no essential qualities of the nature of mind that at first do not exist and are newly produced at the time of a Buddha. Furthermore, Longchenpa states as follows in his *Responses to Mind and Wisdom:*

> These days most virtuous spiritual friends and all meditators are in accord in advocating the ground as a mere absence that is nothing at all, which is not in accord with the viewpoint of the meaning of the essential nature. Through practicing a ground that is nothing at all, the Buddha endowed with all qualities will not arise (1) because the three—ground, path, and fruition—are confused and (2) because the Buddha—with qualities that are unconditioned and spontaneously present—is manifested as a freed effect. Therefore, the view of the summit of existence appears to be in accord with them; here we assert luminous clarity itself—unconditioned and spontaneously present—as the ground.[30]

In this way, Longchenpa asserts a ground that is not a mere absence. Rather, he affirms the ground as luminous clarity—unconditioned and spontaneously present. Longchenpa says: "The ground is the wisdom of luminous clarity that exists within oneself at the time of being a sentient being."[31] Moreover, he states:

> The meaning of the ground is explained as follows: the suchness of luminous clarity from the beginning is unconditioned and spontaneously present. From the side of emptiness, it is free from all constructed extremes like space because it is not at all established as an

> entity or a sign, nor is it at all confined to saṃsāra or nirvāṇa, etc. From the side of clarity, it is spontaneously present and luminously clear like the disks of the sun and moon, endowed from the beginning with the nature of the exalted body and wisdom. These two [emptiness and clarity] are neither conjoined nor separable within the suchness abiding from the beginning.[32]

Using descriptive metaphors such as being empty like space and clear like the sun, Longchenpa characterizes the ground as a unity of emptiness and clarity. He also describes an "ultimate universal ground" (*don gyi kun gzhi*) in his autocommentary of his *Wish-Fulfilling Treasury:* "The basic element is called 'the ultimate universal ground' because it co-exists with the unconditioned qualities of the naturally pure nirvāṇa."[33] He says that this ground is the support for both saṃsāra and nirvāṇa, and identifies it with Buddha-nature:

> Due to abiding as the expanse neither conjoined with nor separable from the exalted body and wisdom, it is Buddha-nature; due to supporting all phenomena of saṃsāra and nirvāṇa, it is the abiding reality called "the ultimate universal ground"; it is unconditioned and abides as the great primordial purity. Moreover, it supports the phenomena of saṃsāra—karma and afflictive emotions—in the manner of a non-support (*rten pa med pa'i tshul*), as the sun and space support cloud formations, they abide within its state without contact or connection with the basis. In reality, since there is no intrinsic nature, support and supported are not established; since it appears as such it is so designated [as the support].[34]

Longchenpa explains that the ground supports all phenomena of saṃsāra and nirvāṇa. He states that the ground supports the phenomena of saṃsāra "in the manner of a non-support"; it is merely designated as the support (conventionally), but since there is no intrinsic nature, support and supported are not established (ultimately).

He distinguishes his assertion—that wisdom is simply the ground made manifest—from those who accept wisdom as a new development, a product of *real* transformation. He says that the proponents of Mind-Only accept that the eight collections of consciousness are *transformed* (*gnas 'gyur*) into wisdom. However, he asserts that consciousnesses are removed and the self-existing wisdom just becomes *manifest* (*mngon pa tsam*), being merely imputed as a transformation:

> Proponents of Mind-Only assert that the collection of eight consciousnesses itself transforms into wisdom; here, the self-existing wisdom is merely made manifest through removing the consciousnesses, which is designated as a transformation—the difference between the two is vast.[35]

Thus, he states that the appearances of the exalted body and wisdom are the suchness of mind, only to be manifested. The transformation from consciousness to wisdom is just a designation.

We can see how Mipam's description of Buddha-nature reflects Longchenpa's description of the ground. Mipam also refers to Buddha-nature as the abiding reality of the "ground of the primeval beginning" (*ye thog gi gzhi*) in his *Trilogy of Innate Mind:*

> Buddha-nature is not a mere absence; it is emptiness and luminous clarity. It is the abiding reality of the ground of the primeval beginning of all phenomena, the abiding reality that is the indivisible truth of unity—emptiness endowed with all supreme aspects (*rnam kun mchog ldan gyi stong nyid*).[36]

The abiding reality of the ground, Buddha-nature, is not a mere absence; it is inseparable from the presence of supreme appearing qualities. He describes the ground of the primeval beginning as the consummate suchness: "The luminous clarity of the ground of the primeval beginning—the primordial abiding reality itself—is the consummate suchness."[37]

Mipam characterizes the ground in the language of the Great Perfection as follows:

> The ground itself, from the aspect of lacking any constructs, is primordially pure. Unlike a mere space-like absence, it is self-illuminating (*rang gsal*) without bias, confinement, or partiality—spontaneously present. As the source of all appearances of saṃsāra and nirvāṇa, it is said to be "all-pervasive compassionate resonance." In the language of the Great Perfection tantras, it is called "wisdom abiding within the ground with three endowments."[38]

The three endowments are (1) empty essence (*ngo bo stong pa*), which is primordial purity, (2) natural clarity (*rang bzhin gsal ba*), which is spontaneous presence, and (3) all-pervasive compassion resonance (*thugs rje kun khyab*).

Mipam's interpretation of Buddha-nature reflects the Great Perfection, as seen in his statements in the *Lion's Roar: Exposition of Buddha-Nature:*

> Due to not existing as they appear, conditioned phenomena that appear to arise and cease in this way have never tainted the basic nature of the expanse; therefore, through this essential point that (1) the primordial purity of the causality of saṃsāra and (2) the uncontaminated appearances, which are the luminous clarity of the spontaneously present nature, are neither conjoined nor separable, the undistorted manner of Buddha-nature should be identified.[39]

He associates Buddha-nature with a distinguishing feature of the ground of the Great Perfection—the unity of primordial purity and spontaneous presence. In this way, his interpretation of Buddha-nature reflects the dual quality of empty essence and natural clarity of the Great Perfection.[40]

Following Mipam, Bötrül's representation of the essence of heritage also echoes the Great Perfection:

> The essence of heritage is asserted to be (1) the abiding reality that is the primordially pure property of the essential nature (2) bearing the identity that is the endowment of the three distinctive qualities—the nature of empty essence, natural clarity, and all-pervasive compassionate resonance. In short, the defining character of heritage is: the abiding reality which is the primordially pure property of the essential nature endowed with the three distinctive qualities.[41]

Like Mipam, Bötrül also incorporates the language of the Great Perfection into his interpretation of sūtras. He states that the intended meaning of the middle wheel is the empty essence and the last wheel's intended meaning is natural clarity: "The intended meaning of the middle wheel is empty essence and the intended meaning of the last wheel is natural clarity, the [unity of the] middle and last [wheels] without contradiction indicates all-pervasive compassionate resonance."[42] In this way, the explicit teaching of emptiness in the middle wheel reflects primordial purity, and the presence of wisdom indicated in the last wheel reflects spontaneous presence. The unity of the middle and last wheels, as empty essence and natural clarity, portrays all-pervasive compassionate resonance. Such a unity is represented in Mipam's depictions of emptiness and Buddha-nature.

Appearance and Reality

We will now discuss Buddha-nature in terms of (1) how it is the abiding reality, or mode of reality, and (2) how it appears, the mode of appearance. We will begin with Mipam's depiction of the essence of Buddha-nature.

In his *Lion's Roar: Exposition of Buddha-Nature,* Mipam describes the essence of the Buddha-nature as follows: "The essence of the Buddha-nature itself is free from all conceptual constructs such as existence and nonexistence, permanence and annihilation; it is the equality of the single sphere of indivisible truth."[43]

He describes Buddha-nature as free from all conceptual constructs, in the same language he uses to describe emptiness as the consummate suchness that we saw in the last chapter. Buddha-nature, like emptiness, is the suchness of all phenomena. He also depicts Buddha-nature with affirming descriptive words such as "the single sphere of indivisible truth." He calls Buddha-nature "the great unconditioned" in his *Lion's Roar: Exposition of Buddha-Nature:*

> Even though partial cognitions that cognize objects are necessarily impermanent, the wisdom that is the one taste of the knower and known, "the one with the space-*vajra* pervading space" (*mkha' khyab mkha' yi rdo rje can*), is not like that [impermanent cognition]. This is because in the state of unchanging luminous clarity, which is the self-vibrancy of the unconditioned, all the phenomena of nirvāṇa and saṃsāra are incorporated (*'ub chub*); hence, reasoning that examines the consummate [reality] (*mthar thug dpyod pa'i rig shes*) establishes that there is primordially no arising or ceasing in the essence of that. Therefore, wisdom such as this is "the great unconditioned," which does not abide in either extreme of being conditioned or unconditioned; it is not at all like a mere nonentity. Since entities and nonentities are phenomena and are dependent arisings, or dependent imputations, when authentically analyzed they are hollow, fake, lies, and deceptions; Buddha-nature is the great unconditioned, the suchness of all phenomena that are entities or nonentities, which is authentically nondeceptive. As is said in the *Mūlamadhyamakakārikā* [XV.2]:
>
> > Nature is uncontrived,
> > And does not depend on another.

And [XXV.13],

> Entities and nonentities are conditioned;
> Nirvāṇa is unconditioned.[44]

He explains that partial cognitions are necessarily impermanent; wisdom, however, is beyond the dichotomy of impermanent entities and permanent nonentities. He argues that Buddha-nature is "the great unconditioned"—the suchness of all phenomena that are entities or nonentities. His statements again resemble Dölpopa's depiction of the unique status of suchness as a third category that is neither an entity nor a nonentity.

Similar to Dölpopa, Mipam also says that wisdom is permanent. He states that from the perspective of sentient beings, ordinary conventional valid cognition exclusively observes functional, thus impermanent, entities. However, in the perspective of wisdom, omniscience is permanent:

> In accord with the mental perspectives of others—those to be trained who have not been transformed—the scriptures say that omniscience is impermanent, and there is reason also in the *Pramāṇavārttika* [II.8]:
>
> > There is no permanent valid cognition
> > Because the realization of the existence of entities is valid and
> > Objects of knowledge are impermanent;
> > That [omniscient valid cognition] is only impermanent.
>
> Omniscience arises through causes such as the generation of the mind [of awakening] and meditation on emptiness because it is not reasonable to arise without a cause, and that [omniscience] is the valid cognition that is the direct perception of all phenomena. If valid cognition is a nondeceptive cognition, then there are no permanent phenomena because it is valid cognition that evaluates existent entities as they are. Since its objects are only impermanent objects of knowledge, then the evaluating valid cognition also must be impermanent, occurring sequentially, because it is established by valid cognition that what is permanent is incapable of functioning; hence, it would certainly be incapable of all activities such as evaluating objects. Therefore, it is extremely unreasonable that omniscience is permanent; it is established as impermanent. Likewise, all

> entities are impermanent and although nonentities are designated as "permanent," since there is no basis of something permanent, there are no genuinely permanent phenomena to be found. This fact is necessarily established as such for the perspectives of non-Buddhist heretics and those of the common vehicles who have not trained their minds in the manner of transformation within the essence of inconceivable suchness because they have no method whatsoever for the arising of what is other than the manner of appearance from the perspective of consciousness. However, as for the vision of thoroughly transformed wisdom, omniscience is established as permanent.[45]

That functional entities are necessarily impermanent phenomena is a tenet of the Buddhist epistemological system of valid cognition (*tshad ma, pramāṇa*) developed by Dharmakīrti, where cognition is said to be impermanent because of the mutually exclusive dichotomy of (1) functional entities and (2) permanent nonentities, devoid of functional capacity. However, Mipam contextualizes the statements regarding wisdom as impermanent; he says that the absence of permanent phenomena is necessarily established as such in the perspectives of non-Buddhists and others who have not trained their minds in the manner of "transformation within the essence of inconceivable suchness." He delimits the necessity of cognition being impermanent to only the perspective of consciousness, not the perspective of wisdom. Thus, he makes an epistemological distinction between appearance and reality based on consciousness and wisdom, respectively.

Moreover, Mipam states that there is no arising or ceasing of dualistic phenomena in the basic nature that abides without ever changing. He adds that this basic nature can also be called "permanent" because it (1) exists and (2) is not momentary:

> To an untransformed one who has dualistic perception, there is the incontrovertible and undeniable appearance of inequality—all the changing, adventitious defilements suitable to be removed, occurring sequentially as arising and ceasing moments, saṃsāra and nirvāṇa, good and bad, etc.; however, the basic nature abides as the great equality in which arising, ceasing, and dualistic phenomena are not established. All spatial aspects and temporal changes are incorporated within that state. This exists as the domain of a Sublime One's individual reflexive awareness wisdom and there is no

> pollution by the changes of the three times. So why not give this the name "great permanence"? [It is designated as such] because (1) it exists and (2) it does not arise and cease momentarily.[46]

He affirms that the basic nature (the Buddha-nature) exists, and it does not arise and cease momentarily; therefore, it can be called "permanent" by definition of what it means to be permanent. He denies, however, that suchness is an entity (*dngos po*). He states that when suchness is evaluated from its own side, it is neither observed as a conditioned entity nor an unconditioned nonentity. He explains as follows in his *Trilogy of Innate Mind:*

> When evaluated in terms of suchness from its own side, it is observed as neither of the two—a conditioned entity or an unconditioned nonentity—because suchness, not abiding in the extremes of either the conditioned or the unconditioned, is known through individual reflexive awareness. . . . At the time when primordial suchness is actualized as a Buddha, the wisdom body of the great permanence—like a *vajra* that never deviates from the expanse of phenomena—is the great unconditioned; it is not conditioned. However, in terms of its mode of appearance, it is posited as newly arisen from the aspect of being a freed effect of previous training on the path; and it is posited as conditioned from the aspect of progressively engaging in enlightened activity for beings to be trained, etc.—you will be freed from the web of doubt when you distinguish the respective intended meanings in accord with what is generally proclaimed in scriptures.[47]

He states that suchness from its own side is neither conditioned nor unconditioned; it is "the great unconditioned" free from extremes. However, in terms of the way of appearance, it is posited as newly arisen from the aspect of being a freed effect. It is also posited as conditioned from the aspect of the progressive engagement in enlightened activity for beings to be trained. In this way, Mipam distinguishes the mode of reality, where all is inseparable from great equality, from the mode of appearance, where everything appears distinctly. Furthermore, he explains in his *Trilogy of Innate Mind:*

> Although it is as such, most others assert that the essence of the exalted body and wisdom of a Buddha is impermanent and that it is a permanent continuity. Those who accept the nature of the fruitional

> emptiness that is endowed with all supreme aspects of the exalted body and wisdom assert as follows: the own essence of the exalted body and wisdom is permanent, but in the mode of appearance of those to be trained, it is an impermanent continuity as is said in the *Sūtra That Gathers the Viewpoints*. In this way, in terms of the abiding reality as it is, while no phenomenon subsumed within the three times at all deviates from the non-arising, unceasing equality in the fundamental nature, all phenomena that exist appear as unmixed—such as self and other, saṃsāra and nirvāṇa, conditioned and unconditioned phenomena, phenomena of the past, present, and future. These two are such that through holding one position, the other need not be rejected. As similar to the discourses of the manner of realization endowed with the eight profundities,[48] for the ones in whom the understood meaning of the noncontradiction of the two truths has radiantly[49] dawned, a certainty that is free from doubt in the viewpoints of Mahāyāna Sūtras and tantras easily arises.[50]

In distinction to the way others have asserted wisdom as impermanent (such as the Sakya scholar, Śākya Chokden),[51] Mipam affirms a view that the essence of wisdom is permanent. He argues that according to the mode of reality, nothing ever wavers from the non-arising and unceasing equality. Nevertheless, everything appears distinctly and unmixed according to the mode of appearance. He shows that these two perspectives need not be in conflict, such that if one holds a position according to the abiding reality as it is, then one must reject the mode of appearance, and vice versa. He shows that both views—the views of the ultimate mode of reality and the conventional mode of appearance—can be held in their respective contexts and adds that understanding the meaning of the noncontradiction of the two truths is a key point in understanding the viewpoints of sūtras and tantras.

He states that in both cases of Sūtra and Mantra, in terms of the conventional way of appearance, a distinction can be made between: (1) the way reality is, where appearance and existence is asserted to be primordially Buddha, and (2) the way things conventionally appear, where wisdom appears as a new development:

> Although in terms of the ultimate abiding reality, appearance and existence are asserted to be primordially Buddha and one should meditate as such, in terms of the conventional way of appearance, supreme knowledge can make a distinction of three: (1) the ground,

> the heritage which is the potential to be a Buddha, (2) the path, which is the occasion of practice, and (3) the fruition, which is the consummation of purity; this is accepted all the way up to the Great Perfection.[52]

He affirms the three contexts of: (1) the ground, as the heritage which is the potential to be a Buddha, (2) the path, the occasion of practice, and (3) the fruition, the consummation of purity. He affirms that such a distinction can be made throughout Buddhist traditions, including the Great Perfection. In the context of meditation, however, he advocates meditation done in accordance with the mode of reality, in which everything is primordially the Buddha.

Mipam also explains these three contexts in terms of consciousness and wisdom. In terms of the mode of appearance, he delineates three contexts: (1) the impure, which is the function of only consciousness, (2) the impure/pure, which is the function of a mix of consciousness and wisdom, and (3) the extremely pure, which is the function of only wisdom:

> Although from the beginning there are no obscurations in the essence of the expanse of suchness, since the ground and fruition are established as indivisible, the mode of reality is ascertained as the viewpoint of the primordial Buddha; and in the mode of appearance, when perfecting the strength of meditation, one also becomes a Buddha again through actualizing the concordant modes of appearance and reality. These two are not a contradiction because suchness—which is the indivisibility of (1) the vibrancy of natural luminous clarity and (2) the primordial purity of all constructs from the beginning—pervades all of saṃsāra and nirvāṇa; hence, from suchness, which is nothing whatsoever, anything can arise. The equality of saṃsāra and nirvāṇa is spontaneously present as the Truth Body! Therefore, whatever the transformations of the limitless miraculous displays are—the various appearances of saṃsāra and nirvāṇa—they all arise from only the functions of consciousness and wisdom. Hence, in the mode of appearance, there is a division of three contexts: (1) the context of the impure ground, which is the function of only consciousness, (2) the context of the path endowed with both the impure and pure, which is the function of consciousness and wisdom having been mixed, and (3) the context of the extremely pure fruition, which is the function of only wisdom.[53]

In this way, while he affirms the indivisibility of the ground and fruition in the mode of reality, he delineates three contexts of the ground, path, and fruition in the mode of appearance. The three contexts of impure, impure/pure, and extremely pure are found in the *Uttaratantra*, in terms of (1) impure "sentient beings," (2) both impure and pure "bodhisattvas," and (3) completely pure "Tathāgatas," the Buddhas.[54]

He states that there are distinctions to be made in terms of the way things appear. Nevertheless, at the time of meditating on the nature of reality, one should do so in accord with the way reality is, where all things are equal:

> In terms of the mode of appearance, since one asserts (1) the ground as natural purity and (2) the fruition as qualified by the purity that is freed from the adventitious [defilements], it is not that there is no distinction. Nevertheless, when conclusively settling (*la zlo'i tshe*), one should ascertain in accord with the mode of reality because if one does not, saṃsāra itself will not be realized as nirvāṇa. Even though when making distinctions one accords with the mode of appearance, by that, the equality of saṃsāra and nirvāṇa within the abiding reality is not negated because there is no impurity within the mode of reality.[55]

He argues that even though distinctions are made in accord with the way things appear, that does not undermine how they are in reality. In the mode of reality, saṃsāra and nirvāṇa are equal because there is no impurity within the mode of reality. If one always makes distinctions even when conclusively settling upon the nature of reality, then saṃsāra itself will not be realized as nirvāṇa—the modes of appearance and reality will not accord.

In this way, he delineates two contexts: (1) in terms of the mode of reality, where there are no distinctions and the two truths are indivisible, and (2) in terms of the mode of appearance, where appearances arise as unmixed and distinctions are made. While there are no distinctions within the ultimate mode of reality known by wisdom, supreme knowledge makes distinctions between what is true and what is not conventionally. In his *Lion's Roar: Exposition of Buddha-Nature*, Mipam states:

> In the context of differentiating well by means of the valid cognition analyzing the conventional, the reality of entities in the apprehension of undistorted supreme knowledge is conventionally:

> - Knowing the truth as truth—such as knowing the path of the Sublime Ones to be undeceiving
> - Knowing the false as false—such as knowing those who profess liberation through meditating on the self to be misguided
> - Knowing the impermanent as impermanent—knowing that all conditioned entities are momentary
> - Knowing the permanent as permanent—knowing that Buddha-nature, the self-existing wisdom totality of [supreme] aspects, never changes
> - Knowing the nonexistent as nonexistent—such as knowing that the appearances of self and perceived-perceiver [duality] are not intrinsically established
> - Apprehending the existent as existent—such as knowing that (1) causality is the incontrovertible mode of appearance of dependent arising and (2) the spontaneously present qualities of suchness, the Buddha-nature, naturally abide in all sentient beings;
>
> Therefore, through knowing and abiding as such, vast qualities are attained because this is the non-deluded root of virtue.[56]

He delineates what exists and what does not from the perspective of conventional valid cognition. Even though there are no distinctions between Buddhas and sentient beings in the mode of reality, the mode of appearance is such that sentient beings appear to exist as distinct from Buddhas. Through delineating appearance and reality in this way, he affirms the primordial endowment of the qualities of the Buddha in sentient beings without incurring the consequence that all sentient beings must necessarily appear as manifest Buddhas.

Conclusion

Like emptiness, Buddha-nature is the suchness of reality and the indivisible truth beyond dichotomies. As the heritage of all sentient beings, Buddha-nature is the reality of a Buddha that is obscured in sentient beings. Mipam portrays the qualities of the Buddha as not newly produced, but as merely made manifest through removing the conditions that obscure reality. He makes a distinction between appearance and reality through which he affirms the indivisibility of Buddhas and sentient beings in the mode of reality, and depicts temporal and qualitative distinctions only in the mode of appearance.

We saw how Mipam presents Buddha-nature in a way that is distinct from other sectarian traditions in Tibet. Specifically, he presents Buddha-nature differently from the way Buddha-nature is characterized in the Jonang, Geluk, and Sakya traditions. Since he depicts Buddha-nature with the qualities of the Buddha present at the time of a sentient being, his presentation shares an important feature with the Jonang tradition. His interpretation also shares a quality with the Geluk tradition, given that he equates Buddha-nature with emptiness. However, Mipam's integration of Buddha-nature and emptiness most directly reflects Longchenpa's description of the ground of the Great Perfection, the pinnacle of Buddhist vehicles in his Nyingma tradition, where Buddha-nature represents the unity of primordial purity and spontaneous presence.

CHAPTER FIVE

The Indivisible Ground and Fruition

Every understanding of spiritual things (*Geistwissenschaft*) is circular.
—Paul Tillich, *Systematic Theology*

Introduction

In the previous chapter, we saw how Mipam makes a case for Buddha-nature within an appearance-reality distinction. In this chapter, we will look further into the reality of Buddha-nature and how it is known. While Mipam emphasizes the role of reasoned certainty in his formulation of emptiness, with Buddha-nature (and Mantra) the touchstone of reality is not ordinary reason, but what is known through a Sublime One's experience. The reality of Buddha-nature is known through the wisdom of reflexive awareness, yet, until then, through an appeal to the authority of the words of those with such wisdom (i.e., authoritative texts and quintessential instructions).

We will begin by looking again into Mipam's *Lion's Roar: Exposition of Buddha-Nature* to unpack the arguments he puts forward for the existence of Buddha-nature. We will then address the implications of Mipam's use of reasoning to affirm what he acknowledges to conflict with ordinary perception. Through this, we will be able to appreciate an epistemological conflict within his appearance-reality distinction—the epistemological conflict between a divine ground of being versus a world known by ordinary perception.

In this chapter, we will see how Mipam's treatment of Buddha-nature reflects his approach to Mantra. We will also discuss the integral role of *subjectivity* in Mantra, and see how Buddha-nature and subjectivity are primary factors by which Sūtra and Mantra are distinguished.

ESTABLISHING BUDDHA-NATURE: THE IMMANENT BUDDHA

In his *Lion's Roar: Exposition of Buddha-Nature,* Mipam sets forth reasons to establish that all beings possess Buddha-nature. He bases a discussion of Buddha-nature around a stanza from the *Uttaratantra*, in which he explains three verses as reasons for the existence of Buddha-nature in all beings. The stanza from *Uttaratantra* I.28 reads as follows:

> Because the body of the perfect Buddha is radiant,
> Because thusness (*de bzhin nyid*) is indivisible,
> Because of possessing heritage;
> Therefore, all beings always possess the essential nature of Buddha.[1]

We will look at Mipam's exegesis of this stanza in some detail, then we will explore in more depth some of the implications of his use of reason to establish Buddha-nature. In his explanation of the stanza, he states:

> The meaning of the first verse is as follows: since the Truth Body, the consummate body of a complete and perfect Buddha, as such with the qualities equal to [the extent of] space, later is made clear, radiant, or manifest from a former continuum of a thoroughly bounded ordinary being; therefore, the statement "presently the Buddha-nature exists in the continua of all sentient beings" is established.[2]

He explains the first verse of the stanza as a reason that proves the cause, Buddha-nature, from the effect, the Buddha. He argues that if a future effect is established—that is, the Truth Body of the Buddha which is the unconditioned and unchanging ultimate truth—then the cause also presently must be the nature of the Truth Body present in all beings in the manner of suchness:

> If the wisdom of the consummate Truth Body is established by scriptures of definitive meaning sūtras and reasoning examining the consummate [reality] to be the nature of the immutable ultimate truth, completely pervading nirvāṇa and saṃsāra, equality, and

unconditioned; then the cause, which is able to actualize that at one time, is presently the nature of the Wisdom Truth Body abiding in the manner of suchness without decrease or increase. Although it may or may not be actualized in the mode of appearance free or not free from adventitious defilements, there is not even the slightest qualitative or temporal difference in the mode of reality because it is the intrinsic nature of the immutable unconditioned. In the *Uttaratantra* [I.51]:

> As it was before so it is later—
> The immutable suchness.

And [I.63],

> The luminous clarity that is the nature of mind
> Is immutable like space.
> It is undisturbed by adventitious defilements
> Such as attachments that arise from the imagination of the unreal.[3]

He argues that since there cannot be the slightest qualitative or temporal difference in the nature of what is immutable and unconditioned, then the nature of the Buddha cannot be different at the time of the effect and at the time of the cause.[4] In the mode of appearance, however, this reality may or may not be actualized due to the presence of adventitious defilements that obscure reality. He then compares the mind that does not realize the suchness of reality to consciousness in a dream:

> Although the suchness that is the luminous and clear wisdom is present in everything without distinction, when this adventitious delusion arises in one's mind, the basis of designation of saṃsāra is only this deluded mind together with its object; due to this delusion, one's suchness is not known as it is. For example, when sleeping, due to the power of solely the mental-consciousness, unrestricted appearances arise such as the body, objects, and eye-consciousness, etc. At that time, although the subject and object are observed and apprehended separately, the mental-consciousness itself is not able to know its own mode of being (*yin lugs*), in which the perceived [object] and the perceiving [subject] are not established as different; even though

> it is not known, there is nothing other than that mode of being. Likewise, all phenomena abide as emptiness; even so, merely being as such does not entail that everyone realizes this because there is the possibility of delusion—appearances that do not accord with reality.[5]

He argues that just because the luminous and clear wisdom is present in everything does not mean that everyone must realize this, just as all phenomena being empty does not entail that phenomena are realized as such by everyone.[6] He calls the argument in the first verse "reasoning of dependency" (*ltos pa'i rigs pa*),[7] proving the cause from the effect:

> The evidence of a clear manifestation of the Truth Body at the time of the fruition establishes that the heritage, primordially endowed with qualities, is present at the time of the cause because there is no temporal causality in the mode of reality; nevertheless, in dependence upon the mode of appearance, it is necessarily posited as cause and effect. Therefore, proving the cause from the effect is called "reasoning of dependency."[8]

He states that a manifestation of the Truth Body is posited as the effect of a cause in the mode of appearance—the way things appear. However, this is not the case within the way things are—in the mode of reality. In reality, the heritage, primordially endowed with qualities, is not the prior cause of a later effect.

Mipam continues his explanation of the second verse of the stanza:

> The meaning of the second [verse], "Because suchness is indivisible," is as follows: since all phenomena of saṃsāra and nirvāṇa are of one taste—indivisible within the great primordial luminous clarity of the emptiness that is the abiding reality—Buddhas and sentient beings also are ultimately indivisible due to the equality of existence and peace. Therefore, although appearing as emanated sentient beings due to adventitious delusion, it is established by the reasoning of the nature of things (*chos nyid kyi rigs pa*) that there is not the slightest deviation from the ultimate suchness of abiding reality; hence, the possession of the essential nature of Buddha is certain.[9]

He says that sentient beings appear as "emanated" due to delusion that is adventitious, but in reality there is no deviation from the suchness of reality.

Also, within the abiding reality saṃsāra and nirvāṇa are indivisible; therefore, Buddhas and sentient beings are also ultimately indivisible. He calls this verse "reasoning of the nature of things," or more literally, "reasoning of suchness." Effectively, he is giving the reason for Buddha-nature as: "because that is just the way things are," like a response to a question why fire is hot—*because it is*. We will consider Mipam's use of reasoning after we address his explanation of the third verse:

> The meaning of the third [verse], "Because of possessing heritage," is as follows: all sentient beings have the heritage that is the potential to be a Buddha because it is established that (1) defilements are adventitious and suitable to be relinquished and (2) the Truth Body primordially endowed with qualities exists in everything without distinction. In this way, the possession of the heritage that is the potential to be a Buddha entails that these embodied beings have Buddha-nature because (1) there is a context of them being a Buddha and (2) since the Buddha's Truth Body is also established as essentially unconditioned, there is no temporal or qualitative distinction [between the Truth Body and Buddha-nature] from the aspect of essence. This third reason, knowing the production of the effect from the cause, is reasoning of efficacy (*bya ba byed pa'i rigs pa*).
>
> Here, due to the mere presence of the cause, the emergence of an effect is not merely inferred because, due to the essential fact that it is impossible that the heritage would ever diminish in the event of becoming a Buddha, (1) the heritage that is the suchness itself is unchanging, (2) at the time of the effect there is no qualitative difference in essence, and (3) no matter how long the duration of the adventitious defilements is, they are suitable to be separate.[10]

Mipam agues here that all beings have the potential to be a Buddha because (1) defilements are adventitious; they are accidental and contingent—not inherent within the nature of beings—and (2) the Truth Body pervades everything without distinction. The possession of heritage that is the potential to be a Buddha is called "reasoning of efficacy"; it is a reason that infers the effect from the cause.

Moreover, he argues that this reason is not merely an inference of the *emergence* of an effect because the effect, in essence, is immanent due to there being no qualitative difference in the essence of a sentient being and a

Buddha. Since suchness is unchanging, a continuity—or common ground—of sentient beings and Buddhas is necessitated. Thus, in essence, beings presently participate in the changeless and timeless nature of the Buddha. In this light, heritage can be seen as somewhat like a divine spark in beings. To conclude, he summarizes the three reasons for all beings possessing Buddha-nature:

> In this way, (1) the existence of the cause, heritage, is essentially not distinct from the Truth Body at the time of the fruition, and (2) if the Truth Body at the time of the fruition exists, then at the time of sentient beings it [the heritage that is essentially the Truth Body] also necessarily exists without increase or decrease, and (3) although there is the imputation of causality and temporality, in reality, the expanse of phenomena is one taste within the immutable essence; the three reasons establish that all sentient beings have Buddha-nature due to the authentic path of reasoning that is engaged by the power of fact (*dngos po'i stobs kyis zhugs pa'i rigs pa*).[11]

In this way, he puts forward reasons "by the power of fact" to support Buddha-nature.

It does not take a trained logician, in Buddhist epistemology or modern logic, to see that the status of these reasons is quite spurious.[12] The first reason is based on the assumption of a Buddha, and the last reason is based on another assumption of tradition—the possession of heritage. At best, in consideration of the second reason, the indivisibility of suchness, one could take a skeptical approach toward the experience of a differentiated world. However, even if one were to find the indivisibility hypothesis a workable description of reality, all beings could be said to share the undivided nature of a Buddha *if* one were to accept the assumption of the existence of a Buddha, which brings us back to Buddhist dogma, not reason.

According to his system of valid truth, the rules of ordinary perception, and those of logic, are superseded by the authority of scriptural testimony. Scriptural testimony derives from the privileged perspective of a Sublime One's meditative experience. His arguments for Buddha-nature draw from, and return to, the foundation on which his discourse rests—the authoritative perspective derived from the experience of meditative equipoise.

Looking at Mipam's argument with the modern assumption of a reason-faith dichotomy, we can see that he is involved in an intricate scholastic project of reconciling reason and religion. It is clear, however, that Mipam does not share in a modern notion of reason as an autonomous entity. In his use of reason to establish the existence of Buddha-nature, there is no abstract domain of pure logic or presumed autonomy of reason. Rather, the subject is an integral part of the equation.

Although the conclusions he reaches do not follow as a result of only his logical procedure, his conclusions are not necessarily incompatible with that logical procedure, either. Even classical logic involves presumptions (dogmas) that are not founded by logical means (e.g., "faith" in the law of noncontradiction).[13] In fact, a process of establishing the reality of Buddha-nature through logic, and (reflexively) understanding it, is arguably circular by necessity.[14] What is important here is the nature of the presumptions that are at play within any inquiry into reality and, in particular, the embedded element of *subjectivity*.

Given that Mipam's Buddhist tradition lacks the modern notion of objectivity that is derived from an autonomous entity of reason, rather than simply dismissing his use of reasoning as "bad logic," a fruitful way to read his reasoning here is with an appreciation for the integral role that the subject plays within any inquiry. In the case of Buddha-nature in particular, the place of the subject is brought out of the background and into the foreground because the subject is a constitutive part of Buddha-nature. Buddha-nature is the true nature of being; it represents what we truly are. Hence, it is not simply an object "out there" in objective space, but the subject is an integral part within the nature of this reality. The role of subjectivity is especially important in Mantra, which we will explore next. Before moving into this, however, we will first look at Bötrül's discussion of these three reasons for the existence of Buddha-nature in his *Notes on the Essential Points of [Mipam's] Exposition [of Buddha-Nature]*, which is translated in its entirety in the back of this book (see Appendix 2).

Bötrül takes up Mipam's three reasons and describes the first reason as evidence that is a result (*'bras rtags*) and the last two as evidence of [identical] nature (*rang bzhin gyi rtags*):

> There are three reasonings that establish Buddha-nature: (1) reasoning of dependency [concerning] the effect, (2) reasoning of the nature of things [concerning] the essence, and (3) reasoning of efficacy [concerning] the cause. Moreover, the first is evidence that is an effect (*'bras rtags*) and the latter two are evidence of [identical] nature (*rang bzhin gyi rtags*). The first, through putting forward as evidence the effect—that which is endowed with the twofold

> purity—establishes the presence of the essence of the primordially pure Buddha; it is posited by means of the two separate contradistinctive aspects: (1) the Buddha that is the primordial pure essence and (2) the Buddha that is endowed with the twofold purity. Since the statement, "sentient beings are Buddhas," is [in reference to] the Buddha that is natural purity, it [refers to] the suchness of mind, not the effect which is that [Buddha endowed with the twofold purity]; therefore, there is also no fault of the effect abiding in the cause.[15]

Bötrül shows that the relationship of essential identity[16] between sentient beings and Buddhas refers to (1) the suchness of the mind of a sentient being and (2) the natural purity, or primordial purity, of the Buddha; it does not refer to the twofold purity of a Buddha at the time of the effect when the qualities of a Buddha are manifest. The actualized Buddha is endowed with the twofold purity: (1) natural purity and (2) purity that is free of the adventitious [defilements]. In the case of the essential identity of a sentient being and Buddha, Bötrül states that it is posited by means of the contradistinctive aspect, or conceptual distinction, of only the Buddha's *natural purity*, not the twofold purity. Therefore, he concludes that there is no fault here of accepting an effect as abiding in a cause.[17]

Establishing Appearances as Divine

We saw how Mipam makes a case for the presence of Buddha-nature by drawing upon Buddhist epistemology. We will now see how he extends his use of epistemology to establish a view of Mantra—that all appearances are divine. An important way he does this is through delineating four perspectives, or four valid cognitions: two that are conventional and two that are ultimate.[18] His fourfold scheme of truth adds a second tier to each of the Buddhist two truths; thus, there are two tiers of the two truths. The second tier plays an important part in his comprehensive interpretation of Buddhism that integrates valid cognition, the Middle Way, and tantra. His incorporation of tantra within a theory of valid cognition is an important part of his exegesis, and is a principal factor that distinguishes his Nyingma view.

We addressed the valid cognitions of the categorized and uncategorized ultimate in chapter 2; now we will look into the two conventional valid cognitions. The two conventional valid cognitions are respectively based on: (1)

confined perception (*tshur mthong*) and (2) pure vision (*dag gzigs*). Mipam delineates these two in his *Sword of Supreme Knowledge:*

> Since there are appearances that do not accord with reality,
> With regards to the conventional also there are two thoroughly
> conventional valid cognitions:
> Based upon impure confined perception and
> Based upon pure vision,
> Like a person's eye and a divine eye.[19]

Similar to the distinction he makes between the categorized and the uncategorized valid cognitions analyzing the ultimate truth, his division of two types of conventional valid cognition is also based on two modes of understanding. The conventional valid cognition of pure vision functions to affirm a reality that is otherwise inconceivable and conflicting with ordinary perception. Conventional valid cognition of confined perception, on the other hand, concerns ordinary modes of being in the world.

He argues that it is extremely close-minded to think that only ordinary confined perception is the consummate conventional reality.[20] Ordinary conventional valid cognition is superseded by the conventional valid cognition of pure vision. In *Essential Nature of Luminous Clarity,* his overview of Longchenpa's commentary on the *Guhyagarbhatantra,*[21] Mipam states:

> The unique object of this latter [conventional valid cognition of pure vision] is (1) that which appears such that it conflicts with the objects of ordinary confined perception and (2) that which is an inconceivable domain such as:
>
> - an appearance of as many [Buddha-]fields as dust motes within the breadth of a single dust mote
> - a show of many aeons' activities in one moment of time
> - showing a display of emanations without wavering from the immutable expanse of phenomena
> - knowing all objects of knowledge simultaneously with a non-conceptual mind.[22]

The conventional valid cognition of pure vision allows Mipam to provide a context for valid cognition to affirm what is inconceivable. In this way, the two-tiered structure of conventional valid cognitions is his attempt to affirm a legitimate presence of an inconceivable world without undermining the grounds for an epistemology of pragmatic truths on the level of worldly transactions.

We can see how Mipam's fourfold perspectival epistemology integrates (1) two conceptual approaches to reality, based on confined perception and the categorized ultimate, and (2) two approaches to reality that defy ordinary conceptual modes of being, based on pure perception and the uncategorized ultimate. Here again we see his important distinction between (1) conceptual consciousness and (2) nonconceptual wisdom.

We have seen how Mipam positions his views within the discourse of valid cognition. The conventional valid cognition of pure vision in particular sets apart his Nyingma view. Moreover, Mipam's use of the epistemological discourse of valid cognition supports his agenda to affirm a unified and coherent view of Buddhism. We can see that Mipam's fourfold system of epistemology spans the genres of sūtra and tantra in his *Essential Nature of Luminous Clarity:*

> In this way, one should be learned in the essential point that the profound meanings—all phenomena are primordially Buddha, etc.—are not established by only confined perception, yet are not utterly without a valid means of establishment either.[23]

He disagrees with the position that the authentic path is incompatible with reason in his *Lion's Roar: Exposition of Buddha-Nature:*

> It is necessary to be learned in the essential point of the manner of accomplishing the path, having expelled the obscured stupidity of thinking: "Even though it is the authentic path, since it cannot be proved through reason, it has to be understood through experience," or, "If it is not the path of confined perception, then it is not an authentic path."[24]

Here we can see that he disagrees with the beliefs that (1) the authentic path cannot be established through reason, but must be realized through experience, and (2) if it is not the path of confined perception, it is not authentic. The former reveals his emphasis on establishing a view of reality that is compatible with reason, whereas the latter reveals his appeal to a higher authority, an authority that is incompatible with, or rather is not limited to, (ordinary) reason. He is working with a delicate balance that seeks to sustain the legitimacy of both (1) reason and (2) a higher authority of scriptural testimony and meditative experience that trumps (ordinary) reason.

Bötrül elaborates on Mipam's four valid cognitions.[25] He describes conventional valid cognition of confined perception as that which is laid out in the works of Dharmakīrti, while the conventional valid cognition of pure vision is found in such texts as the *Uttaratantra*, and in tantras such as the *Guhyagarbha*.[26] Following Mipam, Bötrül states that without the conventional valid cognition of pure vision, the view of the relative as great purity taught in tantras such as the *Guhyagarbha* would be a mere assertion without support. He says that such divine appearances cannot be established by ultimate valid cognition because if they were said to exist from the ultimate perspective, then they would be truly established. Also, the divine nature of appearances cannot be established by ordinary conventional valid cognition:

> As soon as there is no conventional valid cognition of pure vision, there is no valid cognition found as a means to establish the existence of the great purity of the relative, as shown in the *Māyājāla Guhyagarbha* and so forth, other than a mere assertion because (1) ultimate valid cognition is not only simply unable to establish that; even if it were said to just exist as not empty in that perspective [of ultimate valid cognition], it would be truly established, and (2) confined conventional valid cognition establishes only the impurity of the aggregates, fire to be hot and burning, and earth to be hard and obstructive, etc. How could confined conventional valid cognition establish the five aggregates to be the five Buddha families and the five elements to be the maṇḍalas of the five goddesses?[27]

Bötrül shows how the conventional valid cognition of pure vision functions to affirm the purity of appearances by establishing the purity of relative phenomena—such as the five aggregates as the five Buddha families and the five elements as the maṇḍalas of the five goddesses.[28] Furthermore, he states that such conventional valid cognition is different from "ordinary other-emptiness" (*gshan stong phal*):

> This is unlike ordinary other-emptiness
> Because [it] cannot bear the analysis of ultimate valid cognition;
> Due to being the object found by the valid cognition of pure
> [vision],
> It is not rivaled by the ordinary emptiness of true existence.[29]

Following Mipam, Bötrül draws from the discourse of valid cognition to establish the purity of appearance. Mipam also sets forth an argument in a classical form of inference to establish the purity of appearances:

> It follows that the subject, all these appearances, are established in the mode of reality as the maṇḍala of the exalted body and wisdom because the Sublime Ones free from distorting pollutants see [appearances] as pure; like someone with unimpaired vision seeing a conch as white.[30]

People with undefiled perception see reality as it is, while people infected by defilements perceive a distorted reality; this is evident in the fact that ordinarily people see a conch as white, while someone with jaundice sees it as yellow. Mipam argues here that even though the way things appear may not be pure, appearances are pure in the undistorted vision of a Sublime One. Furthermore, he shows a parallel here with the reasons that establish the emptiness of phenomena:

> For example, when ascertaining that all phenomena are empty, no matter what phenomena are set forth as a means to prove (*sgrub byed*) the non-empty—the causality of karma, saṃsāra, nirvāṇa—that very means of proof is similar to what is established (*bsgrub bya*) in the former [i.e., empty]; it also can be proven to lack intrinsic nature. Hence, whatever is put forward as a means to prove the non-empty also goes to assist the reasoning that establishes emptiness—like adding kindling to the fire. Therefore, just as nothing is found within the sphere of what can be known that can refute emptiness, here as well, anything whatsoever that is put forward to prove phenomena to be impure, that very means of proof also is itself what is established as pure. Therefore, an argument that is able to refute the reasoning that establishes all phenomena as pure in the mode of reality is not found within the sphere of what can be known.[31]

He states that just as all the same reasons that are set forth to show that reality is not empty (e.g., because there is cause and effect, there is no emptiness), in fact support the case for emptiness (e.g., things arise dependently and thus lack intrinsic nature), in the same way, all the reasons that are set forth to show that reality is not pure (e.g., because of impure appearance) actually support the case for purity (e.g., impure appearances appear due to the distorted perception of what is pure). Moreover, he argues that since reality does not appear the way it is due to delusion, one must cultivate the path to actualize it, just as the case with emptiness:

> It does not appear as the mode of reality because of arising from pollutants due to delusion; therefore, in order to remove delusion one needs to train—just as the nature of all phenomena is emptiness, even so, one needs to tread the path in order to actualize that.[32]

Mipam, along with other Nyingma exegetes, enlists reason in Mantra to establish what is "extremely hidden" (*shin tu lkog gyur*), what is typically portrayed as the exclusive domain of scriptural authority.[33] Buddhist epistemology relies upon the foundations of principles of validity—inference and direct perception. Yet in the context of Mantra, direct perception no longer presumes *ordinary* direct perception, so what then becomes of inference? Here we are confronted with an epistemological conflict in Mantra's peculiar relationship with reason. In contrast to the certainty induced by reason in the ascertainment of emptiness—a firm conclusion as to the absence of true existence that Mipam emphasizes is necessary in order to understand primordial purity[34]—in the context of the purity of appearance, reason apparently plays a different role. As mentioned earlier, one way to interpret his use of reasoning in this context is to recognize a shift to the role of the subject, in which the role that the subject plays (as an integral part in the equation) is now brought into focus. In any case, it is important to recognize that reason in the context of Mantra, while still useful, is not enough for complete understanding.

Despite his use of inference in the context of Mantra, Mipam explicitly affirms that reason alone is not sufficient for understanding the divine nature of appearances. He says that the view that all phenomena are primordially divine cannot be realized without relying upon scripture and quintessential instructions. He states this in his *Discourse on the Eight Commands:*

> Concerning how to establish the proclamation within scriptures of Secret Mantra that "all phenomena are primordially divine"; it is to be established by scripture, reasoning, and quintessential instruction . . . without scripture and quintessential instruction, one cannot ascertain Secret Mantra.[35]

Furthermore, he says that conviction in the ultimate is necessary to have the view that the relative is divine:

> Without the conviction in the ultimate,
> Then merely meditating on the relative as divine
> Is just an aspiration; it is not the view.[36]

The conviction that the relative is divine comes through an understanding of ultimate reality:

> The belief that the relative is divine
> Comes through the realization of the ultimate abiding reality;
> Otherwise, through abiding in the deluded mode of appearance
> How would [the relative] be established as divine?[37]

Furthermore, he argues that even though the claim that reality necessarily appears as *only* divine appearance cannot be established, it cannot be invalidated either through analysis into reality:

> Regarding this, although one cannot singlely establish that
> "The expanse of consummate equality
> Appears as only divine appearance";
> Due to the expanse, which is naturally pure from the beginning,
> And the appearing aspect, which is the wisdom body, being neither conjoined nor separable,
> One can neither invalidate the appearing aspect—primordially pure as divine—
> Through analysis into the abiding reality.[38]

He concludes that it is his tradition of the Nyingma alone that establishes the nature of appearances to be divine in this way through valid cognition:

> Therefore, establishing the nature of all appearances as divine
> Through this manner of valid cognition
> Is exclusively our tradition of the early translations—
> The lion's roar that is the elegant discourse
> Of the omniscient scholar, Rongzom.[39]

He states that only his Nyingma tradition uses this manner of valid cognition to establish appearances as divine, which he attributes to the works of Rongzom. Along with Rongzom, Longchenpa is the other Tibetan figure with whom Mipam mainly aligns his Nyingma tradition.[40] We will briefly turn again to Longchenpa to introduce Mipam's depiction of Buddha-nature in Mantra.

Buddha-Nature and a Difference Between Sūtra and Mantra

In the Nyingma tradition, the interpretation of Buddha-nature is a primary means by which the Resultant Vehicle of Mantra is distinguished from the Causal Vehicle of Sūtra. In particular, the *immanence* of Buddha-nature in Mantra distinguishes it from Buddha-nature as it is represented in Sūtra. Longchenpa states that the "Causal Vehicle" is so called because of accepting temporal causality (*rgyu 'bras snga phyi*). In the Causal Vehicle, Buddha-nature is seen as a seed that develops into Buddha. In Mantra, on the other hand, the essential nature exists as spontaneously present in all beings:

> It is called the "Causal Vehicle" because of asserting temporal causality—due to accepting that the basic element, the Buddha-nature, is merely a seed that is further developed through the conditions of the two accumulations, by which one attains Buddhahood. [In contrast,] that essential nature of Mantra exists in all sentient beings—inherently and spontaneously present—complete with vast qualities.[41]

Mipam comments on Longchenpa's text as follows:

> In the Causal Vehicle, temporal causality is asserted because of accepting the existence of Buddha-nature as a seed that is further developed through the conditions of the two accumulations, by which after a long time one accomplishes the fruition of Buddhahood; the Vajrayāna . . . professes the philosophy (*grub mtha'*) of the indivisible cause and fruition.[42]

I will not go into the details here on the differences between the paths of Sūtra and Mantra,[43] but it is important for our discussion of Buddha-nature to address this distinction because the status of Buddha-nature is a central part of the way that Mipam shows the superiority of Mantra. Mipam expresses a distinction between Sūtra and Mantra as follows in his *Trilogy of Innate Mind:*

> Since most Middle Way meditations have a strong adherence to the emptiness that is a freedom from constructs, they are like what is said in the *Kālacakra*, "that which is free from the immutable. . . ." Here [in Mantra], awareness (*rig pa*) itself is the consummate great bliss because of being awareness-wisdom—the ultimate immutable bliss—which transcends the eight collections [of consciousness] that are the bases of designation of mind (*blo*), awareness (*rig*), and consciousness (*shes*). Therefore, the path of Mantra is superior to Sūtra.[44]

He states that most Middle Way meditations adhere to emptiness as a freedom from constructs, whereas in the path of Mantra, awareness plays a more fundamental role. Emptiness concerns the quality of objects, as well as the cognitions of the subject; however, awareness specifically concerns subjective cognitions:

> If it is asked, "Is there a difference in the views of Sūtra and Mantra, or not?" Although there is no difference in the mere ascertainment of the object of evaluation—which is the expanse of phenomena free from constructs—there is a difference in subjectivity (*yul can*), which is the manner of perceiving the expanse of phenomena. Since the view is posited from the side of the subject, there is a great difference [in view]. Regarding this, if the object ascertained by the view—the thusness expanse of phenomena—were not the same, then it would [absurdly] follow that: (1) there would be different types of thusness(es) of phenomena, (2) Sūtra's Path of Seeing would not perceive thusness, and (3) reasoning would have to establish a construct to be eliminated in addition to the constructs of the four extremes. Consequently, all scholars and accomplished adepts are in accord in accepting the single essential point that Sūtra's and Mantra's Path of Seeing directly perceives suchness.[45]

He states that Mantra is not distinct concerning the object, the expanse of phenomena;[46] it is the quality of the *subject* that differentiates the respective views of Sūtra and Mantra. Mantra is distinguished by the role ascribed to subjectivity, where reality is not described in the abstract, but as something in which the subject is integrally a part of, and participates in. With this turn to the subject, a new discourse also emerges, the discourse of tantra, where "bliss" characterizes the subject. Mipam states that "bliss" is synonymous with "appearance," "clarity," and "awareness":

From only the aspect of being free from constructs
The two are said to not be distinct;
In order to avert adherence to emptiness
Great bliss is taught in Mantra.
The nondual expanse of empty bliss
Is experienced through a manner
That is free from subject and object.
"Appearance" (*snang ba*), "clarity" (*gsal ba*), and "awareness" (*rig pa*)
Are the synonyms for this "bliss" (*bde ba*).[47]

Here he affirms that Mantra is distinguished by means of the subjective manner of experiencing nonduality. As such, Mantra involves a new ascription of subjectivity. This wisdom, as the optimized subjectivity that is discovered within, is the unique subject matter of Mantra.

Moreover, not only is appearance indivisible from emptiness, as he points out in his interpretation of emptiness in Sūtra, but here in his explanations of Mantra, awareness is also inseparable from emptiness. He says that if there is an awareness that is separate from emptiness, then that is not suitable as suchness; and likewise, if there is an emptiness that is distinct from awareness, then that is not suitable as suchness:

> In the authentic abiding reality, if there is bliss, clarity, or awareness that is separate from emptiness, then that is counted as an entity; it is a phenomenon, but is not suitable as suchness and is not beyond the domain of consciousness. If there is an emptiness that is distinct from bliss, clarity, or awareness, then it is counted as a nonentity; it also is a phenomenon, but is not suitable as suchness and is not beyond the aspect of the absence of mind.[48]

In this way, Mipam portrays suchness as the unity of emptiness and awareness. He affirms again that this is beyond the domain of consciousness and is beyond the mere aspect of the nonexistence of mind. Here we can see a parallel between the way he treats suchness as the unity of *appearance* and emptiness in the context of Sūtra and suchness as the unity of *awareness* and emptiness in Mantra. Appearance and awareness both share the quality of *clarity*.

Elaborating on Mipam's interpretation, Bötrül affirms a difference between the luminous clarity (*'od gsal*) taught in the Causal Vehicle of Sūtra and the Resultant Vehicle of Mantra by stating that Mantra has the distinctions of indicating luminous clarity: (1) clearly (*gsal ba*), (2) extensively (*rgyas*), and (3) completely (*rdzogs*).[49] He states:

> Such distinctions are not present in the Causal Vehicle because [luminous clarity] is not taught other than: (1) as a mere illustration by means of a metaphor, (2) as a mere brief summary of the possession of Buddha-nature, and (3) as a mere luminous clarity that is the suchness of mind.[50]

Although addressed in the middle and last wheels of sūtra, luminous clarity is not as fully developed as it is in Mantra. While the subject matter of Sūtra and Mantra is shared, we can see how the language used shifts from "emptiness" in the middle wheel of sūtra, to "Buddha-nature" in the last wheel of sūtra, to "luminous clarity" in the tantras. Similar to the affirmations of Buddha-nature in the last wheel, an affirmed *presence* of luminous clarity is the emphasis of Mantra. Bötrül states:

> In short, the four philosophies of the Causal Vehicle
> Have the profound distinction of the manner of completing the
> absence of self;
> The four tantra sets of Secret Mantra
> Have the profound distinction of the view of spontaneous
> presence.[51]

In the philosophies within the Causal Vehicle, in which the Middle Way is supreme, the absence of the self is emphasized—the emphasis is on emptiness, or the quality of *transcendence*. In the tantras of Secret Mantra, in which the Great Perfection is supreme, the emphasis is (also) on the view of spontaneous presence—an *immanent* presence.

We can see how the uncategorized emptiness that is emphasized in Prāsaṅgika-Madhyamaka is the culmination of ineffable reality—the top of a philosophical hierarchy of views based on a progression of the increasingly transcendent. In Mantra, however, we can see how the hierarchy of views shifts: it is not a progression toward an increasingly *transcendent* reality, but is a progression toward an increasingly *immanent* presence of the divine—in the nature of (objective) pure appearances and (subjective) wisdom. From the outer-tantras to the inner-tantras, and within the inner-tantras—from Mahāyoga to Atiyoga—the presence of the divine, as pure appearance and wisdom, is increasingly immanent. In this light, the distinction between the Causal and Resultant Vehicles can be seen in a shift from the transcendence of emptiness to the immanence of the divine. These two modalities of truth—transcendent emptiness and immanent presence—are integrated within Mipam's exegesis of Buddha-nature and the Great Perfection.

Furthermore, Mipam states that although the middle wheel of sūtra teaches the ascertainment of a mere unity of appearance and emptiness, it does not affirm the presence of self-existing luminous clarity—the exalted body and wisdom—that is not produced by the causes of karma and afflictive emotions:

> Also in sūtra, in the middle wheel all phenomena are ascertained as a mere unity of the emptiness that is a lack of intrinsic nature and interdependently-arising appearance. However, the presence of the exalted body and wisdom—the self-appearance (*rang snang*) of self-existing luminous clarity which is not produced by the causes of karma and afflictive emotions—is not taught. Therefore, [in the middle wheel] the exalted body and wisdom must be accomplished anew by a cause; the accumulations of great compassion are asserted because the sole realization of emptiness, or suchness, cannot [accomplish] that.[52]

In this way, he shows that the middle wheel affirms the development of the exalted body and wisdom through the causes of the accumulations of the merit of great compassion. However, the presence of the exalted body and wisdom—as the self-existing luminous clarity, primordially present and not produced by causes—is not taught in the middle wheel.

The last wheel indicates the suchness of mind as primordially inseparable from the exalted body and wisdom; therefore, all living beings are potential Buddhas because they are pervaded by Buddha-nature, the heritage of the Mahāyāna:

> In the last wheel, since the suchness of mind, which is the expanse of phenomena, is itself taught to be primordially inseparable from the appearance of the exalted body and wisdom, all sentient beings are pervaded by Buddha-nature—the heritage of the Mahāyāna; hence, they are potential Buddhas. However, it is taught in dependence upon the cause of accomplishing the two accumulations—the cause which illuminates that.[53]

He explains that the last wheel teaches that the appearance of the Buddha, which is primordially inseparable from the suchness of mind, is dependent on the cause of accomplishing the two accumulations. In Mantra, however, there is no newly produced Buddha to be sought after that is accomplished by a cause:

> In Mantra, the maṇḍala of the primordially pure Buddha as such naturally abides as spontaneously present; in merely realizing this through the method taken as the path, the Buddha as such is made manifest—without needing to search some other place for a Buddha that is newly established through a cause.[54]

In Mantra, the Buddha is not newly produced, nor is in some other place; the Buddha is *always already* primordially present. Moreover, Mipam portrays the qualities of Buddha-nature present from beginning as the manner of "joining Sūtra and Mantra" (*mdo sngags mtshams sbyor*). In this way, he emphasizes the continuity between Sūtra and Mantra. However, he also reveals an important difference between Buddha-nature in Sūtra and in Mantra:

> In the path of Sūtra, the qualities of Buddha-nature are said to be "present from the beginning," which has been called the manner of joining Sūtra and Mantra. However, regarding that presence, it says [in sūtras] that based upon the teachings of the Buddha, it is to be known through faith, and also by knowing it as such, one abandons the five faults; yet the intrinsic nature of Buddha-nature is not explicitly taught to be a path that is ascertained right now.[55]

Buddha-nature, *explicitly* shown as the present reality to be ascertained right now, is not taught in sūtras, but is fully disclosed in Mantra. In the path of Sūtra, Buddha-nature is taught as what is known by faith,[56] and is also explained in order to remove five faults.[57] Longchenpa explains the five faults as follows:

> If the essential nature of awakening is not seen to exist within oneself, then these faults will arise: (1) one may become discouraged, [thinking] "someone like myself cannot become a Buddha," and not generate the mind of awakening; (2) even if [the awakened mind is]

generated, one may disparage others, [thinking] "I am a bodhisattva, others are ordinary," which will hinder the attainment of the higher path; (3) through holding onto the extreme of emptiness, one will not engage in the ultimate nature of the expanse, and thus not apprehend the authentic; (4) due to falling to an extreme of eternalism or annihilationism, one will denigrate the authentic doctrine; (5) by not seeing other sentient beings and oneself as equal, one will incur the faults of holding onto self and other. . . . [On the other hand,] by knowing that such a basic element exists as spontaneously present in oneself and others: (1) one will be joyous, knowing that the accomplishment of liberating one's mind is without difficulty; (2) with respect for all sentient beings as Buddhas—in addition to not inflicting harm or hurting them—one will benefit them; and one will be able to accomplish the benefit of others through developing: (3) supreme knowledge that realizes the ultimate expanse, (4) wisdom that sees the abiding reality, and (5) the maṇḍala of limitless love . . . this presentation of heritage should be held as only the definitive meaning, not viewed as a provisional meaning.[58]

In this way, Longchenpa explains how the teaching of the basic element removes the five faults. He shows how such a teaching has great purpose and affirms that it is the definitive meaning. Mipam explains that the five faults arise because of not hearing about Buddha-nature. He also says that Buddha-nature is the essential point in the Vajrayāna that the nature of mind (*sems nyid*) is primordially Buddha:

> The five faults arise because of not hearing about Buddha-nature existing in all sentient beings; this is the essential point of establishing one consummate vehicle, and this is also the essential point in the Vajrayāna that the nature of mind is primordially Buddha.[59]

Mipam affirms Buddha-nature as a central topic in Buddhism, in Sūtra and Mantra. He states that: "'The luminous clarity of the expanse of phenomena,' 'self-existing wisdom', 'the luminous clarity of innate mind', and 'Buddha-nature' are the same meaning; this is the heritage of Buddha."[60] Moreover, he says: "'Innate mind', 'Buddha-nature', 'mind of luminous clarity', 'ultimate mind of awakening', 'self-existing wisdom', and 'the expanse of phenomena' are distinct contradistinctions by name; but they are not different in meaning."[61] In this way, the ground, or Buddha-nature, is a common subject matter of Sūtra and Mantra. Furthermore, he states:

> From the aspect of emptiness, that ground itself is indicated by such names as "the expanse of phenomena," "the authentic limit," and "thusness" in scriptures such as the Victorious One's Mother [Perfection of Wisdom Sūtras]. From the aspect of being with the appearance of the exalted body and wisdom, it is indicated by the word "Buddha-nature" in scriptures such as the sūtras that teach the [Buddha-]nature. Here in the definitive meaning Mantrayāna, it is called "the maṇḍala of the primordial ground, the identity of the great purity and equality that is the indivisible truth of empty appearance."[62]

The common ground of Sūtra and Mantra is the indivisibility of Buddha-nature as appearance and emptiness, purity and equality, and spontaneous presence and primordial purity. We can see how all Buddhist doctrines indicate this reality, or show the way to realize it, explicitly or implicitly, directly or indirectly, from different perspectives and in different contexts. Thus, statements of emptiness in the middle wheel and statements of the primordial endowment of the qualities of a Buddha in the last wheel are not only without contradiction, but are simply two descriptions of one ground. Furthermore, he states:

> If the genuine meaning of non-arising that is taught in sūtras is understood, then there is no other unified emptiness endowed with all supreme aspects other than that; therefore, no matter what high and profound words are designated, it is just that meaning, brothers. This is important.[63]

In this way, Mipam shows that the true meaning of non-arising that is taught in sūtras is none other than the meaning of emptiness endowed with all supreme aspects—the fully qualified ultimate truth.

Although the immanence of the Buddha is indicated within sūtras, and particularly in the last wheel doctrines, Buddha-nature as such is most explicitly affirmed in the tantras. Buddha-nature is most fully articulated in Mipam's explanations of the view of Vajrayāna, and in particular the Great Perfection, the pinnacle of the Buddhist vehicles in his Nyingma tradition.

Conclusion

We saw how Mipam uses reason to affirm the presence of Buddha-nature and to support his tradition's claims that all appearances are divine by nature. The reasonings he employs are similar to those that he uses to establish the emptiness of phenomena. Indeed, emptiness has the same meaning as Buddha-nature, but Buddha-nature evokes more of the quality of *presence.* Unlike emptiness' quality of absence, however, the qualities of Buddha-nature's presence are not known through ordinary reason; another approach to truth is necessary: the reflexive awareness of meditative experience. Until directly known as such, Buddha-nature is to be acknowledged through an appeal to scriptural testimony and the experience of Sublime Ones. Such knowledge is not accessible to reason alone, but is not necessarily incompatible with reason either.

We can understand Mipam's use of reasoning to establish the existence of Buddha-nature by appreciating the integral role of the subject. Subjectivity comes to play a particularly important role in Mantra, as Mantra is distinguished from Sūtra by means of the subject. In Mantra, where the subject is wisdom and appearances are divine, we find the culmination of Mipam's interpretation of Buddha-nature. The full disclosure of Buddha-nature is found in Mantra, and the Great Perfection in particular, where Buddha-nature is the immanent Buddha, the present reality to be ascertained right now.

Conclusion

In this book, I have tried to shed some light on the central place of Buddha-nature across Mipam's interpretation of a range of Buddhist doctrines. We have seen how Mipam's depiction of Buddha-nature, as a unified truth, is reflected in his depiction of emptiness. Indeed, Buddha-nature is indivisible with emptiness and, as such, Buddha-nature embodies both the empty and appearing aspects of reality. It is the unity of emptiness and appearance, and the primordial purity and spontaneous presence in the Great Perfection in particular, that he puts forward as most fully representing the nature of reality.

We saw how Mipam delineates two models of the two truths. In his two-truth model of appearance/emptiness, only emptiness is the ultimate and any appearance is necessarily a relative truth. However, emptiness also appears. As such, there is another meaning of emptiness other than solely appearances' lack of true existence; it is the unity of appearance and emptiness. This unity is expressed by Buddha-nature and is embodied in authentic experience.

The appearance/emptiness model of the two truths is reflected in the explicit teachings of emptiness in the middle wheel of doctrine, and accords with Candrakīrti's *Madhyamakāvatāra*. The other two-truth model of authentic/inauthentic experience delineates not only emptiness as the ultimate truth, but also affirms wisdom and appearances from the perspective of wisdom as ultimate. This latter two-truth model accords with the last wheel of doctrine and the *Uttaratantra*, in which Buddha-nature is explicitly taught. The synthesis of the explicit teachings of the *Madhyamakāvatāra* and the *Uttaratantra* is an important part of Mipam's integration of the middle and last wheels of doctrine.

The ultimate within the two truths distinguished as authentic/inauthentic experience is a *presence*, whereas the ultimate within the two truths distinguished as appearance and emptiness is an *absence*. It is the resonance found *in and between* both models, the unity of the two truths, that we find Buddha-nature within a dialectic of presence and absence. The ultimate as only authentic experience has a tendency to be reified as a truly established presence, as the ultimate status of the nondual cognition in the tradition of Mind-Only. Also, emptiness in the appearance/emptiness model of two truths has the danger of becoming reified as an absence, as solely an absence of true existence. It is within the dialectical interplay of both two-truth models that Mipam represents Buddha-nature.

The two truths as authentic/inauthentic experience reflect a Yogācāra delineation of nondual wisdom as ultimate, as opposed to consciousness. This distinction between consciousness and wisdom is an important distinction in the Great Perfection. Mipam also uses the distinction between consciousness and wisdom to demonstrate the difference between Svātantrika and Prāsaṅgika. He shows that Svātantrika discourse emphasizes the categorized ultimate, the ultimate as known by consciousness. In contrast, he depicts the discourse of Prāsaṅgika as emphasizing the uncategorized ultimate, the domain of wisdom. In this way, he makes a distinction between Prāsaṅgika and Svātantrika that reflects the tradition of the Great Perfection.

By affirming wisdom as ultimate, the tradition of Great Perfection might be seen as resembling traditions that affirm some sort of metaphysical realism, as in absolutist traditions and claims of other-emptiness (that do not include an empty essence as a quality of all phenomena). However, Mipam distances himself from naïve metaphysical assertions by emphasizing the *transcendent* quality of ultimate reality. He consistently affirms that the ultimate truth is not a referent of language and thought. He argues that conventionally the ultimate truth can be said to exist, but ultimately there is no difference between the two truths. In this way, he argues that the two truths are not actually distinct. He emphasizes this unity of the two truths in contrast to (1) the claim that the ultimate truth is only the empty quality of phenomena or (2) the claim that the ultimate truth is separate from relative phenomena, as if lying somewhere else behind phenomena.

Mipam consistently criticizes linguistic and conceptual formulations of ultimate reality. An important part of his critical procedure may be called "skepticism."[1] Through reasoning into ultimate reality, he argues that temporality is an illusion; he portrays temporal and spatial distinctions as ultimately superimpositions that are neither intrinsic to reality, nor inevitable in an understanding of reality. Thus, he parts ways with the temporality of understanding and the universality of linguistic experience.[2]

Although the intimate relationship between language and thought, and the endemic place of conceptual experience, is important for Mipam, he uses the dialectical component of philosophy to critique conceptual experience. Thereby, he reaches the conclusion that temporal and linguistic experience is the fabric of reification and delusion (the so-called veil of māyā), which effectively obscures the unified ineffable truth. Such a conclusion is what we may call an *optimistic* response to skepticism. Rather than a cynical skepticism or an uncritical, naïve optimism, it may be called a "skeptical optimism."

Mipam offers an interpretation that he claims is founded upon reason. He consistently shows that the view of Buddhism is supported by, and arrived at, via a reasoned analysis. The product of such reason, he argues, is not necessarily accessible to everyone. He makes a case that even though certain Buddhist doctrines may appear to contradict reason, on another level, they accord with the truth. Reading his texts in light of a modern reason-faith dichotomy, we can see how he is involved in a scholastic project of reconciling reason and Buddhist dogma; he supports the assumptions of doctrine, the Buddhist *mythos*, with a reasoned procedure. Mipam's account of knowledge, however, does not partake in the modern assumptions of autonomous reason and objective truth.

A modern ideal of knowledge—based on the notion of objectively derived truth from explanatory procedures such as science—inevitably entails a process of *distanciation* that abstracts meaning from its necessary context as a unique moment of human experience. Such a process undeniably allows for technological progress and the refinement of descriptive explanations. However, left to itself, as in the case of the *object* of a reductively scientific "modern" consciousness, such models of truth falsely delimit the extent of semantic possibility to something that necessarily remains apart from a subjective mode of being (including the potential relationship with the sacred) in an event of understanding. Without the component of understanding, explanatory procedures by themselves ignore the semantic grounding in subjectivity, and restrict the potential for meaning to the limits of the model.[3] Thus, the potential for evoking an enriched understanding of oneself and one's relationships with others and the world are barren in an enterprise that does not take into account the concrete act of participation—the sine qua non for the possibility of meaning.

In Mipam's case, he represents the path of Buddhism through a process of reasoned analysis, using reason as a tool, but not completely subsuming understanding within that conceptual framework—as in the case of a meditative equipoise that is induced by analysis, yet only preceded by such analysis. Through such means he affirms a process of *subjectively* verified truth, but unlike a scientific method, not necessarily communally verifiable (or falsifiable). In this way, he does not reject language or reason; he portrays them as instrumental to the process of bringing forth true understanding. However, true understanding of Buddha-nature must be (subjectively) discovered in meditative experience. Such truth is most clearly evoked in Mantra, and the Great Perfection in particular. It is here that we find Buddha-nature, the unity of the two truths, most fully articulated—in Mantra—where the perceived appearances are divine and the subjective cognition is wisdom.

Mipam's arguments for Buddha-nature reflect his arguments for the pure and divine nature of reality. In contrast to his treatment of emptiness, he affirms that the divine nature of reality cannot be definitively ascertained by reason, nor can it be definitively proven false. Thus, his claims of a divine reality are explicitly not founded on ordinary reason; they are to be subjectively verified in meditation, or, until then, based on the testimony of authoritative persons and scriptures. It is this appeal that we as modern readers might feel compelled to characterize as a move from (ordinary) reason to faith, and from philosophy to religion. Such a domain of meaningful reality can also be called the indemonstrable realm of the mystical.

An important part of Mipam's affirmations of a meaningful (mystical) presence of the divine is his conventional valid cognition of pure vision. Through a system of four valid cognitions—two concerning the categorized/uncategorized ultimates and two based on confined perception/pure vision—he is able to maintain a critical, intersubjective system of truth that is situated within a mystical, subjective experience of the Great Perfection. Moreover, his truth claims are unique in that his claims are not disembodied, but are grounded within a particular perspective.

Thus, his representation of the authentic experience of truth integrates the presence of subjectivity within an explanatory system of valid cognition. While the structure of valid cognition is abstract and disembodied, it is a descriptive tool that serves as a guide to the discovery of truth that is intimately grounded in subjectivity. Thereby, this vision of truth is a monistic unity but it is not monological; the perspectival system of the fourfold valid cognitions accommodates a dialectical component to an inquiry into the nature of mystical experience. Such a dialectical approach to Buddha-nature and the Great Perfection is a distinctive feature of his Nyingma view.

Translations of Primary Texts

APPENDIX ONE

Lion's Roar: Exposition of Buddha-Nature

In his *Lion's Roar: Exposition of Buddha-Nature*, Mipam presents a concise and lucid discourse on Buddha-nature. The Tibetan text was completed in 1891, after additional supplements were added to an earlier version.[1] The Tibetan editions of the text I consulted were printed from the same woodblocks—the Degé edition of Mipam's Collected Works.

[564] *namo gurave*—Homage to the guru!

> The path of reasoning that ascertains the primordially stainless
> suchness of mind
> As the identity of the definitive meaning hero Mañjuśrī
> Is a continuous onslaught of sharp swords
> That cuts the net of thoroughly afflicted existence.

Concerning this, here is the essence (*snying po*) of the speech of the Victorious Ones of the three times, the foundational viewpoint, and the single essential point of all the doctrines of Sūtra and Mantra—only this all-pervasive Buddha-nature. Since this is extremely profound, it is said to be difficult to realize as it is, like a form in the night, even for the great lords on the ten [bodhisattva] grounds, needless to mention ordinary beings! Moreover, when speaking, the Sugata teacher sometimes elucidated the essence (*ngo bo*) of the

Buddha-nature by means of teaching emptiness, and at other times elucidated the nature (*rang bzhin*) of the Buddha-nature through the aspect of teaching the [Buddha's] qualities of the powers and so forth as a primordial endowment. [565] These two need to be integrated without contradiction. However, due to the influence of not having found conviction in the extremely profound of profound essential points—the indivisibility of the two truths—some people view the Buddha-nature as a permanent phenomenon that is not essentially empty, while others, holding onto a mere void, remain in the denigrating position of a view of annihilation that cannot posit the primordial endowment of the inseparable qualities of wisdom. Various chatters of refutation and assertion, like a rumbling ocean, are proclaimed in hopes of establishing each respective claim. However, fortunate ones who are embraced by the quintessential instructions of a teacher—within a state of conviction in the meaning of the noncontradictory unity of the empty expanse and the luminous clarity of wisdom, as if their hearts were satisfied by an excellent nectar extract—abide in the pacification of partial fixation on the extremes of either appearance or emptiness, and speak as follows. [566]

Regarding this in general, the valid measure (*tshad ma*) of the Tathāgata's Word is the authentic, infallible scriptures. However, to ascertain their infallibility, the scriptures in general are determined to be authentic by means of the purity through the three analyses.[2] In particular, concerning the literal meaning indicated by a scripture, it should be regarded as the definitive meaning through (1) a lack of invalidation by reason* and (2) the presence of an authentic means of establishment. Having thrown out reason, the means of [assessing] the purity of a scripture, it is not appropriate to simply believe according to whatever is said because it is undeniable that generally there are authentic scriptures and bogus scriptures, and among authentic scriptures as well there is the distinction between definitive and provisional [meanings]. Therefore, irreversible conviction arises in those ordinary beings who, having cut through misconceptions by study and contemplation, are able to determine the topics to be engaged by means of the three valid cognitions. Conversely, if one is not able to determine by one's own valid cognition nor able to establish for another dissenter's perspective, one is like a person, for whom a ghost is imperceptible, claiming, "There is a ghost in front of here!" Words like these have no ability to generate conviction in oneself or others.

Therefore, discourse in accordance with the path of authentic reasoning is the manner of learned people. If established by reason, dissenters' tongues

* *rig* read *rigs [566.2]*.

will naturally be curtailed and irreversible joy will arise in those maintaining one's own position. [567] In a path that is not established by reason, despite whatever way it may be decorated by many words,* heaps of faults will upsurge like water from a geyser.

Here, adherence to partiality is discarded through engaging, undisturbed by conceptuality, in the tradition of the Victorious Ones together with their lineage of great offspring [bodhisattvas]. When the manners of demonstrating the presentation of Buddha-nature and the authentic reasonings to establish them are assessed with an honest mind,† the assertions that Buddha-nature (1) is permanent,‡ a truly established [phenomenon] that is essentially non-empty or (2) is a void emptiness lacking qualities, are both seen to lack a means of establishment and have a means of invalidation. Also, the existence of the [Buddha-]nature as the basic element of beings—an empty essence with a nature primordially endowed with qualities—is seen to lack a means of invalidation and have a means of establishment.

Regarding this, someone may first ask: "What is the means of establishing the existence of the basic element of Buddha-nature in the continua of beings?" In the *Mahāyāna-Uttaratantra* [I.28]:

> Because the body of the perfect Buddha is radiant,
> Because thusness (*de bzhin nyid*) is indivisible,
> Because of possessing heritage;
> Therefore, all beings always possess the essential nature of Buddha.

There is a twofold presentation ascertaining the meaning of this statement by means of reason: (1) stating other traditions and (2) presenting our authentic tradition.

Stating Other Traditions

The early generations (*snga rabs pa*) in Tibet explained "The body of a perfect Buddha is radiant" as merely the Wisdom Truth Body encompassing all objects, "thusness" as being similar in type as a mere void, and "possessing heritage" as merely the potential to become a Buddha. They spoke few

---

* *sma ba* read *smra ba [567.1].*

† *glus* read *blo [567.2].*

‡ *brtag* read *rtag [567.3].*

words, failing to evoke the crucial point from the standpoint of the essential nature in the *Uttaratantra* scripture.

[568] Regarding this, the genuine heritage is not established by merely the Truth Body encompassing [all] objects because the Buddha's wisdom—which perceives that which is comprised by others' continua—simply encompassing all objects is present in all entities. However, merely by this presence there is no reason for all this to become Buddha. As for the Truth Body of one's own continuum, due to not being manifest now, the evidence is doubtful.

Also, the mere categorized emptiness does not at all have the meaning of heritage. This follows because from the perspective of this thinking, one asserts that this heritage is the potential to newly produce [a Buddha] when conjoined with the conditions of the path despite now having no qualities of Buddha whatsoever—like a seed that is transported to a sprout.* Yet such a quality [of potential transformation] is not at all feasible in the contradistinctive aspect of a non-implicative negation, which is an emptiness of true existence—an unconditioned phenomenon that lacks the ability to perform a function. It is like the way that the aspect of a conditioned seed may conventionally transform into a sprout, but the aspect of a seed's lack of true existence can never transform into a sprout.

Moreover, [the assertion that] the essential point of the lack of true existence establishes the potential to be a Buddha is also nonsense. Although it is true that if the mind were truly established, there would simply be no potential to be a Buddha, even so, in lacking true establishment, [the potential of] being Buddha is undetermined because even though all phenomena—earth, rocks,† etc.—also lack true existence, who is able to establish that everything that lacks true existence is a potential Buddha? Also, asserting as heritage only the potential to remove obscurations by observing a lack of true existence is nonsense because by only observing emptiness—without reason for cognitive obscurations (*shes sgrib*) to be relinquished—again it is necessary to become decorated with limitless accumulations according to your position.‡ Calling such a non-implicative negation [569] "Buddha-nature" is a senseless assertion because it becomes a heritage shared with Auditors and Self-Realized Ones. Through this, the potential to be a Buddha is not established

* *myur gu* read *myu gur [568.2]*.

† *rgo* read *rdo [568.5]*.

‡ *dog* read *'dod [568.6]*.

because: (1) there is no ability in merely this to establish any legitimacy for the occurrence of omniscient wisdom after abandoning cognitive obscurations, and (2) since there is no cognitive quality within the essence of a non-implicative negation, it is impossible for that to know anything whatsoever even at the time of being Buddha.

Therefore, in considering this manner of the transforming conditioned heritage (*gnas 'gyur 'dus byas kyi rigs*), rather than asserting a non-implicative negation as the heritage, it is better to assert a seed of wisdom, love, and powers in the mental-continua of all beings from beginningless time—even wild beasts, ogres, etc. possess such [qualities] of love for their children and recognition of benefit and harm—such that when further developed, through conjoined with the path and freed from obstacles, it is merely that which is the potential to become a Buddha endowed with limitless knowledge, love, and powers. This follows because once the causality of production is necessitated, to disregard the momentary entity which is a productive cause and assert an unproductive, unconditioned nonentity as the cause is indeed astonishing!

Some people think as follows: "Everything lacking true existence is not the heritage, but only the mind's lack of a true intrinsic existence is reasonable to be the heritage."

Even if it were the mind's lack of true existence, it would have no ability for the slightest activity of production—since the quality-bearers (*chos can*), the instants of mind, are potential producers of later [instances], the unconditioned heritage is seemingly not need by you, so get rid of it!

If one thinks, [570] "[Heritage] is not posited having distinguished the two truths because heritage is asserted as the abiding reality that is the indivisibility of (1) the quality-bearer, which is the clarity of mind, and (2) suchness, which is emptiness."

If this also is asserted as the unconditioned, immutable wisdom, which is wisdom (*ye shes*) as distinguished from consciousness (*rnam shes*), then since this is established as such by scripture and reasoning, then it certainly is [heritage]. However, making the claim that the quality-bearer that is a unity with emptiness is the aspect of momentary consciousness, then thinking, "this progressively transports to a Buddha" is senseless because it would [absurdly] follow that the heritage would have both a conditioned and an unconditioned aspect. That being the case, the unconditioned, which has no use or ability, would become the nominal heritage, and the conditioned would become the genuine heritage capable of producing effects. Consequently, the viewpoint of all of the Mahāyāna Sūtras—which assert that the unconditioned naturally abiding heritage (*rang bzhin gnas rigs*) is the expanse of phenomena—would be relinquished.*

Therefore, by claiming a heritage posited in terms of a produced effect and a producing cause that the mind is not able to relinquish, although one may speak of the pure expanse of phenomena as the naturally abiding heritage, it is nothing but merely the blatant evidence of the incompatibility† of one's words and beliefs. Hence, as soon as the immutable expanse of phenomena is asserted as the heritage of the Buddha, one should first identify that which is the basis of the designation of "expanse of phenomena"—the uncategorized ultimate that is the great unity of the two truths, the meaning of the thoroughly non-abiding Middle Way itself. Misidentifying this, to assert [the expanse of phenomena] as merely the categorized ultimate, like seeing a group of monkeys in a forest and mistaking them for the gods of the Heaven of the Thirty-Three, [571] what is not the expanse of phenomena is apprehended‡ as the expanse of phenomena. Consequently, all presentations are established as a path of Mahāyāna artifice, such as:

- the assertion of that [categorized ultimate] as the heritage of the Buddha
- the meditation on the perfection of wisdom through observing just that [categorized ultimate]
- the assertion of that [categorized ultimate] as the cause of the Essential Body (*ngo bo nyid sku*).

This is also taught in this way in [scriptures] such as the Perfection of Wisdom Sūtras.

Therefore, the expanse which is the unity of the two truths, the meaning that is distinct from all the webs of conceptual constructs [and] known by the individual reflexive awareness, is called "the naturally pure expanse of phenomena" and "emptiness"; this is said in all the Mahāyāna Sūtras and commentaries on the viewpoint to be the genuine heritage of the Buddha as well as the Essential Body endowed with the twofold purity. Hence, this naturally abiding heritage is not suitable to be asserted as anything other than unconditioned. Being unconditioned, henceforth the qualities of the

* *stong* read *stor [570.4].*

† *'ga'* read *'gal [570.5].*

‡ *'byung* read *bzung [571.1].*

Truth Body are also not suitable to be asserted as anything other than a freed effect—by its essential nature it is not reasonable for itself to cease and produce another effect. Since it is asserted as such by the great being of the tenth ground, the regent [Maitreya], in the *Uttaratantra,* and is also clearly stated by the glorious protector, the sublime Nāgārjuna, in the *Dharmadhātustotra,* our tradition asserts the unconditioned expanse of phenomena as the heritage following these scriptures. This expanse itself is the abiding reality of all phenomena, its essence is without arising or ceasing, and [572] it abides as the identity of indivisible appearance and emptiness; it does not fall to partiality.

Due to not existing as they appear, conditioned phenomena that appear to arise and cease in this way have never tainted the basic nature of the expanse. Therefore, through this essential point that (1) the primordial purity of the causality of saṃsāra and (2) the uncontaminated appearances, which are the luminous clarity of the spontaneously present nature, are neither conjoined nor separable, the undistorted manner of Buddha-nature should be identified.

Presenting Our Authentic Tradition

The Meaning of the First Verse "Because the body of the perfect Buddha is radiant"

Then for the second part, stating our tradition, the meaning of the first verse ["Because the body of the perfect Buddha is radiant"] in the previous [stanza] is as follows: since the Truth Body, the consummate body of a complete and perfect Buddha, as such with the qualities equal to [the extent of] space, later is made clear, radiant, or manifest from a former continuum of a thoroughly bounded ordinary being; therefore, the statement "presently the Buddha-nature exists in the continua of all sentient beings" is established. The justification of how this is established is twofold: common and extraordinary.

The first* [common justification] is as follows: if there are sentient beings who actualize the Wisdom Truth Body, then the mind necessarily possesses the heritage which is the potential to be a Buddha because it is unreasonable as such without a heritage at all, as said in the *Dharmadhātustotra* [v. 11]:

* *dngos po* read *dang po [572.5].*

> If there is the basic element, then through action
> The pure gold will be seen.
> If there is no basic element, then even action
> Will only generate afflictive emotions.

The second [extraordinary justification] is a demonstration of the justification of that [statement that Buddha-nature presently exists in the continua of sentient beings].

[573] Someone may think, "Although the mind is established as a mere cause which is the potential to be a Buddha, like the example of crops potentially growing on a field, how can you establish the distinctive heritage that is primordially endowed with Buddha's qualities?"

This is also established because the Blessed Ones, the Buddhas, have the wisdom body that is the identity distinguished by the unconditioned; it is established through scriptures and reasoning that they do not have the nature of conditioned, impermanent phenomena. Regarding this, as for scriptures, the *Mahāparinirvāṇasūtra* states:

> O Monk of perfect discipline, it is better to die than to become a non-Buddhist by calling the unconditioned Tathāgata a conditioned Tathāgata.

And,

> Noble child, now see the permanent body of the Tathāgata, the indestructible body, the *vajra*-body, as the Truth Body, not a body of flesh.

Furthermore,

> It is better to die having touched this blazing heap of wood with your tongue everywhere than to utter the words "the Tathāgata is impermanent." Do not heed those words.

Also, merely the aspect of a non-implicative negation is not suitable as nirvāṇa; again from the scripture [*Mahāparinirvāṇasūtra*]:

> "Emptiness, emptiness"—at the time you search, you find nothing at all. The Nirgrantha also have "nothing at all," but liberation is not like that.

And,

> That which is liberation is the basic element which is uncontrived; it is the Tathāgata.

[574] And from the *Vajracchedikā* also:

> Those who see me as form [and]
> Those who hear me as sound
> Have entered the wrong path;
> They do not see me.
> The Buddhas' view of suchness,
> The Guides' Truth Body, [and]
> Suchness are not objects of knowledge;
> Hence, they cannot be known.[3]

As is shown, [the unconditioned wisdom body of the Buddha] is extensively taught in the definitive meaning sūtras.

As for reasoning as well, if the omniscient wisdom itself—the consummate fruition of equal taste, nondual with the primordial expanse of phenomena—were an impermanent entity that is newly formed by causes and conditions, then there would be the faults of [absurd] consequences such as:

- It would not be the self-existing wisdom
- It would not have relinquished the pains of change
- It would have the aspects of again ceasing and again arising
- It would be deceptive due to disintegrating by its own essence
- It would not be the perpetual refuge
  (1) because of ceasing as soon as it arises and
  (2) because there is [only] a limited domain where there is a complete gathering of causes
- It would not be of equal taste in all phenomena
- It would not have transcended all extremes
- It would not have ceased such [events] as taking a birth that is of mental nature
- It would be without independence, being a dependent entity which is conditioned.

Therefore, by asserting in this way, the view of the *vajra*-body as impermanent brings about enormous faults. Hence, having abandoned this inferior path, the nondual wisdom body should be viewed as unconditioned and as the sacred permanence (*rtag pa dam pa*).

[575] Through evaluating by means of merely an awareness based on ordinary confined perception, one may think: "Unconditioned wisdom is impossible because there is no common locus of a cognition and a permanent entity."

This is nonsense because even though partial* cognitions that cognize objects are necessarily impermanent, the wisdom that is the one taste of the knower and known, "the one with the space-*vajra* pervading space" (*mkha' khyab mkha' yi rdo rje can*), is not like that [impermanent cognition]. This is because in the state of unchanging luminous clarity,† which is the self-vibrancy of the unconditioned, all the phenomena of nirvāṇa and saṃsāra are incorporated (*'ub chub*); hence, reasoning that examines the consummate [reality] (*mthar thug dpyod pa'i rig shes*) establishes that there is primordially no arising or ceasing in the essence of that. Therefore, wisdom such as this is "the great unconditioned," which does not abide in either extreme of being conditioned or unconditioned; it is not at all like a mere nonentity. Since entities and nonentities are phenomena and are dependent arisings, or dependent imputations, when authentically analyzed they are hollow, fake, lies, and deceptions; Buddha-nature is the great unconditioned, the suchness of all phenomena that are entities or nonentities, which is authentically nondeceptive. As is said in the *Mūlamadhyamakakārikā* [XV.2]:

> Nature is uncontrived,
> And does not depend on another.

And [XXV.13],

> Entities and nonentities are conditioned;
> Nirvāṇa is unconditioned.

In this way, if the wisdom of the consummate Truth Body is established by scriptures of definitive meaning sūtras and reasoning examining the consummate [reality] to be the nature of the immutable ultimate truth, completely pervading nirvāṇa and saṃsāra, equality, and unconditioned [576]; then the cause, which is able to actualize that at one time, is presently the nature of the

---

* *nye tsho* read *nyi tshe [575.1–575.2].*

† *gsel* read *gsal [575.2].*

Wisdom Truth Body abiding in the manner of suchness without decrease or increase. Although it may or may not be actualized in the mode of appearance free or not free from adventitious defilements, there is not even the slightest qualitative or temporal difference in the mode of reality because it is the intrinsic nature of the immutable unconditioned. In the *Uttaratantra* [I.51]:

> As it was before so it is later—
> The immutable suchness.

And [I.63],

> The luminous clarity that is the nature of mind
> Is immutable like space.
> It is undisturbed by adventitious defilements
> Such as attachments that arise from the imagination of the unreal.

All the phenomena of saṃsāra are changing and unstable. While there appears to be transformations within the state of the suchness of all this, it should be known as was frequently taught that the purity of mind, the Buddha-nature, is without change, like space. In this way, the unconditioned expanse of luminous clarity is naturally pure and untainted by delusion; within the self-vibrancy of the basic nature of the non-deluded, the qualities of fruition, such as the powers, abide without separation—like the sun and light rays. Furthermore, in the *Uttaratantra* [I.155]:

> The basic element is empty of those adventitious [phenomena] that have the character of separability
> But not empty of the unexcelled properties that have the character of inseparability.

[577] All of the faults of saṃsāra arise from the deluded mind which apprehends a personal self or a self of phenomena. Since this deluded mind also is adventitious like clouds in the sky, from the beginning neither mixing nor polluting the luminous clarity of the primordial basic nature, these faults are individually distinguished from the basic element and are suitable to be removed. Therefore, the essence of the basic element is empty of these faults; it is untainted. Without depending on the polluting delusion, it is luminous and clear by its own nature; self-existing wisdom permeates the thusness of all phenomena. It is not empty of that which it is inseparable from, the basic

element of consummate qualities, because in its essence this is the basic nature from which it is inseparable—like the sun and light rays.

In this way, the naturally abiding heritage is established as the unconditioned essence of the Truth Body primordially endowed with qualities. Due to the potential to be a Buddha, the Wisdom Truth Body, without decrease or increase, necessarily resides in the continua of all sentient beings because in training in the path, the potential to be a Buddha is established by the power of fact (*dngos stobs kyis grub*). Also, since the Truth Body at the time of being a Buddha is unconditioned due to the impossibility of being a conditioned phenomenon newly formed by causes and conditions, it is established that "it presently resides as the essence of the Buddha."

Regarding this, some people think, "If it presently resides as the essence of the Buddha, then why does that omniscient wisdom not dispel the obscurations of these sentient beings?" Or, fixating upon the range of meanings of the common vehicle, they think, "Since the Buddha is the effect and sentient beings are the cause, [578] if the effect is present in the cause, then there is invalidation by reason such as the reasoning that eating food would [absurdly entail] the eating of excrement."

For you who have not trained in the meaning of the extremely profound definitive meaning sūtras, having been guided by merely a limited understanding of the common scriptures, it is no wonder* that such qualms have arisen! However, that [what you have said] is not the case because although the suchness that is the luminous and clear wisdom is present in everything without distinction, when this adventitious delusion arises in one's mind, the basis of designation of saṃsāra is only this deluded mind together with its object; due to this delusion, one's suchness is not known as it is. For example, when sleeping, due to the power of solely the mental-consciousness, unrestricted appearances arise such as the body, objects, and eye-consciousness, etc. At that time, although the subject and object are observed and apprehended separately, the mental-consciousness itself is not able to know its own mode of being (*yin lugs*), in which the perceived [object] and the perceiving [subject] are not established as different; even though it is not known, there is nothing other than that mode of being. Likewise, all phenomena abide as emptiness; even so, merely being as such does not entail that everyone realizes this because there is the possibility of delusion—appearances that do not accord with reality.

---

* *khags* read *khag [578.2]*.

Therefore, since* mind and the wisdom of the essential nature are [respectively] phenomenon (*chos can*) and suchness (*chos nyid*), also the Buddha and sentient beings are taught in terms of the mode of reality (*gnas tshul*) and the mode of appearance (*snang tshul*); for this reason, showing invalidation with the reason that the effect is present in the cause is simply not understanding the position. In this way, this reasoning is that the evidence [579] of a clear manifestation of the Truth Body at the time of the fruition establishes that the heritage, primordially endowed with qualities, is present at the time of the cause because there is no temporal causality in the mode of reality; nevertheless, in dependence upon the mode of appearance, it is necessarily posited as cause and effect. Therefore, proving the cause from the effect is called "reasoning of dependency" (*ltos pa'i rigs pa*).

The Meaning of the Second Verse "Because thusness is indivisible"

The meaning of the second [verse], "Because thusness is indivisible," is as follows: since all phenomena of saṃsāra and nirvāṇa are of one taste—indivisible within the great primordial luminous clarity of the emptiness that is the mode of reality—Buddhas and sentient beings also are ultimately indivisible due to the equality of existence and peace. Therefore, although appearing as emanated sentient beings due to adventitious delusion, it is established by the reasoning of the nature of things (*chos nyid kyi rigs pa*) that there is not the slightest deviation from the ultimate suchness of abiding reality; hence, the possession of the essential nature of Buddha is certain. Sūtras also state that all phenomena are primordially luminous clarity, are primordially nirvāṇa, and are primordially the nature of the actual Buddha.

Someone may think, "Well, as you previously expressed to another, if the heritage is established by merely being indivisible as thusness, then it [absurdly] follows† that the earth and rocks, etc. also have the heritage."

If "heritage" is necessarily posited as the faultless cause[4] of a Buddha, which—through the complete abandonment of the two obscurations that arise due to the power of a deluded mind—develops awareness (*blo*) that is not deluded concerning the nature of knowledge, then because it is not a mind, material such as earth and rocks cannot accomplish the path. [580] Hence, even though conventionally it is indivisible as thusness, it is not necessary that it be said to possess heritage because earth and rocks, etc. appear

* *las* read *pas [578.5].*
† *thol* read *thal [579.5].*

due to the power of mind; the mind does not arise due to the power of external objects such as earth and rocks. This should be known as illustrated by the example of the appearances in a dream and the cognition at the time of that [dream]. Through knowing that the suchness that is the Buddha-nature—with the uncontaminated nature of ultimate virtue—resides in this mind that is the producer of the three realms like wetness within water, the appearances of saṃsāra and nirvāṇa are merely the play of consciousness and wisdom; therefore, they need not be separate. Concerning the authentic meaning, I emphatically assert that all these appearances, too, which do not deviate from the state of suchness that is primordially Buddha, are not beyond the essential nature (*ngang tshul*) of the Tathāgata. As is said in the *Condensed* [*Prajñāpāramitāsūtra*]:

> The purity of form should be known as the purity of the fruition.
> The purity of form and the fruition are the purity of omniscience.
> The purity of omniscience, the effect, and form
> Are like space—indivisible and inseparable.[5]

The purity of the subject (*yul can*) free from obscurations is the purity, or nature, of objects (*yul*) such as form because other than the manner of perception progressively freed from the obscurations of self-appearance (*rang snang*), the essential meaning abides primordially free from obscurations. Therefore, when the defilements of the basic element of the subjective awareness are exhausted, being a Buddha, no impure* objective entities remain left over, [581] like when an eye-disorder is cured, the distorted images are automatically cleared.

Someone may think, "Well, at the time of one person becoming a Buddha, all impure appearances [for everyone] will cease."

It is not so because the obscurations of each individual's self-appearance† obscures him or herself; there is perception in which appearance conflicts with reality.

One may think, "Well, if appearance is completely in accord with reality at the stage of the Buddha, then does a Buddha experience all these impure appearances or not? If a Buddha does, then all phenomena are not actually

* *bos* read *bo ma [580.6]*.

† *bar snang* read *rang snang [581.1]*.

perfected as Buddha. If not, then it is impossible for a Buddha to know the path of all transmigrations[6] and so forth."

Omniscient wisdom effortlessly and spontaneously knows from within a state of equal taste of itself and the whole entirety of phenomena of saṃsāra and nirvāṇa. In this, while not transgressing the vision of the great purity of everything from its own perspective, omniscient wisdom perceives the appearances of the six classes of beings also, in the way they respectively appear. Due to the power of exhausting all obscurations of the dualistic appearances of subject and object, all phenomena that exist—through the essential point of being encompassed within the expanse of suchness in the manner of an unmixed, complete entirety—are spontaneously perceived by the wisdom of equal taste that is free from arising and ceasing. This is difficult to fathom for even those abiding on the [bodhisattva] grounds, needless to mention beings with confined perception! The meaning of this is also explained in the *Bodhisattvapiṭaka*:[7]

> The equality of all phenomena as equal
> Is known by the self-existing [wisdom].
> Therefore, the vision of the Tathāgatas, [582]
> The complete actual Buddhas, are equal.

And,

> By the natural luminous clarity of mind known as such, the supreme knowledge of a single instant of mind is called the unexcelled, complete and perfect awakening of an actual, perfect Buddha.

As said in the words of the master Candrakīrti:

> There are divisions of vessels yet no divisions in space.
> Likewise, there are divisions of entities yet no divisions in thusness.
> Therefore, understanding authentically the equality of taste
> You of good wisdom understand the objects of knowledge
> instantly.[8]

Due to the power of exhausting all obscurations and actualizing as it is the suchness residing within the ground, which is the self-existing luminous clarity of wisdom, the great wisdom which is nondual with the expanse pervades* everything and effortlessly perceives all phenomena—pervasive in the manner of stars shining in the ocean—from the state of the thorough pacification of conceptuality. Therefore, by relying on the authentic reasoning of the nature of things that examines the consummate [reality], an irreversible conviction is found. Otherwise, through evaluating with a limited intellect, I see an influx of contradictions and a lot of impurity of thoroughgoing conceptuality taken up, such as:

- There being no wisdom at the stage of the Buddha; or, even though there is, affirming it to be equivalent to an ordinary, transient mind
- Accepting that the realm of sentient beings is not perceived [by the Buddhas], or [that Buddhas] have impure perceptions
- Lacking the ability to establish the equal taste of [the wisdom that knows] what is and [the wisdom that knows] whatever there is.

The Meaning of the Third Verse "Because of possessing heritage"

[583] The meaning of the third [verse], "Because of possessing heritage," is as follows: all sentient beings have the heritage that is the potential to be a Buddha because it is established that (1) defilements are adventitious and suitable to be relinquished and (2) the Truth Body primordially endowed with qualities exists in everything without distinction. In this way, the possession of the heritage that is the potential to be a Buddha entails that these embodied beings have Buddha-nature because (1) there is a context of them being a Buddha and (2) since the Buddha's Truth Body is also established as essentially unconditioned, there is no temporal or qualitative distinction [between the Truth Body and Buddha-nature] from the aspect of essence. This third reason, knowing the production of the effect from the cause, is reasoning of efficacy (*bya ba byed pa'i rigs pa*).

Here, due to the mere presence of the cause, the emergence of an effect is not merely inferred because, due to the essential fact that it is impossible that the heritage would ever diminish in the event of becoming a Buddha, (1) the heritage that is the suchness itself is unchanging, (2) at the time of the effect there is no qualitative difference in essence, and (3) no matter

* *bya ba* read *khyab [582.3].*

how long the duration of the adventitious defilements is, they are suitable to be separate.*

In this way, (1) the existence of the cause, heritage, is essentially not distinct from the Truth Body at the time of the fruition, and (2) if the Truth Body at the time of the fruition exists, then at the time of sentient beings it [the heritage that is essentially the Truth Body] also necessarily exists without increase or decrease, and (3) although there is the imputation of causality and temporality, in reality, the expanse of phenomena is one taste within the immutable essence; the three reasons establish that all sentient beings have Buddha-nature due to the authentic path of reasoning that is engaged by the power of fact (*dngos po'i stobs kyis zhugs pa'i rigs pa*).

[584] In this way, this reasoning that establishes that all sentient beings have Buddha-nature establishes that the consummate liberation, the Tathāgata, and the ultimate abiding reality of all phenomena are nondistinct. Furthermore, a single consummate vehicle is established if it is known to arise through the power of the Buddha-nature itself. Otherwise, one will part ways with the reasoning that establishes the single consummate vehicle in the traditions of those who turn their back on the Mahāyāna, such as the ones who assert that: (1) "Buddha-nature" is not in the basic element of sentient beings, (2) it does not exist at the time of the Buddha, and (3) there are no qualities at the time of the cause; the qualities are newly possessed at the time of the effect. Therefore, those who aspire to the topic of the supreme vehicle should train intelligently with regards to this topic.

In this way, since positing the existence of the basic element primordially endowed with qualities at the time of sentient beings is a profound and inconceivable topic, even the Buddha spoke to his audience in a manner that they should trust his words, that they are nondeceptive, even though it is difficult to comprehend by one's own power. Therefore, since it is taught as the consummate of profundity, small-minded logicians (*rtog ge*) consistently make objections to this, no matter how many faults in dependence upon the conventional—such as the consequence that there would be a common locus of the minds of Buddhas and sentient beings—that talk is nonsense. [585] The *Saṃdhinirmocanasūtra* states:

> The character of the conditioned realm and the ultimate,
> Is the character free from being the same or different,

---

* *bras* read *'bral [583.4]*.

> Thus, those who conceive [them] as the same or different
> Have entered into an improper [view].[9]

As is said, (1) the suchness of mind (*sems kyi chos nyid*), the basic element which is the essential nature, and (2) the phenomenon of mind (*chos can kyi sems*) do not need to be asserted as either the same or different. Even though the mode of reality is not other than the meaning of suchness, as for the mode of appearance, there is the possibility of delusion. In this, there is not only no contradiction, but otherwise there would be faults such as the nonexistence of liberation or the impossibility for anyone to be deluded. Thus, since there is appearance that does not accord with reality, there is the possibility of deluded sentient beings, and through their relinquishing delusion by the path, the existence of Buddhas is also established.

Even though the reasoning that analyzes the ultimate establishes the emptiness of all phenomena, it does not negate the qualities of [Buddha-] nature because although the sublime qualities exist, they are also claimed to be essentially empty. Therefore, the meaning demonstrated by the middle wheel that all the phenomena of thorough affliction and complete purification are taught to be empty is established as such because Buddha-nature is also the nature of emptiness. However, since this teaching of [Buddha-] nature—characterized as neither conjoined with nor separable from the appearances of the empty-natured exalted body and wisdom—is [586] the viewpoint of the definitive meaning sūtras of the last wheel, then by merely this fact it is superior to the middle wheel. Although the meaning of the last wheel is praised in the sūtras and commentaries, [this does] not [refer to] everything in the last wheel, but is spoken in this way concerning the definitive meaning position of demonstrating the [Buddha-]nature. This can be clearly ascertained as such through other sūtras such as those that teach the basic element of heritage* through the metaphor of cleansing a jewel. Therefore, the emptiness taught in the middle wheel and the exalted body and wisdom taught in the last wheel should be integrated as a unity of emptiness and appearance. Without dividing or excluding† the definitive meaning subject matters of the middle and last wheels, both should be held to be the definitive meaning in the way of just this assertion by the omniscient Longchen Rapjam.

---

* *rig* read *rigs [586.2].*

† *gsal* read *bsal [586.3].*

By maintaining both of these [wheels] to be the definitive meaning, there is not only no contradiction that one [wheel] must be held as the provisional meaning, but having integrated them, there is the essential point of the quintessential instructions of the Vajrayāna through the Buddha-nature as such taken as the meaning of the causal continuum (*rgyu rgyud*). Therefore, you should know how the teachings of the Buddha converge on this single essential point and that this consummate meaning is the single viewpoint of the Sublime Ones such as Nāgārjuna and Asaṅga, for it can be clearly understood through [Nāgārjuna's] *Dharmadhātustotra, Bodhicittavivaraṇa,* etc., and [Asaṅga's] commentary on the *Uttaratantra* and so forth. As master Nāgārjuna states:

> All the sūtras demonstrating emptiness
> That the Victorious One taught [587]
> Were all uttered to avert afflictive emotions,
> Not to diminish the basic element.[10]

In this way, the consummate outcome of examination through ultimate analysis is the *vajra*-like meaning of the indivisible truth. Since the expanse is impenetrable to logical cognition (*rtog ge'i shes pa*), there are no grounds for the entrance of faults in dependence upon the ultimate.

Now for the explanation of how these basic elements abide in the continua of sentient beings: in terms of the essence of the mode of reality itself, all phenomena are encompassed within the expanse of suchness and the essence of suchness itself abides, without arising or ceasing, as equality; without temporal distinctions such as the past or future, or aspects such as the good or bad, here or there, self or other, greater and lesser, in saṃsāra and nirvāṇa, etc.—the expanse of phenomena is the unchanging, single sphere (*thig le nyag gcig*). Although the abiding reality is as such, in accord with the perspective of the appearances of adventitious delusion, even when bodies, minds, and domains of the three realms of saṃsāra appear in this way and the nature of suchness is not seen, it is not that suchness does not exist; it exists without deviating in the slightest from its own nature. Therefore, although the suchness of mind is as such, it is not actualized due to being enclosed by adventitious defilements. Even so, it abides in the manner of an extract or an essential core in the center and is called the "heritage" or the "essential nature" (*snying po*); for example, it is said to be known by illustration through the nine metaphors such as the underground treasure, etc.[11] [588] Even though it is posited in three contexts depending on the adventitious defilements: (1) impure, (2) variously impure and pure, and (3) extremely pure, there is no distinction in the essence of the basic element itself. In the *Uttaratantra* [I.27]:

> Since the Buddha's wisdom permeates the assembly of sentient beings,
> That nature is stainless and nondual.
> The heritage of Buddha is designated upon that effect,
> All beings are said to possess the essential nature of Buddha.

And [I.144],

> Its* nature is the Truth Body,
> Thusness, and also the heritage . . .

And likewise [I.47],

> According to the progression of impure, impure/pure,
> And extremely pure,
> The names "sentient beings," "bodhisattvas,"
> And "Tathāgatas" are given.[12]

Without knowing this, one negates and affirms, holding in the mind "Buddha-nature" [residing] in some uncertain place in the snare of the aggregates like a juniper berry supported in a bowl—as the character of a mind deluded and non-deluded associated like light and darkness. However, in accordance with this there will only be the lamentation of oneself not having gone at all in the direction of the intended meaning of the Mahāyāna. Therefore, in a crowd of negative logicians who have not trained in the Mahāyāna, even though the discourse of the essential nature is proclaimed, it is futile. Such profound discourse as this is not to be taught to immature people or non-Buddhists because they are not suitable receptacles to hear this profound doctrine. To them, the doctrine should be taught beginning with selflessness and impermanence and so forth, and that should be established by reasoning. [589] Otherwise, demonstrating the essential nature is futile because it cannot be established through only confined perception; hence, it

---

* *yang* read *yi [588.2].*

becomes a topic of superimposition and denigration. If the discourse of the Buddha-nature is progressively taught to those who have trained from the lower Buddhist philosophies and have generated a distinctive certainty in the uncategorized great emptiness, then they will believe.

Therefore, it is necessary to be learned in the essential point of the manner of accomplishing the path, having expelled the obscured stupidity of thinking: "Even though it is the authentic path, since it cannot be proved through reason, it has to be understood through experience," or, "If it is not the path of confined perception, then it is not an authentic path."

Now, to refute a few wrongly conceived positions with regards to the nature of the basic element: (1) refuting the view that it is truly established and not empty, (2) refuting the view that it is a void emptiness, and (3) refuting the apprehension of it as impermanent and conditioned.

Refuting the View that [the Basic Element] Is Truly Established and Not Empty

The *Laṅkāvatārasūtra* states as follows:

> The bodhisattva Mahāmati spoke to the Blessed One, "How is the permanent, steadfast, and eternal Buddha-nature abiding in the enclosure of defilements, which is spoken in the Buddha's sūtras, different from the Self of the non-Buddhists? The non-Buddhists also speak of a Self that is without qualities, etc." In response to the question, the Blessed One spoke, "It is not the same. The Buddhas show the Buddha-nature in [590] the meanings of the words 'three gates of liberation,' 'nirvāṇa,' and 'non-arising.' In order for immature beings to abandon the domain of fear due to no-self, by means of Buddha-nature they demonstrate the realm that is non-appearing and nonconceptual. Mahāmati, bodhisattvas and great beings of the present and future should not fixate upon a self."[13]

Moreover, it is said that there is no liberation for one with a notion of real entities. Also, emptiness of other while not empty of its own essence is not sufficient as emptiness because the emptiness of something in another is an inferior emptiness among the seven types of emptiness, and that is said "to be abandoned . . ."[14] extensively. Moreover,

> Mahāmati, the Tathāgata is neither permanent nor impermanent. If it is asked why, it is because in both there are faults.

And,

> Constructs are the hold of demons;
> One should transcend existence and nonexistence.

And,

> If there is something beyond the supreme truth, nirvāṇa, then that also is like an illusion and a dream . . .

In accord with the meaning of these scriptures, also by reasoned analysis, due to the essential point that Buddha-nature is essentially empty, [591] it impartially appears in all aspects of quality: it is suitable to be the suchness of mind, all-pervasive everywhere, permanent as long as time, inconceivable. However, while not empty of its own essence, being truly established it is completely impossible to be the suchness of an extrinsic phenomenon, etc. It also cannot be the outcome of ascertainment by the valid cognition of ultimate analysis because the affirmation of something truly established is not accurate as a handprint [result] of the analysis of all phenomena lacking true existence—like darkness [arising] from light. True establishment is not established by conventional valid cognition either because even though [it may appear to be] truly established from that [conventional] perspective, by merely that there is never an ability to establish phenomena to be non-empty. Without being able to be established by the two valid cognitions, the means of establishment has gone the way of a [nonexistent] space-flower; therefore, establishing this becomes meaninglessly tiresome.

Refuting the View that [the Basic Element] Is a Void Emptiness

By holding a mere non-implicative negation that is the categorized ultimate as the basic element, the expanse of phenomena, and emptiness, those who do not understand the standpoint of the expanse that is a unity of appearance and emptiness establish contradiction in scriptures that state the qualities as a primordial endowment. This is extremely inappropriate. In the *Jñānamudrāsamādhisūtra:*

> Without longing for truth, seeking gain
> Those without restraint claim to be "training in awakening."
> Later they will come,
> These ones who delight in speech and say "everything is empty."[15]

And,

> Emptiness is non-arising; no one produced it.
> It is not seen, does not arrive, nor move. [592]
> Those who abide with a referent object, saying "we train well in emptiness"
> Are warts who are thieves of the doctrine.[16]

And,

> Conceptualizing the doctrine of absence
> Is the movement that ensnares immature beings.

In the *Condensed* [*Prajñāpāramitāsūtra*]:

> Even in realizing "the aggregates are empty," bodhisattvas
> Engage in signs without faith in the domain of non-arising.[17]

In the *Samādhirājasūtra:*

> "Existence" and "nonexistence" are both extremes;
> "Pure" and "impure" are also extremes.
> Therefore, completely abandoning the extremes of both,
> The wise do not remain even in the middle.[18]

In the *Aṅgulimālīyasūtra*:[19]

> Alas! There are two [types of] beings who destroy the sacred doctrine in this world: those who view an extreme emptiness and those who profess a self in the world. These two destroy the sacred doctrine and turn the sacred doctrine upside down.

It is often said in the sūtras and śāstras that fixating upon emptiness, the antidote which extracts all views, as an entity or a nonentity is an incorrigible view. Also, it is said that it is necessary to relinquish all that is not beyond reference upon anything empty or non-empty. Moreover, in examining through reasoning, it is not necessary to say a lot here because it is easy to gain confidence that merely the designation by a conceptual apprehension of the elimination of the object of negation—the contradistinctive aspect of a non-implicative negation only eliminating true establishment—has not gone in the direction of the abiding reality free from superimpositions. [593] The mere aspect of a non-implicative negation that is the emptiness of true existence is not the genuine expanse of phenomena or the abiding reality; however, it is appropriate for novices to contemplate as merely a gateway to that [abiding reality]. A sūtra says:

> Mañjuśrī, the merit generated by a bodhisattva who gives the three jewels* whatever is needed for a hundred god-years is surpassed by the countless greater merit generated by another bodhisattva who contemplates, for even the time of a finger snap, that in existence all conditioned phenomena are impermanent, all conditioned phenomena are suffering, all conditioned phenomena are empty, all conditioned phenomena are selfless.

Refuting the Apprehension of [the Basic Element] as Impermanent and Conditioned

One may wonder whether the omniscient wisdom that actualizes the ground—the Buddha-nature as it is, like the sun free from clouds—is permanent or impermanent. Sometimes in the sūtras omniscience is said to be permanent and sometimes it is also said to be impermanent; the meaning is as follows: in accord with the mental perspectives of others—those to be trained who have not been transformed—the scriptures say that omniscience is impermanent, and there is reason also in the *Pramāṇavārttika* [II.8]:

> There is no permanent valid cognition
> Because the realization of the existence of entities is valid and

* *dko* read *dkon [592.2].*

> Objects of knowledge are impermanent;
> That [omniscient valid cognition] is only impermanent.

Omniscience arises through causes such as the generation of the mind [of awakening] and meditation on emptiness [594] because it is not reasonable to arise without a cause, and that [omniscience] is the valid cognition that is the direct perception of all phenomena. If valid cognition is a nondeceptive cognition, then there are no permanent phenomena because it is valid cognition that evaluates existent entities as they are. Since its objects are only impermanent objects of knowledge, then the evaluating valid cognition also must be impermanent, occurring sequentially, because it is established by valid cognition that what is permanent is incapable of functioning; hence, it would certainly be incapable of all activities such as evaluating objects. Therefore, it is extremely unreasonable that omniscience is permanent; it is established as impermanent. Likewise, all entities are impermanent and although nonentities are designated as "permanent," since there is no basis of something permanent, there are no genuinely permanent phenomena to be found. This fact is necessarily established as such for the perspectives of non-Buddhist heretics and those of the common vehicles who have not trained their minds in the manner of transformation within the essence of inconceivable suchness because they have no method whatsoever for the arising of what is other than the manner of appearance from the perspective of consciousness.

However, as for the vision of thoroughly transformed wisdom, omniscience is established as permanent because that which is put forward to prove the impermanence of that [omniscience], (1) the arising and ceasing of instances of knowable objects and (2) the subjective wisdom also arising sequentially and so forth, are only the appearances as such from the perspectives of those who have not thoroughly transformed. [595] However, in terms of the meaning of the mode of reality, it is not established as only this because when there is no phenomenon whatsoever that even arises momentarily, then needless to mention that the sequence of time and so forth, which derive from that, are not established. For example, like the appearances from one's own perspective in a dream, although there are unrestricted appearances of various temporal limits and spatial aspects, they are not established as such. Therefore, the consummate wisdom that has thoroughly transformed in accord with the meaning of the non-arising, unceasing suchness is the wisdom body that is the indivisibility of the knower and the object known, and at the time without transformation also, the basic nature of mind—suchness, unity, naturally luminous clarity—is unchanging.

Without distinction as to before and after, it is called the "naturally abiding heritage." To an untransformed one who has dualistic perception, there is the incontrovertible and undeniable appearance of inequality—all the changing, adventitious defilements suitable to be removed, occurring sequentially as arising and ceasing moments, saṃsāra and nirvāṇa, good and bad, etc.; however, the basic nature abides as the great equality in which arising, ceasing, and dualistic phenomena are not established. All spatial aspects and temporal changes are incorporated within that state. This exists as the domain of a Sublime One's individual reflexive awareness wisdom and there is no pollution by the changes of the three times. So why not give this the name "great permanence"? [It is designated as such] because (1) it exists and (2) it does not arise and cease momentarily.

[596] In this way, all objects of knowledge of space and time, all changing entities and nonentities such as space, are subsumed as an equal taste within this suchness. However, this suchness is not at all subsumed within the phenomena that change and so forth. For example, although clouds are subsumed within space, space is not subsumed within clouds. Therefore, the basic nature—the luminous and clear expanse of great equality that is suchness—is the single self-existing wisdom that co-emergently abides, naturally pervading all entities; however, for someone temporarily defiled, one's own nature is not manifest. Through eliminating the defilements through the power of realization and abandonment comprised by the five paths, one attains the great wisdom that is the indivisibility of the knower and the object known. One attains the omniscient wisdom that spontaneously knows, without conceptualizing and without effort, the equal taste that is the basic nature of the suchness of all cognitions—the unchanging self-existing wisdom.

However, by this fact, self-existing wisdom is not produced by a cause because actually, the Truth Body freed from adventitious defilements is a freed effect (*bral ba'i 'bras bu*). Although it appears to be newly produced by a cause, it merely appears as such in the way of appearance for those who are untransformed (*gnas ma gyur pa'i snang tshul*). However, in terms of the actual meaning, in the essence of the Truth Body, which is the nature of suchness without arising or disintegration, from the beginning all phenomena are—as equality—the actual Buddha, [597] primordially nirvāṇa, naturally luminous and clear, etc. This consummate viewpoint of the profound sūtras is a topic that is difficult to fathom for pure beings, needless to mention ordinary people! Nevertheless, if proper belief arises, it is praised as equal to receiving a prophecy of a Non-Returner so you should aspire to this fact. In this way, there is merit in viewing the Tathāgata's wisdom body as permanent. In the *Praśantaviniścaya-prātihāryasamādhisūtra:*[20]

> Mañjuśrī, compared to any noble son or daughter who offers whatever is desired to the four assemblies[21] in each of the worldly realms of the ten directions for ten million god-aeons, another noble son or daughter who stirs for the purpose of acting accordingly, saying, "The Tathāgata is permanent. The Tathāgata is steadfast." That [latter] one generates countless greater merit than the other.

And in the *Mahāparinirvāṇasūtra:*

> Kāśyapa, noble sons and daughters should persist, always with a one-pointed mind, in these two phrases: "The Buddha is permanent and the Buddha abides."

And,

> Whoever persistently perceives that the inconceivable [598] is permanent is a source of refuge . . .

Those who view the Tathāgata's body as impermanent have not even gone for refuge, and there are limitless faults in viewing the *vajra*-body as impermanent. Having acknowledged this as is said in the sūtras, the authentic meaning should be respected.

In this way, the essence of the Buddha-nature itself is free from all conceptual constructs such as existence and nonexistence, permanence and annihilation; it is the equality of the single sphere of indivisible truth. In the state of that abiding reality, seeing as it is the thusness of one taste of all phenomena of appearance and existence is the meaning of seeing authentically with nothing to add or remove. Therefore, freedom from all grasping is the good view that realizes the ultimate. In the *Bodhipakṣanirdeśasūtra:*

> Mañjuśrī, whoever sees, without duality, the equality (*mi mnyam pa med*) of all phenomena as nondual, sees authentically.[22]

In the *Gaganagañjaparipṛcchāsūtra:*

> Entities, nonentities, consciousness, and
> Whatever abides in the authentic limit—

> The view of entities and nonentities
> Is not held by the wise.[23]

In the *Bodhisattvapiṭika:*

> Ultimately, there is no phenomenon whatsoever in front of a Sublime One's supreme knowledge or wisdom that is any phenomenon that is thoroughly known, actualized, cultivated, or abandoned.

[599] However, in the context of differentiating well by means of the valid cognition analyzing the conventional, the abiding reality of entities in the apprehension of undistorted supreme knowledge is conventionally:

- Knowing the truth as truth—such as knowing the path of the Sublime Ones to be undeceiving
- Knowing the false as false—such as knowing those who profess liberation through meditating on the self to be misguided
- Knowing the impermanent as impermanent—knowing that all conditioned entities are momentary
- Knowing the permanent as permanent—knowing that Buddha-nature, the self-existing wisdom totality of [supreme] aspects, never changes
- Knowing the nonexistent as nonexistent—such as knowing that the appearances of self and perceived-perceiver [duality] are not intrinsically established
- Apprehending the existent as existent—such as knowing that (1) causality is the incontrovertible mode of appearance of dependent arising and (2) the spontaneously present qualities of suchness, the Buddha-nature, naturally abide in all sentient beings;

Therefore, through knowing and abiding as such, vast qualities are attained because this is the non-deluded root of virtue.

In this way, also in sūtras many doctrines are taught in general and specific ways. In particular, although a self of persons does not exist, the Buddha-nature transcending both conceptual constructs of self and no-self [600] is said to be the great self, and so forth; the supreme qualities of the perfection of purity, bliss, permanence, and self are taught in order to know the existent as existent—the unchanging consummate quality of peace, coolness (*bsil ba*), and perfection which is the non-abiding great nirvāṇa. In the *Mahāparinirvāṇasūtra:*

> The "self" is the authentic permanence of whatever it is that is true.
> That which is sovereign, unchanging, [and] unmoving is called "self."

Having heard the explanation of the manner of the profound Buddha-nature in this way, limitless benefit ensues in merely being inspired. It is said in the *Uttaratantra* [V.2–5]:

> An intelligent one aspiring to the domain of the Victorious Ones*
> Is a vessel for the accumulation of the qualities of the Buddha;
> Through manifest joy in the inconceivable qualities
> One surpasses the merit of all sentient beings.
>
> Through seeking awakening, one may, with golden fields adorned with jewels,
> Constantly make daily offerings to the Victors of doctrine in Buddha-fields equal in number to dust motes.
> Any other who hears mere words of this, and also is inspired having heard,
> Through this virtue gains much more merit than through generosity.
>
> An intelligent one wishing for awakening, also for many aeons may
> Uphold immaculate discipline of body, speech, and mind effortlessly.
> Any other who hears mere words of this, and also is inspired having heard,
> [601] Through this virtue gains much more merit than through discipline.
>
> One whose concentration drives out the fire of afflictive emotions of the three realms may,

* *brgya* read *rgyal [600.3].*

> In meditation on the method of unshaken awakening, complete the perfections of the abodes of the gods and Brahma.
> Any other who hears mere words of this, and also is inspired having heard,
> Through this virtue gains much more merit than through concentration.

Thus, there is great purpose in knowing and aspiring to what is so profound and difficult to fathom. This demonstration of the discourse of Buddha-nature—the roar of the non-returning lion that is the essential nature of the supreme vehicle—is the excellence of immense profundity; hence, for those who have little previous training and are mentally deficient, it is difficult to aspire to. In the *Tathāgatasaṃgatisūtra:*

> This wisdom of mine
> Is doubted by those with immature minds;
> It does not abide,
> Like an arrow shot in the sky falling down.[24]

And in the *Sarvavaidalyasaṃgrahasūtra:*

> Thus, since stupid people go to the lower realms due to the blessings of demons, they think of the faults of that also. Likewise, they think of the faults of the spoken doctrines bestowed by the Tathāgata.[25]

And in the *Brahmadattaparipṛcchā:*

> When the well-spoken doctrine is taught
> Those within the realm of evil hold it as [602] unreasonable.
> Without faith, when doubts in the doctrine are generated
> One becomes crazy for billions of aeons.
> Through thinking without faith, one becomes an evildoer;
> The mind of an angered one also cannot be protected.
> Having abandoned everything with an essence
> The faithless hold onto the dregs;
> They become boastful and constantly haughty.
> The faithless do not bow down to others.[26]

And,

> They contradict with meaningless words
> The teachings of the Victorious Ones;
> Through the defilements, they have doubts and qualms as a non-Buddhist.
> Having squandered and contradicted the doctrine,
> The faithless even abandon the doctrine.[27]

In the *Duḥśīlanigrahīsūtra:*[28]

> Śāriputra, this world will become filled by such unholy beings who drown in the path of sustenance, are attached to dispute, and harm themselves and others.

Considering the fact of what has been said, the degenerate time is booming and those beings born at the end of the teaching, through the manner of a perverted understanding of the four reliances,[29] have come to mostly denigrate the essential point of the tradition of the supreme vehicle, and contrive the doctrine. It is also extremely rare for a mind to cherish this which is like the life-force of the path of the Mahāyāna. However, through the power of being born at the end of the teachings of the lineage of awareness-holders (*rig 'dzin, vidyādhara*) in the school of early translations, I saw and heard many precious oral instructions of the lineage. [603] Although I am of an age and intellect that is not mature, I have gained a bit of confidence in this profound topic through the power of having the good fortune to take upon the crown of my head the lotus feet of many authentic virtuous spiritual friends such as the powerful victor and regent of Padma[sambhava], the youthful Mañjuśrī displayed in human form, the omniscient *vajra*-splendor [Jamyang Khyentsé Wangpo]. In this way, the well-spoken meaning of the naturally abiding heritage—the expanse of phenomena in the manner of the thoroughly non-abiding unity free from all extremes—is the lion's roar. In the *Brahmaviśoṣacintaparipṛcchāsūtra*:[30]

> Divine child, whatever doctrines are spoken without attachment to anything are the lion's roar (*seng ge'i sgra*). Those spoken with attachment to something are not the lion's roar; they are a fox's chatter (*wa'i sgra*). Teaching a view to be taken up is not the lion's roar.

In the *Mahāparinirvāṇasūtra:*

> Proclaiming the lion's roar is definitively stating that all sentient beings have the nature of Buddha and that the Tathāgata is always abiding and is immutable.

And,

> Noble child, although they state the empty topics a lot, they do not "proclaim the lion's roar"; proclamations in the midst of a large assembly of wise scholars are "proclamations of the great lion's roar." Regarding this, proclaiming the lion's roar is not professing that all phenomena are impermanent, suffering, selfless, and completely impure; it is professing only that the Tathāgata is permanent, bliss, the self, and completely pure.

[604] There are extensive statements on the meaning of the metaphor of proclaiming the lion's roar; it should be known as illustrated.

Even if there is discord with others in speaking the own path of the Sugatas truthfully as such, since it is a presentation of the authentic path, do not make others disturbed. In the *Madhyamakāvatāra* [VI.118]:

> The śāstras demonstrate thusness for the sole purpose of liberation,
> Not for the sake of attachment to analysis and disputation.
> If in explaining thusness other scriptures are destroyed
> There is no fault.

This manner is also protecting the doctrine. In the *Samādhirājasūtra:*

> Regarding this, if it is asked, "What is protecting the doctrine?" It is, in accordance with the doctrine, defeating those who disparage the doctrine of the Buddha.

It is also upholding the doctrine. In the *Gaganagañjaparipṛcchā:*

> The character of the doctrine completely upholds
> Whatever character the Victorious Ones' awakening possesses.
> Whoever knows the extent of the stainless [doctrine]
> Upholds the doctrine of all the Buddhas.[31]

In this way, upholding the doctrine is repaying the actions of the Buddhas and also gaining immeasurable merit. In the *Tathāgatamahākaruṇānirdeśasūtra*:[32]

In this way, by closely abiding by the Victorious One's doctrine and
Through the doctrine, having renunciation and lacking disturbance,
Through this, one upholds the doctrine of the Sugatas and
Repays the actions of all the Buddhas.

[605] And in the *Gaganagañjaparipṛcchā:*

Although expressed for ten billion aeons
There is no limit to Buddha's wisdom.
Likewise, there is no measure to the merit
Of upholding the sacred doctrine of the Tathāgata.[33]

Thus it is said.

Although I have developed a little confidence here
In the scriptural tradition of the supreme vehicle,
I am young in age and immature in training—
Who would rely upon the speech of a crazy monk [like] myself?

These days, following after famous people
And lacking an intellect that discriminates the proper and improper,
Most are possessed by the demon of jealousy—
I know this is not a time to deliver elegant speeches.

However, with constant devoted worship to the supreme teacher
And exalted deity on the lotus of my heart
The clear aspects of the words and meanings of the excellent scriptures
Have clearly dawned in the expanse of awareness.

At that time, prolonged joy arose
In persistent intimacy (*goms*) with elegant sayings. From this,
At a later time and in another land also
Sacred joy in the Victorious One's doctrine will become like the waxing moon.

From this discourse of consummate profundity
The joy that arises in intelligent ones

Is not like the happiness that falls to the extremes of existence or peace.
Therefore, this is a feast for the gathering of fortunate ones!

May the unity of appearance and emptiness that relinquishes all grasping,
The lion's roar of the supreme vehicle,
[606] Overwhelm the hordes of beasts with bad views, and
May the essential nature of the Victorious One's teaching spread across the ten directions!

At the request of my brother in the doctrine named Guṇa, bearing the treasury of jewels of the three trainings,[34] who said, "Write an explanation of 'Because the body of the perfect Buddha is radiant . . . ,' whatever comes to mind," this was precisely written down by the monk Lodrö Drimé.[35] May it be virtuous!

APPENDIX TWO

Notes on the Essential Points of [Mipam's] Exposition [of Buddha-Nature]

Bötrül's *Notes on the Essential Points of [Mipam's] Exposition [of Buddha-Nature]* addresses a number of issues found within Mipam's *Lion's Roar: Exposition of Buddha-Nature*. The short text is thematically organized around a list of topics, which are discussed as the issues are raised. He composed this text at the hermitage of his teacher, Chöying Rangdröl (*chos dbyings rang grol*, 1872–1952) near Serta.[1] For this translation, I used the edition of the text published in his Collected Works, in addition to a photocopy of a digital input of the text that I obtained from Zhechen monastery in Nepal. I included this translation because it is a useful supplement to the translation of Mipam's *Lion's Roar: Exposition of Buddha-Nature*. Also, I have consistently found Bötrül's systematization of Mipam's works very helpful.

[262] *namo guru mañjuśrīye*—Homage to the guru Mañjuśrī!

My object of veneration is the one with the maṇḍala of wisdom and love endowed with the twofold purity—
The natural purity of the essential basic element of awakening [and]
The Truth Body completely devoid of adventitious defilements—
Radiant with thousandfold light [rays] of benefit and happiness!

Regarding this, the definitive meaning Buddha-nature is directly and indirectly the consummate topic of all Sūtra and Mantra. The meaning complete with the essential points of all Sūtra and Mantra is as follows: due to the essential point of the indivisibility of appearance and emptiness, all the essential points of Sūtra and Mantra are complete in this, such as:

- In the path of Sūtra—in all the contexts of ground, path, and fruition—the nature of the Middle Way, which is the unity of appearance and emptiness, is not transgressed; and in particular, there is the essential point of actualizing the qualities of the path and fruition through abandoning the two obscurations;
- In the common Unexcelled Mantra, there is the view of the ground, which is the realization of the indivisibility of purity and equality, and the unity of the two stages[2] of the path; as well as the essential point of actualizing the qualities of the path and fruition through applying the key points of the channels (*rtsa*), winds (*rlung*), and seminal essences (*thig le*);
- In the uncommon Mantra [the Great Perfection], there is the realization of the ground, which is the indivisibility of primordial purity and spontaneous presence; the path of liberation without hardship through sustaining the state of break-through (*khregs chod*); and the appearances of direct-crossing (*thod rgal*), which are not produced by the mind or impure winds.

[263] The following is the manner of how the nature of this is realized: while the aspect of natural purity is directly realized from the first [bodhisattva] ground, the qualities of the purity that is free from the adventitious [defilements] is a topic difficult to realize even for the lords on the tenth ground. The essence of the object (*yul*) itself in the former [natural purity] does not have the aspects of being seen or not; the latter [purity that is free from adventitious defilements] is distinguished by the realization being perfected or not through the power of the purity of the subject's (*yul can*) adventitious [defilements].

Moreover, the manner how its essence is indicated in sūtras is as follows: the manner that the middle Word indicates the empty essence is through indicating the divisions of the quality-bearers (*chos can*) such as the twenty emptinesses.[3] Also, from the aspect of suchness, the expanse of phenomena is taught as the naturally abiding heritage; thereby, the empty essence is clearly shown. Since the last Word indicates the exalted body and wisdom from the contradistinctive aspect of the luminous and clear nature of mind, it also becomes that which joins Sūtra and Mantra. However, there is no fault of the absurd consequence that there would thus be no difference between Sūtra and Mantra because the aggregates, constituents, and sense-fields are not taught [in Sūtra] as the divine maṇḍalas in a manner in which they are perfected right now.

In accord with the intended meaning of the middle wheel, it abides as the empty essence when evaluated by the valid cognition that analyzes the ultimate; therefore, it is free from the extreme of permanence. In accord with the intended meaning of the last Word, its nature is luminous clarity when evaluated by the thoroughly conventional valid cognition based upon pure vision, [264] so it is free from the extreme of nonentity annihilation. Therefore, it is the great unity free from extremes.

Concerning the meaning of this, there are two valid cognitions—ultimate and conventional analyses—which ascertain the two truths. Within the first, there are two: (1) valid cognition that analyzes the categorized and (2) valid cognition that analyzes the uncategorized.

The first [valid cognition that analyzes the categorized] distinguishes the two truths and applies the qualifier "ultimately not established." Since conventional production by its own characteristics is not negated, it is limited emptiness; it does not become the genuine emptiness which is the indivisible two truths. This is because of being distinct and unmixed with appearance due to: (1) an appearing entity not mixing with a non-implicative negation that is an absence of true existence, and (2) a nonentity that is a non-implicative negation rejecting appearance.

The second [uncategorized] is as follows: as is said, "Through this reasoning [production] is not reasonable even conventionally . . . ,"[4] without dividing the two truths, even mere appearances—from form to omniscience—are unable to withstand analysis through reasoning and are ascertained as the great emptiness. Therefore, (1) a nonentity emptiness, which is separate from appearance, and (2) an appearance that is not empty are impossible; hence, it is the genuine unity. If having divided the two truths one also negates appearance, there ensues the fault of the over-pervasion (*khyab ches ba'i skyon*) of the object of negation. However, due to the essential point of not dividing the two truths, there is not only no ensuing fault of the over-pervasion of the object of negation, but it is this which hits the essential point that evokes [265] the genuine indivisibility of the two truths.

Second, there are two conventional valid cognitions: (1) thoroughly conventional valid cognition based on pure vision and (2) thoroughly conventional valid cognition based on impure confined perception. The first is the wisdom of a Sublime One's continuum and the second is the mind of an ordinary being; the first is unmistaken valid cognition and the second is mistaken cognition. Therefore, the indicated meaning of the middle Word as it is should be ascertained as the great emptiness which is the uncategorized ultimate—the essence of Buddha-nature that does not in the slightest degree withstand ultimate analysis. That emptiness also is not a limited nonentity that is posited from a valid cognition of confined perception; it is established by the power of fact (*dngos stobs kyis*) to be the nature that is neither conjoined with nor separable from appearance and emptiness. Moreover, its aspect of appearance also is not like a limited entity posited by confined perception. In accord with the intended meaning of the last Word, it is the object found as it is—appearance in accord with reality—by the thoroughly conventional valid cognition based on pure vision; it is ascertained as the identity of the great luminous clarity.

In short, the definitive meaning Buddha-nature—the single essential point of the noncontradictory viewpoint of the middle and last Words—accords with the statement [266]:

> The mind is devoid of mind;
> The nature of mind is luminous clarity.[5]

(1) From the aspect of the empty essence, it does not in the slightest degree withstand analysis in the evaluation of ultimate analysis, and (2) from the aspect of the nature of clarity, it is the object found by the valid cognition of pure vision; Buddha-nature is taught as the unity* of appearance and emptiness which is neither conjoined with nor separable from the exalted body and wisdom. Otherwise, if it is asserted to be not empty or to withstand analysis even from the perspective of ultimate analysis, it becomes a permanent and true existence. Also, if one does not know how to establish its existence from the perspective of the conventional valid cognition of pure vision, then that heritage is not suitable as anything other than what has fallen to the extreme of nonentity annihilation.

---

* *zug [266]* read *zung 'jug* [Zhechen ed., 9.3].

Therefore, how the valid cognition of pure vision is established is as follows: Candrakīrti states,

> Compared to that mind [with defective sight], they both [distorted subject and object] are true;
> Compared to the clear vision of objects, they both are also false.[6]

Since the appearances of the six classes of beings are distorted perceptions and the perception of pure wisdom is undistorted, [the latter] is necessarily the conventional mode of reality.

If someone asks, "Well, since pure wisdom knows both pure and impure objects of knowledge, which is the conventional mode of reality?"

The wisdom that knows whatever there is perceives both the pure and the impure. Although it knows the impure, that is not its self-appearance (*rang snang*) because that is the distorted perception of the six classes of beings, not the conventional mode of reality. [267] In wisdom's self-appearance, there is the perception of only great purity and equality; hence, that is posited as the conventional mode of reality.

If someone asks, "Well, are all objects of knowledge the nature of Buddha?"

In this context of the Vehicle of Characteristics, all appearances such as pots are the mind's self-appearance; therefore, they are not established in reality. Also, the nature of mind is established to have the essential nature of Buddha, as is said:

> The mind is devoid of mind;
> The nature of mind is luminous clarity.

The nature of mind is posited as the heritage which is the basic element—the Buddha-nature.

If is it said, "Well, if this is posited as ultimate, it becomes truly established, and if posited as relative, then because 'the ultimate Buddha-nature' states it as ultimate, it is not posited as relative."

In accord with the viewpoint of the great scriptures, there are two manners: (1) by means of the object found by ultimate valid cognition being authentic or not, two truths are posited in which the aspect of appearance is relative and the aspect of emptiness is ultimate, and (2) by means of the object of conventional valid cognition of pure vision being authentic or not, nirvāṇa, appearance which accords with reality, is posited as ultimate and saṃsāra, appearance which is in discord with reality, is posited as relative. According to the former [appearance/emptiness model], [Buddha-nature] has aspects of both truths; however, it is posited as ultimate according to the latter [authentic/inauthentic experience model].

[268] If it is asked, "Well, which is the manner of positing the two truths in the Prāsaṅgika tradition?"

Both are posited without contradiction. Moreover, Candrakīrti, emphasizing the former [appearance/emptiness model], elucidated the empty essence of all phenomena. The *Uttaratantra*, although emphasizing the latter [authentic/inauthentic experience model], is in accord with the former because the nature of emptiness is established as luminous clarity. Therefore, this is the reason why both the *Madhyamakāvatāra* and the *Uttaratantra* fall to one essential point, without contradiction, as Prāsaṅgika scriptures. Therefore, being empty of mistaken phenomena that are separable, and not empty of phenomena that are inseparable from emptiness, and so forth, is not from the perspective of ultimate analysis because if something withstands analysis from that perspective, it is truly established. Consequentially, it is posited by means of whether or not it exists as the consummate object found by the valid cognition of pure vision. Whatever statements there are of the presence of the exalted body and wisdom are not in the slightest degree [concerning] an entity found by a valid cognition of confined perception; hence, there is no occasion for a common locus (*gzhi mthun*) of a permanent phenomenon and an entity.

If one says, "How can the viewpoints of the middle and last wheels not contradict? Their provisional and definitive sūtras are distinct."

Concerning the manner of positing the provisional and the definitive in general, sūtras are provisional meanings when the meaning of the literal teaching has all three complete: a basis within an [other] intention, a purpose, and explicit invalidation. [269] The opposite of this is posited as the definitive meaning. Therefore, in accord with the viewpoint of the *Samādhirājasūtra*[7] and so forth, by means of what is or is not invalidated by the valid cognition of ultimate analysis, Candrakīrti accepts sūtras that mainly express the topic of emptiness as the definitive meaning, and sūtras that mainly express the topic of the conventional, [or] relative, truths as provisional meanings:

> Whatever sūtras have the meaning that does not explain thusness
> Know those to also explain the relative, what is provisional.

> Know those that have the meaning of emptiness as the definitive meaning.[8]

Therefore, the manner of positing is by means of the topic: the first Word is provisional, the middle is definitive, and the last is a mix of provisional and definitive meanings. Hence, it does not follow that a meaning taught in a sūtra that Candrakīrti has said to be a provisional meaning is necessarily nonexistent conventionally because all presentations of relative truth are the expressed meanings of a provisional meaning.

In accordance with sūtras that show the heritage, the basic element, through the metaphor of cleansing a jewel, the *Uttaratantra* and the *Dharmadhātustotra* and so forth assert sūtras that teach the consummate definitive meaning, Buddha-nature, as the definitive meaning by means of whether there is or is not invalidation through the [conventional] valid cognition of pure vision in accord with what is found by the valid cognition of pure vision. Hence, the last Word teachings in which the definitive meaning Buddha-nature is the topic—the nature of [270] inseparable appearance and emptiness, the ultimate that is appearance in accord with reality—are the definitive meaning because [Buddha-nature] is the object found by the valid cognition of pure vision.

However, if you understand the essential point that this does not contradict the viewpoints of the sūtras and śāstras that teach (1) the great emptiness, the object found by ultimate valid cognition, as the consummate definitive meaning, and (2) the provisional meaning from the aspect of appearance, which is the contradistinctive aspect of the relative, then the scriptures of the middle and last Words and the commentaries on the viewpoint such as the *Uttaratantra* and the *Madhyamakāvatāra* will have an indivisible viewpoint. In particular, without having an influx of contradictions as to the respective provisional and definitive meanings of the beginning and end of the *Uttaratantra*, there is the essential point of releasing the seal of the difficult points of the indicated meanings of scripture, such as understanding nothing to divide or exclude (*dbye bsal med*).

Regarding this, (1) since whatever indications of Buddha-nature, together with the exalted body and wisdom, are not [concerning] an entity posited by confined perception, there is no common locus of a permanent phenomenon and an entity; and (2) since whatever indications of empty essence are not [concerning] a nonentity like a rabbit horn posited by confined perception, it is free from the extreme of annihilation. Therefore, it is the nature of indivisible appearance and emptiness like the statement [271]:

The mind is devoid of mind;
The nature of mind is luminous clarity.

The manner of purifying the defilements of the basic element is as follows: the two obscurations are divided into two: imputed obscurations (*kun brtags*) and innate obscurations (*lhan skyes*). The aspect of the imputed are discards of the Path of Seeing. The nine aspects within the innate cognitive obscurations (*shes sgrib*) are progressively abandoned by the nine grounds of the Path of Meditation. The aspect of the extremely subtle latency of that is abandoned by the *vajra*[-like] meditative stabilization. Emotive obscurations (*nyon sgrib*), among the twofold division [of obscurations that are] emotive or cognitive, are completely abandoned up to the seventh ground. Their latencies are abandoned on the three pure grounds. Their extremely subtle habitual tendencies (*bag chags*) are abandoned by the *vajra*[-like] meditative stabilization. The latencies of the obscurations that are afflictive emotions, which are cognitive obscurations, are also indicated by the name "afflictive emotion" in sūtras and śāstras. Therefore, the viewpoints of the great chariots are in accord: asserting that afflictive emotions are abandoned up to the seventh ground and asserting that emotive obscurations are abandoned until the end of the continuum (*rgyun mtha'*).

There are three reasonings that establish Buddha-nature: (1) reasoning of dependency [concerning] the effect, (2) reasoning of the nature of things [concerning] the essence, and (3) reasoning of efficacy [concerning] the cause. Moreover, the first is evidence that is an effect (*'bras rtags*) and the latter two are evidence of [identical] nature (*rang bzhin gyi rtags*). [272] The first, through putting forward as evidence the effect—that which is endowed with the twofold purity—the presence of the essence of the primordially pure Buddha is established; it is posited by means of two separate contradistinctive aspects: (1) the Buddha that is the primordial pure essence and (2) the Buddha that is endowed with the twofold purity. Since the statement, "sentient beings are Buddhas," is [in reference to] the Buddha that is natural purity (*rang bzhin rnam dag*), it [refers to] the suchness of mind, not the effect which is that [Buddha endowed with the twofold purity]; therefore, there is also no fault of the effect abiding in the cause. The evidence put forward as an effect is from the contradistinctive aspect of being the effect endowed with the twofold purity; in any case, it also is not contradictory.

If one thinks, "Does the Buddha that is the mode of reality (*gnas tshul gyi sangs rgyas*) abandon the obscurations to be discarded or not?"

If you speak concerning the basic nature of the Buddha that is the mode of reality called "the essential Buddha of primordial purity," since its essence is primordially pure of defilements, what defilements are there to be abandoned? The defilements to be abandoned are not established. There are obscurations in the mode of appearance for sentient beings, yet an adventitiously deluded person is not able to abandon the obscurations due to not realizing the nature of the mode of reality. At the time when the selfless abiding reality of mind is realized through the power of cultivating the path, all the obscurations, which are rooted in the adventitious apprehension of self, will be progressively abandoned; the fruition which is the endowment of twofold purity will be actualized.

The following is an investigation into whether the Buddha that is the mode of reality perceives objects of knowledge or not: [273] although the manner of the primordially pure essence—the essence which is the nature of luminous clarity—resides as the identity of knowledge, love, and powers in the mode of reality, by only this the twofold purity is not asserted. Therefore, a person so endowed does not become omniscient because of being a person for whom appearances do not accord with reality. Through the power of cultivating the path, when such a person is free from the defilements of deluded self-appearances together with their habitual tendencies, then that one becomes a Buddha endowed with the twofold purity due to actualizing the infinite mode of reality of the two wisdoms: knowing what is and knowing whatever there is. Also, through this essential point one can know whether or not the Buddha is [the actualized Buddha] endowed with the twofold purity.

Through the virtue of Dongak Tenpé Nyima,[9] the one from the eastern region of Dakpo,[10]
Having written this in accord with the words spoken by the lord of refuge, the lord of the expanse of phenomena free from activity,[11]
May all beings actualize the Truth Body of the Sugatas!

May it be virtuous! *sarva mangalaṃ*

NOTES

INTRODUCTION

1. The term *sugatagarbha* "the essential nature (*garbha*) of the one gone well (*sugata*)" is also used as a synonym for the *tathāgatagarbha*. "Tathāgata" and "Sugata" are synonymous with "Buddha."
2. David Seyfort Ruegg, "On the Knowability and Expressibility of Absolute Reality in Buddhism," *Indogaku Bukkyōgaku Kenkyū* 20, no. 1 (1971), 1–7.
3. David Seyfort Ruegg, "The Term *Gotra* and the Textual History of *Ratnagotravibhāga*," *Bulletin of the School of Oriental and African Studies* 39, no. 2 (1976), 341–342.
4. Florin Giripescu Sutton, *Existence and Enlightenment in the Laṅkāvatāra-sūtra: A Study in the Ontology and Epistemology of the Yogācāra School of Mahāyāna Buddhism* (Albany: SUNY Press, 1991), 52; 76–78.
5. *Uttaratantra* I.35: *gtsang bdag bde dang rtag nyid kyi/ /yon tan pha rol phyin pa 'bras*. In *theg pa chen po rgyud bla ma'i bstan bcos*, published in *rgyud bla ma rtsa 'grel* (Sichuan: Nationalities Press, 1997), 6.
6. Cyrus Stearns, *The Buddha from Dolpo: A Study of the Life and Thought of the Tibetan Master Sherab Gyaltsen* (Albany: SUNY Press, 1999), 49.
7. Cited from Hajime Nakamura, *A History of Early Vedānta Philosophy* (Delhi: Motilal Banarsidass, 1983), 154.
8. Sallie King, *Buddha Nature* (Albany: SUNY Press, 1991), 104–107.
9. Nathan Katz, "Tibetan Hermeneutics and the Yāna Controversy," in *Contributions on Tibetan and Buddhist Religion and Philosophy*, ed. E. Steinkeller and H. Tauscher (Wien: Arbeitskreis für Tibetische und Buddhistische Studien, 1983), 110.

10. An excellent source for the life and works of Dölpopa is Cyrus Stearns's *The Buddha from Dolpo.*
11. Khenpo Lodrö Drakpa is from Dzamtang (*'dzam thang*) in eastern Tibet, where a prominent Jonang monastery has remained active to the present day.
12. See, for instance, Tsongkhapa's statement that: "The ultimate truth is posited as solely the negation of truth [that is, inherent existence] upon a subject that is a basis of negation." Tsongkhapa, *The Lesser Exposition of the Stages of the Path* (*lam rim chung ba*), 396.6: *don dam bden pa ni dgag gzhi chos can la bden pa bkag pa tsam la 'jog pa'i phyir.*
13. Nāgārjuna also targets the epistemological systems of *pramāṇa* in his *Vigrahavyāvartanī* v. 30–51. See Sanskrit edition and English translation of these verses in Kamaleswar Bhattacharya, *The Dialectical Method of Nāgārjuna* (Delhi: Motilal Banarsidass, 1990), 15–21; 114–124. For a discussion of Candrakīrti's critiques of epistemology, see Dan Arnold, *Buddhists, Brahmins, and Belief: Epistemology in South Asian Philosophy of Religion* (New York: Columbia University Press, 2005), 143–183.
14. Georges Dreyfus cites three ways in which Tibetan commentators have integrated Candrakīrti and Dharmakīrti: (1) those who see Dharmakīrti's view as inferior to Candrakīrti's, (2) early Tibetan epistemologists who view Dharmakīrti as a proponent of the Middle Way, and (3) those who synthesize Dharmakīrti's Yogācāra with Candrakīrti's Middle Way. Georges Dreyfus, *Recognizing Reality* (Albany: SUNY Press, 1997), 428.
15. Mipam, *Words That Delight Guru Mañjughoṣa: Commentary on the Madhyamakālaṃkāra* (*dbu ma rgyan gyi rnam bshad 'jam dbyangs bla ma dgyes pa'i zhal lung*), published in *dbu ma rgyan rtsa 'grel* (Sichuan: Nationalities Press, 1990), 77. My translation of "*dbu tshad seng ge mjing bsnol*" follows Karma Phuntsho's suggestion of "two lions intertwining their necks." See Karma Phuntsho, *Mipham's Dialectics and the Debates on Emptiness*, 18. See also Khenpo Pelden Sherap (*mkhan po dpal ldan shes rab*, b. 1941), *Lamp of the Blazing Sun and Moon: A Commentary on [Mipam's] Sword of Supreme Knowledge* (*don rnam nges 'grel pa shes rab ral gri'i 'grel pa shes rab nyi zla 'bar ba'i sgron me*), (Varanasi: Nyingmapa Students' Welfare Committee, 2000), 26.
16. Mipam, *Words That Delight*, 75: *theg chen mdo sngags mtha' dag gi bzhed pa'i rtsa bar 'gyur ba'i gnad ston pa ni gzhung 'di yin.*
17. Ibid., 76: *'di lta bu'i gzhung ni theg chen spyi'i lam po che yin te/ shing rta rnam pa gnyis kyi gzhung dgongs pa chu bo gcig 'dres su sbyar zhing/ khyad par don dam pa'i tshad ma dpal ldan klu yis ji ltar bzhed pa dang/ tha snyad kyi tshad ma dpal chos kyi grags pas ji ltar bzhed pa gnyis rigs pa'i rgya mtsho chen po ro gcig tu skyil.*
18. Paul Williams, *The Reflexive Nature of Awareness: A Madhyamaka Defence* (London: Curzon Press, 1998).
19. See Williams, *The Reflexive Nature of Awareness*, 199–206.

20. Matthew Kapstein, "We Are All Gzhan stong pas," *Journal of Buddhist Ethics* 7 (2000), 121.
21. The *Guhyagarbhatantra* was not included in the Buddhist canon compiled in Tibet in the fourteenth century by proponents of the "new schools" of translations.
22. Rongzom, *Commentary on the Guhyagarbhatantra* (*rgyud rgyal gsang ba'i snying po dkon cog 'grel*), Rongzom's *Collected Works*, vol. 1 (Sichuan: Nationalities Press, 1999), 33–253.
23. Rongzom, *Establishing Appearances as Divine* (*gsang sngags rdo rje theg pa'i tshul las snang ba lhar bsgrub pa*), Rongzom's *Collected Works*, vol. 1 (Sichuan: Nationalities Press, 1999), 557–568.
24. Longchenpa, *Dispelling Darkness in the Ten Directions: Commentary on the Guhyagarbhatantra* (*dpal gsang ba'i snying po de kho na nyid nges pa'i rgyud kyi 'grel pa phyogs bcu'i mun pa thams cad rnam par sel ba*), (reproduction of *a 'dzom* xylographic edition), (Paro: Ngodup, 1975).
25. The "Seven Treasuries" (*mdzod bdun*) are: *Precious Treasury of Philosophies* (*grub mtha' rin po che'i mdzod*), *Precious Wish-Fulfilling Treasury* (*yid bzhin rin po che'i mdzod*), *Precious Treasury of the Abiding Reality* (*gnas lugs rin po che'i mdzod*), *Precious Treasury of the Expanse of Phenomena* (*chos dbyings rin po che'i mdzod*), *Precious Treasury of Words and Meanings* (*tshig don rin po che'i mdzod*), *Precious Treasury of the Supreme Vehicle* (*theg pa'i mchog rin po che'i mdzod*), and *Precious Treasury of Quintessential Instructions* (*man ngag rin po che'i mdzod*). See Longchenpa (*klong chen rab 'byams*, 1308–1364), *Seven Treasuries* (*mdzod bdun*), 7 vols. (Tarthang Tulku ed.).
26. Mipam, *Flower Garland: Catalogue of Rongzom's Collected Works* (*rong zom gsung 'bum dkar chag me tog phreng ba*), published in Rongzom's *Collected Works*, vol. 1 (Sichuan: Nationalities Press, 1999), 1–22.
27. Mipam, *Precious Mirrorr: Catalogue of the "Seven Treasuries"* (*mdzod bdun spar du bsgrubs pa'i dkar chag rin chen me long*), published in *nges don rdzogs pa chen po'i man ngag phyogs bsgrigs zab don nor bu'i mdzod khang* (Serta: Serta Buddhist Academy of the Five Arts, n.d.), 7–44.
28. Throughout Mipam's works we find references to Longchenpa's writings. Mipam also wrote texts that were explicit commentaries on Longchenpa's texts, such as three short texts that include commentaries on the twelfth and eighteenth chapters of *Wish-Fulfilling Treasury* (*yid bzhin mdzod*), and an "overview" (*spyi don*) of Longchenpa's commentary on the *Guhyagarbhatantra*.
29. Dudjom Rinpoché (*bdud 'joms 'jigs bral ye shes rdo rje*, 1904–1988), *Dudjom's History of Buddhism* (*bdud 'joms chos 'byung*), (Sichuan: Nationalities Press, 1996), 399–410; 497.
30. Nyoshül Khenpo (*smyo shul mkhan po 'jam dbyangs rdo rje*, 1931–1999), *Garland of Lapis* (*rang bzhin rdzogs pa chen po'i chos 'byung rig 'dzin brgyud pa'i rnam*

thar ngo mtshar nor bu baiduryaʼi phreng ba), (Thimphu: Indraprastha Press, 1996), vol. 2, 504.1–504.2.

31. Two important commentaries Lochen Dharmaśrī wrote on the *Guhyagarbhatantra* are his *Ornament of the Lord of Secrets' Viewpoint* (*gsang bdag dgongs rgyan*) and *The Lord of Secrets' Words* (*gsang bdag zhal lung*). Lochen Dharmaśrī, *dpal gsang baʼi snying po de kho na nyid nges paʼi rgyud kyi ʼgrel pa gsang bdag dgongs rgyan*, *Collected Works* (Dehra Dun: D. Kochhen Tulku, 2000), vol. 8 (*nya*), 90–337; *dpal gsang baʼi snying po de kho na nyid nges paʼi rgyud kyi rgyal po sgyu ʼphrul drwa ba spyi don gyi sgo nas gtan la ʼbebs par byed paʼi legs bshed gsang bdag zhal lung*, *Collected Works*, vol. 9–10.
32. Lochen Dharmaśrī, *Cluster of Supreme Intentions: Commentary on "Ascertaining the Three Vows"* (*sdom pa gsum rnam par nges paʼi ʼgrel pa legs bshad ngo mtshar dpag bsam gyi snye ma*), (Bylakuppe: Ngagyur Nyingma Institute, n.d.).
33. See Getsé Paṇchen (*dge rtse paṇ chen, ʼgyur med tshe dbang mchog grub,* 1761–1829), *Ornament of Buddha-Nature* (*nges don dbu ma chen poʼi tshul rnam par nges paʼi gtam bde gshegs snying poʼi rgyan*), *Collected Works*, vol. 1, 95.4.
34. Tsewang Norbu gave Situ Paṇchen Chökyi Jungné (*si tu paṇ chen chos kyi ʼbyung gnas,* 1699–1774) extensive teachings on an other-emptiness view. He also gave transmissions of Jonang teachings to the Thirteenth Karmapa, Düdül Dorjé (*bdud ʼdul rdo rje,* 1733–1797), and the Tenth Zhamar, Chödrup Gyatso (*chos grub rgya mtsho,* 1742–1792). See Khenpo Lodrö Drakpa (*ʼdzam thang mkhan po blo gros grags pa*), *History of the Jonang* (*jo nang chos ʼbyung zla baʼi sgron me*), (Qinghai: Nationalities Press, 1992), 536–537.
35. Ibid., 539.
36. Gene Smith, *Among Tibetan Texts* (Boston: Wisdom Publications, 2001), 250; see also 20, 90.
37. See Smith, *Among Tibetan Texts*, 265; 338n.888. A text that deals specifically with Kongtrül's other-emptiness view is Kongtrül, *Stainless Light Rays of the Vajra-Moon: Teachings on the View of the Middle Way of Other-Emptiness* (*gzhan stong dbu ma chen poʼi lta khrid rdo rje zla ba dri ma med paʼi ʼod zer*), published in *The Collected Works of ʼJam-mgon Kong-sprul* (*rgya chen bkaʼ mdzod*), vol. 8 (Paro: Ngodup, 1976), 581–611.
38. Kongtrül, *Encyclopedia of Knowledge* (*shes bya kun khyab*), (Beijing: Nationalities Press, 2002).
39. Smith, *Among Tibetan Texts*, 237. Kongtrül played an important role in bringing together various compilations of numerous scholars in Tibet. Notably, he compiled the *Treasury of Practical Instructions* (*gdams ngag mdzod*) and the voluminous *Treasury of Precious Treasures* (*rin chen gter mdzod*), which is a sixty-volume compilation of texts gathered from various treasure cycles that had been revealed in Tibet. See Smith, *Among Tibetan Texts*, 263–264.
40. The first line of this text reads: "To briefly explain the assertion of the great omniscient one of the Jonang, the tradition of the middle way of other-empti-

ness" (*kun mkhyen jo nang pa chen po'i bzhed pa gzhan stong dbu ma'i srol cung zad 'chad na*). Jamyang Khyentsé Wangpo (*'jam dbyangs mkhyen brtse'i dbang po*, 1820–1892), *Essential Summary of the Presentation of the Middle Way of Other-Emptiness* (*gzhan stong dbu ma'i rnam bzhag snying por dril ba*), *Collected Works*, vol. 6 (Gangtok: Gonpo Tseten, 1977), 214.4–221.2.

41. Jamyang Khyentsé Wangpo, *Brief Sketch of Tsongkhapa's View and Philosophy* (*lce btsun blo bzang grags pa'i lta grub kyi bzhed tshul mdo tsam bzhugs so*), *Collected Works*, vol. 6, 221.2–225.3.
42. While not widely used in association with Buddhist tantra, "pantheism" conveys the Nyingma view quite well. Alasdair MacIntyre characterizes pantheism as follows: "Pantheism essentially involves two assertions: that everything that exists constitutes a unity and that this all-inclusive unity is divine." Alasdair MacIntyre, "Pantheism," *Encyclopedia of Philosophy* (New York: Macmillan, 1971), 34.
43. Gyelwang Chökyi Nyima (*rgyal dbang chos kyi nyi ma*), *History of Dzokchen Monastery* (*mdo khams rdzogs chen dgon gyi lo rgyus nor bu'i phreng ba*), (Delhi: Konchhog Lhadrepa, 1986), 138.3–142.2. See also Tulku Thondup, *Masters of Meditation and Miracles* (Boston: Shambhala Publications, 1996), 177; 198–199.
44. For more on the monastic college at Dzokchen monastery and its affiliates, see Tenzin Lungtok Nyima (*bstan 'dzin lung rtogs nyi ma*, b. 1974), *The Great History of Dzokchen* (*snga 'gyur rdzogs chen chos 'byung chen mo*), (Beijing: Nationalities Press, 2004), 304–318.
45. Nyoshül Khenpo, *Garland of Lapis*, vol. 2, 263.3–265.3. For a description of the monastic college at Kaḥtok, see Jamyang Gyeltsen (*'jam dbyangs rgyal mtshan*), *A Short History of Kaḥtok* (*rgyal ba kaḥ thog lo rgyus mdor bsdus*), (Sichuan: Nationalities Press, 1996), 154–162.
46. Khenpo Zhenga taught at Gemang monastery (*dge mang dgon*), and was invited by the Fifth Dzokchen Rinpoché, Tupten Chökyi Dorjé (*thub bstan chos kyi rdo rje*, 1872–1935), to be a professor at the Śrī Singha college at Dzokchen around the year 1902, where he taught for about seven years. He later was invited to Pelpung, a Karma Kagyü monastery near Degé, and founded a monastic college there. There is some controversy with regards to Khenpo Zhenga's tenure as a professor at the monastic college of Pelpung. In contrast to Kongtrül, the luminary of Pelpung in the previous century, Khenpo Zhenga did not teach a view of "other-emptiness." Khenpo Zhenga reportedly preferred self-emptiness to other-emptiness. Dilgo Khyentsé (*dil mgo mkhyen brtse*, 1910–1991) is cited as saying that Khenpo Zhenga stated that the bad karma of a hunter is better than someone who holds a view of other-emptiness. See Achim Bayer, "The Life and Works of mKhan-po gZhan-dga' (1871–1927)" (Master's Thesis, University of Hamburg, 2000), 33; 173–174. For more on Khenpo Zhenga, see David Jackson, *A Saint in Seattle* (Boston: Wisdom Publications, 2003), 27–28; Georges Dreyfus, "Where Do Commentarial Colleges Come From?" *Journal of the International Association of Buddhist Studies* 28, no. 2 (2005), 288–292.

47. Nyoshül Khenpo, *Garland of Lapis,* vol. 2, 266.6–267.3: *snga 'gyur phyogs 'dir rgya 'grel dang bod 'grel gyi bshad pa'i gsung rgyun chen po khag gnyis bzhugs pa las/ dang po gzhung chen bcu gsum sogs rgya gar mkhas pa'i legs bshad rgya gzhung gi bshad tshul mkhan chen gzhan phan snang bar bka' babs pa dang/ rong klong rnam gnyis dang mnga' ris paṇ chen sogs bod kyi gzhung 'grel rnams gtso cher 'jam mgon mi pham rin po cher bka' babs pa las bshad srol phyi ma gtso bor gdan sa 'di nas byung ba mang ngo.*

48. The thirteen great scriptures include two Vinaya texts: *Vinayasūtra* and *Prātimokṣasūtra;* two Abhidharma texts: *Abhidharmakośa* and *Abhidharmasamuccaya;* four texts of the profound view (of the Middle Way): *Mūlamadhyamakakārikā, Madhyamakāvatāra, Catuḥśataka,* and *Bodhicaryāvatāra;* and the "five treatises of Maitreya" (*byams chos sde lnga*): *Abhisamayālaṃkāra, Mahāyānasūtrālaṃkāra, Uttaratantra, Dharmadharmatāvibhāga,* and *Madhyāntavibhāga.* Although Khenpo Zhenga's *Interlinear Commentaries on the Thirteen Great Scriptures* (*gzhung chen bcu gsum gyi mchen 'grel*) contains more than thirteen interlinear commentaries, Padma Namgyel (*padma rnam rgyal,* twentieth century) identifies the ones listed above as the thirteen texts. See Padma Namgyel, *Ornament of Speech: A Teaching Manual for the Thirteen Great Scriptures* (*gzhung chen bcu gsum gyi mchad thabs dang mtshan don 'grel ba blo gsal ngag gi rgyan*), (Gangtok: Dodrup Sangyey Lama, 1976), 1.1–1.3.

49. In his colophon of his interlinear commentary of the *Madhyamakāvatāra,* Khenpo Zhenga states that he wrote his commentary "without mixing even a hair of the individual opinions of the Tibetan masters" (*bod gyi slob dpon so so'i 'dod pa dang spu tsam yang ma bsres par*), and in his commentary on the *Uttaratantra,* that he "did not make anything up himself" (*rang bzo med par*). Khenpo Zhenga, *Interlinear Commentary on the Madhyamakāvatāra* (*dbu ma la 'jug pa zhes bya ba'i mchan 'grel*), published in *gzhung chen bcu gsum gyi mchan 'grel,* vol. 5 (Dehra Dun: D. G. Khocchen Tulku, 1978), 284.5; and Khenpo Zhenga, *Interlinear Commentary on the Uttaratantra* (*theg pa chen po rgyud bla ma'i bstan bcos zhes bya ba'i mchan 'grel*), published in *gzhung chen bcu gsum gyi mchan 'grel,* vol. 3 (Dehra Dun: D. G. Khocchen Tulku, 1978), 581.2–581.3.

50. See Smith, *Among Tibetan Texts,* 232–233.

51. Nyoshül Khenpo, *Garland of Lapis,* vol. 2, 393.1–393.4: *'jam dgon mi pham rin po ches kho bos gzhung 'grel 'di tsam brtsams pa rnams snga 'gyur pa'i bstan par phyi rabs rnams la rgyal bstan rin po che yun du gnas pa'i pha phog tu bzhag pa yin/ dpal ldan zla grags dang rong klong rnam gnyis kyi dgongs pa srog tu bzung ste phyogs kun tu bshad sgrub kyi rgyun spel ba la gzhan dga' rin po cher dka' babs pa 'di rgyal sras gzhan phan pa'i sngon gyi thugs smon dang skye sprul yin pa'i dbang gis yin zhes.*

52. Georges Dreyfus, *The Sound of Two Hands Clapping,* 148; Anne Klein, *Meeting the Bliss Queen* (Boston: Beacon, 1995), 150; 262n.2.

53. Gorampa (*go rams pa bsod nams seng ge,* 1429–1489) characterizes Tsongkhapa's position on the Middle Way as "annihilationism" (*chad mtha'*). Gorampa, *Dis-*

tinguishing the Views (*lta ba'i shan 'byed*), (Sarnath: Sakya Students' Union, 1988), 3; English translation in José Cabezón and Geshe Lobsang Dargyay, *Freedom from Extremes: Gorampa's "Distinguishing the Views" and the Polemics of Emptiness* (Boston: Wisdom Publications, 2007).

54. *padma badzra* (1867–1934). See Smith, *Among Tibetan Texts*, 327n.778.
55. See Lauren Hartley, "A Socio-Historical Study of the Kingdom of Sde-dge (Derge, Kham) in the Late Nineteenth Century: Ris-med Views of Alliance and Authority" (Master's Thesis, Indiana University, 1997), 66.
56. See Smith, *Among Tibetan Texts*, 249.
57. Most of the information on Mipam's life and works is drawn from Künzang Chödrak (*sa manta bhadra dharma kirti*), *Mipam's Essential Hagiography and Catalogue of Works* (*gangs ri'i khrod kyi smra ba'i seng ge gcig po 'jam dgon mi pham rgya mtsho'i rnam thar snying po bsdus pa dang gsung rab kyi dkar chag snga 'gyur bstan pa'i mdzes rgyan*), Mipam's *Collected Works*, vol. 8 (*hung*), 621–732. John Pettit translates a portion of this hagiography in *Mipham's Beacon of Certainty*, 23–39. The author of this text is unclear. Pettit attributes the author to Khenpo Künpel, Mipam's student; however, he states that there is some doubt that Khenpo Künpel is in fact the author. See John Pettit, *Mipham's Beacon of Certainty* (Boston: Wisdom Publications, 1999), 27, 467n.59.
58. Mipam is reported by traditional Tibetan scholars to have written his *Beacon of Certainty* (*nges shes sgron me*) when he was seven years old. See Karma Phuntsho, *Mipham's Dialectics and the Debates on Emptiness* (London: RoutledgeCurzon, 2005), 226n.22.
59. Künzang Chödrak, *Mipam's Essential Hagiography*, 627.4–629.5.
60. Ibid., 629.6–630.4.
61. Details of Mipam's life can be found in an English translation of Mipam's hagiography, along with a summary of Mipam's life and works, in John Pettit, *Mipham's Beacon of Certainty*, 19–39. See also Dudjom Rinpoche, *The Nyingma School of Tibetan Buddhism*, trans. and ed. by Gyurme Dorje and Matthew Kapstein (Boston: Wisdom Publications, 1991), vol. 1, 869–880; Nyoshul Khenpo, *A Marvelous Garland of Rare Gems: Biographies of Masters of Awareness in the Dzogchen Lineage*, trans. Richard Barron (Junction City: Padma Publishing, 2005), 415–425.
62. In particular, Pari Rapsel (*dpa' ris blo bzang rab gsal*, 1840–1910) and Drakar Trülku (*brag dkar dpal ldan bstan 'dzin snyan grags*, 1866–1928) wrote refutations of Mipam's commentary. Mipam subsequently wrote rejoinders to their critiques. For a study of the issues at stake in these debates, see Karma Phuntsho, *Mipham's Dialectics and the Debates on Emptiness*.
63. Künzang Chödrak, *Mipam's Essential Hagiography*, 632.2–632.4.
64. Ibid., 633.6–634.2.
65. Mipam did write a topical outline (*sa bcad*) for a treasure text of Chokgyur Lingpa, the *zhal gdams lam rim ye shes snying po'i bsdus don*, Mipam's *Collected*

Works, vol. 8 (*hung*), 435–462. Another short text Mipam wrote concerning the treasure tradition describes how to tell good treasure revealers from charlatans. See Mipam, *gter ston brtag ba chu dwangs nor bu*, Mipam's *Collected Works*, vol. 14, 475–487. For a critical edition, translation, and analysis of this text, see Andreas Doctor, *The Tibetan Treasure Literature: Revelation, Tradition, and Accomplishment in Visionary Buddhism* (Ithaca: Snow Lion Publications, 2006). It is noteworthy that Mipam states: "I also have no hope for the fortune of a new treasure doctrine because I know that there is not the slightest thing missing (*ma chog pa rdul rtsam med*) from sūtras, tantras, and commentarial treatises." Mipam, *Shedding Light on Thusness* (*gzhan gyis brtsad pa'i lan mdor bsdus pa rigs lam rab gsal de nyid snang byed*), published in *spyod 'jug sher 'grel ke ta ka* (Sichuan: Nationalities Press, 1993), 339: *gsar du gter gyi chos skal la re ba'ang med de/ mdo rgyud dgongs 'grel dang bcas pa 'di dag gis ma chog pa rdul tsam med par shes pa lags.*

66. For a description of the breadth of Mipam's writings, see Karma Phuntsho, *Mipham's Dialectics and the Debates on Emptiness*, 13–19. See also Smith, *Among Tibetan Texts*, 229–233.
67. For instance, he wrote a massive two-volume commentary on the *Kālacakra*, as well as composed texts on *Hevajra, Guhyasamāja, Cakrasaṃvara*, et al.
68. See Künzang Chödrak, *Mipam's Essential Hagiography*, 668.3–675.1.
69. See ibid., 676.2–678.3.
70. See ibid., 678.3–681.1.
71. See ibid., 681.6–685.1.
72. See ibid., 685.1–687.6.
73. See ibid., 687.6–688.6.
74. See ibid., 689.2–689.6.
75. See ibid., 689.6–696.5.
76. See ibid., 696.5–703.4.
77. See ibid., 703.4–707.1.
78. See ibid., 707.1–708.5.
79. Mipam, *Words That Delight*, 494: *'jam dbyangs mkhyen brtse'i dbang po zhes snyan pa'i ba dan srid par yongs su grags pa de nyid kyis/ rgya bod kyi 'grel pa'i yig cha rnams gnang nas zhib tu ltos la 'brel bshad cig gyis zhes.*
80. Künzang Chödrak, *Mipam's Essential Hagiography*, 635.6–636.4.
81. When I stayed at Larung Gar in the summer of 2006, the population there was around 10,000. For further information about Larung Gar, see David Germano, "Re-membering the Dismembered Body of Tibet," in *Buddhism in Contemporary Tibet*, ed. Melvyn Goldstein and Matthew Kapstein (Berkeley: University of California Press, 2003), 53–94.
82. The curriculum of the Ngagyur Nyingma Institute is printed in a pamphlet published at the monastery that I got there in the summer of 2004, entitled *snga*

'gyur mtho slob mdo sngags rig pa'i 'byung gnas gling gi sgrig gzhi rtsa khrims chen po, 19–33. See also Dreyfus, *The Sound of Two Hands Clapping*, 128–132.

83. The English translations of Mipam's biography by John Pettit, Gyurme Dorje and Matthew Kapstein, and Richard Barron all use the terms "refutation and proof" here, which does not adequately convey the important dichotomy of negation and affirmation in Buddhist epistemology. John Pettit, *Mipham's Beacon of Certainty*, 28; *The Nyingma School of Buddhism*, trans. Gyurme Dorje and Kapstein, vol. 1, 874; *A Marvelous Garland of Rare Gems*, trans. Richard Barron, 419.
84. Künzang Chödrak, *Mipam's Essential Hagiography*, 639.6–640.2.
85. In chapter 5, we will see how Mipam offers "pure vision" as a conventional valid cognition that is an alternative to ordinary "confined perception."
86. Künzang Chödrak, *Mipam's Essential Hagiography*, 644.6–645.5. It is noteworthy that Lochen Dharmaśrī commented on "the universal form of the Great Perfection," the first line of the first stanza in Ngari Paṇchen's *Ascertainment of the Three Vows*, as corresponding to Buddha-nature. See Lochen Dharmaśrī, *Cluster of Supreme Intentions*, 51.2–53.4.
87. We can see two types of "dialectic" in Mipam's work: (1) a Hegelian dialectic, in which there is a synthesis in a final resolution (closure), and (2) a Ricoeurian or Derridian dialectic, where the two seemingly opposed sides of the dialectic are not resolved and the dialectical tension remains (open-ended). Mipam's dialectic is closed in that he affirms a monistic unity as the ontological ground of existence; however, it is open in that he maintains contexts for the deconstruction of reified notions of such a ground. Mipam sustains a tension, or resonance, between an open-ended dialectical inquiry (e.g., in Prāsaṅgika-Madhyamaka) and the closure of an ultimately indivisible ground. However, when we take into account his esoteric works (e.g., the Great Perfection) and the fact that his dialectic reaches a culminating synthesis (Buddha), it is closer to Hegel's than to Derrida's. For a discussion of Ricoeur's dialectic, see Paul Ricoeur, "Language and Discourse" and "Explanation and Understanding," in *Interpretation Theory: Discourse and the Surplus of Meaning* (Fort Worth: Texas Christian University Press, 1976), 1–23; 71–95.
88. Tupten Tsültrim Namdak (*thub bstan tshul khrim rnam dag*), *Nourishment for Faith: A Short Hagiography of Bötrül* (*rje kun gzigs bod sprul bstan pa'i nyi ma'i rnam thar bsdus pa dad pa'i gsos sman*), Bötrül's *Collected Works*, vol. 1 (Sichuan: Nationalities Press, 2004), 13.
89. For an excellent discussion of this topic, see *The Svātantrika-Prāsaṅgika Distinction*, ed. Georges Dreyfus and Sarah McClintock (Boston: Wisdom Publications, 2003).
90. I capitalize "Sūtra" when it is distinguished as a vehicle in contrast to "Mantra" or "Vajrayāna." I leave "sūtra," as a genre of text like "tantra," in lowercase.

91. Caveat: I use the term "monism" to describe an important aspect of Mipam's view; however, we should bear in mind a distinction between monism and non-dualism. See for instance, Sallie King, *Buddha Nature* (Albany: SUNY Press, 1991), 99–115. Monism is an affirmation of a single reality (closure) and nondualism is a negation of the entire framework of single/plural (open-ended) without affirming either/or/both/neither. We can thus say that the "non" in nondualism is a non-implicative negation, or an illocutionary negation. Although Mipam's view certainly has such a nondual character, I use the term "monism" to evoke the important aspect of his emphasis on unity (*zung 'jug*). Mipam states: "The meaning of unity is the single sphere of equal taste of all dualistic phenomena." Mipam, *Precious Vajra Garland* (*gnyug sems zur dpyad skor gyi gsung sgros thor bu rnams phyogs gcig tu bsdus rdo rje rin po che'i phreng ba*), Mipam's *Collected Works*, vol. 24, 743.4: *gnyis chos thams cad ro gcig ni zung 'jug gi don.*
92. This term is used in a different context by Jean Paul Sartre in *Critique de la Raison Dialectique* (Paris: Editions Gallimard, 1960); English edition translated by Alan Sheridan-Smith in *Critique of Dialectical Reasoning* (London: NLB, 1976), 1.
93. On the premodern worldview as a "sacred cosmos," see David Klemm, *Hermeneutical Inquiry*, vol. 1 (Atlanta: Scholars Press, 1986), 5.
94. David Klemm, *Hermeneutical Inquiry*, vol. 1, 23.
95. The better phrase here is "Buddha-nature knowing *oneself*" rather than "itself" because *itself* is a third-person abstraction, connoting an objectified thing rather than the subjective agent that hits closer to home in "oneself."
96. Paul Ricoeur, *The Symbolism of Evil*, trans. Emerson Buchanan (New York: Harper and Row, 1967), 352; cited from David Klemm, *Hermeneutical Inquiry*, vol. 1, 24.

Chapter One.
Buddha-Nature and the Unity of the two Truths

1. The articulation of a unified, comprehensive view of Buddhist thought is a daunting task indeed when we consider that the Peking edition of the Tibetan canon of Buddha's Word in translation (*bka' 'gyur*) is 108 volumes, and the translated commentaries (*bstan 'gyur*) contain 3,626 texts in 224 volumes!
2. P.774 (Peking ed.), vol. 29.
3. Tibetan and English editions printed in John Powers, *Wisdom of the Buddha: The Saṃdhinirmocana Mahāyāna Sūtra* (Berkeley: Dharma Publishing, 1995), 138–141. This translation, and all subsequent translations unless otherwise noted, are mine.
4. Longchenpa, *Responses to Mind and Wisdom* (*sems dang ye shes kyi dri lan*), published in *gsung thor bu*, vol. 1 (Delhi: Sanje Dorje, 1973), 377.5–378.5: *dka'*

dang po bden pa bzhi'i chos kyi rnam grangs las/ /gtso bor las dang po pa dang blo cung zad dman pa rnams 'jug pa la dgongs te/ spang gnyen gyi rim pas nyams su len pa'i thabs gsal bar gsungs shing/ /bka' bar pa mtshan nyid med pa'i chos kyi rnam grangs las/ /gtso bor cung zad sbyang pa dang dbang po 'bring po rnams 'jug pa'i rim pa la dgongs te/ /ngo bo nyid med pa'i rnam grangs kyi gnyen po la bdag tu 'dzin pa rnams skye ba med par gsungs la/ /bka' tha ma nges pa don gyi chos kyi rnam grangs las/ gtso bor yongs su rdzogs pa'i theg pa rnams dang dbang po rnon po rnams 'jug pa'i rim pas gshis la ji ltar gnas pa'i rnam grangs rgya cher gsungs te/ dang pos 'khor ba'i mtshan nyid spang bya las ldog pa'i lam bstan/ bar bas spang bya las 'dzin pa'i rang bzhin ngo bo med pas shes sgrib spang bar bstan/ tha mas yin lugs snying por bstan te. Longchenpa also states this in abbreviated form in his *Dispelling Darkness in the Ten Directions*, 128.5–129.1.

5. Longchenpa, *Great Chariot: Auto-Commentary of Resting in the Nature of Mind* (*sems nyid ngal gso'i 'grel pa shing rta chen po*), published in *rdzog pa chen po ngal gso skor gsum dang rang grol skor gsum* (reproduction of *a 'dzom* xylographic edition), (Gangtok, 1999), 330.3–330.5.
6. Longchenpa, *Precious Treasury of Words and Meanings* (*gsang ba bla na med pa 'od gsal rdo rje snying po'i gnas gsum gsal bar byed pa'i tshig don rin po che'i mdzod*), 897.1–897.4: *bcom ldan 'das kyis bka' 'khor lo gsum du gsungs pa las gnas 'di ni tha ma don dam rnam par nges pa'i chos kyi 'khor lor gsungs pa yang khyod kyis ma shes/ stong nyid rkyang pa don dam yin na/ 'khor lo gsum la tha dad du bstan pa'ang ji ltar 'thad de/ stong nyid drang don du gsungs kyi de yang gnas lugs kyis skrag pa dang/ las dang po pas bdag tu 'dzin pa dgag tsam la dgongs pa ste.*
7. Longchenpa, *Great Chariot*, 330.6–331.1: *khyed kyi bdag med pa dang/ stong pa nyid la zhen pa'ang bdag dang mi stong pa'i gnyen po tsam yin gyi nges pa'i don ni ma yin te.*
8. Longchenpa, *Precious Treasury of Philosophies* (*theg pa mtha' dag gi don gsal bar byed pa grub mtha' rin po che'i mdzod*), 898.2–898.5: *de'ang don dam pa'i bden pa dbyings yin la/ 'di'i rang bzhin mthong bas don dam bden pa mthong zhes bya'i/ cir yang med pa'i stong nyid kyang don dam bden pa ma yin no/ de'ang byis pa so so skye bo dang/ las dang po dag bdag tu zhen pa'i gnyen por bdag med pa la sogs pa bstan pa yin gyi/ don la dbyings 'od gsal ba 'dus ma byas shing lhun grub tu yod pa shes par bya ste.*
9. I use the singular for "exalted body" (*sku*) and "wisdom" (*ye shes*) because I feel that it conveys Mipam's interpretation better than the plural. The singular conveys the multiple wisdoms and bodies (e.g., two or five wisdoms and two, three, or four bodies) as internal divisions of what is essentially indivisible. Mipam characterizes wisdom(s) as follows: "Although the consummate wisdom is the identity of the unity of the expanse and awareness, free from duality and conceptuality . . . divided from its contradistinctive aspects (*ldog chas phye*), there are said to be the enumeration of five wisdoms." Mipam, *Shedding Light on Thusness*, 354–355: *mthar thug gi ye shes ni dbyings rig zung du 'jug pa'i bdag nyid gzung 'dzin rnam rtog dang bral yang . . . ldog chas phye na ye shes rnam pa lngas*

rnam grangs su gsungs. See also Mipam, *Commentary on the Words of the Eighteenth Chapter [of the Wish-Fulfilling Treasury]* (*le'u bco brgyad pa'i tshig 'grel*), Mipam's *Collected Works*, vol. 21, 570.2–570.3.

10. Mipam, *Lion's Roar: Exposition of Buddha-Nature* (*bde gshegs snying po'i stong thun chen mo seng ge'i nga ro*), Mipam's *Collected Works*, vol. 4, 586.2–586.4: *'khor lo bar bar bstan pa'i stong pa nyid dang/ tha mar bstan pa'i sku dang ye shes dag snang stong zung du chud par bya dgos pas/ bar ba dang tha ma'i nges don gyi skor rnams dbye gsal* [read *bsal*] *med par gnyis ka nges don du kun mkhyen klong chen rab 'byams kyis bzhed pa 'di kho na ltar bzung bar bya*. Nearly the same text is also found in Mipam's *Uttaratantra* commentary compiled by his students, *Words of Mipam: Interlinear Commentary on the Uttaratantra* (*theg pa chen po rgyud bla ma'i bstan bcos kyi mchan 'grel mi pham zhal lung*), Mipam's *Collected Works*, vol. 4, 382.1–382.2.
11. One of Mipam's teachers, Kongtrül, also states that both wheels are definitive: "The middle and last wheels are both equally the definitive meaning; there is said to be a difference between the definitive meaning [in the former] eliminating the temporary conceptual concepts and [in the latter] indicating the consummate mode of reality." Kongtrül, *Encyclopedia of Knowledge*, 686: *'khor lo bar tha nges don yin mnyam yin la/ gnas skabs spros pa gcod pa dang/ mthar thug gnas lugs ston pa'i nges don gyi khyad par du bzhed do*.
12. Mipam, *Lion's Roar: Exposition of Buddha-Nature*, 585.4–586.2: *don dam rigs pas chos thams cad stong pa nyid du grub kyang des snying po'i yon tan 'gog par mi 'gyur te yon tan bla na med par yod kyang ngo bo stong par 'di pas yang zhal gyis bzhes pa'i phyir ro/ /des na 'khor lo bar bas bstan don kun byang gi chos thams cad stong par bstan pa ni de de bzhin du grub ste bde gshegs snying po'ang stong pa nyid kyi rang bzhin yin pa'i phyir ro/ /'on kyang stong pa'i rang bzhin can gyi sku dang ye shes kyi snang ba dang 'du 'bral med pas khyad par du byas pa'i snying po bstan pa 'di 'khor lo tha ma'i nges don gyi mdo sde rnams kyi dgongs pa yin pas/ tshul de tsam gyi cha nas 'khor lo bar pa las lhag pa'i phyir/ mdo sde dgongs 'grel las 'khor lo tha ma'i don la mchog tu sngags pa'ang 'khor lo tha mar gtogs tshad ma yin gyi snying po bstan pa'i nges don gyi phyogs nas de ltar gsungs*. This text (with slight variation) is also found in *Words of Mipam*, 381.2–382.1. See also Bötrül, *Ornament of Mañjugoṣa's Viewpoint: An Explanation of the Words and Meanings of "Distinguishing the Views and Philosophies: A Torch of the Essential Points"* (*lta grub shan 'byed gnad kyi sgron me'i tshig don rnam bshad 'jam dbyangs dgongs rgyan*), published in *lta grub shan 'byed gnad kyi sgron me'i rtsa 'grel* (Sichuan: Nationalities Press, 1996), 92–93.
13. Commenting on Mipam's work, Bötrül makes a distinction within the last wheel by separating the sūtras of the last wheel into those of (1) Mind-Only and (2) Middle Way. He states that the Mind-Only refers to the four Mind-Only Sūtras, such as the *Saṃdhinirmocana*—the tradition of vast activity—in which the definitive meaning is accepted as:

- sūtras that teach three consummate vehicles, and
- sūtras that mainly teach the three natures in the Mind-Only tradition.

In contrast, the Middle Way in the last wheel refers to the ten Buddha-Nature Sūtras, such as the *Dhāraṇīśvararāja*—the tradition of profound view—in which the definitive meaning is accepted as:

- sūtras that teach a single consummate vehicle, and
- sūtras that mainly teach Buddha-nature.

Bötrül, *Ornament of Mañjugoṣa's Viewpoint*, 88–89. Kongtrül cites the four Mind-Only Sūtras as the *Laṅkāvatārasūtra, Saṃdhinirmocanasūtra, Avataṃsakasūtra,* and *Gaṇḍavyūha*. Kongtrül says that these are renowned as four "Mind-Only Sūtras," but also are definitive meaning sūtras. See Kongtrül, *Roar of the Non-Returning Lion: Commentary on the Uttaratantra* (*theg pa chen po rgyud bla ma'i bstan bcos snying po'i don mngon sum lam gyi bshad srol dang sbyar ba'i rnam par 'grel pa phyir mi ldog pa seng ge'i nga ro*), (Varanasi: Kagyud Relief & Protection Committee, 2002/1999), 6; see also Shenpen Hookham, *The Buddha Within* (Albany: SUNY Press, 1991), 266–267. In his *zhu don gnang ba,* Dölpopa lists the ten Buddha-Nature Sūtras as follows: the *Tathāgatagarbhasūtra,* the *Avikalpapraveśadhāraṇī,* the *Śrīmālādevīsiṃhanādasūtra,* the *Mahābherīhārakaparivartasūtra,* the *Aṅgulimālīyasūtra,* the *Mahāśūnyatāsūtra,* the *Tathāgataguṇajñānācintyaviṣayāvatārasūtra,* the *Mahāmeghasūtra,* the *Tathāgatamahākaruṇānirdeśasūtra* (*Dhāraṇīśvararājasūtra*), and the *Mahāparinirvāṇasūtra.* Cited from Cyrus Stearns, *The Buddha from Dolpo*, 178n.12.

14. The "causal continuum" (*rgyu rgyud*), or "ground-continuum" (*gzhi rgyud*), is the first of a threefold division, along with "method-continuum" (*thabs kyi rgyud*), or "path-continuum" (*lam rgyud*), and "result-continuum" (*'bras bu'i rgyud*). Sources for this threefold division are found in the exegeses on the *Guhyagarbhatantra*, as well as the *Guhyasamājatantra*. See Nathaniel Garson, "Penetrating the Secret Essence Tantra: Context and Philosophy in the Mahāyoga System of rNyingma Tantra" (Ph.D. Thesis, University of Virginia, 2004), 55–56; 96.
15. Mipam, *Lion's Roar: Exposition of Buddha-Nature*, 586.4–586.6: *de gnyis gcig nges don byas na gcig drang don bya dgos pa'i 'gal ba med par ma zad/ zung du tshogs par byas nas bde gshegs snying po de lta bu la rgyu rgyud kyi don du byas nas rdo rje theg pa'i man ngag gi gnad 'byung bas sangs rgyas kyi bstan pa de dag gnad gcig tu 'bab par shes dgos shing/ mthar thug gi don 'di la klu thogs rnam gnyis sogs 'phags pa rnams dgongs pa gcig ste chos dbyings bstod pa dang sems 'grel la sogs pa dang/ rgyud bla ma'i 'grel pa sogs kyis gsal bar rtogs pa'i phyir.* Pettit mistranslated this passage when he wrote "it is not contradictory to take one of these [wheels] as definitive and one as provisional," *Mipham's Beacon of Certainty,* 121–122.

16. Nāgārjuna and Asaṅga wrote treatises (*śāstra*) that made important contributions to systematized Mahāyāna thought in India. In Tibet, they are known as the two "great chariots": Nāgārjuna is the chariot of profound view and Asaṅga is the chariot of vast activity.
17. Mipam, *Lion's Roar: Exposition of Buddha-Nature*, 564.2–565.3: *mdo dang sngags kyi chos kun gyi gnad gcig pu ni kun khyab bde gshegs snying po 'di kho na yin . . . ston pa bde bar gshegs pas gsung gi skabs la lar stong pa nyid bstan pa'i sgo nas bde gshegs snying po'i ngo bo gsal bar mdzad/ la lar stobs sogs yon tan ye ldan du bstan pa'i cha nas bde gshegs snying po'i rang bzhin gsal par mdzad de/ de gnyis 'gal med zung du 'thug pa dgos bden kyang/ bden gnyis dbyer med pa'i gnad zab pa las shin tu zab pa la yid ches ma rnyed pa'i dbang gis/ la las ni bde gshegs snying po ngo bo mi stong pa'i rtag par blta/ la las ni stong rkyang tsam la bzung nas sku dang ye shes kyi yon tan 'bral med ye ldan du bzhag tu med pa'i chad lta skur 'debs kyi phyogs la gnas par gyur.*
18. The unity of the empty essence and the luminous nature reflects language that is typically used to describe the ground of the Great Perfection, which we will see in chapter 4. Also, we can see that Anne Klein misrepresented Mipam when she made the false claim that Mipam does not take the Perfection of Wisdom teaching of emptiness in the second wheel as the literal expression of the final view, but, rather, interprets the final view as Buddha-nature in the last wheel. Anne Klein, "Mental Concentration and the Unconditioned: A Buddhist Case for Unmediated Experience," in *Paths of Liberation*, Robert Buswell and Robert Gimello, eds. (Kuroda Institute: University of Hawaii Press, 1992), 272.
19. Mipam, *Words That Delight*, 55–56: *bka' dang bstan bcos rnams na bden gnyis 'jog tshul gnyis su gnas te/ gnas lugs don dam la dpyod pa'i tshad ma'i dbang du byas de/ stong pa la don dam dang/ snang ba la kun rdzob ces bzhag pa dang/ snang tshul la dpyod pa kun tu tha snyad pa'i tshad ma'i dbang du byas te/ gnas snang mthun pa mi bslu ba'i yul dang yul can la don dam dang/ ldog phyogs la kun rdzob tu 'jog pa'i tshul gnyis.* See also Mipam, *Light of the Sun* (*brgal lan nyin byed snang ba*), published in *spyod 'jug sher 'grel ke ta ka* (Sichuan: Nationalities Press, 1993), 549; Bötrül, *Notes on the Essential Points of [Mipam's] Exposition [of Buddha-Nature]* (*stong thun gnad kyi zin thun*), *Collected Works*, vol. 1 (Sichuan: Nationalities Press, 2004), 267.
20. Mipam, *Commentary on the Wisdom Chapter of the Bodhicaryāvatāra* (*sher 'grel ke ta ka*), 6: *kun rdzob ni skye sogs kyi rang bzhin du med bzhin der snang ba sgyu ma dang rmi lam skra shad lta bu'i snang tshul 'di yin la/ snang ba de'i rang bzhin brtags na skye sogs kyi rnam par dben pa'i gnas tshul don dam pa yin te.*
21. The object that is evaluated by means of ultimate valid cognition is the ultimate ontological status of the object, that is, its status as inherently existent or not.
22. Bötrül, *Ornament of Mañjugoṣa's Viewpoint*, 120: *gnas tshul la dpyod pa don dam dpyod pa'i tshad mas gzhal don yang dag yin min gyi sgo nas/ gzhal don yang dag pa'i stong nyid la don dam bden pa dang/ yang dag min pa'i snang ba la kun rdzob ces snang stong gi sgo nas bden pa gnyis su dbye bar mdzad do.*

23. Mipam, *Commentary on the Wisdom Chapter*, 11: *sems dang ngag gi spyod yul du gyur pa'i chos de ni brtags na rnam par dben pas sgyu ma bzhin du stong pa yin gyi dpyad bzod pa nam yang mi srid do.*
24. Mipam, *Words That Delight*, 368: *blos rten 'cha' ba'i yul gang yin pa dbu ma'i rigs pas sun phyin mi nus pa mi srid.*
25. Mipam, *Concise Summary of the Philosophies from the Wish-Fulfilling Treasury* (*yid bzhin mdzod kyi grub mtha' bsdus pa*), Mipam's *Collected Works*, vol. 21, 483.5–483.6: *chos kun rten cing 'brel bar 'byung ba tsam ste/ dngos po rnams brten nas skye ba dang/ dngos med rnams brten nas btags pa'o/ de ltar rten 'brel gyis bsdus pa'i chos thams cad rang bzhin med de/ rang bzhin yod na brten nas 'byung ba mi 'thad la.* See also Mipam, *Precious Vajra Garland*, 742.1–742.2; Khenpo Künpel, *Opening the Door of Intelligent Presence: A Short Commentary Elucidating the Meaning of the Words of "Beacon of Certainty"* (*nges shes rin po che'i sgron me'i tshig gi don gsal ba'i 'grel chung blo gros snang ba'i sgo 'byed*), published in *nges shes sgron me rtsa 'grel* (Sichuan: Nationalities Press, 1997), 155.
26. For more on the status of dependent imputations, see Mipam's discussion of "the genuine evaluated object posited exclusively as entities capable of performing a function" (*gzhal bya mtshan nyid pa don byed nus pa'i dngos po kho na la 'jog pa*) in Mipam, *Words That Delight*, 82–83; English translation in Thomas Doctor, trans., *Speech of Delight: Mipham's Commentary on Śāntarakṣita's* Ornament of the Middle Way (Ithaca: Snow Lion Publications, 2004), 93–97.
27. Mipam, *Words That Delight*, 407: *gal te snang ba'ang med na de'i stong pa'ang med pas/ stong pa dang snang ba gnyis po phan tshun gcig med na gcig mi srid la/ gcig yod na gcig yod pas.*
28. Mipam, *Beacon of Certainty*, 27: *yang dag dpyod pa'i shes rab ngor/ /snang dang stong pa 'di gnyis po/ /yod mnyam med mnyam ngo bo gcig/ /ldog pa tha dad dbye bar 'dod.* Tsongkhapa also depicts the relationship between the two truths as "essentially the same with different contradistinctions, like an impermanent phenomenon and a product." Tsongkhapa, *Thoroughly Illuminating the Viewpoint* (*dgongs pa rab gsal*), (Sarnath: Central Institute of Higher Tibetan Studies, 1998), 176: *ngo bo gcig la ldog pa tha dad pa byas pa dang mi rtag pa lta bu.*
29. Emptiness here should be understood to be emptiness as only a quality of appearance, not emptiness as the unity of emptiness and appearance. This is an important distinction for Mipam that will be discussed in chapter 3.
30. Mipam, *Beacon of Certainty*, 27: *snang kun btags pa tsam zhig la/ /stong pa'ang blo yis btags pa tsam.*
31. The word I translate as "relative" (*kun rdzob, saṃvṛti*), reflects only one of its meanings, "interdependent"—it also has the meanings "conventional" and "concealing," as expressed by Candrakīrti in his *Prasannapadā*. Here Mipam is stressing the *concealing* connotation. Although the term "relative" does not express the full range of meanings of *kun rdzob*, I use the single term "relative" to maintain consistency in translation. For a discussion of the meaning of *kun rdzob*, see Guy Newland, *The Two Truths* (Ithaca: Snow Lion Publications, 1992), 76–80.

32. Mipam, *Words That Delight*, 57: *snang ba dang kun rdzob don du gcig ste/ snang ni snang yang snang ba ltar bden par grub pa med pa la go dgos/ bden pa med ces rjod pa des kyang phyin ci log gi snang ba yin par ston mi dgos te/ stong pa yin pa la bden pa med ces btags pa go dgos/ de de ltar snang ba ltar grub/ snang ba ltar bden na kun rdzob ces gdags par mi rung la/ de ltar na mi stong bar 'gyur zhing/ mi stong pa'i dngos po zhig shes byar mi srid pa'i tshul rigs pas yang dag par grub pa des na shes bya'i khong 'di na snang stong gnyis ris su chad pa'i phyogs gcig kho nar gyur pa'i chos zhig mi srid la.*
33. Mipam, *Difficult Points of Scriptures in General* (*dbu ma sogs gzhung spyi'i dka' gnad skor gyi gsung sgros sna tshogs phyogs gcig tu bsdus pa rin po che'i za ma tog*), Mipam's *Collected Works*, vol. 22, 431.4–432.2: *snang ba yod na de stong pa la stong nyid du btags kyi/ snang ba med pa ri bong gi rwa la sogs pa ni stong pa nyid kyi don ma yin te/ tha snyad du med pa yin pas/ ri bong gi rwa rwa stong gi tha snyad sbyar yang gtan med kyi don yin no/ stong pa nyid ni tha snyad du yod pa'i chos rnams kyi chos nyid yin te . . . des na stong pa nyid 'di tha snyad du yod pa'i chos thams cad kyi rang bzhin nam gnas lugs su bsgrub par bya ba yin gyi/ tha snyad du med pa zhig gi chos nyid du bsgrub bya ni gtan min no.*
34. Mipam delineates two types of lower Svātantrikas (*rang rgyud 'og ma*) in his summary of the philosophies (*grub mtha'*) of Longchenpa's *Wish-Fulfilling Treasury:* those who establish illusion by reason (*sgyu ma rigs grub pa*) and those who hold appearance and emptiness as different (*snang stong tha dad pa*). Mipam, *Concise Summary of the Philosophies from the Wish-Fulfilling Treasury*, 479.5–479.6. The higher Svātantrika (*rang rgyud gong ma*) refer to masters such as Jñānagarbha, Kamalaśīla, and Śāntarakṣita. Mipam, *Concise Summary of the Philosophies from the Wish-Fulfilling Treasury*, 481.4.
35. Mipam, *Shedding Light on Thusness*, 262: *rgyal ba'i dbang po klong chen rab 'byams kyis yid bzhin rin po che'i mdzod du/ rang rgyud 'og ma'i bye brag slob dpon dpal sbas sogs snang stong tha dad du 'dod pa dag gi lugs bkag pa'i skabs su/ snang ba ma yin pa'i stong pa bden pa gnyis char mi srid pa dang/ rtogs byar mi rung ba dang/ tha dad du gyur na spang gnyen du mi 'thad de/ dgra la zhe sdang skyes pa la nam mkha' stong par shes pas mi phan pa ltar/ gzhi rdzun snang la zhen nas logs su stong par zhes pas ci yang mi phan pa'i de 'dra'i stong pa de rtogs pa la dgos pa med par 'gyur pa'i rigs pa gsungs pa bzhin no.* See Longchenpa, *White Lotus: Auto-Commentary of the Precious Wish-Fulfilling Treasury* (*theg pa chen po'i man ngag gi bstan bcos yid bzhin rin po che'i mdzod kyi 'grel pa padma dkar po*), 1125.2–1126.2. See also Mipam, *Concise Summary of the Philosophies from the Wish-Fulfilling Treasury*, 480.3–481.4; and a statement by Mipam's student, Khenpo Künpel, which is nearly verbatim as Mipam's translated above, in Khenpo Künpel, *Opening the Door of Intelligent Presence*, 74–75.
36. Mipam, *Beacon of Certainty*, 27: *kun rdzob spangs pa'i pha rol na/ /don dam med la don dam pa/ /spangs pa'i kun rdzob gzhan med nyid/ /gang snang stong pas khyab*

pa dang/ gang stong snang bas khyab pa ste/ /snang na mi stong mi srid cing/ /stong de'ang ma snang mi grub phyir.

37. Mipam, *Words That Delight*, 57–58: *mi bden pa'i snang ba la kun rdzob ces gdags shing/ rang bzhin ma grub pa'i stong pa la don dam zhes btags pa/ de gnyis po la rtsis che chung med par gzugs nas rnam mkhyen gyi bar du mgo snyoms su sbyor ba 'di shes na shes bya'i khong na de las shes rgyu gal che ba gcig kyang med par nges so.*
38. Mipam, *Difficult Points of Scriptures in General*, 465.3–465.4: *gnas tshul dang snang tshul mthun par 'gyur ba'i yul yul can gnyis ka don dam/ gnas snang mi mthun pa'i yul yul can gnyis ka kun rdzob tu bzhag pa ni/ tha snyad du bslu mi bslu'i dbang gis de ltar 'jog dgos te.* See also Mipam, *Words That Delight*, 56.
39. Bötrül, *Ornament of Mañjugoṣa's Viewpoint*, 122: *snang tshul la dpyod pa dag kyang tha snyad tshad mas gzhal tshe de'i gzhal don yang dag yin min gyi sgo nas yang dag pa'i gnas lugs gang zhig gnas snang mthun par 'gyur pa'i yul stong nyid yul can ye shes lta bu snang stong gnyis ka don dam dang/ yang dag min pa'i snang lugs gang zhig gnas snang mi mthun par 'gyur pa'i yul yul can lta bu 'khrul pa'i cha kun rdzob tu 'jog pa'i sgo nas bden pa gnyis su dbyer mdzad do.*
40. This Tibetan word for "perception" (*snang ba*) also means "appearance." "Appearance" connotes an objective aspect and "perception" connotes a subjective aspect of "perceived appearance." In attempt to convey both aspects of "perceived-appearance," and translate the import of its meaning here, I use the word "experience."
41. Mipam, *Difficult Points of Scriptures in General*, 466.2–466.3: *gnas snang mthun pa'i stobs kyis thob pa'i myang 'das kyi chos thams cad don dam yin la/ mi mthun pa'i stobs kyis byung ba'i chos thams cad kun rdzob tu bzhag rung.*
42. Ibid., 452.2–452.4: *snang ba kun rdzob kyi phyogs su gtogs pa'i chos la'ang/ 'khrul ma 'khrul bslu mi bslu'i khyad phyed dgos kyi/ kun rdzob yin tshad 'khrul snang yin mi dgos so/ /don dam pa'i ming btugs* [read *btags*] *tshad stong rkyang yin mi dgos te/ kun rdzob dang don dam la gzhal lugs kyi ming so sor 'ong ba'i tshul gnyis 'di mdo dang bstan bcos chen po rnams la yongs su grags pa yin no.* See also Karma Phuntsho, *Mipham's Dialectics and the Debates on Emptiness*, 114–120.
43. Mipam, *Words That Delight*, 56: *phyi ma'i don dam yin kyang ngo bo stong pa yin la.*
44. Mipam, *Shedding Light on Thusness*, 304: *gzhung chen po rnams su bden pa gnyis kyi 'jog tshul mi 'dra ba gnyis bshad pa'i dang po gnas tshul skye med la don dam dang/ snang tshul tha snyad la kun rdzob kyi ming gis bstan pa de yin la/ gnyis pa gnas snang mthun par gyur pa'i yul dang yul can gnyis ka la don dam dang/ mi mthun par gyur pa'i yul dang yul can gnyis ka la kun rdzob kyi ming gis bstan pa ni tha snyad nye bar bzung ba'i dbang du yin la/ lugs 'di'i dbang du byas na mdo sngags gang yin kyang yul can la'ang don dam gyi ming 'jug pa dang . . . lugs de gnyis kun rdzob dang don dam zhes ming mthun yang don gyi rnam gzhag byed tshul mi 'dra bas so so'i lugs kyi dgongs pa phye nas 'chad ma shes na gzhung chen po rnams khab mig ltar dog pa'i blos nam mkha' gzhal bas 'jal re zad par 'gyur ro.*

45. The "meaning-commentary" is Candrakīrti's *Madhyamakāvatāra;* the "word-commentary" is Candrakīrti's *Prasannapadā.*

46. Candrakīrti, *Madhyamakāvatāra* VI.23. In the second verse, the *Madhyamakāvatāra* reads "thusness" (*de nyid*) rather than "ultimate" (*don dam*) as in Bötrül's citation. See *Madhyamakāvatāra* published with autocommentary in *Auto-Commentary of the Madhyamakāvatāra* (*dbu ma la 'jug pa'i rang 'grel*), (Sarnath: Sakya Students' Union, 1999), 104. See also Guy Newland, *The Two Truths*, 95.

47. The "Collection of Reasonings" (*rigs tshogs*) refers to six texts of Nāgārjuna: *Prajñāmūlamadhyamakakārikā* (*dbu ma rtsa ba'i shes rab*), *Ratnāvalī* (*rin chen phreng ba*), *Vigrahavyāvartanī* (*rtsod zlog*), *Śūnyatāsaptati* (*stong nyid bdun cu pa*), *Vaidalyaśūtra* (*zhib mo rnam 'thag*), and *Yuktiṣaṣṭikā* (*rigs pa drug cu pa*).

48. Bötrül, *Ornament of Mañjugoṣa's Viewpoint*, 121–122: *bstan bcos chen mo dbu ma rtsa ba shes rab kyi don 'grel zla ba'i gzhung rtsa 'grel gyi dgongs pa yang snang stong gi bden pa gnyis po 'di las gzhan du ma dmigs te/ 'jug pa las/ dngos kun yang dag rdzun par mthong ba yis/ /dngos rnyed ngo bo gnyis ni 'dzin par 'gyur/ /yang dag mthong yul gang de don dam de/ /mthong ba rdzun pa kun rdzob bden par 'dod/ /zhes yang dag mthong ba mnyam bzhag ye shes kyi yul du gyur pa'i stong nyid kho na don dam du bzhag cing/ mthong ba rdzun pa sgyu ma rmi lam lta bu'i snang cha thams cad la kun rdzob tu bzhag cing/ de lta bu'i stong nyid don dam bden pa de mtha' bzhi skye 'gog sogs gnas lugs la dpyod pa don dam dpyod pa'i tshad mas gtan la phab par mdzad kyi/ de las gzhan du snang tshul la dpyod pa tha snyad dag pa'i tshad mas 'khor ba kun rdzob dang/ myang 'das don dam du 'jog pa'i bden gnyis kyi rnam bzhag dbu ma rigs tshogs dang/ 'jug pa rtsa 'grel sogs las ni tshig gcig kyang mi 'byung bas na/ snang stong gnyis su dbye tshul 'di ni gzhung de dag gi dgongs pa bla na med par grub bo.*

49. Ibid., 120: *snang stong gi sgo nas bden pa gnyis su bzhag pa'i tshul 'di ni nges don zab mo yum rgyas 'bring bsdus gsum sogs bka' bar ba mtshan nyid med pa'i mdo sde rnams kyi dgongs pa yin te/ gzugs nas rnam mkhyen bar gyi snang ba thams cad kun rdzob chos can du bzhag ste/ de dag gi ngo bo ma grub pa'i stong nyid don dam bden pa brjod bya gtso bor bstan pa'i phyir te.*

50. Ibid., 122–123: *gnas snang mthun mi mthun gyi sgo nas bden pa gnyis su 'jog pa'i tshul 'di ni/ snying po'i mdo bcu lta bu bka' 'khor lo tha ma'i nges don gyi mdo sde rnams las/ nges don bde gshegs snying po'i khyad par stong cha nas yul chos kyi dbyings ngo bo stong par rnam thar sgo gsum ldan gyi bdag nyid dang/ snang cha nas yul can ye shes kyi rang bzhin 'od gsal ba mkhyen brtse nus pa'i yon tan dang dbyer med gyur pa gnas snang mthun pa'i don dam dang 'khrul snang 'khor ba'i rang bzhin dri ma glo bur ba'i cha yul yul can thams cad gnas lugs gyi gshis la ma zhugs pa'i rnam par dbyer yod pa gnas snang mi mthun pa'i kun rdzob tu bzhed de.*

51. Ibid., 126: *rigs khams snying po sogs kyi snang stong gi cha gnyis ka gnas snang mthun pa'i cha nas don dam du bzhag mod kyang/ 'on kyang snang cha nas kun rdzob dang/ stong cha nas don dam du dbye ba'i tshul gyis snang stong gi bden pa gnyis char yod do.* See also Bötrül, *Notes*, 267.

52. Ibid., 119: *deng dus snang stong gi bden pa gnyis zhes yongs su grags pa tsam las gnas snang gi bden gnyis zab mo mkhyen pa ni shin tu dkon par snang zhing tshul des nges don mdo rgyud kyi dgongs don zab mo bde bar gshegs pa'i snying po snang stong zung 'jug don dam du bzhag pa dang/ ma hā yo ga'i lugs kyi dag mnyam bden pa dbyer med don dam bden par 'jog pa sogs snang stong dbyer med don dam du bzhed pa'i phyogs rnams ring du byas pa snang ngo.*

53. Pettit, *Mipham's Beacon of Certainty,* 122. Pettit consistently misrepresents Bötrül in *Mipham's Beacon of Certainty.* He also cites Bötrül as agreeing that "sūtra and tantra do not differ with respect to the view," which is actually a statement Bötrül makes with regards to *other traditions* in contrast to his own view. Pettit, *Mipham's Beacon of Certainty,* 66.

54. Bötrül shows how both of Mipam's two-truth models of appearance/emptiness and authentic/inauthentic experience apply to the inner-tantras (*nang rgyud*) of Nyingma. In the former delineation of the two truths as appearance/emptiness, in terms of what is found from the perspective of ultimate valid cognition being authentic or not, he states that:

- in Mahāyoga, the relative is "great purity" (*dag pa chen po*) from the aspect of appearance, and from the aspect of emptiness, the ultimate is "great equality" (*mnyam pa chen po*),
- in Anuyoga, the relative is "the maṇḍala of the deities of the three seats" (*gtan gsum lha'i dkyil 'khor*) from the aspect of appearance, and from the aspect of emptiness, the ultimate is "the primordial maṇḍala as it is" (*ye ji bzhin pa'i dkyil 'khor*), and
- in Atiyoga, the relative is "ground-appearance that is spontaneously present by nature" (*gzhi snang rang bzhin lhun gyis grub pa*) from the aspect of appearance, and from the aspect of emptiness, the ultimate is "the nature of the primordially pure essence of the ground-expanse" (*gzhi dbyings ngo bo ka nas dag pa'i rang bzhin*).

Furthermore, in the latter two-truth model of authentic/inauthentic experience, from the perspective of conventional valid cognition of pure vision, Bötrül states that from the aspect of whether experience is authentic or not:

- in Mahāyoga, the indivisibility of the truths of purity and equality is the ultimate and is called "the great seven ultimate treasures" (*don dam dkor bdun chen po*), the opposite of the ultimate is called "the relative of imputed delusion" (*'khrul pa btags pa'i kun rdzob*),
- in Anuyoga, the great ultimate that is the unity of the two truths is called "the maṇḍala of the awakened mind" (*byang chub sems kyi dkyil 'khor*), the opposite of the ultimate is called "the relative of impure delusion" (*ma dag 'khrul pa'i kun rdzob*), and

- in Atiyoga, the unity of primordial purity and spontaneous presence is called "the ultimate truth of self-existing wisdom abiding within the ground" (*gzhi gnas rang 'byung ye shes don dam bden pa*), while the deluded phenomena of dualistic perception are called "the relative of impure ground-appearance" (*gzhi snang ma dag pa'i kun rdzob*).

Bötrül, *Ornament of Mañjugoṣa's Viewpoint*, 120–124.

55. For instance, in the *Great Exposition of Tenets* (*grub mtha' chen mo*) by the Geluk scholar, Jamyang Zhepa (*'jam dbyangs bzhad pa ngag dbang brtson grus*, 1648–1722), he characterizes the ultimate truth as "the mode of appearance in accord with the mode of reality." In an annotated commentary on this text, another Geluk scholar, Ngawang Pelden (*ngag dbang dpal ldan,* b. 1797), states that relative truths are false and deceptive, meaning that there is discord between the mode of appearance and the mode of reality. See English translation of Jamyang Zhepa's text, and Ngawang Pelden's annotated commentary, in Jeffrey Hopkins, *Maps of the Profound* (Ithaca: Snow Lion Publications, 2003), 904.
56. Bötrül, *Ornament of Mañjugoṣa's Viewpoint*, 125: *thal 'gyur pa'i lugs kyi gzhung du ni bshad ma thag pa ltar bka' bar pa'i dgongs 'grel rigs tshogs dang/ 'jug pa rtsa 'grel sogs las ni/ snang stong gi sgo nas 'jog par mdzad cing/ bka' tha ma'i dgongs pa rgyud bla ma rtsa 'grel sogs kyis ni gnas snang mthun mi mthun gyi sgo nas bden gnyis 'jog par mdzad pas bden gnyis kyi 'jog tshul gnyis ka 'gal med gnad gcig tu zhal gyi[s] bzhed kyi gang rung kho na las gzhan spang bar ma mdzad pa'i phyir ro/ /rgyu mtshan de nyid kyi phyir na 'jug pa rtsa 'grel sogs zla ba'i gzhung dang/ rgyal tshab chen po byams mgon mchog gi rgyud bla ma'i gzhung gnyis ka yang/ theg chen thal 'gyur pa'i gzhung du 'gal med gnad gcig tu 'gyur pa lags so.* See also Bötrül, *Ornament of Mañjugoṣa's Viewpoint*, 127.
57. Bötrül, *Notes*, 267–268: *'on na thal 'gyur pa'i lugs la bden gnyis 'jog tshul 'di gnyis gang yin zhe na/ 'di gnyis ka 'gal med du 'jog ste/ de yang zla bas dang pos rtsal du bton te chos thams cad kyi ngo bo stong pa nyid gsal bar mdzad/ rgyud blas phyi ma rtsal du bton kyang snga ma dang dgongs mthun du grub ste/ stong pa'i rang bzhin 'od gsal ba grub pa des na 'jug pa dang rgyud bla gnyis ka thal 'gyur ba'i gzhung du 'gal med gnad gcig tu babs pa'i rgyu mtshan de yin.*
58. Mipam considers the *Uttaratantra* a Middle Way text but does not delineate it as exclusively Prāsaṅgika. This was confirmed to me by Khenpo Kātyāyana in a private conversation in 2004.
59. *Uttaratantra* I.155: *rnam dbyer bcas pas mtshan nyid can/ /blo bur dag gis khams stong gi/ /rnam dbyer med pa'i mtshan nyid can/ /bla med chos kyis stong ma yin. rgyud bla ma rtsa 'grel*, 20.
60. Mipam, *Lion's Roar: Exposition of Buddha-Nature*, 577.1–577.3: *'khor ba'i nyes pa thams cad ni nga dang chos kyi bdag tu 'dzin pa 'khrul pa'i sems las byung la/ 'khrul sems de yang gdod ma'i gshis 'od gsal la ye nas ma gos ma 'dre par mkha' la sprin ltar glo bur ba yin pas skyon de dag ni khams dang so sor 'byed cing 'bral rung ba yin pas*

khams kyi ngo bo la skyon des stong pa ste ma gos pa yin la/ 'khrul pas bslad pa la mi ltos par rang gi ngang gis 'od gsal zhing chos kun gyi de kho na nyid du zhugs pa'i rang byung gi ye shes las rnam dbyer byar med pa'i mthar thug gi yon tan rnams kyi khams de mi stong ste/ rang gi ngo bo la 'bral med kyi gshis yin pas nyi ma dang zer bzhin no.

61. Bötrül, *Ornament of Mañjugoṣa's Viewpoint*, 124: *gzhan yang theg pa chen po rgyud bla ma'i skabs su yang/ rnam dbyer med pa'i mtshan nyid can/ /bla med chos kyis stong ma yin/ /zhes ngo bo stong pa'i rang gdangs 'od gsal ba bral 'bras chos sku'i yon tan dang dbyer med pa'i rigs khams bde gshegs snying po don dam du bstan cing/ rnam dbyer bcas pa'i mtshan nyid can/ /glo bur dag gis khams stong gis/ /zhes dri ma gshis la ma zhugs pa gnyen po'i lam bsgom stobs kyis dbyer yod pa'i gzung 'dzin 'khrul pa'i chos kun rdzob tu bstan.*
62. See Mipam, *Lion's Roar: Exposition of Buddha-Nature*, 589.3–590.2.
63. Candrakīrti under *Madhyamakāvatāra* VI.95, in *Auto-Commentary of the Madhyamakāvatāra*, 196. See also D. T. Suzuki, trans., *The Laṅkāvatāra Sūtra* (London: Routledge, 1968), 68–69; Jeffrey Hopkins, *Meditation on Emptiness* (London: Wisdom Publications, 1983), 615–616.
64. The Nirgrantha, which Bötrül refers to as the Sky-clad Ones (*nam mkha' gos can*), are also known as "the Nudists" (*gcer bu pa*). The Nirgrantha refers to the Jain tradition. Mipam also references the Nirgrantha in distinguishing Buddha-nature from a mere absence in a citation from the *Mahāparinirvāṇasūtra*. He states: "Merely the aspect of a non-implicative negation (*med dgag*) is not suitable as nirvāṇa, again from the scripture [*Mahāparinirvāṇasūtra*]: "'Emptiness, emptiness'—at the time you search, you find nothing at all. The Nirgrantha also have 'nothing at all,' but liberation is not like that." Mipam, *Lion's Roar: Exposition of Buddha-Nature*, 573.5–573.6.
65. Bötrül, *Ornament of Mañjugoṣa's Viewpoint*, 95: *snang cha nas nam mkha'i gos can pa'i lugs ltar ma yin par rang bzhin 'od gsal ba'i yon tan mkhyen brtse nus gsum gyi khyad par du byas pa de yang stong cha nas mu stegs byed kyi bdag ltar ma yin par ngo bo stong pa chen po rnam thar sgo gsum gyi khyad par du byas pa.*
66. Khenpo Künpel, *Opening the Door of Intelligent Presence*, 69: *spyir de bzhin gshegs pa'i snying po rang gi ngo bos mi stong par gyur na phyi rol pa'i rtag bdag dang khyad par med pas rnam thar sgo gsum gyi rang bzhin du bstan pa dang/ 'od gsal ba'i ye shes kyang med pas stong pa phyang chad nam mkha' lta bur gyur na gcer bu pa dang khyad par med pas 'od gsal ba'i ye shes 'dus ma byas par bstan pas ston pa'i bka' bar tha nges pa'i lung gis ngo bo stong pa dang rang bzhin gsal bar bstan pa.*
67. Bötrül, *Notes*, 268–269: *spyir drang nges 'jog tshul la sgra ji bzhin pa'i bstan don la/ dgongs gzhi dgos pa dngos la gnod byed gsum tshang ba'i mdo de drang don dang/ de las ldog pa nges don du 'jog go.* See also Bötrül, *Ornament of Mañjugoṣa's Viewpoint*, 89.
68. *Samādhirājasūtra* VII.5: "Know the specific sūtras of definitive meaning in accord with the teaching of emptiness by the Buddha. Know all the doctrines of

a sentient being, a person, and a being as the provisional meaning." P.795, vol. 31, p. 281, 22a.5–22a.6.

69. *Madhyamakāvatāra* VI.97.

70. Bötrül, *Notes*, 269: *mdo ting 'dzin rgyal po sogs kyi dgongs pa ltar/ zla bas don dam dpyod byed kyi tshad mas gnod pa yod med kyi sgo nas don dam stong nyid brjod bya'i gtso bor ston pa'i mdo nges don dang/ tha snyad kun rdzob brjod bya'i gtso bor ston pa'i mdo drang don du bzhed de/ mdo gang de nyid ma yin bshad don can/ /kun rdzob gsung pa'ang shes nas drang bya zhing/ /stong nyid don can nges don shes par gyis/ zhes gsungs so/ des na brjod bya'i dbang gis bka' dang po drang don dang/ bar ba nges don/ tha ma drang nges phyed ma'i tshul du 'jog go/ /de'i phyir zla bas drang don du bzhag pa'i mdo yis bstan don yin na tha snyad du med pas ma khyab ste/ kun rdzob bden pa'i rnam bzhag thams cad drang don gyi brjod don yin pa'i phyir ro.*

71. Bötrül, *Ornament of Mañjugoṣa's Viewpoint*, 90: *brjod bya snang stong gi sgo nas bka' bar ba nges don du bzhed tshul ni/ stong nyid don dam dpyod byed kyi tshad ma'i rnyed don yang dag mchog gyur yin min gyi sgo nas/ snang ba'i cha la kun rdzob kyi chos dang/ stong pa'i cha la don dam pa'i chos kyi bden pa gnyis su dbye tshul las mdo gang zhig stong pa nyid don dam bden pa brjod bya'i gtso bor dngos bstan gyi bka' 'khor lo bar ba sher phyin gyi mdo rnams nges don.*

72. P.2010, vol. 46.

73. Bötrül, *Notes*, 269–270: *rigs khams nor bu sbyong pa'i dpes bstan pa'i mdo yis bstan don ltar/ rgyud bla ma dang chos dbyings bstod pa sogs kyis dag pa'i gzigs pa tshad mas gnod pa yod med kyi sgo nas dag gzigs tshad mas rnyed don ltar mthar thug nges don bde gshegs snying po bstan pa'i mdo rnams nges don du bzhed pa/ des na nges don bde gshegs snying po snang stong dbyer med kyi rang bzhin gnas snang mthun pa'i don dam brjod byar bstan pa'i bka' tha ma nges don du bzhed de/ dag gzigs tshad mas rnyed don yin pa'i phyir.*

74. Bötrül, *Ornament of Mañjugoṣa's Viewpoint*, 91: *brjod bya gnas snang gi sgo nas bka' tha ma nges don du bzhed tshul ni/ rnam dag tha snyad tshad ma'i rnyed don yang dag mchog gyur yin min gyi sgo nas gnas snang mi mthun pa'i cha kun rdzob kyi chos dang/ gnas snang mthun pa'i cha don dam pa'i chos kyi bden gnyis dbyer med tshul las/ mdo gang zhig 'od gsal don dam bden pa brjod bya'i gtso bor dngos bstan gyi bka' 'khor lo tha ma snying po bstan pa'i mdo rnams nges don du bzhed.*

75. Ibid., 93: *mdor na bka' bar tha gnyis brjod bya/ snang cha bde gshegs snying po dang stong cha chos kyi dbyings dngos bstan gyi brjod bya'i gtso bor mdzad tshul gyi khyad par las drang nges rnam par dbye ba'i tshul gyi sgo nas/ bka' 'khor lo bar ba nges don du 'jog pa dang/ tha ma nges don du 'jog pa'i rang bzhin dag ni/ gnas skabs brjod bya gtso che chung gi sgo nas so sor dbye tshul kyi khyad par tsam las mthar thug gi don la gnyis ka'ang nges don gyi mdor 'gal med gnad gcig tu bzhed pa lags so.*

76. This is the first part of a famous verse in the Perfection of Wisdom Sūtras (Bötrül cites the second part of the verse two stanzas down). One version of these famous lines is found in the *Prajñāpāramitā Sūtra in Eight-Thousand Lines*

(*Aṣṭasāhasrikāprajñāpāramitā, 'phags pa shes rab kyi pha rol tu phyin pa brgyad stong pa*), D.10, vol. 33, 5.3. English translation in Edward Conze, *The Perfection of Wisdom in Eight Thousand Lines & Its Verse Summary* (Bolinas, CA: Four Seasons Foundation, 1973), 84.

77. Bötrül, *Distinguishing the Views and Philosophies: A Torch of the Essential Points* (*lta grub shan 'byed gnad kyi sgron me*), published in *lta grub shan 'byed gnad kyi sgron me'i rtsa 'grel* (Sichuan: Nationalities Press, 1996), 36–37: *'khor lo bar pa'i nges don mchog/ /rnam thar gsum ldan chos kyi dbyings/ /sems la sems ma mchis pa ste/ sems nyid ngo bo stong par gnas/ /snang stong chos kyi bden gnyis las/ /stong nyid don dam mtha' bral mchog /don dpyod tshad ma'i rnyed don phyir/ /rtag dngos bden pa'i mtha' las grol/ /'khor lo tha ma'i nges don mchog /mkhyen brtse nus ldan bde gshegs rigs/ sems kyi rang bzhin 'od gsal ba'i/ /rang bzhin 'od gsal chen por gnas/ /gnas snang chos kyi bden gnyis las/ /gnas snang mthun pa'i don dam mchog /rnam dag tshad ma'i rnyed don phyir/ /cang med chad pa'i mtha' las grol/ /'khor lo bar tha 'gal med mchog /snang stong zung 'jug snying po'i khams/ /sems nyid dag dang ma dag las/ /thugs rjes rten 'byung chen por gnas/ /snang stong dang ni gnas snang gi/ /bden gnyis 'gal med don gyi mchog /tshur mthong tshad ma'i yul min phyir/ /glo bur spros chos kun las grol.* See also Bötrül, *Ornament of Mañjugoṣa's Viewpoint*, 206–208.

78. The *Akṣayamatisūtra* states: "Sūtras that teach an owner where there is no owner for instance, and describe objects with various words [such as] self, sentient being, living being, sustainer, being, person, human being, individual, agent, and experiencer are 'the provisional meaning.' Sūtras that teach the gates of liberation, the emptiness of entities, signlessness, wishlessness, no composition, no arising, no sentient beings, no living beings, no persons, and no owners are 'the definitive meaning.'" P.842, vol. 34, p. 64, 156a.4–156a.7.

79. The *Dhāraṇīśvararāja* states: "Noble child, observe this: a person skilled in gemstones, for instance, knowing well the manner of refining gems, takes an unrefined gemstone from the class of valuable jewels. After washing it in a strong astringent fluid, he scrubs it with a black haircloth. However, he does not cease his efforts with just this; after that, he washes it in a strong solution containing mercury and rubs it with wood and wool. However, he does not cease his efforts with just this; after that, he washes it in a great medicinal serum and then rubs it with a fine cloth. Having polished it, the jewel is free from the various defilements and is called a '*vaiḍūrya*' (star-gem). Noble child, likewise a Tathāgata as well, knowing the constituents of thoroughly impure sentient beings, by means of the disquieting discourse of impermanence, suffering, selflessness, and unpleasantness, makes sentient beings who delight in saṃsāra give rise to disillusionment, causing them to enter into the disciplinary doctrine of Sublime Ones. However, a Tathāgata does not cease his efforts by just this; after that, by means of the discourse of emptiness, signlessness, and wishlessness, he causes them to realize the manner of the Tathāgatas. However, a Tathāgata does not cease his efforts by just this; after that, by means of the discourse on the wheel of the

irreversible doctrine and the discourse on the complete lack of the threefold conceptualization (*'khor gsum*), he causes those sentient beings to enter the realm of the Tathāgatas. Those sentient beings of various predispositions and natures, having entered equality, realize the suchness of the Tathāgatas; thus, they are known as 'the unexcelled place of offering.'" *Dhāraṇīśvararāja* (*Tathāgatamahākaruṇānirdeśasūtra*), P.814, vol. 32, p. 300–301, 176b.4–177a.3.

80. Bötrül, *Ornament of Mañjugoṣa's Viewpoint*, 92: *dbu ma chen po'i lugs la blo gros mi zad pa sogs kyi mdo dang 'jug pa rtsa 'grel sogs bstan bcos chen po'i dgongs don ltar bka' bar ba nges don du bzhed pa dang/ gzungs dbang rgyal po sogs kyi mdo dang rgyud bla sogs bstan bcos chen po'i dgongs don ltar bka' tha ma'i snying po bstan pa'i mdo rnams nges don du bzhed pa'i dgongs don 'gal med gnad gcig tu rnying gzhung spyi.*
81. Mipam, *Shedding Light on Thusness*, 419: *dmigs pa med pa'i stong nyid ston pa de dag nges don gyi mdo sde yin la/ dmigs pa can kun rdzob ston pa drang don du mdo 'di nyid kyis bstan.*
82. See Bötrül, *Ornament of Mañjugoṣa's Viewpoint*, 68. Khenpo Künpel also makes a similar statement in his commentary on Mipam's *Beacon of Certainty*. See Khenpo Künpel, *Opening the Door of Intelligent Presence*, 70.

Chapter Two. Middle Way of Prāsaṅgika and Yogācāra

1. Longchenpa associates Prāsaṅgika with the Great Perfection as follows: "The manner of assessing the freedom from extremes, etc. in this tradition of the natural Great Perfection is mostly in accord with Prāsaṅgika-Madhyamaka." Longchenpa, *Treasure Trove of Scriptural Transmission: Commentary of the Precious Treasury of the Expanse of Phenomena* (*chos dbyings rin po che'i mdzod kyi 'grel ba lung gi gter mdzod*), 322.4–322.5: *rang bzhin rdzogs pa chen po 'di'i lugs kyis mtha' bral la sogs pa'i 'jal tshul phal cher/ dbu ma thal 'gyur dang mtshungs.* Longchenpa also affirms that Prāsaṅgika is the summit of the dialectical vehicle: "the summit of the dialectical vehicle of the Mahāyāna, Prāsaṅgika-Madhyamaka." Longchenpa, *White Lotus*, 1141.3: *mtshan nyid theg pa chen po'i rtse mo dbu ma thal 'gyur.*
2. Mipam, *Words That Delight*, 366: *don dam rnam grangs pa bden grub med par dgag pa tsam ni blo'i yul yin sgra'i yul yin/ rnam grangs min pa la ni snang stong re re'i phyogs su ma lhungs pa'i snang stong zung 'jug bden gnyis zung 'jug spros bral dbu ma sogs ming btags pa ni mtshon byed tsam ste mdzub mos zla ba bstan pa dang 'dra ba las don du sgra rtog gi yul las shin du 'das pa yin no.*
3. Ibid., 54: *mdor na mnyam bzhag sgra dang rtog pa'i yul las 'das pa'i gzhal don ltar mthar thug gi gnas tshul bden pa dbyer med kyi dbang du byas na ni bden gnyis phye mi dgos pas 'di ltar snang ba'i chos thams cad ye nas yod med yin min sogs dgag sgrub kyi khas len gang yang med pas ci'ang mi gsung ba'i tshul gyis lan btab pa dang 'dra*

bar yang dag par na tha snyad thams cad las 'das shing brjod du med pa dang spros pa dang bral ba dang mnyam pa nyid kyi phyir khas len med par grub kyang/ rjes thob sgra rtog gi yul du gyur pa snang tshul gyi dbang du byas te gzhi lam 'bras bu sogs kyi rnam gzhag zhig rang gis bsam zhing gzhan la'ang smra dgos na ni tshad ma gnyis phye ste dgag sgrub kyi tshul la 'jug pa las 'da' ba mi srid do.

4. Ibid., 360–361: *des na dgag bya bcad tsam gyi bden stong med dgag gi cha dang/ rten 'byung gi cha so sor rang sa na ma 'dres par yod pa lta bu'i phyir na lugs de la 'dzin pa'ang yod khas len kyang yod la.*
5. Ibid., 91: *las dang po pa'i dgag bya bkag pa'i med rkyang tsam zhig blo yul du 'char srid kyang/ dbu mas dpyad pa gnad du song ba'i gang zag gis/ rang bzhin med pa dang/ med pa tsam gyi khyad legs par phyed pa'i sgo nas/ rang bzhin med pa dang rten 'byung don du dbyer med pa'i nges shes khyad par can gyi 'dzin stangs ni/ g.yang sa lta bu rtag chad kyi mtha' gnyis sel ba'i gnyen po yin mod/ ji srid dgag sgrub kyi 'dzin stangs dang bcas pa de srid du rnam par rtog pa'i spros pa mtha' bzhi bral ba'i rang bzhin ma yin no.*
6. Other-exclusion (*gzhan sel, anyāpoha*) refers to how words represent meaning through negative reference, an idea developed in the Buddhist epistemological tradition of Dignāga (480–540) and Dharmakīrti. For more on other-exclusion, see Masaaki Hattori, "*Apoha and Pratibhā,*" in *Sanskrit and Indian Studies: Essays in Honour of Daniel H. H. Ingalls,* ed. M. Nagatomi et al. (Dordrecht: Reidel, 1980), 61–73.
7. Mipam, *Words That Delight,* 362: *dngos po dgag bya rnam par bcad pa 'di ni yod pa bsal ba'i gzhan sel rtog pa'i gzugs brnyan tsam yin pas spros pa las ma 'das la.*
8. Ibid., 332: *stong nyid med dgag nyid tha snyad kun bral gyi don dam mtshan nyid pa la ltos te kun rdzob tu bzhag gi.*
9. Georges Dreyfus, "Would the True Prāsaṅgika Please Stand? The Case of 'Ju Mipham," in *The Svātantrika-Prāsaṅgika Distinction,* ed. Georges Dreyfus and Sarah McClintock (Boston: Wisdom Publications, 2003), 323.
10. Mipam, *Light of the Sun*, 544: *blo'i spyod yul yin min dpyad pa sogs kyi skabs su rnam grangs min pa la brjod kyi rnam grangs pa'i don dam la brjod don med de/ rnam grangs pa'i don dam ni las dang po pas stong nyid la rim gyis 'jug pa'i skabs su rtog ngor byas pa tsam las 'phags pa'i mnyam bzhag ye shes rtogs* [read *rtog*] *bral lta bu gnyis snang nub pa'i blo la kho 'dra ba rgyu ba'i sa ga la yod de/ 'khor los sgyur pa'i khri la mu to ba 'dug pa'i dbang med pa bzhin no.*
11. Mipam, *Shedding Light on Thusness*, 265: *tha snyad kyi chos la yod pa'am med pa rtag mi rtag sogs gang rung du khas len pa las/ gnyis ka dang gnyis min du smra ba mi rung ngo/ tha snyad las 'das pa spros pa nye bar zhi ba'i gnas lugs la mtha' bzhi'i khas len med par brjod tshe/ bsdus tshan gyi gzhung gis sangs rgyas kyi bka' sun 'byin dgos pa ni ha cang yang thal ma ches sam.* See also Karma Phuntsho, *Mipham's Dialectics and the Debates on Emptiness*, 93.
12. Mipam, *Shedding Light on Thusness*, 303–304: *yul can gyi dbang du byas na gnyis snang log ma log gi sgo nas rnam grangs min pa dang yin pa'i don dam gyi tha snyan*

[read *snyad*] *kyang 'thad par bdag cag gis kyang 'dod de yul gyi dbang du byas na spros pa nyi tshe ba'i spyod yul dang bral ba dang/ spros pa'i spyod yul mtha' dag dang bral ba de gnyis la don dam gnyis po'i khyad par du bshad cing/ yul can gyi dbang du byas na spros bral gyi don la ji lta bar gzigs nas gnyis snang log pa'i yul can de la rnam grangs min pa'i don dam pa dang/ de las gzhan du gnyis snang dang bcas pa la rnam grangs pa'i don dam gyi brda mdzad pa yod de.*

13. Mipam, *Light of the Sun*, 472: *thal 'gyur pas rnam grangs min pa khas len thams cad bral ba'i dbu ma chen po rtsal du bton nas bshad pa'i tshe don dam dpyod pa gzhir bzhag gi dbang du byas te...ji ltar snang ba thams cad spros bral dmigs pa med pa mnyam gzhag dam pa'i spyod yul dang mthun par gtan la 'bebs pa yin te.*
14. Mipam, *Words That Delight*, 102: *de'i phyir thal rang de dag mnyam bzhag bden gnyis ro gcig pa'i ye shes dang/ rjes thob bden gnyis so sor 'byed pa'i shes rab la rtsal du bton nas 'chad pa'i tshul de ltar yin par shes par bya.*
15. Ibid., 99: *rnam grangs pa'i don dam khas len dang bcas pa de rtsal du bton nas 'chad pa rang rgyud pa'i mtshan nyid yin la/ rnam grangs ma yin pa'i don dam khas len kun bral rtsal du bton nas 'chad pa thal 'gyur ba yin pa shes par bya'o// 'di gnyis kyi mtshan nyid 'jog pa'i skabs su tha snyad du rang mtshan gyis grub pa 'dod mi 'dod dang gtan tshigs 'god tshul sogs kyi khyad par phyes te 'jog pa ni yan lag gi dbye ba tsam ste gong gi mtshan nyid 'dir 'du ba yin te/ khas len yod med/ tha snyad du rang mtshan gyis grub pa zhal gyis bzhes mi bzhes/ rang bzhin med sgrub kyi gtan tshigs thal rang du 'god tshul/ dgag bya la don dam gyi khyad par sbyar mi sbyar gyi gnad kyang bshad ma thag pa'i tshul de nyid kyi dbang gis yin no.*
16. Mipam, *Light of the Sun*, 576: *thal 'gyur ba'i gzhung gis rnam grangs pa'i don dam tsam las mi ston na/ thal rang gnyis las dgongs pa rang rgyud pa mtho bar khas len dgos te.*
17. Mipam, *Beacon of Certainty*, 42: *de ltar gnas lugs mthar thug don/ /khas len med kyang snang tshul la/ /tha snyad bden gnyis so sor yang/ /khas blang yod de de gnyis kyang/ /bden gnyis dbyer med gnas lugs la/ /ltos na so so'i snang tshul tsam/ /dbyer med don mthong ye shes la/ /ltos na tshad ma gnyis po yang/ /nyi tshe'i gnas yin de gcig gis/ /bden gnyis 'dzin pa mi srid phyir.*
18. Mipam, *Light of the Sun*, 473: *rnam grangs min pa khas len thams cad dang bral ba'i don dam 'phags pa'i mnyam gzhag gi yul du snang zhing/ rnam grangs pa'i don dam rjes kyi nges pa la snang la snga ma ye shes dang phyi ma rnam shes kyi spyod yul yin . . . de ltar don dam btags pa ba dang mtshan nyid pa gnyis po dang mnyam rjes sbyar rgyu 'dir go ba'i gnad chen po yod cing 'di go na lta ba'i 'dzin stangs zhig ma zhig gi gnad kyang go nus.*
19. Mipam, *Beacon of Certainty*, 42–43: *nged kyis khyad par phyes nas su/ /shan 'byed lam gyi dbu ma dang/ /dngos gzhi mnyam bzhag dbu ma gnyis/ /rags dang phra ba'am rgyu 'bras sam/ /rnam shes ye shes gnas skabs kyi/ /dbu ma che chung khyad phyes nas.*
20. Ibid., 47: *de phyir bden gnyis so so yi/ /khas len dang bcas dbu ma de/ /'bras ming rgyu la btags pa yi/ /res 'jog dbu ma chung ngu yin.*

21. Mipam, *Words That Delight*, 99, op. cit.
22. Mipam states: "In the perspective of authentic vision—a perspective like the sight of the absence of floating hairs for which nothing at all is found—there are no commonly appearing objects; and due to that essential point, a qualifier [e.g., 'ultimately'] does not need to be applied to the object of negation." Mipam, *Eliminating Doubts* (*dam chos dogs sel*), published in *dbu ma rgyan rtsa 'grel* (Sichuan: Nationalities Press, 1990), 503: *yang dag pa'i gzigs ngor ci yang ma rnyed pa skra shad med pa'i mthong ba lta bu'i ngor chos can mthun snang med pa dang/ gnad de las dgag bya la khyad par sbyar mi dgos pa*. See also Mipam, *Eliminating Doubts*, 502.
23. Mipam, *Words That Delight*, 99, op. cit.
24. Mipam, *Light of the Sun*, 473, op. cit.
25. Mipam, *Shedding Light on Thusness*, 253: *spros bral gyi don rim dang cig car gyi 'chad tshul tsam las mthar thug spros bral nyid du dgongs pa gcig par 'dod pas.*
26. Mipam, *Words That Delight*, 97: *de ltar bden gnyis so sor zhen pa'i cha de thal 'gyur ba'i dgag bya thun mong ma yin pa yin te/ gal te rang rgyud pa dag bden gnyis so sor zhen pa'i dgag bya dang bral bar gyur na/ thal 'gyur ba sogs la'ang lta ba de las skyed cung zad kyang 'don rgyu med par shes par bya ste.*
27. Mipam, *Commentary on the Wisdom Chapter*, 9: *thal 'gyur ba'i skabs 'dir zung 'jug spros pa dang bral ba'i dbu ma chen po nyid rtsal du 'don pas 'di'i lugs la rnam grangs dang rnam grangs min pa'i don dam gnyis su dbye ba med par shes par bya'o.*
28. Mipam, *Light of the Sun*, 472: *rang rgyud pas rnam grangs pa'i don dam rtsal du bton nas 'chad pa'i skabs su don dam bden stong tsam la bzhed pa dang/ tha snyad tshad grub bzhed pa'i gnad kyis khas len dang bcas pa'i dbu ma rjes kyi nges pa dang mthun par gtan la phab pa yin la.*
29. Tsongkhapa argued that Prāsaṅgikas are distinct from Svātantrika due to rejecting that which is established by its own essence conventionally: "The Svātantrika-Madhyamaka and the Prāsaṅgika-Madhyamaka are not distinguished by means of whether or not the qualifier 'ultimately' is applied to the object of negation; rather, there is a difference in whether or not they negate the nature of what is established by its own essence (*rang gi ngo bos grub*) conventionally." Tsongkhapa, *The Great Exposition of the Stages of the Path*, 668–669: *des na dbu ma rang rgyud pa dang thal 'gyur ba gnyis dgag bya la don dam gyi khyad par sbyar mi sbyar gyi sgo nas mi phyed kyang rang gi ngo bos grub pa'i rang bzhin tha snyad du 'gog mi 'gog gi khyad par yod pas.*
30. Mipam, *Light of the Sun*, 474–475: *don dam dpyod pas dpyad pa'i tshe yul rang ngos nas grub pa rdul tsam rnyed na'ang de bden grub du 'gyur mod/ don dam dpyod pa'i ngor rang ngos nas grub pa ni rang rgyud pas kyang khas mi len la len na dbu ma par mi rung zhing thar ba'i lam yang de la med par 'gyur ro/ tha snyad dpyod pa'i ngor yul rang gi ngo bos grub par snang yang des yul de bden grub du ga la 'gyur te tha snyad tshad mas grub pa 'thad dgos la/ de tha snyad dpyod byed kyi ngor yang ma grub na gang du'ang grub par mi 'gyur ro.*

31. Mipam, *Shedding Light on Thusness*, 314: *tha snyad kyi skye ba 'di rang rgyud pas tshad grub tu 'dod cing don dam dpyod pas dpyad kyang de la gnod pa med de/ don dam par skye ba 'gog pa'o zhes bzung nas tha snyad du skye ba med na tha snyad bden pa med par 'gyur ro snyam du dgongs pa'o/ thal 'gyur bas don dam dpyod pas dpyad na dpyad bzod du yod pa gang yang med do.*
32. Ibid., 306–307: *de ltar mtha' bzhi'i tshul gyis dpyad na skye ba ni don dam par ma zad/ tha snyad du yang med par gtan la phab pa'i rigs pa des 'di ltar rten 'byung gi snang ba bslu med du yod pa 'di rnams ye nas skye ba dang 'gag pa med pa'i rang bzhin du gtan la phab pa yin pas/ rnam grangs pa'i bden med tsam las 'das te rnam grangs min pa'i don dam bden gnyis dbyer med spros bral chos kyi dbyings nyid du bstan pa yin no.*
33. Bötrül, *Notes*, 264–265: *bden gnyis phyed te snang ba yang bkag na/ dgag bya khyab ches ba'i skyon 'jug kyang bden gnyis ma phyes pa'i gnad kyis dgag bya khyab ches pa'i skyon mi 'jug pa ma zad bden gnyis dbyer med mtshan nyid pa 'ong ba'i gnad 'di thug.*
34. On this point, Mipam is similar to the fifteenth-century Sakya scholar, Gorampa. In direct contrast to Tsongkhapa, Gorampa explicitly states that the Svātantrika-Prāsaṅgika distinction is not made concerning the presentation of conventional truth: "In the presentation of the conventional, Prāsaṅgika and Svātantrika are not distinguished because Prāsaṅgikas also accept autonomous reasons in the presentation of the conventional." Gorampa, *Distinguishing the Views* (*lta ba'i shan 'byed*), (Sarnath: Sakya Students' Union, 1988), 109: *thad snyad kyi rnam bzhag la/ thal rang gi khyad par 'byed pa ni min te/ tha snyad kyi rnam bzhag la rang rgyud kyi gtan tshigs thal 'gyur ba rnams kyis kyang khas len pa'i phyir te.* See English translation in José Cabezón and Geshe Lobsang Dargyay, *Freedom from Extremes,* 193. Mipam does part ways with Gorampa on the Svātantrika-Prāsaṅgika distinction. Mipam makes a distinction between the two by means of a gradual versus instantaneous elimination of constructs. Gorampa, however, does not make a distinction in terms of the manner of generating the view of the ultimate: "In terms of the manner of generating the view of the ultimate, there is no difference between the manner of asserting the ultimate for Prāsaṅgikas and Svātantrikas." Gorampa, *Completely Elucidating the Definitive Meaning* (*rgyal ba thams cad kyi thugs kyi dgongs pa zab mo dbu ma'i de kho na nyid spyi'i ngag gis ston pa nges don rab gsal*), *Collected Works*, vol. 5 (Dehra Dun: Sakya College, 1979), 57.4: *don dam pa'i lta ba bskyed tshul gyi sgo nas thal 'gyur ba dang/ rang rgyud pa gnyis te/ don dam gyi 'dod tshul la ni khyad par med do.*
35. Mipam, *Words That Delight,* 76: *dpal ldan zla ba'i dgongs pa snang ba 'di kun thad kar rang sar dag pas tha snyad kyi rdzun ris dbyings su yal ba'i zab mo'i lta ba ni/ rdzogs chen gyi gzhung nas ka dag gtan la 'bebs tshul dang mtshungs.*
36. The two are: (1) primordial purity of the Great Perfection and (2) the emptiness of the Prāsaṅgika—freedom from constructs. In his commentary on these verses, Khenpo Künpel states: "It is said that there is not the slightest distinction

between the two: (1) primordial purity of the Great Perfection and (2) the freedom from constructs, which is the emptiness of the Prāsaṅgika, from the aspect of the expanse of phenomena being empty of essence." Khenpo Künpel, *Opening the Door of Intelligent Presence*, 129: *rdzogs chen ka dag dang thal 'gyur ba'i stong pa nyid spros bral de gnyis la khyad par ci yang med do zhes yul chos kyi dbyings ngo bos stong pa'i cha nas gsungs so*. The underlined text, printed in the edition, delineates Mipam's words in the *Beacon of Certainty*, which Khenpo Künpel gives an interlinear commentary on.

37. Mipam, *Beacon of Certainty*, 19: *ka dag bdar sha chod pa la/ /thal 'gyur lta ba mthar phyin dgos/ /spros bral tsam gyi cha nas ni/ /de gnyis khyad par med do gsungs.*
38. Ibid., 17: *mtha' bzhi'i spros pa cig car du/ /khegs pa blo 'das gnyug ma'i dbyings/ /so so'i skye bo'i sa nyid na/ /car phog tshul gyis mthong dka' bas/ /mtha' bzhi'i spros pa res 'jog tu/ /'gog pa thos bsam lta ba'i lugs.*
39. Mipam, *Words That Delight*, 408–410; 95. The text in *Words That Delight* is nearly verbatim as the text in *Overview: Essential Nature of Luminous Clarity* (*spyi don 'od gsal snying po*), published in *bka' brgyad rnam bshad dang spyi don 'od gsal snying po yang dag grub pa'i tshig 'grel bcas bzhugs* (Sichuan: Nationalities Press, 2000), 461–462. For more on these four stages, see Yönten Gyatso (*yon tan rgya mtsho*, fl. nineteenth century), *Moonlamp: Commentary on the Precious Treasury of Qualities* (*yon tan rin po che'i mdzod kyi 'grel pa bden gnyis gsal byed zla ba'i sgron ma*), vol. 3, 80.1–80.5; Karma Phuntsho, *Mipham's Dialectics and the Debates on Emptiness*, 150.
40. Mipam, *Overview: Essential Nature of Luminous Clarity*, 462: *de bzhi po snga ma snga ma la brten nas phyi ma phyi ma'i tshul la 'jug gi/ snga ma la nges par ma rnyed bar phyi ma gtan la pheb pa mi 'byung ngo.*
41. Ibid., 461: *las dang po bas gcig du bral sogs stong nyid sgrub pa'i rigs pa rnams kyis tshul bzhin brtags tshe/ bum sogs ma grub pa'i don la bsams nas/ ma dpyad pa'i ngor yod kyang dpyad na mi rnyed pa'i phyir/ ma grub pa nyid gnas lugs so snyam pas snang stong res 'jog gi tshul du stong pa'i rnam pa zhig 'char.*
42. Ibid., 461: *de'i tshe de'i med pa nyid kyang btags pa tsam las don la ma grub pa'am/ ye nas stong bzhin du snang ba yin pa'i tshul la bsam pas chu zla ltar snang bzhin stong la stong bzhin snang ba'i nges pa khyad par can skye ste/ de'i tshe rang bzhin med pa dang rten 'byung 'gal med du shar ba'am zung 'jug tu go ba zhes bya.*
43. Ibid., 461: *de dus rang bzhin med pa dang rten 'byung de gnyis tshig gis brjod tshul la tha dad yod kyang ngo bo la tha dad cung zad med par dbyer med pa'i tshul la nges shes bskyed pas/ dgag gzhi snang ba dang dgag bya bcad pa sbyar nas 'dzin pa'i rnam rtog rang sar zhig ste/ dgag sgrub bsal bzhag med par sor bzhag tu nus pa lta bu'i spros bral gyi rnam par 'char.*
44. Mipam also depicts emptiness and appearance as conceptually distinct—"essentially the same with different contradistinctions" (*ngo bo gcig [la] ldog pa tha dad*): "Both appearance and emptiness—together present, together absent—are asserted as the same entity, divisible into different contradistinctions." Mipam,

Beacon of Certainty, 27: *snang dang stong pa 'di gnyis po/ /yod mnyam med mnyam ngo bo gcig/ /ldog pa tha dad dbye bar 'dod.*

45. Mipam, *Overview: Essential Nature of Luminous Clarity*, 462: *de 'dra'i spros bral la yang nas yang du goms pas/ chos can re re ba la ltos pa'i chos nyid so so lta bu'i ris chad kyi dmigs pa'i spyod yul gnyis chos kyi rnam pa thams cad dag nas chos thams cad rang bzhin mnyam pa nyid la nges shes khyad par can skye bas mthar phyin to.*
46. Mipam describes two methods of realization: (1) through certainty generated by the explanations of one who sees the definitive meaning, a scholar with extensive study, contemplation, and meditation, or (2) through having the nature of mind pointed out well by a teacher who has experience in the quintessential instructions, even without great knowledge of training in study and reflection. See *Vajra Essence* (*gnyug sems 'od gsal ba'i don rgyal ba rig 'dzin brgyud pa'i lung bzhin brjod pa rdo rje snying po*), Mipam's *Collected Works*, vol. 24, 355.3–356.2. A contemporary Nyingma scholar, Khenpo Namdröl (*mkhan po rnam grol*, b. 1953), in a private conversation contrasted the "quintessential instructions approach" (*man ngag lugs*) with the "study and contemplation approach" (*thos bsam lugs*). A similar distinction can be found in the respective approaches of the Kusāli (hermit) and Paṇḍita (scholar). For a discussion of these two approaches in a parallel context of the Great Perfection in the Bön (*bon*) tradition, see Anne Klein and Geshe Tenzin Wangyal Rinpoche, *Unbounded Wholeness: Dzogchen, Bon, and the Logic of the Nonconceptual* (Oxford: Oxford University Press, 2006), 11–12.
47. Mipam, *Overview: Essential Nature of Luminous Clarity*, 461: *dbang rnon kha cig sems la byung gnas 'gro gsum tsam dpyad pas rgyu 'bras ngo bo nyid gsum gyis stong pa'i rnam thar sgo gsum gyi rang bzhin du myong ba'i stobs tsam las snang stong mnyam nyid kyi don la gcig car du nges pa skye ba'ang yod mod.* See also Yönten Gyatso, *Moonlamp*, vol. 3, 79.6–80.1.
48. Mipam, *Beacon of Certainty*, 14: *sems ni gzugs can ma yin pas/ /sus kyang mdog sogs mthong mi srid/ /ma mthong tsam la stong pa nyid/ /ngo 'phrod snyam na shin tu gol.*
49. The distinction here between what I call "precritical" and "postcritical," a qualitative distinction that Mipam is careful to distinguish, is similar to a distinction that Ken Wilber makes between what he characterizes as "prerational" and "transrational." He calls the mistake of conflating the two "the pre/trans fallacy." See Ken Wilber, *Sex, Ecology, and Spirituality* (Boston: Shambhala Publications, 1995), 205–208; and Ken Wilber, *Eye to Eye: The Quest for the New Paradigm* (New York: Anchor Books, 1983), 201–246.
50. Mipam, *Beacon of Certainty*, 13: *lta ba'i dngos gzhi skyong ba'i dus/ /kha cig ci yang mi 'dzin zer/ /cir yang mi 'dzin zhes pa'i don/ /legs par rtogs dang log rtog gnyis/ /dang po mtha' bzhi'i spros bral te/ /'phags pa'i ye shes kyi 'dun na/ /gang yang gnas pa med mthong bas/ /'dzin stangs ngang gis zhig pa ste/ /stong gsal mkha' la lta dang mtshungs/ /gnyis pa dran med hva shang lugs/ /ma dpyad tse ner bzhag pa yis/ /lhag mthong gsal ba'i cha med par/ /mtsho gting rdo bzhin tha mal gnas/ /dper na ci yang*

med ces pa/ /dbu mas med par mthong ba dang/ /gzugs med med par mos pa ltar/ /tshig tsam mtshungs pa 'di dag kyang/ /don la mi mtshungs gnam sa bzhin.

51. Ken Wilber states this type of distinction well: "Since *pre*rational and *trans*rational are both, in their own ways, *non*rational, then they appear quite similar or even identical to the untutored eye. Once this confusion occurs—the confusion of the "pre" and "trans"—then one of two things inevitably happens: the transrational realms are *reduced* to prepersonal status, or the prerational realms are elevated to transrational glory." Ken Wilber, *Eye to Eye: The Quest for the New Paradigm*, 202. In Mipam's case, these two ways of conflating the prerational and transrational, "the pre/trans fallacy," can be seen in Mipam's characterization of the Great Perfection: the claim that the Great Perfection is simply Hvashang's (prerational) "non-thought" mistakenly reduces the sublime (transrational) Great Perfection to simple (prerational) oblivion; on the other hand, the claim that Hvashang's "non-thought" is the Great Perfection mistakenly elevates simple (prerational) oblivion to the sublime (transrational) Great Perfection.
52. Mipam, *Beacon of Certainty*, 17: *cir yang mi 'dzin lta ngan la/ /dngos po cir yang ma grub pa'i/ /nges shes skye ba ga la yod/ /des na sgrib pa spong mi nus/ /de phyir 'di gnyis khyad par yang/ /du ba'i rtags las me bzhin du/ /spang rtogs bog skyed tshul las shes/ /gang phyir blun sgom tha mal pa/ /spangs dang rtogs pa'i rgyu min la/ /yon tan skye pa'i gegs yin phyir.*
53. Mipam, *Words That Delight*, 88: *mtha' gang du'ang zhen mi rung ngo zhes smras na/ srid pa'i rims nad mtha' dag gi gnyen po stong nyid zab mo'i bdud rtsi'i 'byung gnas rigs pa'i rnam dpyod gyis drangs pa'i nges shes ni bor te/ ji yang yid la byas na mi rung ngo snyam du dran med mun pa'i 'thibs por zhugs pa de lta bus na/ chos zab mo 'di lta zhing mthong ba rtog cing nyams su myong dka' ba yin te.*
54. Ibid., 471–472: *tshig tsam la sgyu ma lta bu dang/ dngos po med pa dang/ spros bral sogs zer yang/ rigs pas drangs pa'i nges shes phu thag chod pa'i sgo nas nyi tshe ba'i stong pa mu stegs rnams kyi bla na 'phags pa'i de bzhin gshegs pa'i stong pa nyid kyi tshul ma shes na ci'ang mi phan la . . . phyi nang gi grub mtha' 'di tshig tsam gyi phye mi nus par zab mo'i gnad gnam sa ltar mi mtshungs pa yod.*
55. The "three analyses" refers to the process of determining the validity of a scripture. They are: (1) that the demonstration of what is evident (*mngon gyur*) is not invalidated by direct perception (*mngon sum*), (2) that the demonstration of what is hidden (*lkog gyur*) is not invalidated by inference (*rjes dpag*), and (3) that the demonstration of what is extremely hidden (*shin tu lkog gyur*) is not contradicted (internally) by previous or later statements.

    Mipam, *Words That Delight*, 347: *sangs rgyas . . . dngos po'i gnas tshul ma nor bar don bzhin bstan pa yin la/ rjes 'jug rnams kyis kyang de bzhin rigs pas gtan la phab dgos pa ni shākya'i ring lugs ma nor ba yin gyi/ spyir rigs pas dpyad pa dang/ khyad par du tshad ma sogs nang rig pa la mi mkho zhes zer ba ni/ dpyad pa gsum gyis dag pa'i sangs rgyas kyi bka' tshad ma'i myang bya phun sum tshogs pa nyams su bstar ba la bar du gcod pa'i bdud kyi gsang tshig rngam chen po ste.*

56. Mipam, *Words That Delight*, 360: *don dam mtshan nyid pa ni med rkyang tsam ma yin te/ mtha' bzhi'i spros bral yin na'ang gzhan sel gyi rtog pa'i blo'i yul na gnas pa'i dngos po'i bden med tsam po ba rnam grangs pa'i don dam 'di med na don dam chen po rtogs pa'i thabs med la/ de rtogs byed kyi thabs sam rgyu yin cing de la gtogs pa yin pas don dam zhes brda sbyar ba yin te.*
57. Mipam, *Commentary on the Wisdom Chapter*, 15–16: *chos thams cad mi bden pa sgyu ma lta bu yin na sbyin sogs lam la'ang slob par mi rigs te sgyu ma'i rta nyo ba'i ngal ba lta bu 'dis ci bya zhe na/ . . . 'khor 'das kyi snang cha rgyu ma lta bu ni rten 'brel ba'i dbang gis bslu med du yod pa des na ji srid gzung 'dzin gyi 'jug pa dbyings su ma nub kyi bar du sems can rnams la snang ba 'di rgyun mi 'chad cing phan gnod byed pa yin pas.*
58. See Mipam, *Eliminating Doubts*, 525–528.
59. For instance, Mipam wrote commentaries on the *Mahāyānasūtrālaṃkāra, Mahāyānasaṃgraha, Abhidharmasamuccaya, Madhyāntavibhāga, Dharmadharmatāvibhāga, Viṃśatikā,* and *Triṃśikā*.
60. Mipam's own most important Middle Way commentaries are on the *Madhyamakālaṃkara* and the ninth chapter of the *Bodhicaryāvatāra*. Much of Mipam's Middle Way views can be found in the "three rejoinders" (*brgal lan rnam gsum*) that he wrote in response to criticisms of his commentaries on these two texts. The commentaries on texts such as the *Madhyamakāvatāra*, the *Madhyamakakārikā*, and the *Uttaratantra*, which are included within Mipam's *Collected Works*, were posthumously assembled by his students from notes and outlines.
61. Mipam, *Words That Delight*, 66: *tha snyad sems tsam du 'dod pa 'di theg chen spyi lugs la grub pa yin no*. See also *Words That Delight*, 50, 85.
62. Mipam, *Overview: Essential Nature of Luminous Clarity*, 407: *de la'ang bdag med kyi lta ba yongs su rdzogs pa dbu ma pa dang/ gnyis stong gi rang rig bden par khas len pas chos bdag phra ba ma rdzogs pa'i sems tsam pa gnyis su yod do.* Kongtrül presents a similar distinction: "The main difference between the two schools of Mahāyāna is whether or not the self-aware, self-illuminating cognition free from perceived-perceiver duality is accepted as ultimately established." Kongtrül, *Encyclopedia of Knowledge*, 550: *gzung 'dzin gnyis kyis stong pa'i shes pa rang rig rang gsal don dam du grub par 'dod pa dang mi 'dod pa theg chen sde gnyis kyi khyad par gyi gtso bo yin te.*
63. Mipam, *Eliminating Doubts*, 544–545: *dbu sems gnyis phyi don yod med la mi rtsod kyang/ rnam shes bden par grub ma grub la rtsod pa yin.*
64. Mipam, *Words That Delight*, 48: *sems tsam pa'i tshul 'di kun rdzob tha snyad kyi de kho na nyid shin tu bden mod/ 'on kyang 'di'i rnam shes rang gsal gyi rang bzhin la bden grub tu zhen pa'i cha de dgag bya yin no.*
65. Mipam, *Light of Wisdom: Commentary on the Dharmadharmatāvibhāga* (*chos dang chos nyid rnam 'byed 'grel pa ye shes snang ba*), Mipam's *Collected Works*, vol. 4, 626.2–627.2: *de ltar gzung bar snang ba de ni rang gi ngo bos 'dzin pa las gzhan du med par grub na/ 'dzin par snang ba de yang med par grub bo/ /de ci'i phyir na 'dzin*

pa ni gzung ba la ltos te grub kyi yan gar du nam yang mi grub po/ de ltar na gzung ba dang 'dzin pa gnyis kyi rnam pa thams cad dang bral te yul dang yul can med pa'i rig pa rang bzhin gyis 'od gsal ba brjod du med pa tsam ni bdag gnyis kyis stong pa'i yongs grub de bzhin nyid dang tha mi dad pa de ni sems tsam pas kyang rtogs dgos na dbu ma pas lta ci smos so . . . brjod med kyi shes pa de yi ngo bo la bden grub du 'jog tshul gyi grub mtha' phra mo tsam zhig lhag mar lus pa de nyid rigs pas sun phyungs te gzung 'dzin med pa'i shes pa nyid kyang bden pa med pa'i stong pa dang zung du zhugs pa'i rang sems gdod nas dag pa'i 'od gsal nyid du 'dod na dbu ma yang dag pa yin te/ des na theg chen dbu sems 'di gnyis zhen pa'i gnad phra mo zhig chod ma chod kyi khyad par las/ mnyam rjes kyi nyams len phyogs 'dra ba lta bur 'ong bas. An edition of Mipam's complete commentary on the *Dharmadharmatāvibhāga*, along with an English translation, can be found in Jim Scott, trans., *Maitreya's Distinguishing Phenomena and Pure Being* (Ithaca: Snow Lion Publications, 2004).

66. The three natures are: (1) the imagined nature (*kun btags, parikalpita*), the dependent nature (*gzhan dbang, paratantra*), and the thoroughly established nature (*yongs grub, pariniṣpanna*).
67. The eight consciousnesses are: (1–5) the five sense consciousnesses, (6) the mental consciousness, (7) the afflicted mind, and (8) the universal ground consciousness.
68. *Laṅkāvatārasūtra: chos lnga dang ni rang bzhin gsum/ /rnam shes brgyad po nyid dag dang/ /bdag med don ni rnam gnyis por/ /theg chen thams cad bsdus pa yin.* Cited in Mipam, *Words That Delight,* 58. See also Mipam, *Light of Wisdom,* 611B.1–611B.4.
69. Mipam, *Shedding Light on Thusness,* 270: *bdag med gnyis dang/ rnam shes tshogs brgyad kyang chos lnga'i nang du 'du la/ de lnga yang rang bzhin gsum gyi nang du 'dus.*
70. Mipam, *Words That Delight,* 58.
71. Mipam, *Garland of Light Rays: Commentary on the Madhyāntavibhāga* (*dbu dang mtha' rnam par 'byed pa'i bstan bcos kyi 'grel pa 'od zer phreng ba*), Mipam's *Collected Works,* vol. 4, 709.5–709.6: *ming ni ka ba dang bum pa sogs brda'i sgo nas btags pa tsam mo/ rgyu mtshan ni ming gi gdags gzhi gdung 'degs sogs kyi don byed pa dang/ lto ldir ba la sogs par snang ba lta bu'o.*
72. Mipam, *Words That Delight,* 59: *de gnyis ni kun btags yin te sgra rtog gi spyod yul can gzung 'dzin gnyis su snang ba brtags na mi bden pa'i phyir ro.*
73. Mipam, *Garland of Light Rays,* 709.6–710.1: *rnam par rtog pa ni rnam shes tshogs brgyad do.*
74. Mipam, *Words That Delight,* 59: *de ni gzhan gyi dbang nyid yin te tha snyad tsam du snang ba sna tshogs kyi snang gzhir gyur pa'o.*
75. Mipam, *Garland of Light Rays,* 669.5–669.6: *kun tu rtog pa'i ngor gzung 'dzin gnyis su snang ba yod kyang/ ji ltar snang ba de kho na ltar gnyis su grub pa ma yin pa'i rnam par rig pa la gzhan dbang zhes bya ste kun brtags 'khrul pa skye ba'i gzhi yin pa'i phyir.*

76. Mipam, *Words That Delight*, 59: *phyi ma yul yul can 'di gnyis ni yongs su grub zhes bya ste.*
77. Ibid., 59: *phyi nang gis bsdus pa'i chos de dag la bdag gnyis kyi rang bzhin cung zad grub pa med pa'i chos kyi dbyings ni de bzhin nyid yin la.*
78. Ibid., 59: *de'i rjes su zhugs pa yang dag min rtog dang bral ba'i yul can so so rang rig pa ni yang dag pa'i ye shes zhes bya'o.*
79. Mipam, *Garland of Light Rays*, 669.5–669.6: *yang dag ma yin kun rtog ces bya ba gang yin na/ de ni gzung 'dzin gnyis su snang ba can/ khams gsum gyis bsdus pa yi sems dang sems byung ba thams cad do.*
80. Ibid., 709.3–709.4: *dag pa'i ye shes kyi yul nyid kun btags dang gzhan dbang gnyis ma yin la/ yongs grub gcig bu kho na yin par brjod de/ de spyod yul du byas tshe gnas snang mthun pa'i phyir.*
81. Ibid., 706.5–707.1: *don dam pa'am dam pa'i don ni ngo bo nyid gsum gyi nang nas yongs grub gcig pu yin gyi gzhan gnyis ma yin te/ gnyis snang med pa'i rang bzhin can tha mal pa'i shes brjod las 'das pa'am/ gnas snang mthun pa ni 'di kho na yin pa'i phyir.*
82. Mipam, *Difficult Points of Scriptures in General*, 466.6–467.1: *gnas snang mthun par gyur pa'i yul can la ye shes zhes bya ste gzung 'dzin med pa'o/ mi mthun par 'dzin pa la rnam shes zhes bya ste gzung 'dzin can no.*
83. Mipam, *Words That Delight*, 59–60: *phyi ma yul yul can 'di gnyis ni yongs su grub zhes bya ste/ ngo bo bden par grub pa ni min gyi yin lugs ma nor bas na tshig de skad bla dwags su btags pa yin no.*
84. Getsé Paṇchen, *Discourse of the Four Reliances: Realizing the Victorious One's Teaching of the Three Wheels as One Viewpoint* (*rgyal bstan 'khor lo gsum dgongs pa gcig tu rtogs pa ston pa bzhi ldan gyi gtam*), *Collected Works*, vol. 1, 119.4–119.5: *de phyir chos kun stong gzhi'i chos nyid gang/ /'phags pa rnams kyi ye shes ma 'khrul bas/ /nyams su myong bya nyid phyir bden par grub/ /'gyur ba med phyir rtag brtan ther zug go.*
85. Getsé Paṇchen, *Ornament of Buddha-Nature*, 95.4: *rdzogs pa chen po'i bzhugs tshul dang/ gzhan stong dbu ma chen po gcig tu mthun.*
86. Getsé Paṇchen, *Discourse of the Four Reliances*, 116.3–116.5: *'di na rgyal ba'i chos 'khor rim gsum gyi/ /dang pos kun rdzob rgyu bcas bslu med dang/ /gnyis pas kun rdzob rang stong gsum pa yis/ /don dam gzhan stong chos nyid zab mo bstan/ /yul gyi 'khrul snang med bzhin kun tu brtags/ /yul can 'khrul sems tshogs brgyad gzhan dbang las/ /rnam grol rig pa'i ye shes yongs grub che/ /'di ni nges don rdzogs chen khyad par chos.*
87. Getsé Paṇchen also says that the viewpoint free from assertions that is stated by Prāsaṅgikas accords with the essence of primordial purity's mode of abiding. He goes on to say that the aspect of spontaneous presence lies in the viewpoint of the last wheel and the doctrines of Maitreya. Getsé Paṇchen, *Elucidating the Definitive Meaning Viewpoint: A Short Explanation of the Four Great Philosophies* (*grub mtha' chen po bzhi'i rnam par gzhag pa mdo tsam phye ba nges don dgongs pa*

gsal byed), *Collected Works*, vol. 1, 70.7–71.2. He also juxtaposes (1) "the subtle inner Middle Way" (*phra ba nang gi dbu ma*) that is other-emptiness with (2) the "gross outer Middle Way of Svātantrika and Prāsaṅgika" (*thal rang rags pa phyi yi dbu ma*), which expresses the relative in accord with Auditors and Self-Realized Ones. We can see here how he positions other-emptiness as superior to a Prāsaṅgika view. See Getsé Paṇchen, *Ornament of Buddha-Nature*, 79.7–80.3; see also Getsé Paṇchen, *Elucidating the Definitive Meaning Viewpoint*, 52.2–53.3.

88. Bötrül, *Ornament of Mañjugoṣa's Viewpoint*, 185–186.
89. Also, it is important to recognize the fact that appearances as they are explained in the *Guhyagarbhatantra*—as divine—is an important part of Nyingma exegesis. We might say that in the Nyingma tradition Mipam inherited, conventional truth in Prāsaṅgika is supplemented by tantra. We will look into the role of tantra in Mipam's interpretation in chapter 5.

Chapter Three. The Present Absence

1. Dölpopa, *The Mountain Doctrine: Ocean of Definitive Meaning* (*ri chos nges don rgya mtsho*), (Gangtok: Dodrup Sangyey Lama, 1976), 194.6: *gnas lugs la yod pa ni gzhan stong dang med pa ni rang stong ngo.*
2. Sixteen types of emptiness are found in the Perfection of Wisdom Sūtras; the fifteenth and sixteenth are referenced in the *Madhyāntavibhāga*. The sixteen are: (1) the emptiness of the internal, (2) the emptiness of the external, (3) the emptiness of the external and internal, (4) the emptiness of the great, (5) the emptiness of emptiness, (6) the emptiness of the ultimate, (7) the emptiness of the conditioned, (8) the emptiness of the unconditioned, (9) the emptiness of the limitless, (10) the emptiness of the beginningless and endless, (11) the emptiness of the non-discarded, (12) the emptiness of intrinsic nature, (13) the emptiness of own characteristics, (14) the emptiness of all phenomena, (15) the emptiness of nonentities, and (16) the emptiness that is the nature of nonentities. Mipam states that the last two subsume the first fourteen, and that the fifteenth, emptiness of nonentities (*dngos po med pa'i stong pa nyid*), is a negation of perceived-perceiver duality through exclusion (*rnam bcad du khegs*), and that the sixteenth, emptiness that is the nature of nonentities (*dngos po med pa'i dngos bo nyid kyi stong pa nyid*), is established through inclusion (*yongs gcod du grub*). Mipam, *Garland of Light Rays*, 673.5–674.1; 679.3–679.5. Kongtrül states that these last two emptinesses necessarily encompass the other fourteen emptinesses (*khyab byed du 'gro dgos*) and are conceptually distinct (*ldog pas phye ba*). He states: "The emptiness of nonentities is posited from the aspect of the negation of the object of negation—the imagined phenomena and the imagined self; the emptiness that is the nature of nonentities is posited from the aspect of the

existence of the entity of the suchness of phenomena and self implied within (*shul na*) the elimination of that object of negation." Kongtrül, *Encyclopedia of Knowledge*, 706: *dgag bya kun brtags kyi chos dang bdag bkag pa'i cha nas dngos po med pa'i stong pa nyid dang/ dgag bya de bkag pa'i shul na chos nyid kyi chos dang gang zag gi dngos po yod pas cha nas dngos po med pa'i ngo bo nyid stong pa nyid du bzhag go*. There is a variation in the enumeration of sixteen emptinesses cited by Candrakīrti in *Madhyamakāvatāra* VI.180–223; see *Auto-Commentary of the Madhyamakāvatāra,* 301–336. Candrakīrti cites "the emptiness of the unobserved" (*mi dmigs pa stong pa nyid*) for the fifteenth instead of "the emptiness of nonentities" as in the *Madhyāntavibhāga.* Although Candrakīrti uses the same term as the one used in the *Madhyāntavibhāga* for the sixteenth, "the emptiness that is the nature of nonentities," a better translation to reflect his explanation of it would be "the emptiness of the nature of nonentities." These two interpretations of the sixteenth, reflected in the translations as "the emptiness *of* . . ." (Candrakīrti) or "the emptiness *that is* . . ." (*Madhyāntavibhāga*), reveal the crucial distinction between emptiness interpreted as a quality (in the former) or a substrate (in the latter); the distinction here prefigures the "self-emptiness versus other-emptiness" controversy in Tibet.

3. Dölpopa's "frequent statement" can be found in Vasubandhu's definition of emptiness in his commentary on the *Madhyāntavibhāga* under verse 2, D.4027, 2a.2–2a.3.
4. Dölpopa, *Ocean of Definitive Meaning,* 300.5–300.6: *bco lnga pa dngos po med pa stong pa nyid ni gang zhig gang na med pa de des stong ngo zhes yang yang gsungs pa'i don te rang gi dngos po stong pa nyid gang yin pa kun rdzob rang stong ngo/ /bcu drug pa dngos po med pa'i de nyid stong pa nyid ni de la lhag mar gyur pa gang yin pa de ni 'dir rtag tu yod pa'o/ /zhes yang yang gsungs pa'i don te gzhan gyi dngos po stong pa nyid gang yin pa don dam gzhan stong ngo.*
5. Ibid., 88.2–88.3: *sngar gdul bya'i dbang gis thar pa la sogs pa thams cad med cing stong pa dang bdag med pa la sogs par gsungs pa ni gang zhig gang na med pa la dgongs pa yin la/ phyi nas mi stong pa dang bdag yod pa la sogs par gsungs pa rnams ni med pa'i lhag ma gang yin pa la dgongs pa yin pas gsung rab snga phyi 'gal 'dra yang legs par brtags na mi 'gal ba.*
6. An implicative negation is characterized as an explicit negation that implicates something else; for instance, like the classic example, "the fat Devadatta does not eat during the day." This negation implies something else, namely, that Devadatta eats at night. In contrast, a non-implicative negation is characterized as an explicit negation that does not imply anything else, for instance, "Brahmins should not drink alcohol." In contrast to implicative negations, the connotative force of a non-implicative negation is denial rather than an implied affirmation.
7. Dölpopa, *Ocean of Definitive Meaning,* 88.3–88.4: *med dgag gi gzhi la ma yin dgag yod pa'i phyir dang/ skyon thams cad kyis gdod nas rang bzhin gyis dag cing spangs pa'i gzhi la gnyug ma'i yon tan thams cad tshang ba'i ye shes mkha' khyab yongs su grub par bzhugs pa'i phyir ro.*

8. Ibid., 434.6: *stong gzhi don dam gyi yon tan . . . thams cad gnas lugs la rnam yang bzhugs pa'i phyir.*
9. Ibid., 313.7–314.1: *yod med la sogs pa'i mtha' thams cad dang bral ba'i gzhi chos kyi dbyings kun tu 'gro ba ni gnas lugs kyi sangs rgyas so.*
10. Ibid., 366.6–366.7: *don dam gyi sems ni gnas lugs la yod pa'i sems so/ /kun rdzob kyi sems ni gnas lugs la med pa'i sems so/ /de'i phyir sems gang zhig yod pa'i sems zhes pa don dam byang chub kyi sems rang bzhin 'od gsal ba ste.*
11. Ibid., 166.4–166.5: *gzhan yang chos nyid la sogs pa rnam grangs mang po can gyi bde gsheg* [read *gshegs*] *snying po de bzhin nyid gang yin pa de nyid chos thams cad kyi gzhi yin pa'i phyir.*
12. Ibid., 431.5–431.6: *gnas lugs la don dam chos sku med pa ma yin te de bzhin nyid bdag dag pa'i bdag tu gyur pa sangs rgyas kyi bdag nyid chen po'i bdag ma chad pa'i phyir/ /gnas lugs la kun rdzob gzugs sku yod pa ma yin te kun rdzob kyi chos gang yang ma grub pa'i phyir.*
13. Ibid., 483.7–484.1: *sems can rnams kyis las snang 'khrul pa 'di ni sems can pa nyid kyi dgos* [read *sgos*] *chos yin gyi/ gnas lugs la ri bong gi rwa dang mo sham kyi bu dang nam mkha'i me tog la sogs pa ltar gtan mi srid pa'i phyir.*
14. Ibid., 303.5–303.6: *yod pa'i mtha' ni kun rdzob kyi chos rnams gnas lugs la gtan nas med pa yin yang yod do zhes sgro 'dogs pa gang yin pa'o/ /med pa'i mtha' ni chos kyi dbyings kyi ye shes cha med kun 'gro kun la khyab par rtag tu bzhugs kyang med cing ma grub la rang gi ngo bos stong ngo zhes skur 'debs pa gang yin pa'o/ /mtha' de dag dang bral ba'i dbus gang yin pa de ni yod med dang sgro skur dang rtag chad la sogs pa mtha' thams cad dang bral ba'i gzhi yin pa'i phyir dbu ma chen po mthar thug pa ste.* See also Dölpopa's *bka' bsdu bzhi pa'i rang 'grel,* cited in Stearns, *The Buddha from Dolpo,* 248n.11.
15. Dölpopa, *Ocean of Definitive Meaning,* 313.1–313.2: *shes bya thams cad dngos po dngos med gnyis su kha tshon chos par smra ba rnams kyis ni chos nyid don dam pa'i gnas lugs ma rtogs pa nyid du zad de/ de ni shes bya yin yang dngos po dang dngos med gang yang ma yin pa'i phyir ro/ /des na de ni phung po gsum pa dang dbus ma'am bar ma nyid du yang grub bo.*
16. Ibid., 384.4–384.5: *thams cad kyis stong pa mi srid de chos nyid kyis stong pa mi srid pa'i phyir ro/ chos thams cad kyis stong pa'i gzhi ni srid de chos nyid do/ chos nyid kyis stong pa'i gzhi ni mi srid de ha cang thal ba dpag tu med pas gnod pa'i phyir ro/ des na thams cad kyis stong pa dang chos thams cad kyis stong pa ni khyad par shin tu che ste/ gnas lugs la chos kyi[s] stong yang chos nyid kyis mi stong pa'i phyir ro/ 'dis ni chos dang chos nyid ngo bo gcig la ldog pa tha dad du 'dod pa dang/ tha dad gtan med du 'dod pa yang bsal ba yin te/ de gnyis ni ngo bo gcig pa bkag pa'i tha dad yin pa'i phyir.*
17. Dölpopa denies that the ultimate and relative are expressible as essentially the same or different. He states: "The two truths are not expressible as essentially the same or different; they are different in the sense of not being one." Dölpopa, *The Sun Elucidating the Two Truths (bden gnyis gsal ba'i nyi ma), Collected Works,* vol. 6, 711.1–711.2: *bden gnyis ngo bo de nyid dang/ gzhan du brjod du med pa gcig pa bkag pa'i tha dad pa yin.*

18. Khenpo Lodrö Drakpa, *The Beautiful Ornament of a Clear Mind: A Presentation of Buddhist and Non-Buddhist Philosophies* (*phyi nang grub mtha'i rnam bzhag gi bsdus don blo gsal yid kyi rgyan bzang*), *Collected Works*, vol. 10, 243.7–244.1: *dgag bya bden grub bkag tsam gyi med dgag de stong nyid mthar thug tu smra bas na rang stong zhes brjod do.*
19. Ibid., 270.6–270.7: *stong gzhi don dam gnyis med kyi ye shes de rang ngos nas mi stong par gzhan gzung 'dzin sogs spros pa mtha' dag gis gdod nas stong pa dang/ kun rdzob glo bur gyis bsdus pa'i chos rnams don dam gzhan gyi ngo bos stong pa'i steng du kun rdzob rang gi ngo bos kyang stong par smra bas na dbu ma gzhan stong pa zhes brjod.*
20. Khenpo Lodrö Drakpa, *Roar of the Fearless Lion* (*rgyu dang 'bras bu'i theg pa mchog gi gnas lugs zab mo'i don rnam par nges pa rje jo nang pa chen po'i ring lugs 'jigs med gdong lnga'i nga ro*), (Dharamsala: Library of Tibetan Works and Archives, 1993), 88.1–88.2: *mthar thug pa'i yin lugs thams cad med cing ma grub pa'i stong rkyang tsam du zad pa ma yin par kun rdzob spros pas stong pa med dgag gi gzhi la ma yin dgag gi 'od gsal ba'i chos nyid don dam ye nas bzhugs pas.*
21. Khenpo Lodrö Drakpa, *The Beautiful Ornament of a Clear Mind*, 242.6–243.6; 268.1–270.7.
22. Khenpo Lodrö Drakpa, *Roar of the Fearless Lion*, 60.6–61.2: *kun rdzob kyi tshul gtso bo dang po'i brjod bya dang rnam grangs pa'i don dam gyi tshul gtso bo bar ba'i brjod bya dang rnam grangs min pa'i nges don mthar thug pa gsal bar gtso bo tha ma'i brjod byar byas pas 'khor lo gsum po rim par brjod bya spyi la bsam na drang ba'i don dang gnas skabs kyi nges don dang mthar thug gi nges don gtso bor bjod byar byed pa'i cha nas de lugs su drang nges kyi mdor 'jog pa yin.*
23. Ibid., 51.6–52.1: *dang por kun rdzob thun mong bden bzhi'i tshul dang bar bar mtshan ma'i spros pa kun bral gyi dbyings nges don phyed tsam dang tha mar spros bral gyi gzhi dbyings ye shes chen po nges don don dam.*
24. Ibid., 50.4–50.6: *tha ma don dam rnam par phye pa'i chos 'khor ni gdul bya theg pa mtha' dag gis rgyud sbyangs zin pa'i dbang rnon shin tu smin pa rnams la 'phags pa'i ye shes kyi gzigs ngo'i don dam bden pa nyid dbyings rig dbyer med kyi ngo bo gdod ma nas 'gyur ba med pa'i phyir rtag brtan ther zug pa'i bden par yod pa dang/ kun rdzob gzung 'dzin gyis bsdus pa'i chos rnams ni don dam de'i rnam 'gyur tsam me long gi gzugs brnyan ltar gdod nas ma skyes pa'i bden med du so sor legs par phyes nas gtso bor gsungs.*
25. Ibid., 84.4–84.6: *de gnyis la mdo sde tha dad med pa yin te/ mdo sde gcig la dgongs pa 'grel tshul bzang ngan gyi khyad tsam ma gtogs don mdo so sor 'jog rgyu med pa'i phyir/ dper na bye mdo gnyis la mdo sde tha dad med kyang dgongs pa len lugs tsam yin pa bzhin.*
26. Ibid., 63.3–63.6: *snying po'i mdo sogs bka' tha ma'i mdo mchog rnams chos can/ khyod dag spyis gnyis med ye shes bden grub tu bstan pa tsam gyis dngos smra'i sems tsam pa'i rang lugs su mi 'gyur te/ tha ma'i bstan don gyi ye shes bden grub dang dngos smra'i sems tsam lugs kyi gzhan yongs bden grub gnyis bden par grub lugs gtan nas mi*

'dra ba'i khyad par chen po yod pa'i phyir/ der thal/ tha ma'i bstan don gyi ye shes ni spros bral rang rig dam pa'i yul du gshes [read *gshis*] *kyi gnas lugs su bden pas na bden grub dang/ sems tsam lugs kyi gzhan yongs bden grub ni rnam par shes pa'i snang cha las ma 'das pa'i grub pa'i mtha' las bzhag pa yin pas mtshan ma bden dngos su dmigs pa'i dgag bya yin pa'i cha nas khyad che.* See also ibid., 214.6–223.6.

27. Dölpopa, *Ocean of Definitive Meaning,* 192.3–193.3: *re zhig gzhan dbang du gtogs pa'i phung po khams dang skye mched rnams kun btags bdag dang bdag gi bas stong pa'i gzhi gsungs kyang mthar stong gzhi gzhan dbang gis kyang stong pa'i gzhi chos nyid yongs grub yin . . . de ltar kun btags kyi stong pa'i gzhi ni gzhan dbang ngo/ gzhan dbang gi stong pa'i gzhi ni yongs grub po/ chos nyid yongs grub kyis stong pa'i gzhi ni gtan mi srid de/ de ni nam yang gang na'ang lhun grub tu bzhugs pa de bzhin nyid yin pa'i phyir.*
28. Lochen Dharmaśrī, *Cluster of Supreme Intentions,* 373.5–373.6: *spros pa gcod lugs la/ rang stong dang/ gzhan stong gnyis las/ rang stong ni/ chos can ji ltar snang ba 'di dag snang tsam nyid nas rang rang gi ngo bos stong pas med dgag gi stong nyid don dam par bzhed.*
29. Ibid., 374.1–374.5: *gzhan stong du gtan la 'bebs pa'i dbu ma pa rnams la/ shes bya thams cad mtshan nyid gsum du 'dod pa dang/ kun brtags dang yongs grub gnyis su bsdu ba'i khyad par las/ chos can ngos 'dzin tshul mi 'dra ba gnyis byung ste/ rnal 'byor spyod pa'i gzhung du/ stong gzhi gzhan dbang dgag bya kun btags kyis stong pa'i yongs grub tu bshad pa dang/ rgyud bla ma sogs las chos nyid yongs grub dgag bya kun brtags kyis stong par gsungs so/ des na yongs grub sems kyi chos nyid don dam pa'i dbyings 'di'i ngo bo la dor bya'i dri ma dang sngar med kyi yon tan gsar du sgrub tu med de/ ye nas rang bzhin gyis rnam par dag cing yon tan lhun grub yin pa'i phyir.*
30. Getsé Paṇchen makes a distinction between two ways of identifying the empty-ground in the same way as Lochen Dharmaśrī does here. He asserts the former as the tradition of Mind-Only (*rnam rig smra ba*) and the latter as his own tradition of the Great Middle Way. See Getsé Paṇchen, *Ornament of the Second Buddha's Viewpoint: A Commentary on the Stages of the Inner-Path of Secret Mantra* (*slob dpon chen po padmas mdzad pa'i gsang sngags nang gi lam rim rgya cher 'grel pa sangs rgyas gnyis pa'i dgongs pa'i rgyan*), *Collected Works,* vol. 2, 311.6–311.7.
31. Khenpo Lodrö Drakpa, *Roar of the Fearless Lion,* 51.6–52.1, op. cit.
32. Lochen Dharmaśrī, *Cluster of Supreme Intentions,* 290.5–291.2: *bar tha gnyis drang nges gang yin la bzhed pa mi mthun pa mang yang/ bar ba nges don dang phyi ma drang don du gsal bar ston pa'i mdo sde'i lung med cing/ nad pa'i sman dang yi ge slob pa'i dpe'i dgongs don dang yang 'gal bas/ rang lugs ni bar pa drang nges phyed ma'am gnas skabs pa'i nges don dang/ tha ma nyid nges don du 'dod de/ mdo sde dgongs pa nges 'grel dang/ myang 'das chen po dang/ sor phreng gi mdo sogs las gsal bar bshad pa'i phyir.*
33. Kongtrül states that the traditions that accept the middle wheel as the consummate definitive meaning and the last wheel as mainly teaching provisional

meanings are "proponents of naturelessness" (*ngo bo nyid med par smra ba*); he adds that such a claim has no explicit source in scriptures (*lung khung dngos med*) and its legitimacy is argued through reasoning (*rigs pas 'thad pa sgrub*). Kongtrül, *Encyclopedia of Knowledge*, 686.

34. The metaphor of progressively learning to read can be found in Nāgārjuna's *Ratnāvalī* III.94: "Just as a grammarian first [teaches] reading letters, so the Buddha teaches the doctrine in accord with what disciples can bear." Lochen cites this in his *Desire-Bestowing Vase of Elegant Sayings* (*dam pa'i chos kyi 'bel gtam legs bshad 'dod ster*), *Collected Works*, vol. 19 (*dza*), 20a.1–20a.2. English translation in Jeffrey Hopkins, *Advice for Living and Liberation: Nāgārjuna's Precious Garland* (Ithaca: Snow Lion Publications, 1999), 284.
35. A metaphor of medicine is found in the *Laṅkāvatārasūtra:* "Just as a doctor gives medicine to the ill, the Buddha teaches Mind-Only to sentient beings." *Laṅkāvatārasūtra,* P.775, vol. 29, p. 34, 80b.5; English translation in Suzuki, *The Laṅkāvatāra Sūtra,* 44. Lochen cites a slight variation of this: "Just as a doctor gives medicine to the ill, the Buddha teaches the doctrine in accord with what sentient beings can bear." Lochen Dharmaśrī, *Desire-Bestowing Vase of Elegant Sayings,* 19b.6–20a.1. Another reference to Buddha-nature and medicine is found in Longchenpa's citations of the *Mahāparinirvāṇasūtra*, in which Buddha-nature is explained as a teaching after the nonexistence of self in the way that bile is smeared on an infant's mother's breast to stop him from drinking breast milk while he digests the medicine (no-self), and later he is given the milk (Buddha-nature). See Longchenpa, *Great Chariot*, 331.1–332.5; English translation in Tulku Thondup, *Practice of Dzogchen* (Ithaca: Snow Lion Publications, 1996), 245–246; reprint of *Buddha Mind* (Ithaca: Snow Lion Publications, 1989). See also citation in Longchenpa, *Precious Treasury of Words and Meanings*, 897.4–899.2.
36. The three sūtras Lochen cites are also the sūtras that Khenpo Lodrö Drakpa cites to support the last wheel as the definitive meaning. Khenpo Lodrö Drakpa, *Roar of the Fearless Lion*, 49.5, 79.3. See translation of the first section of Khenpo Lodrö Drakpa's *Roar of the Fearless Lion* in my dissertation, Douglas Duckworth, "Buddha-Nature and a Dialectic of Presence and Absence in the Works of Mipham" (University of Virginia, 2005), 272–312.
37. Lochen Dharmaśrī, *Cluster of Supreme Intentions*, 377.1–377.4: *sgom pas nyams su myong bya'i lta ba la/ 'khor lo bar pa'i dngos bstan rigs tshogs su bkral ba ltar na/ nges don med dgag la bzhed pas/ ci yang mi sgom pa la stong nyid sgom pa dang/ ci yang ma mthong ba la de kho na nyid rtogs par 'chad/ 'khor lo tha ma'i dgongs pa byams chos kyi gzhung thogs med sku mched kyis bkral ba dang klu sgrub zhabs kyis bstod tshogs su/ gzung 'dzin gnyis med kyi ye shes nyid sgom pas nyams su myong byar bshad cing/ de nyid gsang sngags kyi rgyud sde zab mo rnams dang yang dgongs pa mthun pa yin no.*

38. Ibid., 377.4–378.4: *grub mtha' mdzod dang yid bzhin mdzod rtsa 'grel la sogs pa'i gsung rab rnams su thos pas gtan la dbab bya ngos 'dzin pa'i skabs su dbu ma thal 'gyur ba rgyu'i theg pa chen po'i rtse mor sgrub par mdzad cing/ sgom pa nyams myong gis gtan la 'bebs pa'i skabs rnams su myong bya gzung 'dzin gnyis dang bral ba'i so so rang rig pa'i ye shes la bzhed pa gnyis mi 'gal lam snyam na/ mi 'gal te/ so skye'i sar lta ba thos bsam gyis gtan la 'bebs pa'i tshe blo'i mtshan 'dzin gzhig dka' bas/ de thos bsam las byung ba'i shes rab kyis 'gog par byed pa la/ sgro 'dogs gcod byed kyi rig pa thal 'gyur ba rno ba'i phyir dang/ yang sgom byung nyams myong gis gtan la 'bebs pa'i skabs su 'khor lo tha mar gsungs pa'i dbu ma'i lta ba de nyid zab cing ches bzang ba yin te/ dbyings rang bzhin gyis rnam par dag pa don dam pa'i bden pa rang byung gi ye shes de nyid chos thams cad kyi gdod ma'i gnas lugs yin pa gang zhig gsang sngags kyi rgyud sde zab mo rnams nas bshad pa'i lta ba'i nyams len dang yang mthun pa'i phyir.*
39. For more on Lochen's treatment of the differences between the middle and last wheels of doctrine, see Lochen Dharmaśrī, *Desire-Bestowing Vase of Elegant Sayings,* 18a.1–20b.5. Getsé Paṇchen's statements on this issue also concur with Lochen. Like Lochen, Getsé Paṇchen also associates self-emptiness (or Prāsaṅgika) with cutting through misconceptions and other-emptiness with what is experienced in meditation. He states that proponents of other-emptiness accord with the scriptural traditions of self-emptiness in the way of cutting through conceptual constructs in meditative equipoise, and that proponents of self-emptiness accord with the manner of other-emptiness at the times of meditation (*sgom pa*) and conduct (*spyod pa*). See Getsé Paṇchen, *Ornament of the Second Buddha's Viewpoint,* 312.4–312.6; 314.1–314.5.
40. Dölpopa, *Ocean of Definitive Meaning,* 181.2–181.4: *'khor lo phyi ma gnyis dang rdo rje theg pa'i don gcig mod kyi nyams su len pa na la zlo ba chos nyid zab mo la 'khor lo bar ba dang 'thun* [read *mthun*] *par rtog med spros bral du mnyam par bzhag nas rjes thob tu shan 'byed pa'i tshe chos rnams la yang dag par so sor rtog pa na 'khor lo tha ma dang rdo rje theg pa las gsungs pa bzhin du legs par rnam par phye ste.*
41. Lochen Dharmaśrī, *Cluster of Supreme Intentions,* 296.1–296.5: *spyir gsang sngags kyi rgyud sde rnams las gsungs pa'i byang sdom thob tshul dang/ de'i bslab bya'i rkang grangs kyang phal cher klu sgrub kyi lugs dang mthun par 'byung ba'i gnad kyis rang cag slob dpon chen po padma saṃ bha wa'i rjes su 'jug pa snga 'gyur gyi ring lugs pa rnams kyi sems bskyed kyi cho ga'i phyag bzhes kyang nā gardzu na dang mthun par snang mod/ 'on kyang lta ba ni der ma nges te/ klu sgrub kyi bstod tshogs dang mi 'gal yang gtso bor thogs med sku mched kyis ji ltar bkral ba dang mthun te/ rnam grangs ma yin pa'i don dam med dgag la mi byed par ma yin dgag gi stong nyid la byed pa'i phyir dang/ 'khor lo tha ma nges don du bzhed pa'i phyir ro.*
42. Getsé Paṇchen, *Reponse to Sherap's Questions* (*dge ba'i bshes gnyen shes rab mtshan can gyi dris lan*), *Collected Works,* vol. 6, 221.7–223.3.

43. See Getsé Paṇchen, *Ornament of Buddha-Nature,* 95.4–96.7.
44. Mipam, *Eliminating Doubts,* 521: *bdag la gzhan stong sgrub pa'i khur kyang med/ rong klong rnam gnyis klu sgrub gzhung dang mthun.*
45. Mipam, *Lion's Roar: Affirming Other-Emptiness* (*gzhan stong khas len seng ge'i nga ro*), Mipam's *Collected Works,* vol. 12 (*ga*), 359–378. See English translation in John Pettit, *Mipham's Beacon of Certainty,* 415–427.
46. Mipam, *Lion's Roar: Affirming Other-Emptiness,* 361.3–361.4: *dang po mgon po klu sgrub kyi gzhung bzhin du chos thams cad rang bzhin med par gtan la 'bebs dgos te/ de ma shes na kun rdzob rang ngo[s] nas stong tshul dang/ don dam gzhan gyis stong tshul gtan la mi pheb pas/ thog mar spros bral so sor rang gis rig par bya ba'i gtan la dbab par bya'o.*
47. Mipam, *Immaculate Crystal Rosary: Commentary on the Madhyamakāvatāra* (*dbu ma la 'jug pa'i 'grel pa zla ba'i zhal lung dri me shel phreng*), Mipam's *Collected Works,* vol. 1, 813.6: *snang stong mnyam par nges shes rdzogs pa che/ /klu sgrub gzhung lugs bzang po kho nas mthong.*
48. Mipam, *Beacon of Certainty,* 6: *ka ba ka bas mi stong dang/ /chos nyid ka bas stong ngo zhes/ /stong gzhi bzhag nas gzhan stong pa/ /tshig dang don gyi gzhan stong gnyis.* Khenpo Namdröl, in an oral commentary on this text, stated that any emptiness with a substrate (*stong gzhi*) is only a limited (*nyi tshe ba*) emptiness.
49. See Mipam, *Difficult Points of Scriptures in General,* 549.2.
50. See Mipam, *Difficult Points of Scriptures in General,* 548.6. Tsongkhapa, however, denied that such a claim represents other-emptiness. In his commentary on the *Madhyamakāvatāra,* Tsongkhapa says: "The statement, 'That a pot is not empty of pot, but empty of true existence is other-emptiness; therefore, a pot empty of pot is the assertion of self-emptiness,' is utterly unreasonable." Tsongkhapa, *Thoroughly Illuminating the Viewpoint,* 213: *bum pa bum pas mi stong bar bum pa bden pas stong pa ni/ gzhan stong yin pas bum pa bum pas stong pa ni rang stong yin no zhes smra ba ni gtan nas mi rigs te.*
51. Mipam also argues that a view that accepts real entities as an implication of the negation of a separate true establishment is in effect an implicative negation. See Mipam, *Difficult Points of Scriptures in General,* 545.3–545.4; see also, Mipam, *Words That Delight,* 380–381 (cited below).
52. Mipam, *Difficult Points of Scriptures in General,* 548.6–549.4.
53. See D. T. Suzuki, trans., *The Laṅkāvatāra Sūtra,* 67. *The Dictionary of Internal Knowledge* (*nang rig pa'i tshig mdzod*) delineates the seven emptinesses (*stong nyid rnam pa bdun*) as: "(1) emptiness of characteristics, (2) emptiness of the nature of entities, (3) emptiness of existence, (4) emptiness of nonexistence, (5) emptiness which is the inexpressibility of all phenomena, (6) great emptiness which is the ultimate wisdom of Sublime Ones, (7) emptiness of something in another." *nang rig pa'i tshig mdzod,* ed. Purbu Tsering (*phur bu tshe ring*), (Beijing: Nationalities Press, 1994), 515.
54. Mipam, *Difficult Points of Scriptures in General,* 545.4–545.6: *bum pa rang ngos nas ma stong na chos gzhan gyis stong pas bum pa nyid stong pa'i go mi chod de/ rta*

la ba lang med kyang/ rta rang nyid stong pa'i go mi chod pa dang gnag gi rwa ri bong rwas stong yang/ gnag gi rwa stong pa'i go mi chod pa bzhin no/ lang kar gshegs pa las stong pa bdun gyi nang nas tha chad pa lha khang dge 'dun gyis stong pa lta bu 'di spang par bya zhes gsung.

55. Longchenpa, *White Lotus,* 1095.1: *gcig la gcig med pa rnams ni stong pa nyid rnams kyi tha shal lo.*

56. See Asaṅga's commentary on *Uttaratantra* I.155 in *theg pa chen po mdo sde'i rgyan dang rgyud bla rtsa 'grel* (Beijing: Nationalities Press, 1998), 201–202. This text is nearly the same as Vasubandhu's definition of emptiness referred to below, in his commentary on the *Madhyāntavibhāga* under v.2, D.4027, 2a.2–2a.3.

57. It is interesting to note that the word used is "there" (*de la*), as found in the translation of Asaṅga's *Uttaratantra* commentary, rather than "here" (*'dir*), as in Dölpopa usage and the Tibetan translation of Vasubandhu; "there" is more abstract, or more removed, than "here"—"here" in this context can be seen to evoke more of the immanent presence of Buddha-nature. Vasubandhu's *Madhyāntavibhāga* commentary under v.2: *'di lhag ma yod pa gang yin pa de ni 'dir yod.* Vasubandhu's Sanskrit: *yad punaratrāvaśiṣṭam bhavati tat sadihāsti.* Published in Ramchandra Pandeya, *Madhyāntavibhāga-śāstra* (Delhi: Motilal Banarsidass, 1999/1971), 9; Tibetan translation from D.4027, 2a.2.

58. Longchenpa, *Great Chariot,* 334.3–334.5: *de bzhin gshegs pa'i snying po ni rnam par dbye ba yod pa/ bral ba shes pa/ nyon mongs pa'i sbubs thams cad kyis ni stong pa yin la/ rnam par dbye ba med pa bral mi shes pa bsam gyis mi khyab pa'i sangs rgyas kyi chos gangā'i klung gi bye ma snyed las 'das pa ni mi stong ngo zhes so/ de ltar gang zhig gang na med pa de ni des stong ngo zhes yang dag par rjes su mthong la/ gang zhig der lhag par gyur pa de ni/ de la rtag par yod do zhes yang dag pa ji [lta] ba bzhin du shes so zhes so.*

59. The *Rapsel Rejoinder,* called *Shedding Light on Thusness,* is a text that Mipam wrote in response to the criticism of the Geluk scholar, Pari Lozang Rapsel (*dpa' ris blo bzang rab gsal,* 1840–1910), concerning Mipam's commentary on the ninth chapter of the *Bodhicaryāvatāra* (*sher le'u 'grel pa nor bu ke ta ka*).

60. Mipam, *Difficult Points of Scriptures in General,* 450.2–450.3: *rang stong pa'i lugs la don dam par med pa sha stag pas/ don dam par yod pa'i chos mi srid la/ gzhan stong pa'i lugs la/ don dam par med na kun rdzob dang/ don dam par yod la don dam rang nyid yin pa'i phyir ro/ rang lugs rab lan du gsal te rang stong smra ba'i lugs so.*

61. Khenpo Lodrö Drakpa, *The Beautiful Ornament of a Clear Mind,* 243.7–244.1; 270.6–270.7, op. cit.

62. Lochen Dharmaśrī, *Cluster of Supreme Intentions,* 373.5–373.6; 374.1–374.5, op. cit.

63. There is some dispute among interpreters of Mipam, among Tibetan and non-Tibetan scholars, as to whether Mipam's view accords with "other-emptiness" or with "self-emptiness." As I mentioned earlier, it is first of all important to pay

close attention to what these terms mean in the contexts they are used. For a discussion of competing interpretations of Mipam's view, see Matthew Kapstein, "We Are All Gzhan stong pas," *Journal of Buddhist Ethics* 7 (2000): 105–125; John Pettit, "Review of Altruism and Reality," *Journal of Buddhist Ethics* 6 (1999): 120–137; Paul Williams, "A Response to John Pettit," *Journal of Buddhist Ethics* 6 (1999): 138–153; Karma Phuntsho, *Mipham's Dialectics and the Debates on Emptiness,* 16–17.

64. Mipam, *Difficult Points of Scriptures in General*, 450.3–450.4: *gzhan stong gi don dam sgrub tshul de gnas snang mthun mi mthun gyi dbang du byas.*
65. Mipam, *Words That Delight*, 55–56, op. cit.
66. Mipam, *Lion's Roar: Exposition of Buddha-Nature*, 591.1–591.3: *rang gi ngo bo mi stong par bden par grub pa la chos gzhan gyi chos nyid du rung ba sogs rnam pa kun tu mi srid cing don dam dpyod pa'i tshad mas gtan la phab pa'i grub 'bras su yang mi btub ste chos thams cad bden med du dpyod pa'i lag rjes la bden grub gcig 'grub pa ni snang ba las mun pa ltar gnas ma yin pa'i phyir ro/ /tha snyad dpyod pa'i tshad mas kyang bden grub mi 'grub ste/ de'i ngor bden par grub kyang de tsam gyis chos de mi stong par rnam pa kun tu 'grub mi nus pa'i phyir ro/ /tshad ma gnyis kyis sgrub ma nus par gyur pa la sgrub byed nam mkha'i me tog gi rjes su 'gro bas de sgrub pa don med kyi ngal par zad do.*
67. For Mipam, ultimate valid cognition (*don dam dpyod pa'i tshad ma*) apparently concerns only the ultimate in the appearance/emptiness model of the two truths, for which the ultimate is only emptiness. The ultimate in the authentic/inauthentic experience model of the two truths, on the other hand, is the domain of conventional valid cognition when *theorizing about* the ultimate of authentic experience. However, the ultimate of authentic experience is truly realized by wisdom in the context of meditative experience. We can see that this realization by meditative wisdom is what advocates of other-emptiness evoke to support their claims of true establishment: it is truly established "because it is just what is experienced by the undistorted wisdom of the Sublime Ones" (Getsé Paṇchen) or "due to being true in the abiding reality of the basic nature as the object of ultimate reflexive awareness free from constructs" (Khenpo Lodrö Drakpa). However, Mipam emphasizes a universal empty quality and does not affirm anything that is both empty and truly established ultimately.
68. Mipam, *Lion's Roar: Affirming Other-Emptiness*, 370.3–370.4: *bden grub khegs kyang bden med mi khegs mi 'gog bkag mi rung bar 'dod pa ltar/ kun rdzob 'khrul pa rnams khegs kyang don dam ma 'khrul pa mi khegs mi 'gog bkag mi rung bar mtshungs so.*
69. Ibid., 374.5–374.6: *bum pa bum pas stong na bum pa de bum pa min par 'gyur bas bum pa tha snyad du med par mi 'gyur ram zhe na/ 'gyur du chug ste/ de lta na/ don dam bden pa don dam bden pas stong na/ don dam bden pa don dam bden pa min par 'gyur zhing/ don dam pa tha snyad du yang med par 'gyur ba mtshungs so.*
70. Mipam, *Immaculate Crystal Rosary*, 539.6: *tha snyad kyi dbang du byas na/ bum pa bum pas mi stong par 'dod de/ tha snyad du de stong na bum pa med par 'gyur.*

Tsongkhapa makes a similar claim: "If a pot were empty of pot, a pot would have to be nonexistent in itself, and if it were nonexistent in itself, it would be nonexistent everywhere else, too; therefore, a pot would [absurdly] be utterly nonexistent." Tsongkhapa, *Thoroughly Illuminating the Viewpoint*, 213: *bum pa bum pas stong na bum pa la bum pa med dgos na/ rang la rang med na gzhan su la yang med pas bum pa gtan med par 'gyur ro.*

71. Mipam, *Immaculate Crystal Rosary*, 540.1: *tha snyad tshad mas bum pa bum pa nyid du bden par grub dgos te las 'bras bden pa dang dkon mchog gsum bden pa bzhin no.* See also Karma Phuntsho, *Mipham's Dialectics and the Debates on Emptiness*, 101.
72. Mipam, *Gateway to Scholarship* (*mkhas pa'i tshul la 'jug pa'i sgo*), published in *mkhas 'jug* (Qinghai: Nationalities Press, 1994), 129: *tha snyad de la shes brjod 'jug gsum du bzhag pa ni sems dang ngag dang lus kyi sgo nas so.*
73. For a discussion of a similar distinction between existence and truth in the works of Tsongkhapa, see Guy Newland, *The Two Truths*, 93–94; Thupten Jinpa, *Self, Reality and Reason in Tibetan Philosophy* (London: RoutledgeCurzon, 2002), 152–153.
74. Mipam, *Words That Delight*, 74–75: *mdor na tha snyad kyi tshad ma'i ngor yod par grub na de tha snyad du sus kyang dgag mi nus la/ tha snyad pa'i tshad mas gnod pa yod na de tha snyad du yod par sus kyang sgrub mi nus shing/ don dam pa'i tshad mas med par grub pa de don dam par yod do zhes sus kyang sgrub mi nus.*
75. Mipam, *Commentary on the Wisdom Chapter*, 31: *don dam pa gtan la 'bebs pa la rang rig dang kun gzhi mi dgos mod/ tha snyad kyi rnam bzhag dpyod pa la med du mi rung zhing tha snyad dpyod pa'i tshad mas grub na de tha snyad du med ces 'gog pa'i rigs pa ni med do.* See also Bötrül, *Ornament of Mañjugoṣa's Viewpoint*, 187.
76. Mipam states that in the end, inference (*rjes dpag*) comes down to direct perception (*mngon sum*), and direct perception to reflexive awareness; hence, reflexive awareness is indispensable when asserting a presentation of valid cognition of confined perception. Mipam, *Words That Delight*, 208. Regarding the universal ground, Mipam states that the universal ground, along with the other consciousnesses, all need to be accepted to account for their transformation into the five wisdoms according to Sūtra and Mantra. Mipam, *Shedding Light on Thusness*, 356–357. The universal ground becomes "the wisdom of the expanse of phenomena" (*chos dbyings ye shes*), the universal ground consciousness becomes "the mirror-like wisdom" (*me long lta bu'i ye shes*), the afflicted mind becomes "the discerning wisdom" (*so sor rtog pa'i ye shes*), the mental consciousness becomes "the wisdom of equality" (*mnyam nyid ye shes*), and the five sense consciousnesses become "the accomplishing wisdom" (*bya ba grub pa'i ye shes*).
77. Tsongkhapa laid out eight unique assertions of Prāsaṅgika in his *Thoroughly Illuminating the Viewpoint*, 226. The eight listed there are: the unique manners of (1) refuting a universal ground distinct from the six consciousnesses and (2) refuting reflexive awareness; (3) not asserting that autonomous arguments generate the view of thusness in the continuum of an opponent, (4) the necessity of

asserting external objects as one asserts cognitions, (5) the assertion that Auditors and Self-Realized Ones realize the selflessness of phenomena, (6) the assertion that grasping to the self of phenomena is an afflictive emotion, (7) the assertion that disintegration is an entity, and (8) the consequent unique presentation of the three times. Tsongkhapa also lists a different set of unique assertions in his *bka' gnas brgyad kyi zin bris.* See David S. Ruegg, *Two Prolegomena to Madhyamaka Philosophy* (Wien: Arbeitskreis für Tibetische und Buddhistische Studien, 2002), 144–147. For a discussion of the unique assertions of Prāsaṅgika according to the Geluk tradition, see Dan Cozort, *Unique Tenets of the Middle Way Consequence School* (Ithaca: Snow Lion Publications, 1998).

78. Mipam, *Light of the Sun*, 561: *spyir dbu ma thal 'gyur pa'i lugs la rnam shes tshogs drug tu bzhes pa dang/ rang rig gi rnam bzhag sogs ma mdzad pa ni rang gzhung na gsal mod/ der tha snyad du zhal bzhes med pa tsam zhig gis tha snyad du med nges su go dgos pa'i nges pa ga la yod de/ dper na thal 'gyur pa'i lugs la gnyug sems dang bde ba chen po sogs kyi tha snyad sbyar don med kyang de dag tha snyad du mi 'thad pa ma yin pa bzhin no.*

79. Mipam, *Intelligent Presence* (*gnyug sems 'od gsal gyi don la dpyad pa rdzogs pa chen po gzhi lam 'bras bu'i shan 'byed blo gros snang ba*), Mipam's *Collected Works*, vol. 24, 476.1–476.4: *chos nyid dang chos nyid kyi rang rtsal las shar ba'i snang ba dang bcas pa thams cad don dam par dngos dngos med kyi mtha' las 'das kyang/ tha snyad du rtag pa chen po'i tha snyad byed de/ skad cig ma'i mi rtag pa'i dngos po'ang min/ rtag pa ther zug dngos po'ang min/ 'gyur ba med kyang dngos med stong kyang yang min pas/ rtag pa chen por gdags pa'i gzhi yod pas dngos med la rtag par 'dod pa dang mi 'dra ba ste/ mkha' sogs rtag par gdags pa la dpyad na mi rtag pa las log tsam yod kyang/ rtag par gdags pa'i gzhi gang yang med do.*

80. Ibid., 446.5–446.6: *rnam shes kyi chos nyid ni ye shes so.*

81. *Saṃdhinirmocanasūtra*, chapter 3. John Powers, trans., *Wisdom of the Buddha,* 48–49. The last verse is rendered here in a slightly different way than the verse in the *Saṃdhinirmocanasūtra;* Mipam adds the word "view."

82. *Intelligent Presence*, 447.2–448.1: *des na rnam shes tshogs brgyad chos can dang/ de'i rang bzhin chos nyid kyi ye shes gnyis ni/ gcig tha dad gang du'ang khas blangs bya min par/ dgongs 'grel las/ 'du byed khams dang don dam mtshan nyid ni/ /gcig dang tha dad bral ba'i mtshan nyid te/ gcig dang tha dad du yang gang rtog pa/ /de dag tshul min lta la zhugs pa yin/ /zhes gsungs pa'i lung bzhin klong chen rab 'byams kyis gsungs la/ de'i phyir de gnyis tha snyad du gcig ma yin te/ sems rtogs pa tsam gyis sems kyi chos nyid ye shes mi rtogs pa dang/ chos dang chos nyid yin pa sogs kyi phyir ro/ don dam par tha dad min te/ sems kyi rang bzhin ye shes yin pas/ ye shes rtogs dus sems kyang de las tha dad du ma dmigs pa'i phyir dang/ ye shes rtogs tshe sems rang grol du 'char ba.* See also Mipam, *Lion's Roar: Exposition of Buddha-Nature*, 585.1–585.2.

83. Mipam, *Vajra Essence*, 372.3–372.4: *ye shes ni sems las byung ba ma yin te/ sems kyi gnas lugs rang bzhin 'od gsal yin pas/ dngos po kun gyi chos nyid stong pa nyid ni dngos po'i gnas lugs yin gyi dngos po las byung ba min pa ltar go dgos.*

84. Mipam, *Lion's Roar: Affirming Other-Emptiness*, 369.3: *'khrul pa'i 'khor ba dang ma 'khrul pa'i myang 'das gnyis ka yin pa tha snyad du nam yang mi srid la.*
85. As with the distinction between saṃsāra and nirvāṇa, the two truths of authentic/inauthentic experience are conventionally distinct. Ultimately, saṃsāra and nirvāṇa are not distinct and thus neither are the two truths of authentic/inauthentic experience. Mipam addresses the meaning of the indivisibility of saṃsāra and nirvāṇa in a commentary on Longchenpa's *Wish-Fulfilling Treasury*, where he mentions a "dualistic nirvāṇa that is separate from saṃsāra" (*gnyis chos 'khor 'das kyi zlas phye ba'i myang 'das*) that contrasts with an "uncategorized nirvāṇa" (*rnam grangs min pa'i myang 'das*), in which the two truths are not distinct and there is no duality. See Mipam, *An Elucidation of Various Difficult Points in the Precious Wish-Fulfilling Treasury* (*yid bzhin rin po che'i mdzod kyi dka' gnad ci rigs pa gsal bar byed pa*), Mipam's *Collected Works*, vol. 21, 553.3–555.4.
86. Dölpopa, *The Categories of the Possible and the Impossible* (*srid mi srid kyi rab dbye dbu phyogs legs par bzhugs so*), *Collected Works*, vol. 6, 314.2. See also Strearns, *The Buddha from Dolpo*, 51–52.
87. In a private conversation, Khenpo Pema Sherap (*mkhan po padma shes rab*, b. 1936) described the "general ground" as the aspect of suchness (*chos nyid kyi cha*). He also explained that the general ground and the ultimate primordial ground (*ye don gyi gzhi*) are not the universal ground that is to be distinguished from the Truth Body (*chos sku*).
88. See Longchenpa, *Precious Treasury of Words and Meanings*, 792.4–792.5.
89. Longchenpa, *White Lotus*, 151.1–152.1.
90. See Mipam, *Vajra Essence*, 357.4.
91. See Dölpopa, *The Great Assessment of the Doctrine Which Has the Significance of the Fourth Council* (*bka' bsdu bzhi pa don ldan rtsis chen po*), *Collected Works*, vol. 6, 192.5. See also Stearns, *The Buddha from Dolpo*, 161; 266n.120.
92. The difference between the two traditions should not be overemphasized. There is a context for the distinction between mind (*sems*) and awareness (*rig pa*) in the Great Perfection similar to the distinction between consciousness and wisdom in the Jonang tradition. Also, the two traditions can be seen to respectively relate to different contexts (e.g., meditative equipoise and postmeditation), in which the Great Perfection texts that collapse the distinction between the relative and ultimate evoke the ultimate that is phenomenologically known in meditative practice, and the Jonang discourses of other-emptiness that make a sharp distinction between the relative and ultimate describe the ultimate (qua authentic experience) that is theorized in postmeditation.
93. Mipam, *Words That Delight*, 471: *ka dag la nges pa ma rnyed par yod pa'ang min med pa'ang min pa'i gzhi zhig snying la brnag pa tsam gyis ni gar yang mi phyin te/ de 'dra ba'i yod med gnyis kyis stong pa'i stong gzhi logs su ngo bos grub par bzung na/ de'i ming la bsam mi khyab pa'i bdag gam/ tshangs pa'am/ khyab 'jug gam/ dbang phyug gam/ ye shes sogs ji btags kyang ming tsam las don 'dra ba yin no/ mtha'*

bzhi'i spros bral gyi gnas lugs so so rang rig par bya ba'i 'od gsal rdzogs pa chen po ni de 'dra ba zhig yin tshod mi gda' bas.

94. Ibid., 470–471: *lugs de dag kyang mtha' dang bral ba skad du 'chad kyang/ mthar gtugs na bdag gam tshangs pa sogs blo yi gtad so zhig la mu brten nas yod pas dbu ma'i tshul ga la yin.*
95. Mipam, *Shedding Light on Thusness*, 294: *dbus zhes pa mtha' gang la'ang mi dmigs pa la brjod.*
96. Ibid., 291: *dbus zhes pa ka ba gnyis bsgrig gi bar mtshams lta bu dmigs pa can zhig la gnas par bya ba'i yul du ngos ma bzung ste/ dbus mi dmigs par gsungs.*
97. Mipam, *Words That Delight*, 368: *blos rten 'cha' ba'i yul gang yin pa dbu ma'i rigs pas sun phyung mi nus pa mi srid.*
98. Mipam, *Lion's Roar: Affirming Other-Emptiness*, 368.4–368.5: *bden med khas blangs pas stong nyid dngos por med pa'i mtshan mar zhen pa'i gsor mi rung ba'i lta bar 'gyur ba dang/ spros bral khas blangs pas stong nyid ni brjod du med pa'i dngos por dmigs pa'i lta bar 'gyur ba mtshungs so.*
99. Mipam, *Shedding Light on Thusness*, 375: *ji srid dmigs pa can nam gzung 'dzin dang bcas pa'i blo la gnas pa de srid du gnas snang mi mthun te/ chos nyid ni gzung 'dzin dang bcas pa'i blo'i yul min no.*
100. Ibid., 545: *don dam dpyod pa'i rjes dpags sam don dam mngon sum rtogs pa'i ye shes kyi yul gyi ngo bo 'di zhes rnyed pa'ang gzigs so zhes nan gyis khas len pa de dag gis gzhan stong ji ltar bkag kyang rang gi zhe phug gzhan stong gis dbang byas pa ma tshor ba tsam du zad do.* See also Karma Phuntsho, *Mipham's Dialectics and the Debates on Emptiness*, 165.
101. Mipam, *Commentary on the Wisdom Chapter*, 11: *dngos po'i gnas tshul don dam pa ni yod pa dang/ med pa dang/ gnyis ka/ gnyis min gyi mtha' kun dang bral bas na blo yi spyod yul min te/ blo dang sgra ni kun rdzob yin gyi don dam pa ma yin pa'i phyir ro.*
102. In his commentary on the *Madhyamakāvatāra,* Tsongkhapa claimed that the basis of division of the two truths is objects of knowledge: "There are many ways of asserting the basis of division of the two truths; here it is done as objects of knowledge." Tsongkhapa, *Thoroughly Illuminating the Viewpoint*, 176: *bden pa gnyis kyi dbye gzhi la 'dod tshul mi 'dra ba mang mod/ 'dir shes bya la bya ste.* See also Guy Newland, *The Two Truths*, 59.
103. Mipam, *Commentary on the Wisdom Chapter*, 13: *tha snyad du ni 'phags pa'i mnyam bzhag yul can dang/ chos kyi dbyings yul du byas pa la brten nas shes bya yin no zhes brjod rung gi don dam par gzung 'dzin med pa'i mnyam bzhag gis 'di gzung bya'am shes bya yin zer na tshig de dngos shugs mi 'gal lam/ yang bden gnyis kyi dbye gzhi shes bya yin pas don dam shes byar khas blangs pa de yang rnam bcod du yin la/ 'dir shes bya min pa ni yongs gcod du yin pas mi 'gal te/ yongs gcod du'ang shes byar khas len na stong nyid dngos por zhal gyis bzhes par 'gyur.*
104. Śāntideva, *Bodhicaryāvatāra* IX.2: *kun rdzob dang ni don dam ste/ /'di ni bden pa gnyis su 'dod/ /don dam blo yi spyod yul min/ /blo ni kun rdzob yin par brjod.*

Published in *byang chub sems dpa'i spyod pa la 'jug pa rtsa ba dang 'grel ba* (Sichuan: Nationalities Press, 1990), 103.

105. Bötrül, *Ornament of Mañjugoṣa's Viewpoint*, 131: *'jug pa rtsa 'grel du/ yongs gcod kyi sgo nas don dam pa'i mtshan nyid 'jog par mdzad pa dang/ spyod 'jug sher le'u skabs su rnam gcod kyi sgo nas/ don dam pa'i mtshan nyid bstan zhing/ gzhung gnyis kar yongs gcod kyi sgo nas kun rdzob bden pa'i mtshan nyid bstan.*

106. Candrakīrti, *Madhyamakāvatāra* VI.23: "[Buddha] said that all entities found by authentic and false seeing are apprehended as two essences: That which is the object of authentic seeing is thusness; false seeings are relative truths." op. cit.

107. Bötrül, *Ornament of Mañjugoṣa's Viewpoint*, 130: *spyir rang rgyud pa'i lugs kyi rnam grangs dpyod pa'i tshad ma'i yul gyi don dam la ltos pa'i bden gnyis gzhir bzhag na/ bden gnyis ngo bo gcig la ldog pa tha dad du rnam par dbye ba las 'os med kyang/ mthar thug thal 'gyur lta ba'i lugs kyi rnam grangs ma yin pa dpyod pa'i tshad ma'i yul du gyur pa'i don dam la ltos pa'i bden pa gnyis ni ngo bo gcig du bral du bzhed pa lags so/ /'on kyang skabs 'ga' zhig tu ni/ tha snyad dag gzigs tshad ma'i yul du gyur pa'i gnas snang chos kyi bden gnyis ni/ gnas snang mthun pa'i rang bzhin dag pa myang 'das kyi chos dang mi mthun pa'i rang bzhin ma dag 'khor ba'i chos gnyis gnas lugs la grub ma grub kyi sgo nas dngos dngos med ltar gcig pa bkag pa'i zhal bzhes mdzad do/ /'on kyang stong thun sogs las ni 'khor 'das gnyis chos can chos nyid kyi tshul du gcig du bral gyi zhal bzhes kyang snang ngo.*

108. Tsongkhapa depicted the relationship between the two truths as "essentially the same with different contradistinctions, like an impermanent phenomenon and a product." Tsongkhapa, *Thoroughly Illuminating the Viewpoint*, 176: *ngo bo gcig la ldog pa tha dad pa byas pa dang mi rtag pa lta bu.*

109. Dölpopa, *Ocean of Definitive Meaning*, 384.4–384.5, op. cit.

110. Ibid., 88.3–88.4, op. cit.

111. Mipam, *Words That Delight*, 380–381: *dngos po rang bzhin med par bstan pa ni med par dgag pa ste/ ma yin dgag ni chos gzhan kyi ngo bo sgrub pas de 'dra la zung 'jug gi don med la/ snang ba rang bzhin med par gdags pa'ang/ snang ba las logs na stong rgyu yod pa lta bur go na med dgag zer yang ma yin dgag tu song ba yin la/ snang ba nyid med bzhin snang ba ni zung 'jug ste ngo mtshar che zhing/ de ltar snang stong dbyer med brjod bral du gnas pas na mthar thug gi don la dgag sgrub dang bral bas blo 'das pa yin no.*

112. Mipam, *Beacon of Certainty*, 5: *dge ldan lta ba med dgag zer/ /gzhan rnams ma yin dgag tu smra/ /snga 'gyur ring lugs gang zhes na/ /stong tshul kho na bsam nas ni/ /dri na med dgag nyid yin te/ /'phags yul dpal ldan zla ba dang/ /bod na rong zom chos bzang gnyis/ /dgongs pa gcig dang dbyangs gcig gis/ /ka dag stong pa chen po bsgrubs.*

113. Ibid., 49: *sems 'das ye shes yin pa'i phyir/ /rtog pa gzhan gyis bsam mi khyab/ /de ni sgra rtog yul min phyir/ /med dgag ma yin dgag sogs dang/ /tha dad dang ni snang stong sogs/ /ris su chad pa med pa ste.*

114. Ibid., 5: *zung 'jug ye shes chen po'i ngor/ /med ces dgag bya bkag shul gyi/ /med rkyang dang ni ma yin zhes/ /bkag shul chos gzhan ci zhig 'phen/ de gnyis blo yis brtag pa tsam/ /don la gnyis kar khas mi len*. Brackets in translation are taken from gloss in Khenpo Künpel's interlinear commentary, *Opening the Door of Intelligent Presence*, 72.

115. Mipam, *Commentary on the Wisdom Chapter*, 10: *stong pa nyid ston pa'i skabs su gzugs la sogs pa dgag pa ni med dgag kho na yin te/ ma yin par bkag kyang mthar gtugs na dngos por zhen pas stong nyid kyi don du mi rung bas med par dgag pa yin bzhin du/ rten 'byung bslu med du snang bas snang stong zung du 'jug pas na dgag sgrub kyi 'dzin stangs zhig gzhig dgos te*.

116. When I asked the late Jonang scholar, Yönten Zangpo (*yon tan bzang po*, 1928–2002), who was one of Khenpo Lodrö Drakpa's main disciples, whether Mipam is a proponent of self-emptiness (*rang stong pa*) or other-emptiness (*gzhan stong pa*), he replied, "He is a proponent of the Great Perfection" (*rdzogs chen pa*). I asked him twice, and got the same answer both times. I was not completely satisfied with the answer then (hence, I asked him twice), but I am now. Although it depends on how one defines "self-emptiness" and "other-emptiness"—given that Mipam consistently undoes dichotomies such as middle wheel versus last wheel and Yogācāra versus Prāsaṅgika—in terms of self-emptiness versus other-emptiness, we might say that his view is both (or neither); or better yet, that his view is the Great Perfection.

117. Mipam, *Beacon of Certainty*, 14: *don dam rang ngo shes pa la/ /bden stong phu thag chod pa dgos*.

118. Tsongkhapa, *The Great Exposition of the Stages of the Path* (*lam rim chen mo*), (Qinghai: Nationalities Press, 2000/1985), 783: *bdag med pa'i don la phu thag chod pa'i lta ba'i nges pa med na lhag mthong gi rtogs pa mi skye ste*. In the *Four Interlinear Commentaries on "The Great Exposition of the Stages of the Path,"* the meaning of "reaching a firm conclusion" (*phu thag chod*) is explained with an example: when a horse is lost in a valley, one reaches a firm conclusion that the horse is not in the valley after completely searching up and down the valley. Similarly, one reaches a firm conclusion about thusness when thusness is thoroughly sought after by reason, and the self to be negated is concluded to not exist. Jamyang Zhepa (*'jam dbyangs bzhad pa ngag dbang brtson 'grus*, 1648–1722) et al. *lam rim chen mo mchan bzhi sbrags*, vol. 2 (Dharamsala: Tehor Tenzhug Committee, 2005), 131: *phu thag chod pa'i don ni/ dper na lung pa der rta lta bu brlag pa na/ lung pa de'i phu ji tsam yod pa ma rdzogs kyi bar du btsal nas med par thag chod pa'i phu thag chod par btsal ba zhes bya'o// de bzhin du de kho na nyid kyi don 'tshol ba'i tshe yang dgag bya'i bdag de mtha' thams cad nas 'tshol lugs ma tshang ba med pa'i rigs pas btsal ba na med par thag chod pa'i tshe de kho na nyid la phu thag chod pa'o*.

119. Mipam, *Beacon of Certainty*, 15–16: *bdag gzhan dngos 'dzin 'dir brten nas/ /srid pa'i chu bo brgyud mar 'jug /'di dag zlog pa'i gnyen po ni/ /bdag med pa yi 'dzin*

stangs yin/ /de yang med tshul ma shes par/ /med par mos pas mi phan te/ /thag khrar sbrul du 'khrul ba la/ sbrul med snyam pas mi phan kyang/ /med tshul mthong na spangs pa bzhin.

120. Mipam, *Words That Delight*, 88: *thog ma kho nar bden med du ma bstan na ni thog med nas goms pa'i dngos 'dzin phyin ci log 'jil ba'i thabs med la/ de tsam zhig don dam du bstan na ni blo chung ba kha cig dgag bya bkag pa'i med pa tsam gnas lugs so snyam du stong pa nyid la zhen nas gsor mi rung ba'i lta bar 'gyur la/ zhen tshul la'ang stong nyid la dngos por zhen pa dang dngos med du zhen pa gnyis yod.*

121. Mipam, *Beacon of Certainty*, 51: *dngos po stong pa'i gnas lugs dang/ /bden gnyis dbyer med gnas lugs gnyis/ /ming gcig na yang don la ni/ /khyad par gnam sa bzhin du mchis/ /de bzhin chos nyid chos dbyings dang/ /stong nyid spros bral 'gog pa'i mtha'/ /don dam la sogs smra mtshungs kyang/ /mthar thug dang ni nyi tshe ba'i/ /khyad par che phyir skabs so so/ /phye nas ma nor bshad bya ste.*

122. Mipam, *Light of the Sun*, 543: *bden gnyis su phye ba'i ya gyal gyi bden stong dang rten 'byung gi snang ba gnyis po ldog pa tsam gyi cha nas tha dad kyang/ ji ltar byas pa dang mi rtag pa don gyi steng na tha dad med pa bzhin/ stong dang snang gnyis po ngo bo dbyer med pa'i rang bzhin mtha' gang du'ang mi gnas pa bcos min gshis kyi gnas lugs de la bden pa dbyer med dam bden gnyis zung 'jug ces bya ste.*

123. Mipam, *Beacon of Certainty*, 49: *snang ba tha snyad tshad ma'i yul/ /stong pa don dam dpyod pa'i yul/ /zung 'jug de gnyis 'dres pa'i cha/ /de rnams sgra rtog yul yin phyir/ /de las 'das pa'i mnyam bzhag ni.*

124. Ibid., 35: *'dir ni mthong don tha snyad pa'i/ /tshad ma'i rnam bzhag skabs yin pas/ /de'i ngor yod med 'gal ba ste/ /dngos gcig steng gi bden pa gnyis/ /mi 'gal ye shes yul yin phyir.*

125. Mipam, *Precious Vajra Garland*, 599.3–599.5: *rig pa dang 'od gsal ni snang ba'i cha nas bzhag kyang stong pa dang mi phyed la/ stong pa nyid zer yang snang ba dang mi phyed kyi/ don la zung 'jug kho na chos nyid yin gyi snang stong re re ba chos nyid chen po mthar thug gi don dam min pa kun tu gal che'o/ 'di las brtsam ste mdo sngags kun gyi gnad 'grol lo.*

126. Mipam, *Difficult Points of Scriptures in General*, 431.3: *gnas lugs ni ye nas snang stong zung 'jug yin.*

Chapter Four. Buddha-Nature and the Ground of the Great Perfection

1. Mipam, *Lion's Roar: Exposition of Buddha-Nature*, 590.6–591.4: *rigs pas dpyad na yang bde gshegs snying po ngo bo stong pa yin pa'i gnad kyis sems kyi chos nyid du rung ba/ yul thams cad khyab pa/ dus ji srid du rtag pa/ bsam gyis mi khyab pa/ yon tan rnam pa thams cad par ris med du 'char ba yin gyi/ rang gi ngo bo mi stong par bden par grub pa la chos gzhan gyi chos nyid du rung ba sogs rnam pa kun tu mi srid cing don dam dpyod pa'i tshad mas gtan la phab pa'i grub 'bras su*

yang mi btub ste chos thams cad bden med du dpyod pa'i lag rjes la bden grub gcig 'grub pa ni snang ba las mun pa ltar gnas ma yin pa'i phyir ro/ /tha snyad dpyod pa'i tshad mas kyang bden grub mi 'grub ste/ de'i ngor bden par grub kyang de tsam gyis chos de mi stong par rnam pa kun tu 'grub mi nus pa'i phyir ro/ /tshad ma gnyis kyis sgrub ma nus par gyur pa la sgrub byed nam mkha'i me tog gi rjes su 'gro bas de sgrub pa don med kyi ngal par zad do.

2. See chapter 3.
3. We can see how Mipam distinguishes a distinctive Nyingma view through his treatment of Buddha-nature, by positioning his view in contrast to assertions characteristic of the Jonang and Geluk traditions. Such an interpretative move that Mipam makes in his *Lion's Roar: Exposition of Buddha-Nature* resembles the structure of Gorampa's *Distinguishing the Views* (*lta ba'i shan 'byed*) in which Gorampa places his Sakya view, which he aligns with "the proponents of the freedom from extremes as the Middle Way" (*mtha' bral la dbu mar smra ba*) in contrast to the two extremes of "the proponents of eternalism as the Middle Way" (*rtag mtha' la dbu mar smra ba*) of the Jonang and "the proponents of annihilationism as the Middle Way" (*chad mtha' la dbu mar smra ba*) of the Geluk. See Gorampa, *Distinguishing the Views*, 3.
4. See Khedrupjé, *rgyud sde spyi'i rnam par bzhag pa rgyas par bshad pa,* in Ferdinand Lessing and Alex Wayman, *Mkhas grub rje's Fundamentals of the Buddhist Tantras* (The Hague: Mouton, 1968), 52–53. See also David S. Ruegg, "On the dGe Lugs pa Theory of the *tathāgatagarbha*," in *Pratidānam,* ed. J. C. Heesterman (The Hague: Mouton, 1968), 505. For more on Geluk interpretations of Buddha-nature, see David S. Ruegg, *Three Studies in the History of Indian and Tibetan Madhyamaka Philosophy* (Wien: Arbeitskreis für Tibetische und Buddhistische Studien, 2000), 75–76n.171.
5. Mipam, *Lion's Roar: Exposition of Buddha-Nature*, 568.4–569.1: *bden stong yin pa'i gnad kyis sangs rgya rung yin par sgrub pa'ang bab col te/ sems bden grub yin na sangs rgya mi rung ba tsam yin pa bden kyang/ bden grub med pa yin na sangs rgya ba'i nges pa med de/ sa rgo* [read *rdo*] *la sogs pa chos thams cad kyang bden med yin kyang/ bden med yin tshad sangs rgya rung bar sus sgrub par nus.*
6. Mipam, *Precious Vajra Garland*, 579.1–579.2: *spyir bden stong med dgag gi cha tsam bde gshegs snying por mi rung ste/ de la mkhyen cha med pas bde gshegs snying po'i don med.*
7. Mipam, *Lion's Roar: Exposition of Buddha-Nature*, 568.6–569.2: *med dgag de 'dra la bde gshegs snying po zhes 'dod pa don med de/ 'di nyan rang dang thun mongs pa'i rigs su 'gyur gyi/ 'dis sangs rgya rung mi 'grub ste 'di tsam la shes sgrib spangs nas rnam pa thams cad mkhyen pa'i ye shes 'byung ba'i 'thad pa gang yang sgrub mi nus pa dang/ med dgag rang gi ngo bo la mkhyen cha med pas sangs rgyas dus kyang des ci yang mkhyen mi srid pa'i phyir.*
8. Mipam uses "heritage" (*rigs*) and "Buddha-nature" (*bde gshegs snying po*) interchangeably in this context. For Mipam, as well as Longchenpa, "heritage" has a

smaller range of reference because it refers specifically to Buddha-nature at the time of obscured sentient beings. "Buddha-nature" can refer to both contexts of Buddhas and sentient beings.

9. Mipam, *Lion's Roar: Exposition of Buddha-Nature*, 568.2–568.4: *stong pa rnam grangs pa tsam la rigs kyi don gang yang med de/ khyod kyi bsam ngor rigs 'dis sa bon myur gu* [read *myu gur*] *go 'pho ba bzhin du da lta sangs rgyas kyi yon tan ci yang med kyang/ lam rkyen gyis zin na gzod 'gyur rung yin par 'dod na/ bden stong med dgag gi ldog cha de 'dus ma byas don byed nus pas stong pa la de 'dra'i khyad par gang yang 'thad pa med de/ 'dus byas sa bon gyi cha ni tha snyad du myu gur gnas 'gyur rung gi sa bon gyi steng gi bden med kyi cha ni myu gur gnas 'gyur ba nam yang mi srid pa bzhin no.*
10. A Geluk scholar, Ngawang Pelden (*ngag dbang dpal ldan*, b. 1797), explains how an absence is understood as a cause as follows: "The expanse of phenomena, which is so called because meditation within observing it acts as a cause of generating sublime qualities, is both the earlier voidness of the permeation of the nature [of the mind] by afflictive emotions and the later voidness of those [afflictive emotions brought about by antidotes]." Cited from Jeffrey Hopkins, *Maps of the Profound*, 513. I have slightly modified Hopkins's translation from Ngawang Pelden's *Annotations* (*grub mtha' chen mo'i mchan 'grel dka' gnad mdud grol blo gsal gces nor*). This Geluk interpretation of Buddha-nature, as a cause and as an emptiness that is a non-implicative negation, has a precedent in the works of Ngok Loden Sherap (*rngog blo ldan shes rab*, 1059–1109), the one who translated the *Uttaratantra* into Tibetan and wrote the first Tibetan commentary on it. For Ngok Loden Sherap's statements on Buddha-nature as a cause and as a non-implicative negation, see Kazuo Kano, "rNgog Blo-ldan-shes-rab's Summary of the *Ratnagotravibhāga*" (Ph.D. Thesis, University of Hamburg, 2006), 148–151.
11. Mipam, *Lion's Roar: Exposition of Buddha-Nature*, 569.2–569.5: *gnas 'gyur 'dus byas kyi rigs kyi tshul 'di yid la mdza' na/ sems can thams cad kyi sems kyi rgyud na thog ma med pa nas yod pa'i mkhyen brtse nus gsum gyi sa bon/ gcan gzan dang srin po sogs kyang rang gi bu la brtse ba dang/ phan gnod ngo shes pa sogs yod pa de/ lam gyis zin nas gegs bral te je 'phal du song ba na tshad med pa'i mkhyen brtse nus gsum mnga' ba sangs rgyas su 'gyur rung ba tsam la 'dod na med dgag la rigs su 'dod pa las de legs te/ skyed byed kyi rgyu 'bras yin dgos phan chad/ skad cig can dngos por gyur pa'i rgyu skyed byed yin pa bor nas/ dngos med 'dus ma byas skyed byed min pa la rgyur 'dod pa ni ya mtshan pa'i gnas so.*
12. The Jonang tradition accepts that the qualities of Buddha, such as the ten powers, and so on, are present in the continua of sentient beings. See for instance, Khenpo Lodrö Drakpa, *Roar of the Fearless Lion*, 126.4–126.6. For a discussion of Buddha-nature that is endowed with qualities of a Buddha in the Jonang tradition, see Jeffrey Hopkins, *Reflections on Reality* (Berkeley: University of California Press, 2002), 274–285.

13. In his commentary on the *Uttaratantra,* the Geluk scholar, Gyeltsapjé (*rgyal tshab rje dar ma rin chen,* 1364–1432), states that emptiness is the basis of intention (*dgongs gzhi*) of the Buddha-nature taught as a universal ground separate from the six collections of consciousness, and that such a Buddha-nature is not its literal meaning. Gyeltsapjé, *Commentary on the Uttaratantra* (*theg pa chen po rgyud bla ma'i ṭīka*), *Collected Works*, vol. 3, 75a-78b. Tsongkhapa says that emptiness is the basis of intention of the Buddha-nature that was taught in the *Laṅkāvatārasūtra* and referenced in the *Madhyamakāvatāra* (under VI.95). Tsongkhapa, *Essence of Eloquence* (*drang nges legs bshad snying po*), *Collected Works*, vol. 14, 92a-95b; See also Tsongkhapa, *Thoroughly Illuminating the Viewpoint,* 325–326. For a discussion of several important facets a Geluk view of Buddha-nature, see Jeffrey Hopkins, *Meditation on Emptiness,* 381–383. For an excellent comparison of Jonang and Geluk views on Buddha-nature, see Jeffrey Hopkins, *Reflections on Reality,* 308–315.
14. Ngawang Jorden explains Buddha-nature as the indivisibility of the emptiness and clarity of mind as the view of the Sakya scholar, Gorampa, in "Buddha-nature: Through the Eyes of Go rams pa bsod rnams seng ge in Fifteenth-Century Tibet" (Ph.D. Thesis, Harvard University, 2003), 125. Jorden cites the Sakya scholar Mangtö Ludrup Gyatso (*mang thos klu sgrub rgya mtsho,* 1523–1596) from a manuscript of *rnam bshad nor bu'i phreng ba,* a commentary on Gorampa, in his thesis, p.124n.252: "In short, the unity of clarity and emptiness is posited as Buddha-nature because saṃsāra and nirvāṇa are comprised within the mind (*sems*) and the mind also is free from constructs, empty of true existence; therefore, the abiding nature of objects primordially abides as the unity of clarity and emptiness" (translation mine). Another Sakya scholar, Śākya Chokden (*śākya mchog ldan,* 1427–1508), portrays the ultimate [Buddha-] nature (*don dam pa'i snying po*) as impermanent. See Śākya Chokden, *The Never Seen Sun: The Definitive Meaning of the Uttaratantra* (*rgyud bla ma'i bstan bcos kyi nges don sngon med nyi ma*), *Collected Works*, vol. 13 (Thimphu, Bhutan: Kunzang Tobgey, 1975), 117.6–117.7. Śākya Chokden also characterizes Buddha-nature as an implicative negation and the consummate definitive meaning: "That which has the name 'Buddha-nature' is the consummate definitive meaning, the luminous clarity which is the nature of mind; moreover, it is an implicative negation, not a non-implicative negation because it expresses the meaning of 'the emptiness endowed with all supreme aspects'." Śākya Chokden, *Ocean of Scripture and Reasoning* (*dbu ma rnam par nges pa'i chos kyi bang mdzod lung dang rigs pa'i rgya mtsho*), *Collected Works*, vol. 14 (Thimphu, Bhutan: Kunzang Tobgey, 1975), 393.5–393.7: *nges don mthar thug pa ni bde bar gshegs pa'i snying po zhes bya ba'i ming can sems rang bzhin gyis 'od gsal ba de nyid yin la/ 'dir yang ma yin dgag pa yin gyi/ med par dgag pa ni ma yin te/ rnam pa mchog dang ldan pa'i stong pa nyid ces bya ba'i don du bshad pa'i phyir*. For more on Śākya Chokden's position on Buddha-nature, see Yaroslav Komarovski, "Reburying

the Treasure, Maintaining the Continuity—Two Texts by Śākya Mchok Ldan on the Buddha-Essence," *Journal of Indian Philosophy* 34, no. 6 (December, 2006): 521–570.

15. Mipam, *Lion's Roar: Exposition of Buddha-Nature*, 569.6–570.3: *gal te bden gnyis so sor phye nas mi 'jog ste/ chos can sems kyi gsal ba dang chos nyid stong pa nyid dbyer med pa'i gnas lugs rigs su 'dod do snyam na/ 'di yang rnam shes ye shes kyi zla phye ba'i ye shes 'gyur med 'dus ma byas la 'dod na ni de ltar lung dang rigs pas grub pa'i phyir shin tu yin mod kyi/ stong pa dang zung du 'jug rgyu'i chos can de rnam shes skad cig ma'i cha 'di zhe la bzhag nas 'di rim gyis sangs rgyas su go 'pho'o snyam pa ni gyi na ste/ rigs la 'dus byas dang 'dus ma byas kyi cha gnyis yod par thal zhing/ de lta na dgos nus med pa'i 'dus ma byas ni rigs btags pa ba dang/ 'dus byas ni 'bras bu skyed nus kyi rigs mtshan nyid par 'gro bas rang bzhin gnas rigs 'dus ma byas chos kyi dbyings la bzhed pa'i theg chen gyi mdo sde kun gyi dgongs pa stong* [read *stor*] *par zad do.*
16. Mipam, *Gateway to Scholarship*, 296: *rang bzhin du gnas pa'i rigs ni de bzhin gshegs pa'i snying po ste/ de'i ngo bo ni gdod nas sku dang ye shes dang dbyer med pa'i chos kyi dbyings rig stong zung du 'jug pa rang byung gi ye shes 'dus ma byas pa.*
17. Mipam, *Precious Vajra Garland*, 741.2–741.3: *ye shes yin la gzhan byung ngam rgyus byung min pa'i cha nas rang byung btags kyi/ rang las rang skyes dang/ gsar byung gnyis ka'i byung ba'am skyes pa min te ma skyes pas so.*
18. Mipam, *Lion's Roar: Exposition of Buddha-Nature*, 587.2–588.1: *gnas lugs rang gi ngo bo'i dbang du byas na chos thams cad chos nyid de yi klong du chud cing chos nyid rang gi ngo bo la skye 'gag med par mnyam pa nyid du gnas la 'khor 'das la sogs pa'i bzang ngan dang/ pha rol tshu rol bdag dang gzhan che dang chung ba sogs kyi cha dang/ snga phyi'i dus kyi khyad par sogs med de chos dbyings thig le nyag gcig 'pho 'gyur med pa'o/ gnas lugs la de ltar yin kyang 'khrul pa glo bur ba'i snang ngo dang bstun na 'di ltar khams gsum 'khor ba'i lus sems yul gyi snang ba shar nas chos nyid kyi rang bzhin mi mthong ba'i tshe na'ang/ chos nyid ni med pa ma yin te rang gi rang bzhin las g.yo ba cung zad kyang med par yod pas na/ sems kyi chos nyid de lta bu glo bur gyi dri mas sbubs su byas nas mi mngon yang bcud dam dbus na snying po'i tshul gyis gnas pa la rigs sam snying po zhes brjod de/ dper na sa 'og gi gter la sogs pa'i dpe dgus mtshon nas shes par bya bar gsungs so.*
19. The nine metaphors are found in *Uttaratantra* I.96–97: like the Buddha in a lotus, like honey in a beehive, like grain in a husk, like gold in a dirt heap, like a treasure under a pauper's house, like a sprout that grows from a small seed, like a statue wrapped in an old cloth, like a king in the womb of an ugly woman, like gold in the earth; *rgyud bla ma rtsa 'grel*, 12–13. Richard King points out that with the exception of two metaphors representing the Buddha-nature as an undeveloped cause, the metaphors of the king in the womb and the seed, the other seven metaphors depict the Buddha-nature as a *fully developed* concealed essence. See Richard King, *Early Advaita Vedānta and Buddhism* (Albany: SUNY Press, 1995), 208.

20. Mipam, *Vajra Essence*, 392.6–393.2: *sems can thams cad kyi sems la chos nyid kyi tshul du yod cing sgrib pa spang rung du gnas pa'i skabs na bde gshegs snying po zhes bya ste/ sems kyi chos nyid de rtogs pas sangs rgya bar byed pa'i phyir ro.*
21. Mipam, *Lion's Roar: Exposition of Buddha-Nature*, 596.5–597.2: *rang byung gi ye shes rgyu las skyes par mi 'gyur te/ yang dag par glo bur dri bral gyi chos sku de bral ba'i 'bras bur song ba yin la/ rgyu las gsar du skye ba ltar snang ba yang gnas ma gyur pa'i snang tshul la de ltar snang bar zad kyi/ yang dag pa'i don du chos nyid kyi rang bzhin chos kyi sku'i ngo bo la skye 'jig med par chos thams cad gdod nas mnyam pa nyid du mngon par sangs rgyas pa'am/ gzod ma nas zhi ba mya ngan las 'das pa/ rang bzhin gyis 'od gsal ba sogs zab mo'i mdo sde rnams kyi dgongs pa mthar thug 'di dag pa'i sems dpa' rnams kyi kyang bsam par dka' ba'i gnas yin na phal pas lta ci smros.*
22. The twofold purity is (1) natural purity (*rang bzhin rnam dag*), or primordial purity, and (2) purity that is freed from the adventitious [defilements] (*glo bur bral dag*). The two purities are alternatively rendered as "pure of the two obscurations" (*sgrib pa gnyis dag pa*). The *Tibetan-Chinese Dictionary* (*bod rgya tshig mdzod chen mo*) entry for twofold purity (*dag pa gnyis ldan*) reads: "Free from the two obscurations, cognitive obscurations and the obscurations of afflictive emotions—the state of Buddha" (*nyon mongs pa dang shes bya'i sgrib pa gnyis dag pa ste sangs rgyas kyi go 'phang*). Such a description reflects a more general interpretation and does not evoke the *primordial* purity that is an important part of Mipam's and Longchenpa's particular Nyingma exegesis; it does not highlight a "discovery model" of the path as opposed to a "developmental model." I draw these contrasting terms from Anne Klein's provocative discussion of these two models in Anne Klein, *Meeting the Bliss Queen* (Boston: Beacon Press, 1995), 63–76.
23. Mipam, *Intelligent Presence*, 538.5–539.1: *ji snyed pa'i don kun mkhyen pa'i yon tan mngon du snang ba ni dag pa gnyis ldan la yod kyi/ rang bzhin rnam dag tsam la med kyang/ de'i yon tan ye ldan du khas len dgos par ral gri'i dpe sogs bzhin no/ des na gzhi'i dus na bde gshegs snying po la yon tan mngon du yod rung tsam du shes par bya'o.*
24. Ibid., 537.1–537.3: *stobs sogs kyi yon tan ye ldan/ ral gri tshad ldan la gcod pa'i yon tan/ me long dwangs pa la gzugs snang ba'i yon tan/ nor bu 'od dang dgos 'dod rtsol ba'i yon tan ye nas rang chas lhun grub tu yod kyang/ ral gri shub dang me long sgrom du chud pa/ nor bu 'dam gos bzhin no/ de'i sgrib pa bsal na yon tan gsar bskyed min yang/ mngon du snang ba gsar skye ltar snang ngo.*
25. Mipam, *Difficult Points of Scriptures in General*, 454.2–454.5: *'on na khyi dang phag sogs sems can rnams kyi sems kyi rgyud la stobs bcu'i ye shes yod dam zer na/ stobs bcu'i ye shes kyi yon tan de'i rgyud kyi gshegs snying la ye nas yod de/ kho rang gi chos nyid kyi yon tan yin pas khams yod na yon tan yod mod kyi mngon du mi 'gyur te/ ral gri la gcod pa'i bya ba yod kyang/ shub tu chud pa la gcod pa'i bya ba mngon gyur du med pa dang/ me long la gzugs brnyan 'char rung gi yon tan yod kyang sgrom du bcug pa la mngon gyur du mi 'char ba dang 'dra ste.*

26. *The Dictionary of Internal Knowledge* (*nang rig pa'i tshig mdzod*) references ten powers listed in the Vinaya as: "(1) the power of knowing what is and is not correct (*gnas dang gnas ma yin*), (2) the power of knowing the ripenings of karma, (3) the power of knowing various inclinations (*mos pa*), (4) the power of knowing thorough affliction and complete purification, (5) the power of knowing faculties that are supreme and those that are not, (6) the power of knowing the path of all transmigrations (*thams cad 'gro ba'i lam*), (7) the power of knowing various dispositions (*khams sna tshogs*), (8) the power of remembering previous existences (*sngon gyi gnas*), (9) the power of knowing death, transference, and birth, and (10) the power of knowing the exhaustion of contamination (*zag pa*)." *nang rig pa'i tshig mdzod*, ed. Purbu Tsering, 671.
27. Longchenpa, *Precious Treasury of Philosophies*, 877.4–877.5: *sangs rgyas de'ang bral ba'i rgyu 'bras las/ bskyed bya skyed byed kyi rgyu 'bras kyis bsgrubs pa ma yin te ye nas lhun gyis grub pa'i phyir.*
28. Longchenpa, *Treasure Trove of Scriptural Transmission*, 117.1–117.4: *bsod nams dang ye shes kyi tshogs las byung ba ma yin nam zhe na/ smras pa tshogs gnyis ni ye nas snang ba dang/ stong pa'i yon tan du rdzogs zin pa la lhun grub ces brjod de/ glo bur du bsags pa de ni dri ma sel byed kyi rkyen gyi cha tsam la rgyu tshogs gnyis zhes btags pa tsam ste/ nor bu dri mas gos pa khrus ras dang 'dag chal gyis phyi ba la/ nor bu mthong ba'i rgyu brjod pa bzhin no.*
29. Longchenpa, *Great Chariot*, 312.4–312.6: *sems can pa'i dus na sems kyi chos nyid la snang cha nas gzugs sku'i yon tan dang/ stong cha nas chos sku'i yon tan rdzogs par ldan yang dri mas bsgribs pas mngon sum du mi bsal ba'i phyir khams sam rigs zhes btags shing/ sangs rgyas pa'i tshe dri ma mtha' dag dang bral bas byang chub ces brjod kyang/ ngo bo sems nyid kyi nus pa rdzogs par snang mi snang tsam las dang po sems can gyi dus na med pa'i yon tan phyis gsar du bskyed par 'dod pa ni ma yin te/ 'pho 'gyur med pa'i phyir.*
30. Longchenpa, *Responses to Mind and Wisdom*, 380.3–381.1: *ding sang ni dge ba'i bshes gnyen phal dang/ sgom chen kun mthun par/ stong rkyang ci yang med pa la gzhi byed pa ni snying po'i don gyi dgongs pa dang mi mthun te/ ci yang med pa'i gzhi nyams su blangs pas 'bras bu sangs rgyas yon tan thams cad dang ldan pa mi 'byung ste/ gzhi lam 'bras bu gsum 'dzol ba'i phyir ro/ sangs rgyas de ni 'dus ma byas shing lhun gyis grub pa'i yon tan can bral ba'i 'bras bu mngon du gyur pa zhig yin pa'i phyir ro/ des na srid rtse'i lta ba dang de dag mthun par snang ngo/ 'dir 'dus ma byas shing lhun gyis grub pa'i 'od gsal ba nyid gzhir 'dod pa yin no.*
31. Ibid., 379.2: *sems can pa'i dus kyi 'od gsal ba'i ye shes rang la yod pa ni gzhi'o.*
32. Ibid., 379.4–379.6: *gzhi don bshad pa ni/ ye nas 'od gsal ba chos nyid 'dus ma byas shing lhun gyis grub pa stong pa'i ngos nas dngos po dang mtshan ma gang du'ang ma grub cing 'khor ba dang mya ngan las 'das pa la sogs pa gang du'ang ma chad pas spros pa'i mtha' thams cad dang bral ba nam mkha' lta bu/ gsal ba'i ngos nas sku dang ye shes kyi rang bzhin ye ldan du lhun gyis sgrub cing 'od gsal ba nyi zla'i dkyil 'khor lta bu/ de gnyis ka'ang 'du 'bral med pa'i chos nyid du ye nas gnas pa.*

33. Longchenpa, *White Lotus*, 1066.6–1067.1: *khams ni rang bzhin gyis dag pa mya ngan las 'das pa 'dus ma byas pa'i yon tan dang lhan cig pas don gyi kun gzhi zhes bzhag pa yin no.*

34. Longchenpa, *White Lotus*, 151.4–152.2: *sku dang ye shes 'du 'bral med pa'i dbyings su gnas pas bde bar gshegs pa'i snying po/ 'khor 'das kyi chos rnams brten pas gnas lugs don gyi kun gzhi zhes bya ste/ 'dus ma byas shing ye nas rnam dag chen por gnas pa'o/ /de yang 'khor ba'i chos las dang nyon mongs pa rnams rten pa med pa'i tshul gyis brten pa ni/ nyi mkha'i ngos na sprin phung brten pa ltar/ gzhi la ma reg ma 'byar la de'i ngang la gnas pa ste/ don la rang bzhin med pas rten dang brten par ma grub bzhin du brten par snang bas brtags pa ste.* Longchenpa follows this description with a quote from the *Uttaratantra* I.55–57: "In the way that the earth abides in water, and water in wind, wind completely abides in space, while space does not abide in wind, water, or earth; in the same way the aggregates, constituents, and faculties abide in karma and afflictive emotions, karma and afflictive emotions constantly abide in the distorted mind, and the distorted mind completely abides in the purity of mind, while the nature of mind does not abide in any phenomena." *rgyud bla ma rtsa 'grel*, 8: *sa ni chu la chu rlung la/ /rlung ni mkha' la rab tu gnas/ /mkha' ni rlung dang chu dag dang/ /sa yi khams la gnas ma yin/ /de bzhin phung po khams dbang rnams/ /las dang nyon mongs dag la brten/ /las dang nyon mongs tshul bzhin min/ /yid la byed la rtag tu gnas/ /tshul bzhin ma yin yid byed ni/ /sems kyi dag pa la rab gnas/ /sems kyi rang bzhin chos rnams ni/ /thams cad la yang gnas ma yin.* See also Longchenpa, *Responses to Mind and Wisdom*, 384.2–384.4.

35. Longchenpa, *White Lotus*, 1420.4–1420.5: *sems tsam pas kun gzhi tshogs brgyad de nyid gnas 'gyur bas ye shes su 'dod la/ 'dir de dag bsal bas rang byung gi ye shes mngon pa tsam la gnas 'gyur du btags pa gnyis khyad par shin tu che'o.*

36. Mipam, *Difficult Points of Scriptures in General*, 453.4–453.5: *gshegs snying ni stong kyang tsam min te/ stong nyid 'od gsal yin/ de chos thams cad kyi ye thog gzhi yi gnas lugs yin/ zung 'jug bden pa dbyer med kyi gnas lugs rnam kun mchog ldan gyi stong nyid yin la.*

37. Mipam, *Vajra Essence*, 357.4: *ye thog gzhi'i 'od gsal gdod ma'i gnas lugs de nyid ni chos kun gyi chos nyid mthar thug yin.*

38. Ibid., 358.1–358.2: *gzhi de nyid spros pa gang yang med pa'i cha nas ka dag dang/ stong kyang nam mkha' lta bu min par rang gsal ris med rgya chad phyogs lhung med par lhun gyis grub pa/ 'khor 'das snang ba kun gyi 'byung gnas yin pas thugs rje kun khyab ces gsungs te/ rdzogs chen gyi rgyud kyi chos skad la gzhi gnas kyi ye shes gsum ldan zhes gsungs.*

39. Mipam, *Lion's Roar: Exposition of Buddha-Nature*, 572.1–572.2: *'di ltar skye zhing 'gag par snang ba'i 'dus byas rnams ni snang ba ltar ma grub pa'i phyir dbyings kyi gshis la des gos pa yod ma myong bas/ 'khor ba rgyu 'bras ye nas dag cing rang bzhin lhun gyis grub pa'i 'od gsal zag med kyi snang ba rnams dang 'du 'bral med pa'i gnad 'dis bde bar gshegs pa'i snying po'i tshul phyin ci ma log pa ngos zin par bya dgos so.*

40. One should note that in the triad of empty essence, natural clarity, and all-pervasive compassionate resonance, the word "essence" (*ngo bo*) and the word "nature" (*rang bzhin*) are both words that are used to translate the same Sanskrit word, *svabhāva* "intrinsic nature." Thus, if a proponent of self-emptiness is defined as one holding the view that the nature of reality is *only* empty, then Mipam would not be a proponent of self-emptiness because he also asserts the nature of reality as clarity (*rang bzhin gsal ba*).

41. Bötrül, *Ornament of Mañjugoṣa's Viewpoint*, 205: *rigs kyi ngo bo ni gnas lugs ye dag snying po'i chos su gyur pa gang zhig ngo bo stong pa la rang bzhin gsal ba thugs rje kun khyab kyi rang bzhin ste/ khyad chos gsum ldan gyi bdag nyid can du bzhed pa ste/ mdor bsdus na/ gnas lugs ye dag snying po'i chos su gyur pa gang zhig/ khyad chos gsum dang ldan pa de rigs kyi mtshan nyid du 'dod do.*

42. Ibid., 205–206: *ngo bo stong pa 'khor lo bar ba dang rang bzhin gsal ba tha ma'i dgongs don dang/ thugs rjes kun khyab bar tha 'gal med bstan.*

43. Mipam, *Lion's Roar: Exposition of Buddha-Nature*, 598.2–598.3: *bde bar gshegs pa'i snying po rang gi ngo bo ni yod med rtag chad la sogs pa'i spros pa thams cad bral ba bden pa dbyer med thig le nyag gcig mnyam pa nyid de.*

44. Ibid., 575.1–575.6: *yul shes pa'i shes pa nye tsho* [read *nyi tshe*] *ba la mi rtag pas khyab kyang/ shes dang shes bya ro gcig pa'i ye shes mkha' khyab mkha' yi rdo rje can ni de dang mi 'dra ste/ 'dus ma byas pa'i rang gdangs 'od gsel* [read *gsal*] *mi 'gyur ba'i ngang der 'khor 'das kyi chos kun 'ub chub pas na de'i ngo bo la skye 'gags ye nas med par mthar thug dpyod pa'i rig shes kyis grub pa'i phyir ro/ des na de 'dra ba'i ye shes de ni 'dus byas dang 'dus ma byas kyi mthar gang la'ang mi gnas pa'i 'dus ma byas chen po ste/ dngos med rkyang pa dang gtan mi 'dra la/ dngos dngos med gnyis ka chos yin zhing/ de dag brten nas skyes pa'am brten nas btags pa'i phyir na yang dag par dpyad na 'dus byas dang gsog gsob rdzun pa bslu ba yin la/ bde gshegs snying po ni dngos dngos med kyi chos nyid 'dus ma byas chen po yang dag par mi bslu ba yin te/ rtsa ba shes rab las/ rang bzhin dag ni bcos min dang/ gzhan la ltos pa med pa yin/ zhes dang/ dngos dang dngos med 'dus byas yin/ mya ngan 'das pa 'dus ma byas/ zhes gsungs pa bzhin no.*

45. Ibid., 593.5–594.5: *gnas yongs su ma gyur pa'i gdul bya gzhan gyi bsam ngo dang bstun te rnam mkhyen mi rtag ces lung las gsungs shing/ rigs pa yang rnam 'grel las/ tshad ma rtag pa nyid yod min/ /dngos yod rtogs pa tshad phyir dang/ /shes bya mi rtag pa nyid kyi/ /de mi rtag pa nyid phyir ro/ /zhes gsungs te/ /sems bskyed pa dang stong nyid goms pa la sogs lam gyi rgyu las rnam mkhyen 'byung gi rgyu med du 'byung ba mi rigs pa dang/ de chos thams cad la mngon sum pa'i tshad ma yin pa'i phyir/ tshad ma ste mi bslu ba'i blo yin na rtag pa zhig med de dngos po yod pa la de de bzhin 'jal ba'i tshad ma yin la/ de'i yul shes bya ni mi rtag pa nyid kyi phyir 'jal byed tshad ma de yang mi rtag ste rim can du 'byung gi /rtag pa yin na don byed nus pas stong par tshad mas grub pa'i phyir yul 'jal ba la sogs pa'i byed pa mtha' dag gis stong par nges pas na rnam mkhyen ni rtag par shin tu mi rigs te mi rtag par 'grub la/ de bzhin dngos po thams cad mi rtag pa dang/ dngos med la rtag par btags kyang*

rtag rgyu'i gzhi med pas rtag pa mtshan nyid pa'i chos gang yang mi rnyed par 'gyur ro/ /tshul 'di ni phyi rol mu stegs can dang/ bsam gyis mi khyab pa'i chos nyid kyi ngo bor gnas gyur pa'i tshul la blo ma sbyangs pa'i theg pa thun mongs pa'i ngor de ltar sgrub dgos te/ rnam shes kyi ngor snang tshul la de las gzhan du 'char ba'i thabs ci yang med do/ /'on kyang gnas yongs su gyur pa'i ye shes kyi gzigs pa'i dbang du byas na rnam mkhyen rtag par 'grub ste.

46. Ibid., 595.4–596.1: *'gyur bcas glo bur 'bral rung gi dri ma gang dag skad cig ma'i skye 'gag rim gyis 'byung ba dang/ 'khor 'das dang bzang ngan la sogs pa'i mi mnyam pa 'di ni gnas ma gyur pa'i gnyis snang can la de ltar bslu med bsnyon med du snang yang/ gshis la skye 'gag dang gnyis chos ma grub par mnyam pa chen por gnas pa/ de'i ngang du phyogs kyi cha dang dus kyi 'gyur ba thams cad 'ub chub cing/ de ni 'phags pa rnams kyi so so rang rig pa'i ye shes kyi yul du yod pa yin cing/ dus gsum gyi 'gyur bas bslad med pas na de la rtag pa chen po'i tha snyad cis mi gtags te/ yod pa gang zhig skad cig gi skye 'gag can min pa'i phyir ro.*

47. Mipam, *Vajra Essence*, 404.6–405.6: *chos nyid rang ngos nas gzhal na/ 'dus byas dngos po dang 'dus ma byas dngos med gnyis kar mi dmigs te/ chos nyid 'dus byas dang 'dus ma byas kyi mtha' la mi gnas pa so so rang rig par bya ba yin cing . . . gdod ma'i chos nyid mngon du gyur pa sangs rgyas kyi dus na/ chos kyi dbyings de las nam yang mi g.yo ba'i rdo rje lta bu rtag pa chen po ye shes kyi sku ni 'dus ma byas chen po yin te 'dus byas ma yin mod/ 'di la snang tshul gyi dbang du byas na sngar lam sgom pa'i bral 'bras yin pa'i cha nas gsar byung dang/ gdul bya rnams phrin las rim can du 'jug pa'i cha nas 'dus byas lta bur 'jog pa sogs lung spyi la grags pa ltar so so'i dgongs don shan phyed na the tshom gyi drwa ba bral bar 'gyur ro.*

48. The eight profundities (*zab mo brgyad*) refer to profundity regarding: (1) arising, (2) ceasing, (3) suchness, (4) objects of knowledge, (5) cognition, (6) conduct, (7) nonduality, and (8) skillful means. These are found in the fourth section of the *Abhisamayālaṃkāra*, "joining with the perfect aspects" (*rnam rdzogs sbyor ba*) as signs of the Path of Meditation. See Bötrül, *Words of Maitreya: An Explanation of the Meaning of the Words of the Abhisamayālaṃkāra* (*sher phyin mngon par rtogs pa'i rgyan gyi tshig don rnam par bshad pa ma pham zhal lung*), Bötrül's *Collected Works*, vol. 2 (Sichuan: Nationalities Press, 2004), 208–209.

49. I have used the word "radiantly" here because I feel that it is a more evocative translation of *legs*, which literally means "good" or "excellent"; I find that radiant is a better descriptive word to positively qualify a dawning (*'char ba*), which is the verb that Mipam uses here that literally means "to arise," "to appear," "to dawn."

50. Mipam, *Vajra Essence*, 405.6–406.6: *de ltar yang gzhan phal mo ches sangs rgyas kyi sku dang ye shes ngo bo mi rtag la rgyun gyis rtag par 'dod/ sku dang ye shes rnam kun mchog ldan 'bras bu'i stong nyid kyi rang bzhin du 'dod pa dag gis/ sku dang ye shes rang gi ngo bos rtag kyang/ gdul bya'i snang tshul la rgyun gyis mi rtag par 'dod de mdo dgongs 'dus las gsungs pa bzhin no/ /de ltar gnas lugs ji lta ba'i dbang du byas na dus gsum gyis bsdus pa'i chos gang yang gshis la skye 'gag med par mnyam pa nyid*

las ma g.yos bzhin du/ bdag dang gzhan/ 'khor ba dang myang 'das/ 'dus byas dang 'dus ma byas/ 'das dang da lta ma 'ongs pa'i chos sogs ji snyed pa'i chos kun ma 'dres par 'char ba 'di gnyis gcig gi phyogs bzung nas gcig spang mi dgos par/ zab mo brgyad dang [read *ldan*] *rtogs tshul gsungs pa dang mtshungs par bden gnyis 'gal med kyi go don legs par shar ba rnams la theg chen mdo rgyud kyi dgongs pa rnams la the tshom med pa'i nges shes bde blag tu skye ba yin no.*

51. In contrast to Mipam, Śākya Chokden asserts that wisdom is impermanent and claims that statements of its permanence are spoken intending a "permanent continuity" (*rgyun gyi rtag pa*). Śākya Chokden, *Golden Needle of Elegant Sayings: A Copious Dicourse Ascertaining [Sakya Paṇḍita's] "Clear Differentiation of the Three Vows"* (*sdom gsum gyi rab tu dbye ba'i bstan bcos kyi 'bel gtam rnam par nges pa legs bshad gser gyi thur ma*), *Collected Works*, vol. 6 (Thimphu, Bhutan: Kunzang Tobgey, 1975), 498.2–498.4.
52. Mipam, *Intelligent Presence*, 449.3–449.5: *gnas lugs don dam pa'i dbang du byas na snang srid ye sangs rgyas par khas len zhing de ltar bsgom dgos kyang/ snang lugs tha snyad kyi dbang du byas na/ gzhi sangs rgya rung gi rigs dang/ lam nyams su len pa'i skabs dang/ dag pa mthar phyin pa'i 'bras bu gsum du shes rab kyis shan 'byed du yod pa ni rdzogs pa chen po'i bar gyis 'dod de.*
53. Ibid., 518.1–519.1: *chos nyid dbyings kyi ngo bo la sgrib pa ye nas med par grub pas kyang/ gnas tshul gzhi 'bras dbyer med du grub pas ye sangs rgyas pa'i dgongs pa gtan la phebs shing/ snang tshul la goms rtsal rdzogs pa'i tshe na gnas snang mthun pa'i tshul gyis mngon du gyur pas yang 'tshang rgya ba'ang yin te/ de gnyis mi 'gal lo/ /spros kun ye nas sam ka nas dag pa dang/ rang bzhin 'od gsal ba'i gdangs dbyer med pa'i chos nyid de ni 'khor 'das kun la khyab pas/ chos nyid ci yang ma yin las cir yang 'char rung ba'i phyir/ 'khor 'das dbyer med mnyam pa nyid chos kyi skur lhun gyis grub pa'o/ /de'i phyir 'khor 'das kyi snang ba sna tshogs pa'i cho 'phrul tshad med pa ci bsgyur kyang/ de dag rnam shes dang ye shes kyi byed pa kho na las byung ste/ snang tshul du/ rnam shes kho nas las byed pa ma dag gzhi yi skabs/ rnam shes ye shes 'dre nas las byed pa ma dag dag pa gnyis ldan lam gyi skabs/ ye shes kho nas las byed pa shin tu rnam dag pa'i 'bras bu'i skabs te gnas skabs gsum du dbyer yod.*
54. *Uttaratantra* I.47: "According to the progression of impure, impure/pure, and extremely pure, they are called 'sentient beings,' 'bodhisattvas,' and 'Tathāgatas'." *rgyud bla ma rtsa 'grel*, 8: *ma dag ma dag dag pa dang/ /shin tu rnam dag go rims bzhin/ /sems can byang chub sems dpa' dang/ /de bzhin gshegs pa zhes brjod do.*
55. Mipam, *Intelligent Presence*, 542.3–543.1: *snang tshul gyi dbang du byas na/ rang bzhin rnam dag gzhi dang/ glo bur bral dag gi khyad par du byas pa'i dbyings 'bras bur 'dod pas khyad med pa min yang/ la zlo'i tshe gnas tshul ltar gtan la 'bab dgos kyi/ de ma phab na/ 'khor ba nyid myang 'das su mi rtogs so/ /shan 'byed pa'i tshe snang tshul ltar yin yang/ des gnas lugs la 'khor 'das mnyam nyid yin pa'ang mi khegs te/ gnas tshul la ma dag pa med pas so.*
56. Mipam, *Lion's Roar: Exposition of Buddha-Nature*, 599.1–599.5: *tha snyad dpyod pa'i tshad mas shan legs par 'byed pa'i skabs su bden pa la bden par shes pa 'phags pa'i*

lam mi bslu bar shes pa lta bu dang/ mi bden pa la mi bden par shes pa bdag bsgoms pas grol bar smra ba la log par shes pa lta bu dang/ mi rtag pa la mi rtag par shes pa 'dus byas kyi dngos po thams cad skad cig mar shes pa dang/ rtag pa la rtag par shes pa bde gshegs snying po rang byung gi ye shes rnam pa thams cad pa mi 'gyur bar shes pa dang/ med pa la med par shes pa bdag dang gzung 'dzin du snang ba rang bzhin ma grub par shes pa lta bu dang/ yod pa la yod par 'dzin pa rgyu 'bras bslu med rten 'brel gyi snang tshul dang/ sems can thams cad la chos nyid bde gshegs snying po lhun gyis grub pa'i yon tan rang bzhin gyi gnas par shes pa lta bu la sogs pa ni tha snyad du dngos po'i yin lugs la phyin ci ma log pa'i shes rab 'dzin stangs yin pas de ltar shes shing bzhugs pa las yon tan rgya chen po thob ste gti mug med pa'i dge ba'i rtsa ba yin pa'i phyir ro.

Chapter Five. The Indivisible Ground and Fruition

1. Mipam, *Lion's Roar: Exposition of Buddha-Nature*, 567.4–567.5: *rdzogs sangs sku ni 'phro phyir dang/ /de bzhin nyid dbyer med phyir dang/ /rigs yod phyir na lus can kun/ /rtag tu sangs rgyas snying po can. rgyud bla ma rtsa 'grel*, 6.
2. Ibid., 572.3–572.4: *rkang pa dang po'i don ni/ yang dag par rdzogs pa'i sangs rgyas kyi sku mthar thug pa chos kyi sku yon tan nam mkha' dang mnyam pa de lta bu/ sngon tha mal pa 'ching ba kun ldan du gyur pa'i gang zag gi rgyud de las phyis gsal ba'am/ 'phro ba'am/ mngon du gyur pa yod pas na da lta nas sems can gyi rgyud na bde gshegs snying po yod ces bsgrub pa yin no.*
3. Ibid., 575.6–576.4: *mthar thug chos sku'i ye shes de ni srid zhi kun khyab dang mnyam pa nyid dang 'dus ma byas pa dang/ 'gyur med don dam pa'i rang bzhin du nges pa don gyi mdo sde'i lung dang mthar thug dpyod pa'i rigs pas grub pa na/ de nam zhig mngon du 'gyur rung gi rgyu de ni da lta nas ye shes chos sku'i rang bzhin chos nyid kyi tshul du bri gang dang bral bar bzhugs pa de nyid la/ blo bur gyi dri ma bral ma bral gyi snang tshul la mngon du gyur ma gyur yod kyang/ gnas tshul la snga phyir bzang ngan gyi khyad par til tsam med de/ 'gyur med 'dus ma byas kyi rang bzhin yin pa'i phyir te/ rgyud bla ma las/ ji ltar sngar bzhin phyis de bzhin/ 'gyur ba med pa'i chos nyid do/ zhes dang/ sems kyi rang bzhin 'od gsal gang yin pa/ /de ni nam mkha' bzhin du 'gyur med de/ yang dag min rtog las byung 'dod chags sogs/ glo bur dri mas de nyon mongs mi 'gyur.*
4. We can see this first argument as an argument for the immanence of the divine: if a future is acknowledged when beings are united with a perfect and unchanging divinity, then that unchanging divinity must also in some way participate in the present world because any change between pre- and post-union would by definition contradict the unchanging divinity. A current trend in theology, called "panentheism" (*lit.* God-in-everything), addresses issues of the relationship between the divine and the world in terms such as "inextricable intertwining." The discourses of panentheism are fruitful to consider in light of Mipam's

depictions of Buddha-nature. For a concise introduction to some of the central issues in panentheism, see Michael W. Brierley, "Naming a Quiet Revolution: The Panentheistic Turn in Modern Theology," in *In Whom We Live and Move and Have Our Being: Panentheistic Reflections on God's Presence in a Scientific World,* ed. Philip Clayton and Arthur Peacocke (Grand Rapids: Eerdmans, 2004), 1–15.

5. Mipam, *Lion's Roar: Exposition of Buddha-Nature*, 578.2–578.5: *chos nyid 'od gsal ba'i ye shes kun la khyad med par yod kyang/ rang sems 'khrul pa glo bur ba 'di skyes pa'i tshe 'khrul sems yul dang bcas pa 'di tsam 'khor ba'i gdags gzhi yin la 'khrul pa de rang la yod pa'i chos nyid ji lta ba bzhin du mi shes te/ dper na gnyid kyi dus na yid kyi shes pa gcig bu'i dbang gis lus dang yul dang mig shes la sogs pa'i snang ba mu med pa byung la/ de dus yul yul can so sor 'dzin cing dmigs kyi/ yid shes kho rang gis rang gi yin lugs gzung 'dzin tha dad du ma grub pa shes mi nus la/ ma shes kyang yin lugs de las gzhan du gyur pa med pa dang/ chos thams cad stong pa nyid du gnas kyang de ltar yin pa tsam gyis kun gyis rtogs dgos pa ma yin pa bzhin te gnas snang mi mthun pa'i 'khrul pa srid pa'i phyir ro.*
6. We will see that Mipam uses this type of reasoning to also establish "the great purity" (*dag pa chen po*) of all appearances. Mipam, *Overview: Essential Nature of Luminous Clarity*, 457–459, cited below.
7. Mipam explains each of the first three verses of the stanza from the *Uttaratantra* in terms of three of the four types of reasons from the *Saṃdhinirmocanasūtra*. See *Saṃdhinirmocanasūtra*, in Powers, *Wisdom of Buddha*, 284–285. These same three reasons are found in Rongzom's *Establishing Appearances as Divine*. See Rongzom, *Establishing Appearances as Divine*, 560–561. See also Matthew Kapstein, "Mi-pam's Theory of Interpretation," in *Buddhist Hermeneutics,* ed. Donald Lopez (Honolulu: University of Hawaii Press, 1988), 155–157.
8. Mipam, *Lion's Roar: Exposition of Buddha-Nature*, 578.6–579.2: *'bras dus kyi chos sku mngon du gsal pa'i rtags kyis rgyu dus kyi rigs yon tan ye ldan can yod par sgrub pa ste/ gnas tshul la snga phyi rgyu 'bras su med kyang snang tshul la ltos nas rgyu 'bras su bzhag dgos pa'i phyir 'bras bu las rgyu bsgrub pa ltos pa'i rigs pa zhes bya ba yin no.*
9. Ibid., 579.2–579.4: *rkang pa gnyis pa/ de bzhin nyid dbyer med phyir dang/ zhes pa'i don ni/ 'khor 'das kyi chos thams cad gnas lugs stong pa nyid gdod ma'i 'od gsal chen por dbyer med ro gcig pas na/ sangs rgyas dang sems can kyang don dam par dbye ba med de srid gzhi mnyam pa nyid do/ /de'i phyir 'khrul pa glo bur bas sprul pa'i sems can ltar snang ba rnams kyang gnas lugs don dam pa'i chos nyid las cung zad kyang ma g.yos par chos nyid kyi rigs pas grub pas na sangs rgyas kyi snying po can du nges.*
10. Ibid., 583.1–583.5: *rkang pa gsum pa rigs yod phyir na/ zhes pa'i don ni/ sems can thams cad la sangs rgya rung gi rigs yod de/ dri ma glo bur ba spang rung du grub cing/ yon tan ye ldan gyi chos sku kun la khyad med par yod par grub pas so/ /de ltar sangs rgya rung gi rigs yod na lus can de dag sangs rgyas kyi snying po can du nges te/*

de dag sangs rgyas pa'i gnas skabs yod la/ sangs rgyas chos sku de yang ngo bo 'dus ma byas su grub pas snga phyi la bzang ngan gyi khyad par ngo bo'i cha nas med pa'i phyir ro/ rigs pa gsum pa 'dis rgyu las 'bras bu skyed par shes pa bya ba byed pa'i rigs pa yin no/ /'dir rgyu yod tsam gyis 'bras bu 'byin par dpog pa tsam min te/ chos nyid de bzhin nyid kyi rigs la 'gyur ba med pa dang/ de 'bras dus ngo bo la bzang ngan med pa dang/ glo bur ba'i dri ma rnams yun ji ltar ring yang 'bras [read *'bral*] *rung yin pas rigs de sangs rgya ba la nam yang chud za ba mi srid pa'i gnad kyis so.*

11. Ibid., 583.5–584.1: *de ltar rgyu rigs yod pa de 'bras dus kyi chos sku dang ngo bo khyad med dang/ 'bras dus kyi chos sku yod na de sems can gyi dus na'ang 'phel 'bri med par yod dgos pa dang/ rgyu 'bras dang snga phyir btags kyang don la chos dbyings 'gyur med kyi ngo bor ro gcig pa'i rigs pa de gsum gyis sems can thams cad de bzhin gshegs pa'i snying po can du 'grub ste dngos po'i stobs kyis zhugs pa'i rigs pa yang dag gi lam nas so.*
12. Mikyö Dorjé (*mi bskyod rdo rje,* 1507–1554), the Eighth Karmapa, makes an argument that the three reasons in the *Uttaratantra* do not hold up to analysis in his commentary on the *Abhisamayālaṃkāra.* See Mikyö Dorjé, *shes rab kyi pha rol tu phyin pa'i lung chos mtha' dag gi bdud rtsi'i snying por gyur pa gang la ldan pa'i gzhi rje btsun mchog tu dgyes par ngal gso ba'i yongs 'dus brtol gyi ljon pa rgyas pa* (reproduction of *dpal spungs* xylographic edition), (Delhi: Karmapae Choedhey, 1984), vol. 1, 255.1–256.1.
13. In his book that makes a strong case for *dialetheism* (the view that there are true contradictions), Graham Priest claims that dialetheism is held to be absurd by philosophers due to sociological rather than rational reasons. See Graham Priest, *Beyond the Limits of Thought* (Oxford: Oxford University Press, 2002; reprint of Cambridge University Press, 1995), 5.
14. Such a circularity in the case of Buddha-nature is articulated well in Paul Tillich's "mystical apriori," a foundation of dialectical inquiry in the context of his Christian theology: "In both the empirical and metaphysical approaches, as well as in the much more numerous cases of their mixture, it can be observed that the a priori which directs the induction and the deduction is a type of mystical experience. Whether it is 'being itself' (Scholastics) or 'universal substance' (Spinoza), whether it is 'beyond subjectivity and objectivity' (James) or the 'identity of spirit and nature' (Shelling), whether it is 'universe' (Schleiermacher) or 'cosmic whole' (Hocking), whether it is 'value creating process' (Whitehead) or 'progressive integration' (Wieman), whether it is 'absolute spirit' (Hegel) or 'cosmic person' (Brightman)—each of these concepts is based on an immediate experience of something ultimate in value and being of which one can become intuitively aware. Idealism and naturalism differ very little in their starting point. . . . Both are dependent on a point of identity between the experiencing subject and the ultimate. . . . The theological concepts of both idealists and naturalists are rooted in a 'mystical apriori,' an awareness of something that transcends the

cleavage between subject and object. And if in the course of a 'scientific' procedure this a priori is discovered, its discovery is only possible because it was present from the very beginning. This is the circle which no religious philosopher can escape. And it is by no means a vicious one. Every understanding of spiritual things (*Geistwissenschaft*) is circular." Paul Tillich, *Systematic Theology*, vol. 1 (Chicago: University of Chicago Press, 1951), 9.

15. Bötrül, *Notes*, 271–272: *gshegs snying sgrub byed kyi rigs pa la/ 'bras bu ltos pa'i rigs pa dang/ ngo bo chos nyid kyi rigs pa dang/ rgyu bya ba byed pa'i rigs pa dang gsum gyis sgrub/ de yang dang po 'bras rtags dang/ phyi ma gnyis rang bzhin gyi rtags yin/ dang po dag gnyis ldan gyi 'bras bu rtags su bkod nas ngo bo ye dag gi sangs rgyas yod par sgrub cing ngo bo ye dag dang/ dag pa gnyis ldan gyi sangs rgyas gnyis ldog cha tha dad kyi sgo nas 'jog go sems can sangs rgyas yin zhes pa rang bzhin rnam dag gi sangs rgyas yin pas sems kyi chos nyid yin gyi de'i 'bras bu min pas rgyu la 'bras gnas kyi skyon med do.*
16. The evidence of identical nature that Bötrül references here is such that, for example, if it is a dog, then it is necessarily an animal; or, if it is a product, then it is necessarily an impermanent phenomenon—the two entities have a relationship of essential identity. Moreover, in the case of an impermanent phenomenon and a product, the two are equivalent (*don gcig*). They are not actually distinct, but are merely conceptually distinct; they are said to have "different contradistinctions." Also, there are only two types of affirming evidence (*sgrub rtags*) in Buddhist logic, corresponding to the two types of relations accepted—causal relationships and relationships of essential identity. The observation of a lack of relationship permits the third of the three types of evidence in Buddhist logic, the evidence of non-observation (*ma dmigs pa'i rtags*). For more on these three types of inference, see Bimal Krishna Matilal, *The Character of Logic in India* (Albany: SUNY Press, 1998), 108–116. See also Karma Phuntsho (*slob dpon karma phun tshogs*), *tshad ma rigs pa'i them skas* (Bylakuppe, India: Ngagyur Nyingma Institute, 1997), 18–19; 40–44; 72–82.
17. Such concerns show the similarity of Buddha-nature with doctrines that Buddhists have tended to refute, such as the claim that the effect is present in the cause (*satkāryavāda*) and the claim that change is a transformation of a single substance (*parināṃavāda*). I should note that Mipam affirms that the Sāṃkhya (*grangs can pa*), the classic exemplar of *satkāryavāda* and *parināṃavāda*, is "the best of the non-Buddhist philosophies" (*phyi rol pa'i nang nas grub mtha' legs shos*) and that it has been said to be "very similar to the philosophical slant of the False-Aspectarian Mind-Only" (*grub mtha' bab sems tsam rnam brdzun pa dang ches nye ba*). Mipam, *Words That Delight*, 248.
18. For a discussion of the functions of Mipam's four valid cognitions, see Matthew Kapstein, "Mi-pham's Theory of Interpretation," in *Buddhist Hermeneutics,* ed. Donald Lopez, 159. Bötrül's presentation of these four valid cognitions is also

discussed in Kennard Lipman, "What Is Buddhist Logic?" in *Tibetan Buddhism: Reason and Revelation,* ed. Steven Goodman and Ronald Davidson (Albany: SUNY Press, 1992), 27–39.

19. Mipam, *Sword of Supreme Knowledge* (*don rnam par nges pa shes rab ral gri mchan bcas*), Mipam's *Collected Works*, vol. 4, 800.3–800.5: *tha snyad la yang gnas snang dag/ /mi mthun snang ba yod pa'i phyir/ /ma dag tshu rol mthong ba dang/ /dag pa'i gzigs pa la brten pa'i/ kun tu tha snyad tshad ma gnyis/ /mi dang lha yi mig bzhin no.* See also Mipam, *Overview: Essential Nature of Luminous Clarity*, 447.
20. Mipam, *Overview: Essential Nature of Luminous Clarity*, 447.
21. Longchenpa, *Dispelling Darkness in the Ten Directions: Commentary on the Guhyagarbhatantra* (*dpal gsang ba'i snying po de kho na nyid nges pa'i rgyud kyi 'grel pa phyogs bcu'i mun pa thams cad rnam par sel ba*), (reproduction of *a 'dzom* xylographic edition), (Paro: Ngodup, 1975).
22. Mipam, *Overview: Essential Nature of Luminous Clarity*, 448: *phyi ma 'di rang yul mthun min ni/ rdul gcig gi khyon la rdul snyed kyi zhing snang ba/ dus skad cig la bskal pa mang po'i mdzad pa ston pa/ chos dbyings 'gyur med las ma g.yos bzhin du sprul pa'i rol pa ston pa/ rnam rtog dang bral ba'i thugs kyis shes bya thams cad dus gcig tu mkhyen pa sogs/ bsam gyis mi khyab pa'i spyod yul gang zhig tha mal pa'i tshul mthong gi yul du 'gal ba lta bur snang.* The valid cognition of pure vision seems to stem from yogic direct perception (*rnal 'byor mngon sum, yogi-pratyakṣa*), a special form of awareness among the four types of direct perception. Yogic direct perception is one of four types of direct perception, the others being sense direct perception (*dbang po mngon sum*), mental direct perception (*yid kyi mngon sum*), and reflexive awareness direct perception (*rang rig mngon sum*). With the twofold conventional valid cognitions, we can also see a parallel here with the two types of dependent nature (*gzhan dbang, paratantra*), pure and impure, in Yogācāra discourses.
23. Mipam, *Overview: Essential Nature of Luminous Clarity,* 449: *de ltar chos thams cad ye nas sangs rgyas pa la sogs pa don zab mo rnams tshur mthong kho nas bsgrub pa ma yin zhing/ sgrub byed tshad ma gtan med pa'ang ma yin par gnad kyi don la mkhas par bya'o.*
24. Mipam, *Lion's Roar: Exposition of Buddha-Nature*, 589.2–589.3: *lam rnam dag yin kyang rigs pas sgrub mi nus te myong bas rtogs dgos so zhes pa dang/ tshur mthong gi lam du ma gyur na lam yang dag min no snyam pa'i rmongs mtshang brtol nas lam sgrub tshul gyi gnad la mkhas par bya dgos so.*
25. Bötrül states that because of the division of two ultimate valid cognitions: by means of temporarily (*re zhig*) accepting the valid cognition that analyzes the categorized ultimate, all the views of the lower vehicles and philosophies are not disregarded—from the selflessness of persons in the Vaibhāṣika up to the concordant ultimate (*mthun pa'i don dam*) of the Svātantrika. By means of accepting the valid cognition that analyzes the uncategorized ultimate, the great empty essence is ascertained without superimposition or denigration—from the great

empty ultimate (*don dam stong pa chen po*) of the Prāsaṅgika, through the great equality (*mnyam pa chen po*) of Mahāyoga, all the way up to the primordial purity of the ground-expanse (*gzhi dbyings ka nas dag pa*) of Atiyoga (the Great Perfection). Similarly, he explains that because of the division of two conventional valid cognitions: by means of accepting the valid cognition of confined perception, the mode of appearance of impure phenomena is ascertained without superimposition or denigration—such as aggregates, elements, and sense-fields that constitute the truths of suffering and origin in the tradition of the Vehicle of Characteristics (*mtshan nyid theg pa*). By means of accepting the pure conventional valid cognition (*tha snyad dag pa'i tshad ma*), the distinctive luminous and clear nature of the great purity of the relative is established without superimposition or denigration—from the luminous clarity that is the appearing aspect of Buddha-nature, the definitive meaning of the Vehicle of Characteristics, through the great purity (*dag pa chen po*) of Mahāyoga, all the way up to the spontaneous presence of the ground-appearance (*gzhi snang lhun gyis grub*) of Atiyoga. Bötrül, *Ornament of Mañjugoṣa's Viewpoint*, 109–110.

26. See Bötrül, *Ornament of Mañjugoṣa's Viewpoint*, 112–113.
27. Ibid., 110: *tha snyad dag pa'i tshad ma med du zin na/ sgyu 'phrul gsang ba'i snying po sogs kyi skabs nas bstan pa'i kun rdzob dag pa chen po yod par dam bca' ba tsam las sgrub byed kyi tshad ma mi rnyed de/ don dpyod tshad mas ni de sgrub par mi nus pa tsam du zad/ de'i ngor mi stong par yod pa tsam du smras kyang bden grub du 'gyur zhing tshul mthong tshad mas ni phung lnga ma dag pa dang/ sa sra zhing 'thas pa/ me tsha zhing bsreg pa tsam du 'grub kyi phung lnga rigs lnga dang/ 'byung lnga yum lnga'i dkyil 'khor du bsgrub ga la nus.*
28. The five aggregates are: forms, feelings, perceptions, formations, and consciousnesses; and the five Buddha families are: Tathāgata, Vajra, Padma, Ratna, and Karma. The five elements are: earth, water, fire, wind, and space; and the five goddesses are: Buddhalocanā, Māmakī, Pāṇḍaravāsinī, Samayatārā, and Ākāśadhātvīśvarī.
29. Bötrül, *Distinguishing the Views and Philosophies*, 37: *don dpyod tshad mas dpyad bzod bral/ /gzhan stong phal dang 'di mi 'dra/ /rnam dag tshad ma'i rnyed don phyir/ /bden stong phal gyis do zla min.*
30. Mipam, *Overview: Essential Nature of Luminous Clarity*, 444: *'di ltar snang ba thams cad chos can/ gnas tshul la sku dang ye shes kyi dkyil 'khor du grub ste/ phyin ci log gi bslad pa dang bral ba'i 'phags pa rnams kyis dag par gzigs pa'i phyir/ mig skyon med pas dung dkar por mthong ba bzhin.* See also nearly verbatim text in Yönten Gyatso, *Moonlamp*, vol. 3, 75.5.
31. Mipam, *Overview: Essential Nature of Luminous Clarity*, 457–458: *dper na chos kun stong par gtan la 'bebs pa'i tshe mi stong pa'i sgrub byed du/ las rgyu 'bras dang 'khor ba dang myang 'das kyis chos gang bgod* [read *bkod*] *kyang/ sgrub byed de nyid snga ma bsgrub bya dang mtshungs te kho rang yang rang bzhin ma grub par sgrub nus pas na/ ci tsam mi stong par bsgrub pa'i sgrub byed bkod pa thams cad kyang*

bud shing me la bsnan pa ltar stong nyid sgrub pa'i rigs pa'i grogs su 'gro bas na stong pa nyid sun 'byin pa'i rigs pa shes bya'i khongs nas mi rnyed pa bzhin du/ /'dir yang chos rnams dag pa min pa'i sgrub byed du gang dang ji bkod kyang sgrub byed de nyid kho rang dag par bsgrub bya yin pas na shes bya'i khongs na chos kun gnas tshul la dag par sgrub pa'i rigs pa la sun 'byin nus pa'i gtan tshig mi rnyed de.

32. Ibid., 459: *gnas tshul ltar mi snang ba ni 'khrul pas bslad pa las byung bas na 'khrul pa sel phyir lam goms dgos te chos kun gyi rang bzhin stong pa nyid yin kyang/ de mngon du bya ba'i phyir lam la gom dgos pa bzhin.*
33. In general explanations of valid cognition, what is evident (*mngon gyur*) is the domain of direct perception, what is hidden (*lkog gyur*) is the domain of inference, and what is extremely hidden (*shin tu lkog gyur*) is the domain of scripture.
34. See Mipam, *Words That Delight,* 88; 471–472; and Mipam, *Beacon of Certainty*, 14, op. cit.
35. Mipam, *Discourse on the Eight Commands* (*bka' brgyad rnam bshad*), published in *bka' brgyad rnam bshad dang spyi don 'od gsal snying po yang dag grub pa'i tshig 'grel bcas bzhugs* (Sichuan: Nationalities Press, 2000), 43–44: *gsang sngags pa'i gzhung gis chos thams cad ye nes lha yin no zhes grags pa de ji ltar bsgrub par bya na/ lung dang rig[s] pa man ngag gsum gyis bsgrub par bya ste . . . lung dang man ngag med par gsang sngags gtan la dbab mi nus.*
36. Mipam, *Beacon of Certainty*, 26: *don dam gdeng dang mi ldan par/ /kun rdzob lha ru bsgom pa tsam/ /mos pa tsam yin lta ba min.*
37. Ibid., 28: *don dam gnas lugs rtogs pa yis/ /kun rdzob lha ru yid ches kyi/ /gzhan du 'khrul ba'i snang tshul la/ /gnas nas lha ru ji ltar 'grub.*
38. Ibid., 37: *de la mthar thug mnyam nyid dbyings/ /lha snang kho nar snang ngo zhes/ /phyogs gcig sgrub par mi nus kyang/ /rang bzhin gdod nas dag pa yi/ /dbyings dang snang cha ye shes sku/ /'du 'bral med phyir snang ba'i cha/ /gdod nas lha ru dag pa la/ /gnas lugs dpyad pas kyang mi gnod.*
39. Ibid., 34: *de phyir tshad ma'i tshul 'di yis/ /snang kun rang bzhin lhar sgrub pa/ /snga 'gyur rang lugs kho na ste/ /kun mkhyen rong zom paṇdi ta'i/ /legs bshad seng ge'i nga ro yin.*
40. Mipam characterizes his tradition of exegesis on the *Guhyagarbhatantra* as the "Rong-Long tradition" (*rong long lugs*), the tradition of Rongzom and Longchenpa, in contrast to the "Zur tradition" (*zur lugs*). Mipam, *Overview: Essential Nature of Luminous Clarity*, 388–389.
41. Longchenpa, *White Lotus*, 1169.4–1170.1: *khams bde gshegs snying po sa bon tu yod pa tsam rkyen tshogs gnyis las gong du 'phel bas sangs rgyas thob par 'dod pa'i phyir rgyu'i theg pa zhes bya ste rgyu 'bras snga phyir khas len pa'i phyir ro/ sngags kyi snying po de sems can la rang chas lhun grub tu yon tan rgya chen ma tshang ba med par yod.* Kongtrül also has a nearly verbatim passage as Longchenpa's in Kongtrül, *Completely Spreading the Light of Wisdom* (*lam rim ye shes snying po'i 'grel pa ye shes snang ba rab tu rgyas ba*), 59.6–60.3. Longchenpa characterizes the Resultant Vehicle as taking the effect as the path in his *Precious Treasury of*

Philosophies, 1032.2–1032.3: *'bras bu rang dang 'dra ba lam du byed pas 'bras bu'i theg par gzhag pa.*

42. Mipam, *Concise Summary of the Philosophies from the Wish-Fulfilling Treasury*, 488.1–488.4: *rgyu'i theg par khams bde gshegs snying po sa bon du yod pa rkyen tshogs gnyis las gong du 'phel ba las dus ring zhig 'bras bu sangs rgyas su 'grub par 'dod pas rgyu 'bras snga phyir khas len la . . . rdo rje theg pas ni . . . rgyu 'bras dbyer med pa'i grub mthar smra'o.*
43. I capitalize Sūtra as a path, or vehicle, and leave "sūtra" uncapitalized as a text. Although such a distinction is at times problematic, the metaphor of a vehicle reveals more of the practical means by which the path is traversed, as opposed to a text or a philosophy that simply describes and represents reality. Through this distinction, I wish to point out that the Causal Vehicle of Sūtra and the Resultant Vehicle of Mantra should not necessarily be conflated with a different corpus of *texts*, sūtras versus tantras, but inclusive of a *subjective view*. "Vehicle" (*theg pa*), as a practical means, is reflected in Mipam's depiction of vehicle: "A vehicle is like something you ride; when you remain in it, it takes you to your desired effect." Mipam, *Words That Delight*, 462–463: *theg pa ni bzhon pa dang 'dra ste/ de la gnas na rang 'dod pa'i 'bras bu la phyin par byed pa yin la.*
44. Mipam, *Intelligent Presence*, 462.1–462.3: *dbu ma'i sgom phal cher spros pa dang bral ba'i stong par zhen shas che bas/ gang zhig 'gyur med dang bral sogs dus 'khor nas gsungs pa ltar la/ 'dir rig pa nyid bde ba chen po mthar thug yin te/ blo rig shes gsum gyi gdags gzhi tshogs brgyad las 'das pa'i rig pa ye shes don gyi bde chen 'gyur med yin pa'i phyir/ des na sngags lam mdo las 'phags.*
45. Mipam, *Overview: Essential Nature of Luminous Clarity*, 437–438: *mdo sngags kyi khyad par yod dam med ce na/ gzhal bya chos kyi dbyings spros bral du gtan la 'bebs pa tsam la khyad med kyang/ chos dbyings mthong tshul gyis yul can la khyad yod la/ lta ba ni yul can gyi ngos nas 'jog pas na khyad shin du che'o/ /de la lta bas gtan la dbab bya'i yul chos dbyings de bzhin nyid gcig min na/ chos rnams kyi de bzhin nyid la rigs mi 'dra bar yod par thal ba dang/ mdo yi mthong lam gyis de bzhin nyid ma mthong bar thal ba dang/ mtha' bzhi'i spros pa las lhag pa'i spros pa gcod rgyu rigs pas grub dgos pas na/ mdo sngags kyi mthong lam chos nyid mngon sum mthong ba la gnad gcig par mkhas grub thams cad bzhed pa mthun no.*
46. Kongtrül stated that proponents of self-emptiness claim that the only difference in Mantra is the subject, and not the object that is free from conceptual constructs; on the other hand, proponents of other-emptiness claim that there is a difference in the object as well: "Mantra distinguished by the subject, [through] the method of bliss, and not the object, which is the freedom from constructs, is the tradition of self-emptiness. Proponents of other-emptiness assert that the object also is not merely the freedom from constructs, but is endowed with all the supreme aspects, [appearing] like [reflections in a] divination mirror (*pra phab*)." Kongtrül, *Encyclopedia of Knowledge*, 716: *sngags su yul can bde ba'i thabs kyis khyad/ /spros bral yul la khyad med rang stong lugs/ /gzhan stong yul yang spros*

bral tsam po min/ /rnam kun mchog ldan pra phab lta bur bzhed. Sakya Paṇḍita (*sa skya paṇḍita,* 1182–1251) famously stated that there is no view higher than the freedom of constructs taught in the Perfection Vehicle: "If there were a view superior to the freedom from constructs of the Perfection [Vehicle], then that view would possess constructs; if free from constructs, then there is no difference [in view between Mantra and the Perfection Vehicle]." Sakya Paṇḍita, *Clear Differentiation of the Three Vows* (*sdom gsum rab dbye*), III.255: *pha rol phyin pa'i spros bral las/ /lhag pa'i lta ba yod na ni/ /lta de spros pa can du 'gyur/ /spros bral yin na khyad par med.* Published in Jared Douglas Rhoton, trans., *A Clear Differentiation of the Three Codes* (Albany: SUNY Press, 2002), 308.

47. Mipam, *Beacon of Certainty*, 19: *spros bral tsam gyi cha nas ni/ /de gnyis khyad par med do gsungs/ /stong par zhen pa bzlog phyir du/ /sngags las bde ba chen po bstan/ bde stong gnyis su med pa'i dbyings/ /yul dang yul can bral ba yi/ /tshul gis nyams su myong bar byed/ /snang dang gsal dang rig pa gsum/ /bde ba de yi rnam grangs yin.*
48. Mipam, *Precious Vajra Garland*, 624.5–625.1: *yang dag pa'i gnas lugs la ni stong pa las logs su gyur pa'i bde ba'am gsal ba rig pa zhig yod na/ de dngos po'i grangs su bgrang ste chos can yin gyi chos nyid du mi rung zhing rnam shes kyi sa las ma 'das so/ bde ba'am gsal ba'am rig pa las tha dad pa'i stong pa zhig yod na/ de ni dngos med kyi grangs su bgrang ste/ de yang chos can yin gyi chos nyid du mi rung zhing sems med kyi cha las ma 'das so.*
49. Bötrül, *Ornament of Mañjugoṣa's Viewpoint*, 84.
50. Ibid., 84: *de 'dra'i khyad par mtshan nyid theg par med de/ dpe'i sgo nas mtshon tsam dang/ sangs rgyas kyi snying po can du mdor bsdus pa tsam dang/ sems kyi chos nyid 'od gsal ba tsam kho na las ma bstan pa'i phyir.*
51. Bötrül, *Distinguishing the Views and Philosophies*, 4: *mdor na rgyu yi grub mtha' bzhi/ /bdag med rdzogs tshul zab khyad yod/ /gsang sngags rgyud sde rnam pa bzhi/ /lta ba lhun grub zab khyad yod.*
52. Mipam, *Intelligent Presence*, 490.4–491.1: *mdo las kyang 'khor lo bar par chos kun rang bzhin med pa'i stong pa dang rten 'byung gi snang ba zung 'jug tsam gtan la phab kyang/ las nyon gyi rgyus ma bskyed pa'i rang byung 'od gsal ba'i rang snang sku dang ye shes yod par ma gsungs pas/ sku dang ye shes ni gzod rgyus sgrub ste 'byung gi stong nyid dam chos nyid rtogs pa tsam gyis de mi nus pas snying rje chen po'i tshogs rdzogs par 'dod.*
53. Ibid., 491.1–491.2: *'khor lo tha mar sems kyi chos nyid chos kyi dbyings de nyid sku dang ye shes kyi snang ba dang ye nas 'bral med bstan pas sems can thams cad la theg pa chen po'i rigs bde gshegs snying pos khyab pas sangs rgya rung du bstan kyang/ de'i gsal byed kyi rgyur tshogs gnyis sgrub pa'i rgyu la ltos par bstan.*
54. Ibid., 491.3–491.4: *sngags su de 'dra'i ye nas rnam par dag pa'i sangs rgyas kyi dkyil 'khor rang bzhin lhun grub tu bzhugs pa thabs kyis lam du byas na de rtogs pa tsam gyis sangs rgyas nyid mngon du 'gyur gyi rgyus sgrub pa'i gsar byung gi sangs rgyas logs su 'tshol mi dgos par.*

55. Ibid., 453.5–454.1: *mdo yi lam na bde gshegs snying po yon tan ye ldan yod ces gsungs pa mdo sngags mtshams sbyor gyi tshul du gsungs kyang/ de yod par sangs rgyas kyi gsungs la brten nas dad pas rtogs bya yin la/ de ltar shes pas kyang nyes pa lnga spong bar gsungs kyi/ bde gshegs snying po'i rang bzhin da lta nas gtan la 'babs pa'i lam dngos su gsungs pa med.*
56. The *Uttaratantra* states that the ultimate truth is understood by faith alone. *Uttaratantra* I.153: "The ultimate truth of the self-existing is understood only by faith; the blazing disk of the sun cannot be seen by the blind." *rgyud bla ma rtsa 'grel*, 19: *rang byung rnams kyi don dam de/ /dad pa nyid kyis rtogs bya yin/ /nyi ma'i dkyil 'khor 'od 'bar ba/ /mig med pas ni mthong ba med.*
57. The *Uttaratantra* states that heritage is taught in order to remove five faults: (1) discouragement, (2) disparagement of inferior beings, (3) holding onto the inauthentic, (4) denigration of the authentic truth, and (5) considering ourselves superior. *Uttaratantra* I.157: "The existence [of the basic element] is taught to relinquish these five faults: discouragement, disparagement of inferior beings, holding onto the inauthentic, denigration of the authentic truth, considering ourselves superior." *rgyud bla ma rtsa 'grel*, 20: *sems zhum sems can dman la brnyas pa dang/ /yang dag min 'dzin yang dag chos la skur/ /bdag cag lhag pa'i skyon lnga gang dag la/ /yod pa de dag de spong don du gsungs.*
58. Longchenpa, *Precious Treasury of Philosophies*, 902.3–905.1: *byang chub kyi snying po rang la yod par ma mthong bas/ bdag lta bus sangs rgyas mi thob ces sems zhum nas byang chub tu sems mi bskyed pa dang/ bskyed kyang bdag byang chub sems dpa' gzhan tha mal pa zhes sems can la brnyas pas lam gong ma thob pa'i gegs byed pa dang/ stong nyid mthar 'dzin gyi dbang gis don dam pa'i rang bzhin chos kyi dbyings la mi 'jug pas yang dag par mi 'dzin pa dang/ rtag chad du lhung bas yang dag pa'i chos la skur ba 'debs pa dang/ bdag dang sems can mnyam par ma mthong bas/ bdag gzhan du 'dzin pa'i nyes pa 'byung ba ste . . . de lta bu'i khams rang gzhan la lhun grub tu yod par shes na/ rang gi sems thar bar bsgrub pa la dka' ba med par shes te spro ba dang sems can thams cad la sangs rgyas bzhin du gus pas 'tshe ba dang gnod pa med kyi steng du phan 'dogs pa dang/ don dam pa'i dbyings rtogs pa'i shes rab dang/ gnas lugs mthong ba'i ye shes dang/ byams pa tshad med pa'i dkyil 'khor rgyas pas gzhan don bsgrub par nus pa ste . . . rigs kyi rnam par gzhag pa 'di ni drang don du mi lta bar/ nges pa'i don 'ba' zhig tu bzung ste.* See also Longchenpa, *Great Chariot*, 328.5–329.6; Mipam, *Words of Mipam*, 435.4–437.5.
59. Mipam, *Difficult Points of Scriptures in General*, 456.3–456.4: *nyes pa lnga po gshegs snying sems can thams cad la yod par ma thos pa las 'byung/ mthar thug theg pa gcig 'grub pa'i gnad la de yin la/ rdo rje theg par sems nyid ye sangs rgyas pa'i gnad kyang 'di yin no.*
60. Ibid., 455.6–456.1: *chos kyi dbyings 'od gsal lam/ rang byung ye shes sam/ gnyug sems 'od gsal lam/ bde gshegs snying po zhes pa rnams don gcig te/ 'di sangs rgyas kyi rigs te.*

61. Mipam, *Vajra Essence*, 434.6–435.1: *gnyug sems dang/ bde gshegs snying po/ 'od gsal ba'i sems dang/ don dam byang chub kyi sems dang/ rang byung gi ye shes dang/ chos kyi dbyings rnams ming gi ldog pa tha dad kyang/ don la tha mi dad pa yin.*
62. Mipam, *Overview: Essential Nature of Luminous Clarity*, 399: *de lta bu'i gzhi de nyid la stong pa nyid kyi cha nas rgyal ba'i yum la sogs pa las chos kyi dbyings dang/ yang dag pa'i mtha' dang/ de bzhin nyid la sogs pa'i ming gis bstan cing/ sku dang ye shes kyi snang ba dang bcas pa'i cha nas snying po bstan pa'i mdo la sogs pa nas de bzhin gshegs pa'i snying po zhes pa'i ming gis bstan la/ nges don sngags kyi theg pa 'dir ni snang stong bden pa dbyer med dag mnyam chen po'i bdag nyid gdod ma gzhi yi dkyil 'khor zhes bya'o.*
63. Mipam, *Precious Vajra Garland*, 755.1–755.2: *mdo las gsungs pa'i skye med kyi don rnal ma rtogs na zung 'jug rnam kun mchog ldan gyi stong nyid de las gzhan du med pas mtho mtho zab zab kyi ming ci btags kyang don la de ga rang yin a bo rnams/ 'di gal che.*

Conclusion

1. In particular, I refer here to the epistemological critiques of Mind-Only as empirical skepticism and ontological critiques of the Middle Way as logical skepticism.
2. The emphasis on (and reification of?) temporality is part and parcel of the Judeo-Christian traditions for which God's revelation is quintessentially a *historical* moment of time. The metaphysical assumptions of temporality and finitude have shaped Western philosophical traditions, including the hermeneutic traditions stemming from Heidegger. These assumptions are *not* shared by Buddhists like Mipam.
3. A point of comparison here is with John Searle's distinction between syntax and semantics within the philosophy of mind, and how syntax alone cannot account for semantics. See John Searle, "Minds, Brains, and Programs," in *The Mind's I*, ed. Daniel Dennett and Douglas Hofstadter (New York: Basic Books, 1981), 353–382; originally published in *Behavioral and Brain Sciences* 3 (1980): 417–424.

Appendix One. *Lion's Roar: Exposition of Buddha-Nature*

1. As stated in the colophon of the text. Mipam, *Lion's Roar: Exposition of Buddha-Nature*, 606.2–606.4.
2. See chapter 2, note 55.
3. *Vajracchedikā* (*rdo rje gcod pa*), P.739, vol. 21, p. 255, 74a.4–74a.5.

4. A cause of a freed effect. As stated in an oral commentary on the text by Khenpo Pema Sherap.
5. *Prajñāpāramitāsañcayagāthā* (*shes rab kyi pha rol tu phyin pa sdud pa tshigs su bcad pa*), VIII.1. P.735, vol. 21. p. 189, 7a.3–7a.4. English translation in Edward Conze, *The Perfection of Wisdom in Eight Thousand Lines & Its Verse Summary*, 25.
6. *kun tu 'gro ba'i lam.* This is one of the ten powers of a Buddha.
7. P.760.12, vol. 22–23.
8. *Madhyamakāvatāra* XI.11.
9. *Saṃdhinirmocanasūtra*, chapter 3. John Powers, trans., *Wisdom of the Buddha,* 48–49.
10. *Dharmadhātustotra* v. 22.
11. See chapter 4, note 19.
12. The last verse of Mipam's citation is worded with a slight difference in the *Uttaratantra*. See *rgyud bla ma rtsa 'grel*, 8.
13. See Suzuki, trans., *The Laṅkāvatāra Sūtra,* 68–69.
14. See chapter 3, note 53.
15. *Jñānamudrāsamādhisūtra* (*ye shes phyag rgya'i ting nge 'dzin gyi mdo*), P.799, vol. 32, p. 66, 264b.3–264b.4.
16. *Jñānamudrāsamādhisūtra*, P.799, vol. 32, p. 68, 270b.6.
17. *Prajñāpāramitāsañcayagāthā* I.9. P.735, vol. 21, p. 187, 2a.7. English translation in Edward Conze, *The Perfection of Wisdom in Eight Thousand Lines & Its Verse Summary*, 10.
18. *Samādhirājasūtra* IX.27. P.795, vol. 31, p. 283, 29a.5.
19. P.879, vol. 34.
20. P.797, vol. 32.
21. The four assemblies are: (1) fully ordained monks (*dge slong*), (2) fully ordained nuns (*dge slong ma*), (3) male laypersons (*dge bsnyen*), and (4) female laypersons (*dge bsnyen ma*).
22. *Bodhipakṣanirdeśasūtra* (*byang chub phyogs bstan pa*), P.845, vol. 34, p. 103, 253b.5.
23. P.815, vol. 33, p. 19, 250b.4–250b.5.
24. *Tathāgatasaṃgatisūtra* (*de bzhin gshegs pa 'gro ba'i mdo*), P.895, vol. 35, p. 153, 268a.8–268b.1.
25. *Sarvavaidalyasaṃgrahasūtra* (*rnam pa 'thag pa bsdus pa'i mdo*), P.893, vol. 35, p. 125, 197a.8.
26. *Brahmadattaparipṛcchā* (*tshangs pas byin gyis zhu pa*), P.826, vol. 33, p. 186, 20b.5–20b.6.
27. *Brahmadattaparipṛcchā*, P.826, vol. 33, p. 186, 21a.6–21a.7.
28. P.886, vol. 35.
29. Reliance on the doctrine, not individuals; reliance on the meaning, not words; reliance on the definitive meaning, not provisional meanings; reliance on wisdom, not consciousness.

30. P.827, vol. 33.
31. P.815, vol. 33, p. 16, 242a.3
32. P.814, vol. 32.
33. P.815, vol. 33, p. 36, 292a.2–292a.3.
34. The three trainings are: discipline (*tshul khrims*), meditative stabilization (*ting nge 'dzin*), and supreme knowledge (*shes rab*).
35. Lodrö Drimé (*blo gros dri med*) is one of Mipam's names.

APPENDIX TWO. *NOTES ON THE ESSENTIAL POINTS OF [MIPAM'S] EXPOSITION [OF BUDDHA-NATURE]*

1. Tupten Tsültrim Namdak, *Nourishment for Faith*, 17–18.
2. The two stages are: the generation stage (*bskyed rim*) and the completion stage (*rdzogs rim*).
3. Citing the Perfection of Wisdom Sūtras, Candrakīrti enumerates twenty emptinesses in *Madhyamakāvatāra* VI.180–223. In addition to the enumeration of sixteen emptinesses (see chapter 3, note 2) there are four, which summarize the sixteen: (1) emptiness of entity, (2) emptiness of nonentity, (3) emptiness of nature, and (4) emptiness of another entity. See Edward Conze, trans. *The Large Sutra on Perfect Wisdom* (Berkeley: University of California Press, 1975), 144–148.
4. Candrakīrti, *Madhyamakāvatāra* VI.36.
5. *Prajñāpāramitā Sūtra in Eight-Thousand Lines* (*Aṣṭasāhasrikāprajñāpāramitā, 'phags pa shes rab kyi pha rol tu phyin pa brgyad stong pa*), D.10, vol. 33, 5.3. Conze, trans., *The Perfection of Wisdom in Eight Thousand Lines & Its Verse Summary*, 84.
6. *Madhyamakāvatāra* VI.54.
7. See chapter 1, note 68.
8. *Madhyamakāvatāra* VI.97.
9. Dongak Tenpé Nyima (*mdo sngags bstan pa'i nyi ma*) is one of Bötrül's names.
10. *dwags po*. Presently known as the district of Gyatsa (*rgya tshwa*) in the region of Lhokha (*lho kha*).
11. This refers to Bötrül's teacher, Chöying Rangdröl.

BIBLIOGRAPHY

CANONICAL SOURCES

(P.) Suzuki, Daitetz T., ed. *The Tibetan Tripitika, Peking edition*. Tokyo: Tibetan Tripitika Research Institute, 1957.

(D.) *sde dge mtshal par bka' 'gyur: A Facsimile Edition of the 18th Century Redaction of si tu chos kyi 'byung gnas Prepared under the Direction of H.H. the 16th rgyal dbang karma pa*. Delhi: Delhi Karmapae Chodhey Gyalwae Sungrab Partun Khang, 1976–1979.

sde dge bstan 'gyur. Reproduced from the 18th century *sde dge* blocks edited by *tshul khrims rin chen*. Delhi: Delhi Karmapae Chodhey Gyalwae Sungrab Partun Khang, 1982–1985.

TRANSLATED WORD (*BKA' 'GYUR*)

Aṣṭasāhasrikāprajñāpāramitā (*shes rab gyi pha rol tu phyin pa brgyad stong pa*). P.734, vol. 21; D.10, vol. 33.

Akṣayamatisūtra (*blo gros mi zad pas bstan pa*). P.842, vol. 34.

Aṅgulimālīyasūtra (*sor mo'i phreng ba la phan pa*). P.879, vol. 34.

Bodhipakṣanirdeśasūtra (*byang chub phyogs bstan pa*). P.845, vol. 34.

Bodhisattvapiṭaka (*byang chub sems dpa'i sde snod*). P.760.12, vols. 22–23.

Brahmadattaparipṛcchā (*tshangs pas byin gyis zhu pa*). P.826, vol. 33.

Brahmaviśoṣacintaparipṛcchāsūtra (*tshangs pa khyad par sems kyis zhus pa'i mdo*). P.827, vol. 33.

Dhāraṇīśvararājasūtra (*gzungs kyi dbang phyug rgyal pos zhus pa'i mdo*)/*Tathāgatamahākaruṇānirdeśasūtra* (*de bshin gshegs pa'i snying rje chen po nges par bstan pa'i mdo*). P.814, vol. 32.

Duḥśīlanigrahīsūtra (*tshul khrims 'chal pa tshar gcod pa*). P.886, vol. 35.

Gaganagañjaparipṛcchāsūtra (*'phags pa nam mkha'i mdzod kyis zhus pa'i mdo*). P.815, vol. 33.

Jñānamudrāsamādhisūtra (*ye shes phyag rgya'i ting nge 'dzin gyi mdo*). P.799, vol. 32.

Laṅkāvatārasūtra (*lang kar gshegs pa'i mdo*). P.775, vol. 29.

Mahāparinirvāṇasūtra (*mya ngan las 'das pa chen po'i mdo*). P.788, vol. 31.

Prajñāpāramitāsañcayagāthā (*shes rab kyi pha rol tu phyin pa sdud pa tshigs su bcad pa*). P.735, vol. 21.

Praśantaviniścaya-prātihāryasamādhisūtra (*rab tu zhi ba rnam par nges pa'i cho 'phrul gyi ting nge 'dzin gyi mdo*). P.797, vol. 32.

Samādhirājasūtra (*ting nge 'dzin gyi rgyal po'i mdo*). P.795, vols. 31–32.

Saṃdhinirmocanasūtra (*dgongs pa nges par 'grel pa'i mdo*). P.774, vol. 29.

Sarvavaidalyasaṃgrahasūtra (*rnam pa 'thag pa bsdus pa'i mdo*). P.893, vol. 35.

Tathāgatasaṃgatisūtra (*de bzhin gshegs pa 'gro ba'i mdo*). P.895, vol. 35.

Vajracchedikā (*rdo rje gcod pa*). P.739, vol. 21.

Other Tibetan Sources

Asaṅga. *Commentary on Uttaratantra* (*theg pa chen po'i rgyud bla ma'i bstan bcos kyi rnam par bshad pa*). P.5526, vol. 108; also in *theg pa chen po mdo sde'i rgyan dang rgyud bla rtsa 'grel.* Beijing: Nationalities Press, 1998.

Bötrül (*bod sprul mdo sngags bstan pa'i nyi ma*, 1898–1959). *Collected Works* (*bod sprul mdo sngags bstan pa'i nyi ma'i gsung 'bum*), vols. 1–3. Sichuan: Nationalities Press, 2004.

———. *Distinguishing the Views and Philosophies: A Torch of the Essential Points* (*lta grub shan 'byed gnad kyi sgron me*). *Collected Works*, vol. 1, 1–51.

———. *Distinguishing the Views and Philosophies: Root Text and Commentary* (*lta grub shan 'byed gnad kyi sgron me'i rtsa 'grel*). Sichuan: Nationalities Press, 1996.

———. *Notes on the Essential Points of [Mipam's] Exposition [of Buddha-Nature]* (*stong thun gnad kyi zin thun*). *Collected Works*, vol. 1, 261–274; also in digital edition from Zhechen monastery in Nepal, n.p.n.d.

———. *Ornament of Mañjugoṣa's Viewpoint: An Explanation of the Words and Meanings of "Distinguishing the Views and Philosophies: A Torch of the Essential Points"* (*lta grub shan 'byed gnad kyi sgron me'i tshig don rnam bshad 'jam dbyangs dgongs rgyan*). *Collected Works*, vol. 1, 53–259.

———. *Words of Maitreya: An Explanation of the Meaning of the Words of the Abhisamayālaṃkāra* (*sher phyin mngon par rtogs pa'i rgyan gyi tshig don rnam par bshad pa ma pham zhal lung*). *Collected Works*, vol. 2. Sichuan: Nationalities Press, 2004.

Chandra, Lokesh. *Tibetan-Sanskrit Dictionary*. Delhi: International Academy of Indian Culture, 2000/1961.

Candrakīrti. *Auto-Commentary of the Madhyamakāvatāra* (*dbu ma la 'jug pa'i rang 'grel*). P.5263, vol. 98; also in Sarnath: Sakya Students' Union, 1999.

———. *Madhyamakāvatāra* (*dbu ma la 'jug pa*). P.5261, P.5262, vol. 98.

———. *Prasannapadā* (*tshig gsal*). P.5260, vol. 98.

Dharmakīrti. *Pramāṇavārttika* (*tshad ma rnam 'grel*). P.5709, vol. 130.

Dölpopa (*dol po pa shes rab rgyal mtshan*, 1292–1361). *The Categories of the Possible and the Impossible* (*srid mi srid kyi rab dbye dbu phyogs legs par bzhugs so*). *Collected Works* (*'dzam thang* ed.), vol. 6, 305–316.

———. *The Great Assessment of the Doctrine Which Has the Significance of the Fourth Council* (*bka' bsdu bzhi pa don ldan rtsis chen po*). *Collected Works* (*'dzam thang* ed.), vol. 6, 165–202.

———. *The Mountain Doctrine: Ocean of Definitive Meaning* (*ri chos nges don rgya mtsho*). Gangtok: Dodrup Sangyey Lama, 1976.

———. *The Sun Elucidating the Two Truths* (*bden gnyis gsal ba'i nyi ma*). *Collected Works* (*'dzam thang* ed.), vol. 6, 695–726.

Dudjom Rinpoché (*bdud 'joms 'jigs bral ye shes rdo rje*, 1904–1988). *Dudjom's History of Buddhism* (*bdud 'joms chos 'byung*). Sichuan: Nationalities Press, 1996.

Getsé Paṇchen (*dge rtse paṇ chen, 'gyur med tshe dbang mchog grub*, 1761–1829). *Collected Works*. Chengdu: People's Press, 2001.

———. *Discourse of the Four Reliances: Realizing the Victorious One's Teaching of the Three Wheels as One Viewpoint* (*rgyal bstan 'khor lo gsum dgongs pa gcig tu rtogs pa ston pa bzhi ldan gyi gtam*). *Collected Works*, vol. 1, 105–120.

———. *Elucidating the Definitive Meaning Viewpoint: A Short Explanation of the Four Great Philosophies* (*grub mtha' chen po bzhi'i rnam par gzhag pa mdo tsam phye ba nges don dgongs pa gsal byed*). *Collected Works*, vol. 1, 13–74.

———. *Ornament of Buddha-Nature: A Discourse Ascertaining the Manner of the Definitive Meaning Middle Way* (*nges don dbu ma chen po'i tshul rnam par nges pa'i gtam bde gshegs snying po'i rgyan*). *Collected Works*, vol. 1, 75–104.

———. *Ornament of the Second Buddha's Viewpoint: A Commentary on the Stages of the Inner-Path of Secret Mantra* (*slob dpon chen po padmas mdzad pa'i gsang sngags *nang gi lam rim rgya cher 'grel pa sangs rgyas gnyis pa'i dgongs pa'i rgyan*). *Collected Works*, vols. 2–3.

———. *Reponse to Sherap's Questions* (*dge ba'i bshes gnyen shes rab mtshan can gyi dris lan*). *Collected Works*, vol. 6, 205–260.

Gorampa (*go rams pa bsod nams seng ge*, 1429–1489). *Completely Elucidating the Definitive Meaning* (*rgyal ba thams cad kyi thugs kyi dgongs pa zab mo dbu ma'i de kho na nyid spyi'i ngag gis ston pa nges don rab gsal*). *Collected Works*, vol. 5. Dehra Dun: Sakya College, 1979.

———. *Distinguishing the Views* (*lta ba'i shan 'byed*). Sarnath: Sakya Students' Union, 1988.

Gyeltsapjé (*rgyal tshab rje dar ma rin chen*, 1364–1432). *Commentary on the Uttaratantra* (*theg pa chen po rgyud bla ma'i ṭīka*). *Collected Works* (*lha sa* ed.), vol. 3. Asian Classics Input Project, Release IV, S5434.

Gyelwang Chökyi Nyima (*rgyal dbang chos kyi nyi ma*). *History of Dzokchen Monastery* (*mdo khams rdzogs chen dgon gyi lo rgyus nor bu'i phreng ba*). Delhi: Konchhog Lhadrepa, 1986.

Jamyang Gyeltsen (*'jam dbyangs rgyal mtshan*). *A Short History of Kaḥtok* (*rgyal ba kaḥ thog lo rgyus mdor bsdus*). Sichuan: Nationalities Press, 1996.

Jamyang Khyentsé Wangpo (*'jam dbyangs mkhyen brtse'i dbang po*, 1820–1892). *Brief Sketch of Tsongkhapa's View and Philosophy* (*lce btsun blo bzang grags pa'i lta grub kyi bzhed tshul mdo tsam bzhugs so*). *Collected Works*, vol. 6, 221.2–225.3. Gangtok: Gonpo Tseten, 1977.

———. *An Essential Summary of the Presentation of the Middle Way of Other-Emptiness* (*gzhan stong dbu ma'i rnam bzhag snying por dril ba*). *Collected Works*, vol. 6, 214.4–221.2. Gangtok: Gonpo Tseten, 1977.

Jamyang Zhepa (*'jam dbyangs bzhad pa ngag dbang brtson 'grus*, 1648–1722) et al. *Four Interlinear Commentaries on "The Great Exposition of the Stages of the Path"* (*lam rim chen mo mchan bzhi sbrags*), vols.1–2. Dharamsala: Tehor Tenzhug Committee, 2005.

Karma Phuntsho (*slob dpon karma phun tshogs*). *Steps to Valid Reasoning* (*tshad ma rigs pa'i them skas*). Bylakuppe, India: Ngagyur Nyingma Institute, 1997.

Khedrupjé (*mkhas grub rje dge legs dpal bzang*, 1385–1438). *rgyud sde spyi'i rnam par bzhag pa rgyas par bshad pa.* Published in Ferdinand Lessing and Alex Wayman, trans., *Mkhas grub rje's Fundamentals of the Buddhist Tantras.* The Hague: Mouton, 1968.

Khenpo Künpel (*kun bzang dpal ldan*, 1870/2–1943). *Opening the Door of Intelligent Presence: A Short Commentary Elucidating the Meaning of the Words of "Beacon of*

Certainty" (*nges shes rin po che'i sgron me'i tshig gi don gsal ba'i 'grel chung blo gros snang ba'i sgo 'byed*). Published in *nges shes sgron me rtsa 'grel,* 57–260. Sichuan: Nationalities Press, 1997.

Khenpo Lodrö Drakpa (*'dzam thang mkhan po blo gros grags pa,* 1920–1975). *The Beautiful Ornament of a Clear Mind: A Presentation of Buddhist and Non-Buddhist Philosophies* (*phyi nang grub mtha'i rnam bzhag gi bsdus don blo gsal yid kyi rgyan bzang*). *Collected Works* (*'dzam thang* ed.), vol. 10.

———. *History of the Jonang* (*jo nang chos 'byung zla ba'i sgron me*). Qinghai: Nationalities Press, 1992.

———. *Roar of the Fearless Lion* (*rgyu dang 'bras bu'i theg pa mchog gi gnas lugs zab mo'i don rnam par nges pa rje jo nang pa chen po'i ring lugs 'jigs med gdong lnga'i nga ro*). Dharamsala: Library of Tibetan Works and Archives, 1993.

Khenpo Pelden Sherap (*mkhan po dpal ldan shes rab,* b. 1941). *Lamp of the Blazing Sun and Moon: A Commentary on [Mipam's] Sword of Supreme Knowledge* (*don rnam nges 'grel pa shes rab ral gri'i 'grel pa shes rab nyi zla 'bar ba'i sgron me*). Varanasi: Nyingmapa Students' Welfare Committee, 2000.

Khenpo Zhenga (*mkhan po gzhan dga',* 1871–1927). *Interlinear Commentary on the Madhyamakāvatāra* (*dbu ma la 'jug pa zhes bya ba'i mchan 'grel*). Published in *gzhung chen bcu gsum gyi mchan 'grel,* vol. 5, 149–286. Dehra Dun: D. G. Khocchen Tulku, 1978.

———. *Interlinear Commentary on the Uttaratantra* (*theg pa chen po rgyud bla ma'i bstan bcos zhes bya ba'i mchan 'grel*). Published in *gzhung chen bcu gsum gyi mchan 'grel,* vol. 3, 477–582. Dehra Dun: D. G. Khocchen Tulku, 1978.

Kongtrül (*kong sprul blo gros mtha' yas,* 1813–1899). *Completely Spreading the Light of Wisdom* (*lam rim ye shes snying po'i 'grel pa ye shes snang ba rab tu rgyas ba*). Woodblock print from Ka-Nying She-drup Ling Monastery, Kathmandu, Nepal.

———. *Encyclopedia of Knowledge* (*shes bya kun khyab*). Beijing: Nationalities Press, 2002.

———. *Roar of the Non-Returning Lion: Commentary on the Uttaratantra* (*theg pa chen po rgyud bla ma'i bstan bcos snying po'i don mngon sum lam gyi bshad srol dang sbyar ba'i rnam par 'grel pa phyir mi ldog pa seng ge'i nga ro*). Varanasi: Kagyud Relief & Protection Committee, 2002/1999.

———. *Stainless Light Rays of the Vajra-Moon: Teachings on the View of the Middle Way of Other-Emptiness* (*gzhan stong dbu ma chen po'i lta khrid rdo rje zla ba dri ma med pa'i 'od zer*). Published in *The Collected Works of 'Jam-mgon Kong-sprul* (*rgya chen bka' mdzod*), vol. 8, 581–611. Paro: Ngodup, 1976.

krang dbyi sun, ed. *Tibetan-Chinese Dictionary* (*bod rgya tshig mdzod chen mo*). Beijing: Nationalities Press, 1998/1993.

Künzang Chödrak (*sa manta bhadra dharma kirti*). *Mipam's Essential Hagiography and Catalogue of Works* (*gangs ri'i khrod kyi smra ba'i seng ge gcig po 'jam dgon mi pham rgya mtsho'i rnam thar snying po bsdus pa dang gsung rab kyi dkar chag snga 'gyur bstan pa'i mdzes rgyan*). Mipam's *Collected Works*, vol. 8 (*hung*), 621–732.

Lochen Dharmaśrī (*lo chen dharmaśrī*, 1654–1717). *Cluster of Supreme Intentions: Commentary on "Ascertaining the Three Vows"* (*sdom pa gsum rnam par nges pa'i 'grel pa legs bshad ngo mtshar dpag bsam gyi snye ma*). Bylakuppe: Ngagyur Nyingma Institute, n.d.

———. *Desire-Bestowing Vase of Elegant Sayings* (*dam pa'i chos kyi 'bel gtam legs bshad 'dod ster*). *Collected Works*, vol. 19 (*dza*), 1–67. Dehra Dun: D. Kochhen Tulku, 2000.

———. *The Lord of Secrets' Words: An Overview of the Guhyagarbhatantra* (*dpal gsang ba'i snying po de kho na nyid nges pa'i rgyud kyi rgyal po sgyu 'phrul drwa ba spyi don gyi sgo nas gtan la 'bebs par byed pa'i legs bshed gsang bdag zhal lung*). *Collected Works*, vols. 9–10. Dehra Dun: D. Kochhen Tulku, 2000.

———. *Ornament of the Lord of Secrets' Viewpoint: A Commentary on the Guhyagarbhatantra* (*dpal gsang ba'i snying po de kho na nyid nges pa'i rgyud kyi 'grel pa gsang bdag dgongs rgyan*). *Collected Works*, vol. 8 (*nya*), 90–337. Dehra Dun: D. Kochhen Tulku, 2000.

Longchenpa (*klong chen rab 'byams*, 1308–1364). *Dispelling Darkness in the Ten Directions: Commentary on the Guhyagarbhatantra* (*dpal gsang ba'i snying po de kho na nyid nges pa'i rgyud kyi 'grel pa phyogs bcu'i mun pa thams cad rnam par sel ba.* Reproduced from *a 'dzom* xylographic edition. Paro: Ngodup, 1975.

———. *Great Chariot: Auto-Commentary of Resting in the Nature of Mind* (*sems nyid ngal so'i 'grel pa shing rta chen po*). Published in *rdzog pa chen po ngal gso skor gsum dang rang grol skor gsum.* Reproduced from *a 'dzom* xylographic edition. Gangtok, 1999.

———. *Seven Treasuries* (*mdzod bdun*). 7 vols. (Tarthang Tulku ed.).

———. *Precious Treasury of the Expanse of Phenomena* (*chos dbyings rin po che'i mdzod*).

———. *Precious Treasury of Philosophies* (*theg pa mtha' dag gi don gsal bar byed pa grub mtha' rin po che'i mdzod*).

———. *Precious Treasury of the Supreme Vehicle* (*theg pa'i mchog rin po che'i mdzod*), vols. 1–2.

———. *Precious Treasury of Words and Meanings* (*gsang ba bla na med pa 'od gsal rdo rje snying po'i gnas gsum gsal bar byed pa'i tshig don rin po che'i mdzod*).

———. *Responses to Mind and Wisdom* (*sems dang ye shes kyi dri lan*). Published in *gsung thor bu,* vol. 1, 377–392. Delhi: Sanje Dorje, 1973.

———. *Treasure Trove of Scriptural Transmission: Commentary of the Precious Treasury of the Expanse of Phenomena* (*chos dbyings rin po che'i mdzod kyi 'grel ba lung gi gter mdzod*).

———. *White Lotus: Auto-Commentary of the Precious Wish-Fulfilling Treasury* (*theg pa chen po'i man ngag gi bstan bcos yid bzhin rin po che'i mdzod kyi 'grel pa padma dkar po*).

Maitreya. *Dharmadharmatāvibhāga* (*chos dang chos nyid rnam par 'byed pa*). P.5523, vol. 108.

———. *Madhyāntavibhāga* (*dbus dang mtha' rnam par 'byed pa*). P.5522, vol. 108; D.4027.

———. *Uttaratantra* (*theg pa chen po rgyud bla ma'i bstan bcos*). P.5525, vol. 108; also in *rgyud bla ma rtsa 'grel.* Sichuan: Nationalities Press, 1997.

Mikyö Dorjé (*mi bskyod rdo rje,* 1507–1554). *Lush Grove: Commentary on the Abhisamayālaṃkāra* (*shes rab kyi pha rol tu phyin pa'i lung chos mtha' dag gi bdud rtsi'i snying por gyur pa gang la ldan pa'i gzhi rje btsun mchog tu dgyes par ngal gso ba'i yongs 'dus brtol gyi ljon pa rgyas pa*), vol. 1. Reproduced from *dpal spungs* xylographic edition. Delhi: Karmapae Choedhey, 1984.

Mipam (*'ju mi pham rgya mtsho,* 1846–1912). *Beacon of Certainty* (*nges shes sgron me*). Published in *nges shes sgron me rtsa 'grel,* 1–54. Sichuan: Nationalities Press, 1997.

———. *Collected Works* (Dilgo Khyentsé's expanded redaction of *sde dge* edition). Kathmandu: Zhechen Monastery, 1987.

———. *Commentary on the Wisdom Chapter of the Bodhicaryāvatāra* (*spyod 'jug sher 'grel ke ta ka*). Sichuan: Nationalities Press, 1993.

———. *Commentary on the Words of the Eighteenth Chapter [of the Wish-Fulfilling Treasury]* (*le'u bco brgyad pa'i tshig 'grel*). Mipam's *Collected Works*, vol. 21, 565–578.

———. *Concise Summary of the Philosophies from the Wish-Fulfilling Treasury* (*yid bzhin mdzod kyi grub mtha' bsdus pa*). Mipam's *Collected Works*, vol. 21, 439–500.

———. *Difficult Points of Scriptures in General* (*dbu ma sogs gzhung spyi'i dka' gnad skor gyi gsung sgros sna tshogs phyogs gcig tu bsdus pa rin po che'i za ma tog*). Mipam's *Collected Works*, vol. 22, 427–710.

———. *Discourse on the Eight Commands* (*bka' brgyad rnam bshad*). Published in *bka' brgyad rnam bshad dang spyi don 'od gsal snying po yang dag grub pa'i tshig 'grel bcas bzhugs,* 1–185. Sichuan: Nationalities Press, 2000.

———. *Eliminating Doubts* (*dam chos dogs sel*). Published in *dbu ma rgyan rtsa 'grel,* 498–563. Sichuan: Nationalities Press, 1990.

———. *An Elucidation of Various Difficult Points in the Precious Wish-Fulfilling Treasury* (*yid bzhin rin po che'i mdzod kyi dka' gnad ci rigs pa gsal bar byed pa*). Mipam's *Collected Works*, vol. 21, 501–564.

———. *Flower Garland: Catalogue of Rongzom's Collected Works* (*rong zom gsung 'bum dkar chag med tog phreng ba*). Published in Rongzom's *Collected Works* (*rong zom chos bzang gi gsung 'bum*), vol. 1, 1–22. Sichuan: Nationalities Press, 1999.

———. *Garland of Light Rays: Commentary on the Madhyāntavibhāga* (*dbu dang mtha' rnam par 'byed pa'i bstan bcos kyi 'grel pa 'od zer phreng ba*). Mipam's *Collected Works,* vol. 4 (*pa*), 659–786.

———. *Gateway to Scholarship* (*mkhas pa'i tshul la 'jug pa'i sgo*). Published in *mkhas 'jug*. Qinghai: Nationalities Press, 1994.

———. *Immaculate Crystal Rosary: Commentary on the Madhyamakāvatāra* (*dbu ma la 'jug pa'i 'grel pa zla ba'i zhal lung dri med shel phreng*). Mipam's *Collected Works*, vol. 1 (*oṃ*), 497–837.

———. *Intelligent Presence* (*gnyug sems 'od gsal ba'i don la dpyad pa rdzogs pa chen po gzhi lam 'gras bu'i shan 'byed blo gros snang ba*). Mipam's *Collected Works*, vol. 24, 411–566.

———. *Light of the Sun* (*brgal lan nyin byed snang ba*). Published in *spyod 'jug sher 'grel ke ta ka,* 465–579. Sichuan: Nationalities Press, 1993.

———. *Light of Wisdom: Commentary on the Dharmadharmatāvibhāga* (*chos dang chos nyid rnam 'byed 'grel pa ye shes snang ba*). Mipam's *Collected Works*, vol. 4 (*pa*), 609–658.

———. *Lion's Roar: Affirming Other-Emptiness* (*gzhan stong khas len seng ge'i nga ro*). Mipam's *Collected Works*, vol. 12 (*ga*), 359–378.

———. *Lion's Roar: Exposition of Buddha-Nature* (*bde gshegs snying po'i stong thun chen mo seng ge'i nga ro*). Mipam's *Collected Works*, vol. 4 (*pa*), 563–607.

———. *Overview: Essential Nature of Luminous Clarity* (*spyi don 'od gsal snying po*). Published in *bka' brgyad rnam bshad dang spyi don 'od gsal snying po yang dag grub pa'i tshig 'grel bcas bzhugs*, 381–605. Sichuan: Nationalities Press, 2000.

———. *Precious Mirror: Catalogue of the "Seven Treasuries"* (*mdzod bdun spar du bsgrubs pa'i dkar chag rin chen me long*). Published in *nges don rdzogs pa chen po'i man ngag phyogs bsgrigs zab don nor bu'i mdzod khang*, 7–44. Serta: Serta Buddhist Academy of the Five Arts, n.d.

———. *Precious Vajra Garland* (*gnyug sems zur dpyad skor gyi gsung sgros thor bu rnams phyogs gcig tu bsdus pa rdo rje rin po che'i phreng ba*). Mipam's *Collected Works*, vol. 24, 567–774.

———. *Sanskrit-Tibetan Dictionary* (*skad gnyis shan sbyar*). Mipam's *Collected Works*, vol. 26.

———. *Shedding Light on Thusness* (*gzhan gyis brtsad pa'i lan mdor bsdus pa rigs lam rab gsal de nyid snang byed*). Published in *spyod 'jug sher 'grel ke ta ka,* 133–463. Sichuan: Nationalities Press, 1993.

———. *Sword of Supreme Knowledge* (*don rnam par nges pa shes rab ral gri mchan bcas*). Mipam's *Collected Works*, vol. 4 (*pa*), 787–820.

———. *Treasury Illuminating Elegant Discourse: Commentary on the Pramāṇavārttika* (*tshad ma rnam 'grel gyi gzhung gsal por bshad pa legs bshad snang ba'i gter*), vols. 1–2. Varanasi: Nyingmapa Students' Welfare Committee, 2002.

———. *Trilogy of Innate Mind* (*gnyug sems skor gsum*). Mipam's *Collected Works*, vol. 24, 353–774.

———. *Vajra Essence* (*gnyug sems 'od gsal ba'i don rgyal ba rig 'dzin brgyud pa'i lung bzhin brjod pa rdo rje snying po*). Mipam's *Collected Works*, vol. 24, 353–410.

———. *Words of Mipam: Interlinear Commentary on the Uttaratantra* (*theg pa chen po rgyud bla ma'i bstan bcos kyi mchan 'grel mi pham zhal lung*). Mipam's *Collected Works*, vol. 4 (*pa*), 349–361.

———. *Words That Delight Guru Mañjughoṣa: Commentary on the Madhyamakālaṃkāra* (*dbu ma rgyan gyi rnam bshad 'jam byangs bla ma dgyes pa'i zhal lung*). Published in *dbu ma rgyan rtsa 'grel.* Sichuan: Nationalities Press, 1990.

Nāgārjuna. *Bodhicittavivaraṇa* (*byang chub sems kyi 'grel pa*). P.2665, P. 2666, vol. 61.

———. *Dharmadhātustotra* (*chos kyi dbyings su bstod pa*). P.2010, vol. 46.

———. *Mūlamadhyamakakārikā* (*dbu ma rtsa ba'i shes rab*). P.5224, vol. 95.

———. *Ratnāvalī* (*rin chen phreng ba*). P.5658, vol. 95.

———. *Vigrahavyāvartanī* (*rtsod zlog*). P.5228, vol. 95.

Nyoshül Khenpo (*smyo shul mkhan po 'jam dbyangs rdo rje*, 1931–1999). *Garland of Lapis* (*rang bzhin rdzogs pa chen po'i chos 'byung rig 'dzin brgyud pa'i rnam thar ngo mtshar nor bu baidurya'i phreng ba*), vols. 1–2. Thimphu: Indraprastha Press, 1996.

Padma Namgyel (*padma rnam rgyal,* twentieth century). *Ornament of Speech: A Teaching Manual for the Thirteen Great Scriptures* (*gzhung chen bcu gsum gyi mchad thabs dang mtshan don 'grel ba blo gsal ngag gi rgyan*). Gangtok: Dodrup Sangyey Lama, 1976.

Purbu Tsering (*phur bu tshe ring*), ed. *The Dictionary of Internal Knowledge* (*nang rig pa'i tshig mdzod*). Beijing: Nationalities Press, 1994.

Rongzom (*rong zom chos kyi bzang po, ca.* eleventh century). *Commentary on the Guhyagarbhatantra* (*rgyud rgyal gsang ba'i snying po dkon cog 'grel*). Rongzom's *Collected Works*, vol. 1, 33–253. Sichuan: Nationalities Press, 1999.

———. *Establishing Appearances as Divine* (*gsang sngags rdo rje theg pa'i tshul las snang ba lhar bsgrub*). Rongzom's *Collected Works*, vol. 1, 557–568. Sichuan: Nationalities Press, 1999.

Śākya Chokden (*śākya mchog ldan*, 1427–1508). *Golden Needle of Elegant Sayings: A Copious Dicourse Ascertaining [Sakya Paṇḍita's] "Clear Differentiation of the Three Vows"* (*sdom gsum gyi rab tu dbye ba'i bstan bcos kyi 'bel gtam rnam par nges pa legs bshad gser gyi thur ma*). *Collected Works*, vol. 6. Thimphu, Bhutan: Kunzang Tobgey, 1975.

———. *The Never Seen Sun: The Definitive Meaning of the Uttaratantra* (*rgyud bla ma'i bstan bcos kyi nges don sngon med nyi ma*). *Collected Works*, vol. 13. Thimphu, Bhutan: Kunzang Tobgey, 1975.

———. *Ocean of Scripture and Reasoning* (*dbu ma rnam par nges pa'i chos kyi bang mdzod lung dang rigs pa'i rgya mtsho*). *Collected Works*, vol. 14. Thimphu, Bhutan: Kunzang Tobgey, 1975.

Sakya Paṇḍita. *Clear Differentiation of the Three Vows* (*sdom gsum rab dbye*). Published in Jared Douglas Rhoton, trans. *A Clear Differentiation of the Three Codes.* Albany: SUNY Press, 2002.

Śāntideva. *Bodhicaryāvatāra* (*byang chub sems dpa'i spyod pa la 'jug pa*). P.5272, vol. 99; also in *byang chub sems dpa'i spyod pa la 'jug pa rtsa ba dang 'grel pa.* Sichuan: Nationalities Press, 1995.

Śāntarakṣita. *Madhyamakālaṃkāra* (*dbu ma rgyan*). P.5284, vol. 101; also in *dbu ma rgyan rtsa 'grel.* Sichuan: Nationalities Press, 1990.

Tenzin Lungtok Nyima (*bstan 'dzin lung rtogs nyi ma*, b. 1974). *The Great History of Dzokchen* (*snga 'gyur rdzogs chen chos 'byung chen mo*). Beijing: Nationalities Press, 2004.

Tsongkhapa (*tsong kha pa blo bzang grags pa*, 1357–1419). *Essence of Eloquence* (*drang nges legs bshad snying po*). *Collected Works*, vol. 14. Lhasa: Zhol spar khang. Asian Classics Input Project, Release IV, S5396.

———. *The Great Exposition of the Stages of the Path* (*lam rim chen mo*). Qinghai: Nationalities Press, 2000/1985.

———. *The Lesser Exposition of the Stages of the Path* (*lam rim chung ba*). *Collected Works*, vol. 21, 1–438. New Delhi: Ngawang Gelek Demo, 1979.

———. *Thoroughly Illuminating the Viewpoint* (*dgongs pa rab gsal*). Sarnath: Central Institute of Higher Tibetan Studies, 1998.

Tupten Tsültrim Namdak (*thub bstan tshul khrim rnam dag*). *Nourishment for Faith: A Short Hagiography of Bötrül* (*rje kun gzigs bod sprul bstan pa'i nyi ma'i rnam thar bsdus pa dad pa'i gsos sman*). Bötrül's *Collected Works*, vol. 1, 1–46. Sichuan: Nationalities Press, 2004.

Yönten Gyatso (*yon tan rgya mtsho*, fl. nineteenth century). *Moonlamp: Commentary on the Precious Treasury of Qualities* (*yon tan rin po che'i mdzod kyi 'grel pa bden gnyis gsal byed zla ba'i sgron ma*), vols. 1–3. Bylakuppe: Ngagyur Nyingma Institute, n.d.

Non-Tibetan Sources

Arnold, Dan. *Buddhists, Brahmins, and Belief: Epistemology in South Asian Philosophy of Religion*. New York: Columbia University Press, 2005.

Bayer, Achim. "The Life and Works of mKhan-po gZhan-dga' (1871–1927)." Master's Thesis, University of Hamburg, 2000.

Bhattacharya, Kamaleswar. *The Dialectical Method of Nāgārjuna*. Delhi: Motilal Banarsidass, 1990/1978.

Brierley, Michael W. "Naming a Quiet Revolution: The Panentheistic Turn in Modern Theology." In *In Whom We Live and Move and Have Our Being: Panentheistic Reflections on God's Presence in a Scientific World*, edited by Philip Clayton and Arthur Peacocke, 1–15. Grand Rapids: Eerdmans, 2004.

Cabezón, José. "Two Views on the Svātantrika-Prāsaṅgika Distinction in Fourteenth-Century Tibet." In *The Svātantrika-Prāsaṅgika Distinction*, edited by Georges Dreyfus and Sara McClintock, 289–315. Boston: Wisdom Publications, 2003.

Cabezón, José, and Geshe Lobsang Dargyay. *Freedom from Extremes: Gorampa's "Distinguishing the Views" and the Polemics of Emptiness*. Boston: Wisdom Publications, 2007.

Conze, Edward, trans. *The Large Sutra on Perfect Wisdom*. Berkeley: University of California Press, 1975.

_____, trans. *The Perfection of Wisdom in Eight Thousand Lines & Its Verse Summary*. Bolinas, CA: Four Seasons Foundation, 1973.

Cozort, Dan. *Unique Tenets of the Middle Way Consequence School*. Ithaca: Snow Lion Publications, 1998.

Davidson, Ronald, ed. *Wind Horse: Proceedings of the North American Tibetological Society*, vol. 1. Berkeley: Asian Humanities Press, 1981.

Dharmachakra Translation Committee, trans. *Middle Beyond Extremes: Maitreya's Madhyāntavibhāga with Commentaries by Khenpo Shenga and Ju Mipham*. Ithaca: Snow Lion Publications, 2006.

Doctor, Andreas. *The Tibetan Treasure Literature: Revelation, Tradition, and Accomplishment in Visionary Buddhism*. Ithaca: Snow Lion Publications, 2006.

Doctor, Thomas, trans. *Speech of Delight: Mipham's Commentary on Śāntarakṣita's* Ornament of the Middle Way. Ithaca: Snow Lion Publicatons, 2004.

Dorje, Gyurme, and Matthew Kapstein. *The Nyingma School of Tibetan Buddhism*, vol. 2. Boston: Wisdom Publications, 1991.

Dorji, Wangchuk. "The rÑiṅ-ma Interpretations of the Tathāgatagarbha Theory." *Vienna Journal of South Asian Studies* 28 (2004): 171–213.

Dreyfus, Georges. "Where Do Commentarial Colleges Come From?" *Journal of the International Association of Buddhist Studies* 28, no. 2 (2005): 273–279.

———. "Would the True Prāsaṅgika Please Stand? The Case of 'Ju Mi-pham." In *The Svātantrika-Prāsaṅgika Distinction*, edited by Georges Dreyfus and Sarah McClintock, 317–347. Boston: Wisdom Publications, 2003.

———. *The Sound of Two Hands Clapping: The Education of a Tibetan Buddhist Monk*. Berkeley: University of California Press, 2003.

———. *Recognizing Reality*. Albany: SUNY Press, 1997.

Duckworth, Douglas. "Buddha-Nature and a Dialectic of Presence and Absence in the Works of Mi-pham." Ph.D. Thesis, University of Virginia, 2005.

Dudjom Rinpoche. *The Nyingma School of Tibetan Buddhism*, vol. 1. Translated and edited by Gyurme Dorje and Matthew Kapstein. Boston: Wisdom Publications, 1991.

Ehrhard, Franz-Karl. "Observations on the Prāsaṅgika-Madhyamaka in the rÑiṅ-ma-pa-school." In *Tibetan Studies: Proceedings of the 4th Seminar of the IATS*, edited by Helga Uebach and Jampa Panglung, 139–147. Munich: Schloss Hohenkammer, 1988.

Gadamer, Hans Georg. *Truth and Method*. Translated and revised by Joel Weinsheimer and Donald Marshall. New York: Continuum, 1997.

Garson, Nathaniel. "Penetrating the Secret Essence Tantra: Context and Philosophy in the Mahāyoga System of rNyingma Tantra." Ph.D. Thesis, University of Virginia, 2004.

Germano, David. "Re-membering the Dismembered Body of Tibet." In *Buddhism in Contemporary Tibet*, edited by Melvyn Goldstein and Matthew Kapstein, 53–94. Berkeley: University of California Press, 2003.

———. "Architecture and Absence in the Secret Tantric History of the Great Perfection (*rdzogs chen*)." *Journal of the International Association of Buddhist Studies* 17, no. 2 (1994): 203–335.

Goodman, Steven D. "Mi-pham rgya-mtsho: An Account of His Life, the Printing of His Works, and the Structure of His Treatise Entitled *mKhas-pa'i tshul la 'jug-pa'i sgo*." In *Wind Horse: Proceedings of the North American Tibetological Society*, edited by Ronald M. Davidson, 58–78. Berkeley: Asian Humanities Press, 1981.

Goodman, Steven, and Ronald Davidson, eds. *Tibetan Buddhism: Reason and Revelation*. Albany: State University of New York Press, 1992.

Guenther, Herbert. *Buddhist Philosophy in Theory and Practice.* Baltimore: Penguin Books, 1971.

Hartley, Lauren. "A Socio-Historical Study of the Kingdom of Sde-dge (Derge, Kham) in the Late Nineteenth Century: Ris-med Views of Alliance and Authority." Master's Thesis, Indiana University, 1997.

Hookham, Shenpen. *The Buddha Within.* Albany: SUNY Press, 1991.

Hopkins, Jeffrey. *Mountain Doctrine: Tibet's Fundamental Treatise on Other-Emptiness and the Buddha Matrix.* Ithaca: Snow Lion Publications, 2006.

———. *Maps of the Profound.* Ithaca: Snow Lion Publications, 2003.

———. *Reflections on Reality.* Berkeley: University of California Press, 2002.

———. *Emptiness in the Mind-Only School.* Berkeley: University of California Press, 1999.

———. *Meditation on Emptiness.* London: Wisdom Publications, 1983.

Jackson, David. *A Saint from Seattle.* Boston: Wisdom Publications, 2003.

Kano, Kazuo. "rNgog Blo-ldan-shes-rab's Summary of the *Ratnagotravibhāga.*" Ph.D. Thesis, University of Hamburg, 2006.

Kapstein, Matthew. "We Are All Gzhan stong pas." *Journal of Buddhist Ethics* 7 (2000): 105–125.

———. "Mi-pham's Theory of Interpretation." In *Buddhist Hermeneutics,* edited by Donald S. Lopez, 149–174. Honolulu: University of Hawaii Press, 1988.

Karmay, Samten. *The Great Perfection (rDzogs Chen): A Philosophical and Meditative Tradition in Tibetan Buddhism.* Leiden: E. J. Brill, 1988.

Katz, Nathan. "Tibetan Hermeneutics and the Yāna Controversy." In *Contributions on Tibetan and Buddhist Religion and Philosophy,* edited by E. Steinkeller and H. Tauscher, 107–130. Wien: Arbeitskreis für Tibetische und Buddhistische Studien, 1983.

King, Richard. *Early Advaita Vedānta and Buddhism: The Mahāyāna Context of the Gauḍapāḍīya-kārikā.* Albany: SUNY Press, 1995.

King, Sallie B. *Buddha Nature.* Albany: SUNY Press, 1991.

Klein, Anne. *Meeting the Great Bliss Queen.* Boston: Beacon Press, 1995.

———. "Mental Concentration and the Unconditioned: A Buddhist Case for Unmediated Experience." In *Paths of Liberation,* edited by Robert Buswell and Robert Gimello, 269–308. Kuroda Institute: University of Hawaii Press, 1992.

Klein, Anne, and Geshe Tenzin Wangyal Rinpoche. *Unbounded Wholeness: Dzogchen, Bon, and the Logic of the Nonconceptual.* Oxford: Oxford University Press, 2006.

Klemm, David. *Hermeneutical Inquiry*, vol. 1. Atlanta: Scholars Press, 1986.

Komarovski, Yaroslav. "Reburying the Treasure, Maintaining the Continuity—Two Texts by Śākya Mchok Ldan on the Buddha-Essence." *Journal of Indian Philosophy* 34 (2006): 521–570.

Lipman, Kinnard. "What Is Buddhist Logic?: Some Tibetan Developments of Pramāṇa Theory." In *Tibetan Buddhism: Reason and Revelation,* edited by Steven D. Goodman and Ronald M. Davidson, 25–44. Albany: SUNY Press, 1992.

Magliola, Robert. *Derrida on the Mend.* Indiana: Purdue University Press, 1984.

Matilal, Bimal Krishna. *The Character of Logic in India*. Albany: SUNY Press, 1998.

———. "Is *Prasaṅga* a Form of Deconstruction?" *Journal of Indian Philosophy* 20 (1992): 345–362.

Nakamura, Hajime. *A History of Early Vedānta Philosophy*. Delhi: Motilal Banarsidass, 1983.

Newland, Guy. *The Two Truths*. Ithaca: Snow Lion Publications, 1992.

Ngawang Jorden. "Buddha-nature: Through the Eyes of Go rams pa bsod rnams seng ge in Fifteenth-Century Tibet." Ph.D. Thesis, Harvard University, 2003.

Nyoshul Khenpo. *A Marvelous Garland of Rare Gems: Biographies of Masters of Awareness in the Dzogchen Lineage*. Translated by Richard Barron. Junction City: Padma Publishing, 2005.

Pettit, John. *Mipham's Beacon of Certainty*. Boston: Wisdom Publications, 1999.

———. "Review of Altruism and Reality." *Journal of Buddhist Ethics* 6 (1999): 120–137.

Phuntsho, Karma. *Mipham's Dialectics and the Debates on Emptiness*. London: RoutledgeCurzon, 2005.

Powers, John, trans. *Wisdom of the Buddha: The Saṃdhinirmocana Mahāyāna Sūtra*. Berkeley: Dharma Publishing, 1995.

Ricoeur, Paul. "Hermeneutics and the Critique of Ideology." In *Hermeneutics and the Human Sciences: Essays on Language, Action and Interpretation*. Edited and translated by John Thompson. Cambridge: Cambridge University Press, 1981.

———. *Interpretation Theory: Discourse and the Surplus of Meaning*. Fort Worth: Texas University Press, 1976.

———. *The Symbolism of Evil*. Translated by Emerson Buchanan. New York: Harper and Row, 1967.

Ruegg, David Seyfort. *Two Prolegomena to Madhyamaka Philosophy*. Wien: Arbeitskreis für Tibetische und Buddhistische Studien, 2002.

———. *Three Studies in the History of Indian and Tibetan Madhyamaka Philosophy*. Wien: Arbeitskreis für Tibetische und Buddhistische Studien, 2000.

———. “The Term Gotra and the Textual History of *Ratnagotravibhāga*.” *Bulletin of the School of Oriental and African Studies* 39, no. 2 (1976): 341–363.

———. “On the Knowability and Expressibility of Absolute Reality in Buddhism.” *Indogaku Bukkyōgaku Kenkyū* 20, no. 1 (1971): 1–7.

———. *La Théorie du Tathāgatagarbha et du Gotra*. Paris: École Française d’Extrême Orient, 1969.

———. “On the dGe Lugs Pa Theory of the Tathāgatagarbha.” In *Pratidānam,* edited by J. C. Heesterman. The Hague: Mouton, 1968: 500–509.

Scott, Jim, trans. *Maitreya’s Distinguishing Phenomena and Pure Being*. Ithaca: Snow Lion Publications, 2004.

Smith, E. Gene. *Among Tibetan Texts*. Boston: Wisdom Publications, 2001.

Stearns, Cyrus. *The Buddha from Dolpo: A Study of the Life and Thought of the Tibetan Master Sherab Gyaltsen*. Albany: SUNY Press, 1999.

Sutton, Florin Giripescu. *Existence and Enlightenment in the Laṇkāvatāra-sūtra: A Study in the Ontology and Epistemology of the Yogācāra School of Mahāyāna Buddhism*. Albany: SUNY Press, 1991.

Suzuki, D.T., trans. *The Laṅkāvatāra Sūtra*. London: Routledge, 1968.

Takasaki, Jikido. *A Study on the Ratnagotravibhāga*. Rome: Is. M.E.O., 1966.

Thupten Jinpa. *Self, Reality and Reason in Tibetan Philosophy*. London: Routledge-Curzon, 2002.

Tillich, Paul. *Systematic Theology*, vol. 1. Chicago: University of Chicago Press, 1951.

Tsong-kha-pa. *The Great Treatise of the Stages of the Path to Enlightenment: Lam rim chen mo*. Translated by Lamrim Chenmo Translation Committee, edited by Joshua Cutler, 3 vols. Ithaca: Snow Lion Publications, 2000–2004.

Tulku Thondup. *Masters of Meditation and Miracles*. Boston: Shambhala Publications, 1996.

———. *Buddha Mind: An Anthology of Longchen Rabjam’s Writings on Dzogpa Chenpo*. Ithaca: Snow Lion Publications, 1989.

Vasubandhu. *Madhyāntavibhāga*. Edition in Ramchandra Pandeya, *Madhyāntavibhāga-śāstra*. Delhi: Motilal Banarsidass, 1999/1971.

Wilber, Ken. *Sex, Ecology, and Spirituality*. Boston: Shambhala Publications, 1995.

———. *Eye to Eye: The Quest for the New Paradigm*. New York: Anchor Books, 1983.

Williams, Paul. “A Response to John Pettit.” *Journal of Buddhist Ethics* 6 (1999): 138–153.

———. *The Reflexive Nature of Awareness: A Madhyamaka Defence*. London: Curzon Press, 1998.

Index